MEMOIRS OF LOUIS XIV AND HIS COURT AND OF THE REGENCY

BY THE DUKE OF SAINT-SIMON

VOLUME I

With a Special Introduction and Illustrations

NEW YORK
P F COLLIER & SON
PUBLISHERS

Copyright 1910
By P. F. Collier & Son

CONTENTS

CHAPTER I

My Birth and Family.—Early Life.—Desire to Join the Army.—Enter the Musketeers.—The Campaign Commences.—Camp of Gevries.—Siege of Namur.—Dreadful Weather.—Gentlemen Carrying Corn.—Sufferings during the Siege.—The Monks of Marlaigne.—Rival Couriers.—Naval Battle.—Playing with Fire-arms.—A Prediction Verified 31

CHAPTER II

The King's Natural Children.—Proposed Marriage of the Duc de Chartres.—Influence of Dubois.—The Duke and the King.—An Apartment.—Announcement of the Marriage.—Anger of Madame.—Household of the Duchess.—Villars and Rochefort.—Friend of King's Mistresses.—The Marriage Ceremony.—Toilette of the Duchess.—Son of Montbron.—Marriage of M. du Maine.—Duchess of Hanover.—Duc de Choiseul.—La Grande Mademoiselle . 42

CHAPTER III

Death of My Father.—Anecdotes of Louis XIII.—The Cardinal de Richelieu.—The Duc de Bellegarde.—Madame de Hautefort.—My Father's Enemy.—His Services and Reward.—A Duel against Law.—An Answer to a Libel.—M. de la Rochefoucauld.—My Father's Gratitude to Louis XIII. 57

CHAPTER IV

Position of the Prince of Orange.—Strange Conduct of the King.—Surprise and Indignation.—Battle of Neerwinden.—My Return to Paris.—Death of La Vauguyon.—Symptoms of Madness.—Vauguyon at the Bastille.—Projects of Marriage.—M. de Beauvilliers.—A Negotiation for a Wife.—My Failure.—Visit to La Trappe . . 66

CONTENTS

CHAPTER V

M. de Luxembourg's Claim of Precedence.—Origin of the Claim.—Duc de Piney.—Character of Harlay.—Progress of the Trial.—Luxembourg and Richelieu.—Double-dealing of Harlay.—The Duc de Gesvres.—Return to the Seat of War.—Divers Operations.—Origin of These Memoirs . 77

CHAPTER VI

Quarrels of the Princesses.—Mademoiselle Choin.—A Disgraceful Affair.—M. de Noyon.—Comic Scene at the Académie.—Anger and Forgiveness of M. de Noyon.—M. de Noailles in Disgrace.—How He Gets into Favour Again.—M. de Vendôme in Command.—Character of M. de Luxembourg.—The Trial for Precedence Again.—An Insolent Lawyer.—Extraordinary Decree 86

CHAPTER VII

Harlay and the Dutch—Death of the Princess of Orange—Count Koenigsmarck.—A New Proposal of Marriage.—My Marriage.—That of M. de Lauzun.—Its Result.—La Fontaine and Mignard.—Illness of the Maréchal de Lorges.—Operations on the Rhine.—Village of Seckenheim.—An Episode of War.—Cowardice of M. du Maine.—Despair of the King, Who Takes a Knave in the Act.—Bon Mot of M. d'Elbœuf 98

CHAPTER VIII

The Abbé de Fénelon.—The Jansenists and St. Sulpice.—Alliance with Madame Guyon.—Preceptor of the Royal Children.—Acquaintance with Madame de Maintenon.—Appointment to Cambrai.—Disclosure of Madame Guyon's Doctrines.—Her Disgrace.—Bossuet and Fénelon.—Two Rival Books.—Disgrace of Fénelon 112

CHAPTER IX

Death of Archbishop Harlay.—Scene at Conflans.—"The Good Langres."—A Scene at Marly.—Princesses Smoke Pipes!—Fortunes of Cavoye.—Mademoiselle de Coetlogon.—Madame de Guise.—Madame de Miramion.—Madame de Sévigné.—Father Seraphin.—An Angry Bishop.—Death of La Bruyère.—Burglary by a Duke.—Proposed Marriage of the Duc de Bourgogne.—The

CONTENTS

Duchesse de Lude.—A Dangerous Lady.—Madame d'O.—
Arrival of the Duchesse de Bourgogne 122

CHAPTER X

My Return to Fontainebleau.—A Calumny at Court.—Portrait of M. de La Trappe.—A False Painter.—Fast Living at the "Desert."—Comte d'Auvergne.—Perfidy of Harlay.—M. de Monaco.—Madame Panache.—The Italian Actor and the "False Prude" 136

CHAPTER XI

A Scientific Retreat.—The Peace of Ryswick.—Prince of Conti King of Poland.—His Voyage and Reception.—King of England Acknowledged.—Duc de Condé in Burgundy.—Strange Death of Santeuil.—Duties of the Prince of Darmstadt in Spain.—Madame de Maintenon's Brother.—Extravagant Dresses.—Marriage of the Duc de Bourgogne.—The Bedding of the Princesse.—Grand Balls.—A Scandalous Bird 144

CHAPTER XII

An Odd Marriage.—Black Daughter of the King.—Travels of Peter the Great.—Magnificent English Ambassador.—The Prince of Parma.—A Dissolute Abbé.—Orondat.—Dispute about Mourning.—M. de Cambrai's Book Condemned by M. de La Trappe.—Anecdote of the Head of Madame de Montbazon.—Condemnation of Fénelon by the Pope.—His Submission 158

CHAPTER XIII

Charnacé.—An Odd Ejectment.—A Squabble at Cards.—Birth of My Son.—The Camp at Compiègne.—Splendour of Maréchal Boufflers.—Pique of the Ambassadors.—Tessé's Grey Hat.—A Sham Siege.—A Singular Scene.—The King and Madame de Maintenon.—An Astonished Officer.—Breaking-up of the Camp 170

CHAPTER XIV

Gervaise, Monk of La Trappe.—His Disgusting Profligacy.—The Author of the Lord's Prayer.—A Struggle for Precedence.—Madame de Saint-Simon.—The End of the

CONTENTS

Quarrel.—Death of the Chevalier de Coislin.—A Ludicrous Incident.—Death of Racine.—The King and the Poet.—King Pays Debts of Courtiers.—Impudence of M. de Vendôme.—A Mysterious Murder.—Extraordinary Theft 182

CHAPTER XV

The Farrier of Salon.—Apparition of a Queen.—The Farrier Comes to Versailles.—Revelations to the Queen.—Supposed Explanation.—New Distinctions to the Bastards.—New Statue of the King.—Disappointment of Harlay.—Honesty of Chamillart.—The Comtesse de Fiesque.—Daughter of Jacquier.—Impudence of Saumery.—Amusing Scene.—Attempted Murder . . . 195

CHAPTER XVI

Reform at Court.—Cardinal Delfini.—Pride of M. de Monaco.—Early Life of Madame de Maintenon.—Madame de Navailles.—Balls at Marly.—An Odd Mask.—Great Dancing.—Fortunes of Langlée.—His Coarseness.—The Abbé de Soubise.—Intrigues for His Promotion.—Disgrace and Obstinacy of Cardinal de Bouillon . . . 207

CHAPTER XVII

A Marriage Bargain.—Mademoiselle de Mailly.—James II.—Begging Champagne.—A Duel.—Death of Le Nôtre.—His Character.—History of Vassor.—Comtesse de Verrue and Her Romance with M. de Savoie.—A Race of Dwarfs.—An Indecorous Incident.—Death of M. de La Trappe . 222

CHAPTER XVIII

Settlement of the Spanish Succession.—King William III.—New Party in Spain.—Their Attack on the Queen.—Perplexity of the King.—His Will.—Scene at the Palace.—News Sent to France.—Council at Madame de Maintenon's.—The King's Decision.—A Public Declaration.—Treatment of the New King.—His Departure for Spain.—Reflections.—Philip V. Arrives in Spain.—The Queen Dowager Banished 233

CHAPTER XIX

Marriage of Philip V.—The Queen's Journey.—Rival Dishes.

CONTENTS

—A Delicate Quarrel.—The King's Journey to Italy.—The Intrigues against Catinat.—Vaudemont's Success.—Appointment of Villeroy.—The First Campaign.—A Snuffbox.—Prince Eugène's Plan.—Attack and Defence of Cremona.—Villeroy Made Prisoner.—Appointment of M. de Vendôme 247

CHAPTER XX

Discontent and Death of Barbezieux.—His Character.—Elevation of Chamillart.—Strange Reasons of His Success.—Death of Rose.—Anecdotes.—An Invasion of Foxes.—M. le Prince.—A Horse upon *Roses.*—Marriage of His Daughter.—His Manners and Appearance 262

CHAPTER XXI

Monseigneur's Indigestion.—The King Disturbed.—The Ladies of the Halle.—Quarrel of the King and His Brother.—Mutual Reproaches.—Monsieur's Confessors.—A New Scene of Wrangling.—Monsieur at Table.—He Is Seized with Apoplexy.—The News Carried to Marly.—How Received by the King.—Death of Monsieur.—Various Forms of Grief.—The Duc de Chartres . . . 269

CHAPTER XXII

The Dead Soon Forgotten.—Feelings of Madame de Maintenon.—And of the Duc de Chartres.—Of the Courtiers.—Madame's Mode of Life.—Character of Monsieur.—Anecdote of M. le Prince.—Strange Interview of Madame de Maintenon with Madame.—Mourning at Court.—Death of Henriette d'Angleterre.—A Poisoning Scene.—The King and the Accomplice 282

CHAPTER XXIII

Scandalous Adventure of the Abbesse de la Joye.—Anecdote of Madame de Saint-Herem.—Death of James II. and Recognition of His Son.—Alliance against France.—Scene at St. Maur.—Balls and Plays.—The " Electra " of Longepierre.—Romantic Adventures of the Abbé de Vatteville 295

CHAPTER XXIV

Changes in the Army.—I Leave the Service.—Annoyance of the King.—The Medallic History of the Reign.—Louis

CONTENTS

XIII.—Death of William III.—Accession of Queen Anne.—The Alliance Continued.—Anecdotes of Catinat.—Madame de Maintenon and the King 305

CHAPTER XXV

Anecdote of Canaples.—Death of the Duc de Coislin.—Anecdotes of His Unbearable Politeness.—Eccentric Character.—Président de Novion.—Death of M. de Lorges.—Death of the Duchesse de Gesvres 315

CHAPTER XXVI

The Prince d'Harcourt.—His Character and That of His Wife.—Odd Court Lady.—She Cheats at Play.—Scene at Fontainebleau.—Crackers at Marly.—Snowballing a Princess.—Strange Manners of Madame d'Harcourt.—Rebellion among Her Servants.—A Vigorous Chambermaid 324

CHAPTER XXVII

Madame des Ursins.—Her Marriage and Character.—The Queen of Spain.—Ambition of Madame de Maintenon.—Coronation of Philip V.—A Cardinal Made Colonel.—Favourites of Madame des Ursins.—Her Complete Triumph.—A Mistake.—A Despatch Violated.—Madame des Ursins in Disgrace 332

CHAPTER XXVIII

Appointment of the Duke of Berwick.—Deception Practised by Orry.—Anger of Louis XIV.—Dismissal of Madame des Ursins.—Her Intrigues to Return.—Annoyance of the King and Queen of Spain.—Intrigues at Versailles.—Triumphant Return of Madame des Ursins to Court.—Baseness of the Courtiers.—Her Return to Spain Resolved On 343

CHAPTER XXIX

An Honest Courtier.—Robbery of Courtin and Fieubet.—An Important Affair.—My Interview with the King.—His Jealousy of His Authority.—Madame La Queue, the King's Daughter.—Battle of Blenheim or Hochstedt.—Our Defeat.—Effect of the News on the King.—Public

CONTENTS 9

PAGE

Grief and Public Rejoicing.—Death of My Friend Montfort 355

CHAPTER XXX

Naval Battle of Malaga.—Danger of Gibraltar.—Duke of Mantua in Search of a Wife.—Duchesse de Lesdiguières.—Strange Intrigues.—Mademoiselle d'Elbœuf Carries off the Prize.—A Curious Marriage.—Its Result.—History of a Conversion to Catholicism.—Attempted Assassination.—Singular Seclusion 370

CHAPTER XXXI

Fascination of the Duchesse de Bourgogne.—Fortunes of Nangis.—He Is Loved by the Duchesse and Her Dame d'Atours.—Discretion of the Court.—Maulevrier.—His Courtship of the Duchess.—Singular Trick.—Its Strange Success.—Mad Conduct of Maulevrier.—He Is Sent to Spain.—His Adventures There.—His Return and Tragical Catastrophe 381

CHAPTER XXXII

Death of M. de Duras.—Selfishness of the King.—Anecdote of Puysieux.—Character of Pontchartrain.—Why He Ruined the French Fleet.—Madame des Ursins at Last Resolves to Return to Spain.—Favours Heaped upon Her.—M. de Lauzun at the Army.—His bon mot.—Conduct of M. de Vendôme.—Disgrace and Character of the Grand Prieur 394

CHAPTER XXXIII

A Hunting Adventure.—Story and Catastrophe of Fargues.—Death and Character of Ninon de l'Enclos.—Odd Adventure of Courtenvaux.—Spies at Court.—New Enlistment.—Wretched State of the Country.—Balls at Marly . 405

CHAPTER XXXIV

Arrival of Vendôme at Court.—Character of That Disgusting Personage.—Rise of Cardinal Alberoni.—Vendôme's Reception at Marly.—His Unheard-of Triumph.—His High Flight.—Returns to Italy.—Battle of Calcinato.—Condition of the Army.—Pique of the Maréchal de Villeroy.—Battle of Ramillies.—Its Consequences . . 415

CONTENTS

CHAPTER XXXV

PAGE

Abandonment of the Siege of Barcelona.—Affairs of Italy.—La Feuillade.—Disastrous Rivalries.—Conduct of M. d'Orléans.—The Siege of Turin.—Battle.—Victory of Prince Eugène.—Insubordination in the Army.—Retreat.—M. d'Orléans Returns to Court.—Disgrace of La Feuillade 427

CHAPTER XXXVI

Measures of Economy.—Financial Embarrassments.—The King and Chamillart.—Tax on Baptisms and Marriages.—Vauban's Patriotism.—Its Punishment.—My Action with M. de Brissac.—I Appeal to the King.—The Result.—I Gain My Action 437

CHAPTER XXXVII

My Appointment as Ambassador to Rome.—How It Fell Through.—Anecdotes of the Bishop of Orleans.—A Droll Song.—A Saint in Spite of Himself.—Fashionable Crimes.—A Forged Genealogy.—Abduction of Beringhen.—The *Parvulos* of Meudon and Mademoiselle Choin . . . 448

CHAPTER XXXVIII

Death and Last Days of Madame de Montespan.—Selfishness of the King.—Death and Character of Madame de Nemours.—Neufchâtel and Prussia.—Campaign of Villars.—Naval Successes.—Inundations of the Loire.—Siege of Toulon.—A Quarrel about News.—Quixotic Despatches of Tessé 464

CHAPTER XXXIX

Precedence at the Communion Table.—The King Offended with Madame de Torcy.—The King's Religion.—Atheists and Jansenists.—Project against Scotland.—Preparations.—Failure.—The Chevalier de St. George.—His Return to Court 479

CHAPTER XL

Death and Character of Brissac.—Brissac and the Court Ladies.—The Duchesse de Bourgogne.—Scene at the Carp Basin.—King's Selfishness.—The King Cuts Samuel Bernard's Purse.—A Vain Capitalist.—Story of Léon and

CONTENTS

Florence the Actress.—His Loves with Mademoiselle de Roquelaure.—Run-away Marriage.—Anger of Madame de Roquelaure.—A Furious Mother.—Opinions of the Court.—A Mistake.—Interference of the King.—Fate of the Couple 492

CHAPTER XLI

The Duc d'Orléans in Spain.—Offends Madame des Ursins and Madame de Maintenon.—Laziness of M. de Vendôme in Flanders.—Battle of Oudenarde.—Defeat and Disasters.—Difference of M. de Vendôme and the Duc de Bourgogne 505

CHAPTER XLII

Conflicting Reports.—Attacks on the Duc de Bourgogne.—The Duchesse de Bourgogne Acts against Vendôme.—Weakness of the Duke.—Cunning of Vendôme.—The Siege of Lille.—Anxiety for a Battle.—Its Delay.—Conduct of the King and Monseigneur.—A Picture of Royal Family Feeling.—Conduct of the Maréchal de Boufflers . 514

CHAPTER XLIII

Equivocal Position of the Duc de Bourgogne.—His Weak Conduct.—Concealment of a Battle from the King.—Return of the Duc de Bourgogne to Court.—Incidents of His Reception.—Monseigneur.—Reception of the Duc de Berry.—Behaviour of the Duc de Bourgogne.—Anecdotes of Gamaches.—Return of Vendôme to Court.—His Star Begins to Wane.—Contrast of Boufflers and Vendôme.—Chamillart's Project for Retaking Lille.—How It Was Defeated by Madame de Maintenon 525

CHAPTER XLIV

Tremendous Cold in France.—Winters of 1708-1709.—Financiers and the Famine.—Interference of the Parliaments of Paris and Dijon.—Dreadful Oppression.—Misery of the People.—New Taxes.—Forced Labour.—General Ruin.—Increased Misfortunes.—Threatened Regicide.—Procession of Saint Geneviève.—Offerings of Plate to the King.—Discontent of the People.—A Bread Riot, How Appeased 537

CHAPTER XLV

M. de Vendôme out of Favour.—Death and Character of the Prince de Conti.—Fall of Vendôme.—Puységur's Interview with the King.—Madame de Bourgogne against Vendôme.—Her Decided Conduct.—Vendôme Excluded from Marly.—He Clings to Meudon.—From Which He is also Expelled.—His Final Disgrace and Abandonment.—Triumph of Madame de Maintenon 551

CHAPTER XLVI

Death of Père La Chaise.—His Infirmities in Old Age.—Partiality of the King.—Character of Père La Chaise.—The Jesuits.—Choice of a New Confessor.—Fagon's Opinion.—Destruction of Port Royal.—Jansenists and Molinists.—Pascal.—Violent Oppression of the Inhabitants of Port Royal 563

CHAPTER XLVII

Death of D'Avaux.—A Quarrel about a Window.—Louvois and the King.—Anecdote of Boisseuil.—Madame de Maintenon and M. de Beauvilliers.—Harcourt Proposed for the Council.—His Disappointment.—Death of M. le Prince.—His Character.—Treatment of His Wife.—His Love Adventures.—His Madness.—A Confessor Brought.—Nobody Regrets Him 571

CHAPTER XLVIII

Progress of the War.—Simplicity of Chamillart.—The Imperialists and the Pope.—Spanish Affairs.—Duc d'Orléans and Madame des Ursins.—Arrest of Flotte in Spain.—Discovery of the Intrigues of the Duc d'Orléans.—Cabal against Him.—His Disgrace and Its Consequences . . 584

CHAPTER XLIX

Danger of Chamillart.—Witticism of D'Harcourt.—Faults of Chamillart.—Court Intrigues against Him.—Behaviour of the Courtiers.—Influence of Madame de Maintenon.—Dignified Fall of Chamillart.—He is Succeeded by Voysin. —First Experience of the New Minister.—The Campaign in Flanders.—Battle of Malplaquet 592

CHAPTER L

Disgrace of the Duc d'Orléans.—I Endeavour to Separate Him from Madame d'Argenton.—Extraordinary Reports.

CONTENTS 13

—My Various Colloquies with Him.—The Separation.—Conduct of Madame d'Argenton.—Death and Character of M. le Duc.—The After-suppers of the King . . . 605

CHAPTER LI

Proposed Marriage of Mademoiselle.—My Intrigues to Bring It About.—The Duchesse de Bourgogne and Other Allies.—The Attack Begun.—Progress of the Intrigue.—Economy at Marly.—The Marriage Agreed Upon.—Scene at Saint-Cloud.—Horrible Reports.—The Marriage.—Madame de Saint-Simon.—Strange Character of the Duchesse de Berry 616

CHAPTER LII

Birth of Louis XV.—The Maréchale de la Meilleraye.—Saint-Ruth's Cudgel.—The Cardinal de Bouillon's Desertion from France.—Anecdotes of His Audacity . . 629

CHAPTER LIII

Imprudence of Villars.—The Danger of Truthfulness.—Military Mistakes.—The Fortunes of Berwick.—The Son of James.—Berwick's Report on the Army.—Imprudent Saying of Villars.—" The Good Little Fellow" in a Scrape.—What Happens to Him 636

CHAPTER LIV

Duchesse de Berry Drunk.—Operations in Spain.—Vendôme Demanded by Spain.—His Affront by the Duchesse de Bourgogne.—His Arrival.—Staremberg and Stanhope.—The Flag of Spain Leaves Madrid.—Entry of the Archduke.—Enthusiasm of the Spaniards.—The King Returns.—Strategy of Staremberg.—Affair of Brighuega.—Battle of Villaviciosa.—Its Consequences to Vendôme and to Spain 645

CHAPTER LV

State of the Country.—New Taxes.—The King's Conscience Troubled.—Decision of the Sorbonne.—Debate in the Council.—Effect of the Royal Tithe.—Tax on Agioteurs.—

CONTENTS

Merriment at Court.—Death of a Son of Maréchal
Boufflers.—The Jesuits 658

CHAPTER LVI

My Interview with Du Mont.—A Mysterious Communication.
—Anger of Monseigneur against Me.—Household of the
Duchesse de Berry.—Monseigneur Taken Ill of the Small-
pox.—Effect of the News.—The King Goes to Meudon.—
The Danger Diminishes.—Madame de Maintenon at
Meudon.—The Court at Versailles.—Hopes and Fears.—
The Danger Returns.—Death of Monseigneur.—Conduct
of the King 666

CHAPTER LVII

A Rumour Reaches Versailles.—Aspect of the Court.—
Various Forms of Grief.—The Duc d'Orléans.—The News
Confirmed at Versailles.—Behaviour of the Courtiers.—
The Duc and Duchesse de Berry.—The Duc and Duchesse
de Bourgogne.—Madame.—A Swiss Asleep.—Picture of a
Court.—The Heir-Apparent's Night.—The King Returns
to Marly.—Character of Monseigneur.—Effect of His
Death 680

CHAPTER LVIII

State of the Court at Death of Monseigneur.—Conduct of
the Dauphin and the Dauphine.—The Duchesse de Berry.
—My Interview with the Dauphin.—He is Reconciled with
M. d'Orléans 694

CHAPTER LIX

Warnings to the Dauphin and the Dauphine.—The Dauphine
Sickens and Dies.—Illness of the Dauphin.—His Death.—
Character and Manners of the Dauphine.—And of the
Dauphin 711

CHAPTER LX

Certainty of Poison.—The Supposed Criminal.—Excitement
of the People against M. d'Orléans.—The Cabal.—My
Danger and Escape.—The Dauphin's Casket 727

CONTENTS

CHAPTER LXI

The King's Selfishness.—Defeat of the Czar.—Death of Catinat.—Last Days of Vendôme.—His Body at the Escurial.—Anecdote of Harlay and the Jacobins.—Truce in Flanders.—Wolves 740

CHAPTER LXII

Settlement of the Spanish Succession.—Renunciation of France.—Comic Failure of the Duc de Berry.—Anecdotes of M. de Chevreuse.—Father Daniel's History and Its Reward 751

CHAPTER LXIII

The Bull *Unigenitus*.—My Interview with Father Tellier.—Curious Inadvertence of Mine.—Peace.—Duc de la Rochefoucauld.—A Suicide in Public.—Charmel.—Two Gay Sisters 764

CHAPTER LXIV

The King of Spain a Widower.—Intrigues of Madame des Ursins.—Choice of the Princes of Parma.—The King of France Kept in the Dark.—Celebration of the Marriage.—Sudden Fall of the Princesse des Ursins.—Her Expulsion from Spain 777

CHAPTER LXV

The King of Spain Acquiesces in the Disgrace of Madame des Ursins.—Its Origin.—Who Struck the Blow.—Her Journey to Versailles.—Treatment There.—My Interview with Her.—She Retires to Genoa.—Then to Rome.—Dies 795

CHAPTER LXVI

Sudden Illness of the Duc de Berry.—Suspicious Symptoms.—The Duchess Prevented from Seeing Him.—His Death.—Character.—Manners of the Duchesse de Berry . . 806

CHAPTER LXVII

Maisons Seeks My Acquaintance.—His Mysterious Manner.—Increase of the Intimacy.—Extraordinary News.—The

CONTENTS

Bastards Declared Princes of the Blood.—Rage of Maisons and Noailles.—Opinion of the Court and Country . . 814

CHAPTER LXVIII

The King Unhappy and Ill at Ease.—Court Paid to Him.—A New Scheme to Rule Him.—He Yields.—New Annoyance.—His Will.—Anecdotes Concerning It.—Opinions of the Court.—M. du Maine 821

CHAPTER LXIX

A New Visit from Maisons.—His Violent Project.—My Objections.—He Persists.—His Death and That of His Wife.—Death of the Duc de Beauvilliers.—His Character.—Of the Cardinal d'Estrées.—Anecdotes.—Death of Fénelon . 833

CHAPTER LXX

Character and Position of the Duc d'Orléans.—His Manners, Talents, and Virtues.—His Weakness.—Anecdote Illustrative Thereof.—The "Débonnaire."—Adventure of the Grand Prieur in England.—Education of the Duc d'Orléans.—Character of Dubois.—His Pernicious Influence.—The Duke's Emptiness.—His Deceit.—His Love of Painting.—The Fairies at His Birth.—The Duke's Timidity.—An Instance of His Mistrustfulness . . . 845

CHAPTER LXXI

The Duke Tries to Raise the Devil.—Magical Experiments.—His Religious Opinions.—Impiety.—Reads Rabelais at Church.—The Duchesse d'Orléans.—Her Character.—Her Life with Her Husband.—My Discourses with the Duke on the Future.—My Plans of Government.—A Place at Choice Offered Me.—I Decline the Honour.—My Reason.—National Bankruptcy.—The Duke's Anger at My Refusal.—A Final Decision 860

CHAPTER LXXII

The King's Health Declines.—Bets about His Death.—Lord Stair.—My New Friend.—The King's Last Hunt.—And Last Domestic and Public Acts.—Doctors.—Opium.—The King's Diet.—Failure of His Strength.—His Hopes of Recovery.—Increased Danger.—Codicil to His Will.—Interview with the Duc d'Orléans.—With the Cardinal de

CONTENTS 17

PAGE

Noailles.—Address to His Attendants.—The Dauphin Brought to Him.—His Last Words.—An Extraordinary Physician.—The Courtiers and the Duc d'Orléans.—Conduct of Madame de Maintenon.—The King's Death . . 869

CHAPTER LXXIII

Early Life of Louis XIV.—His Education.—His Enormous Vanity.—His Ignorance.—Cause of the War with Holland.—His Mistakes and Weakness in War.—The Ruin of France.—Origin of Versailles.—The King's Love of Adulation, and Jealousy of People Who Came Not to Court.—His Spies.—His Vindictiveness.—Opening of Letters.—Confidence Sometimes Placed in Him.—A Lady in a Predicament 885

CHAPTER LXXIV

Excessive Politeness.—Influence of the Valets.—How the King Drove Out.—Love of Magnificence.—His Buildings. —Versailles.—The Supply of Water.—The King Seeks for Quiet.—Creation of Marly.—Tremendous Extravagance . 896

CHAPTER LXXV

Amours of the King.—La Vallière.—Montespan.—Scandalous Publicity.—Temper of Madame de Montespan.—Her Unbearable Haughtiness.—Other Mistresses.—Madame de Maintenon.—Her Fortunes.—Her Marriage with Scarron.—His Character and Society.—How She Lived After His Death.—Gets into Better Company.—Acquaintance with Madame de Montespan.—The King's Children.—His Dislike of Widow Scarron.—Purchase of the Maintenon Estate.—Further Demands.—M. du Maine on His Travels. —Montespan's Ill-humour.—Madame de Maintenon Supplants Her.—Her Bitter Annoyance.—Progress of the New Intrigue.—Marriage of the King and Madame de Maintenon 902

CHAPTER LXXVI

Character of Madame de Maintenon.—Her Conversation.— Her Narrow-mindedness.—Her Devotion.—Revocation of the Edict of Nantes.—Its Fatal Consequences.—Saint-Cyr.—Madame de Maintenon Desires Her Marriage to be Declared.—Her Schemes.—Counterworked by Louvois.—

His Vigorous Conduct and Sudden Death.—Behaviour of the King.—Extraordinary Death of Séron 912

CHAPTER LXXVII

Daily Occupations of Madame de Maintenon.—Her Policy.—How She Governed the King's Affairs.—Connivance with the Ministers.—Anecdote of Le Tellier.—Behaviour of the King to Madame de Maintenon.—His Hardness.—Selfishness.—Want of Thought for Others.—Anecdotes.—Resignation of the King.—Its Causes.—The Jesuits and the Doctors.—The King and Lay Jesuits 923

CHAPTER LXXVIII

External Life of Louis XIV.—At the Army.—Etiquette of the King's Table.—Court Manners and Customs.—The Rising of the King.—Morning Occupations.—Secret Amours.—Going to Mass.—Councils.—Thursdays.—Fridays.—Ceremony of the King's Dinner.—The King's Brother.—After Dinner.—The Drive.—Walks at Marly and Elsewhere.—Stag-hunting.—Play-tables.—Lotteries.—Visits to Madame de Maintenon.—Supper.—The King Retires to Rest.—Medicine Days.—King's Religious Observances.—Fervency in Lent.—At Mass.—Costume.—Politeness of the King for the Court of Saint-Germain.—Feelings of the Court at His Death.—Relief of Madame de Maintenon.—Of the Duchesse d'Orléans.—Of the Court Generally.—Joy of Paris and the Whole of France.—Decency of Foreigners.—Burial of the King 933

CHAPTER LXXIX

Surprise of M. d'Orléans at the King's Death.—My Interview with Him.—Dispute about Hats.—M. du Maine at the Parliament.—His Reception.—My Protest.—The King's Will.—Its Contents and Reception.—Speech of the Duc d'Orléans.—Its Effect.—His Speech on the Codicil.—Violent Discussion.—Curious Scene.—Interruption for Dinner.—Return to the Parliament.—Abrogation of the Codicil.—New Scheme of Government.—The Regent Visits Madame de Maintenon.—The Establishment of Saint-Cyr.—The Regent's Liberality to Madame de Maintenon . . 948

CHAPTER LXXX

The Young King's Cold.—*Lettres des Cachet* Revived.—A Melancholy Story.—A Loan from Crosat.—Retrench-

CONTENTS

ments.—Unpaid Ambassadors.—Council of the Regency.—Influence of Lord Stair.—The Pretender.—His Departure from Bar.—Colonel Douglas.—The Pursuit.—Adventure at Nonancourt.—Its Upshot.—Madame l'Hospital.—Ingratitude of the Pretender 962

CHAPTER LXXXI

Behaviour of the Duchesse de Berry.—Her Arrogance Checked by Public Opinion.—Walls up the Luxembourg Garden.—La Muette.—Her Strange Amour with Rion.—Extraordinary Details.—The Duchess at the Carmelites.—Weakness of the Regent.—His Daily Round of Life.—His Suppers.—How He Squandered His Time.—His Impenetrability.—Scandal of His Life.—Public Balls at the Opera 974

CHAPTER LXXXII

First Appearance of Law.—His Banking Project Supported by the Regent.—Discussed by the Regent with Me.—Approved by the Council and Registered.—My Interviews with Law.—His Reasons for Seeking My Friendship.—Arouet de Voltaire 982

CHAPTER LXXXIII

Rise of Alberoni.—Intimacy of France and England.—Gibraltar Proposed to be Given Up.—Louville the Agent.—His Departure.—Arrives at Madrid.—Alarm of Alberoni.—His Audacious Intrigues.—Louville in the Bath.—His Attempts to See the King.—Defeated.—Driven out of Spain.—Impudence of Alberoni.—Treaty between France and England.—Stipulation with Reference to the Pretender 989

CHAPTER LXXXIV

The Lieutenant of Police.—Jealousy of Parliament.—Arrest of Pomereu Resolved On.—His Imprisonment and Sudden Release.—Proposed Destruction of Marly.—How I Prevented It.—Sale of the Furniture.—I Obtain the *Grandes Entrées*.—Their Importance and Nature.—Afterwards Lavished Indiscriminately.—Adventure of the Diamond called "The Regent."—Bought for the Crown of France 998

CONTENTS

CHAPTER LXXXV

                                                      PAGE

Death of the Duchesse de Lesdiguières.—Cavoye and His Wife.—Peter the Great.—His Visit to France.—Enmity to England.—Its Cause.—Kourakin, the Russian Ambassador.—The Czar Studies Rome.—Makes Himself the Head of Religion.—New Desires for Rome.—Ultimately Suppressed.—Preparations to Receive the Czar at Paris.—His Arrival at Dunkerque.—At Beaumont.—Dislikes the Fine Quarters Provided for Him.—His Singular Manners, and Those of His Suite 1008

CHAPTER LXXXVI

Personal Appearance of the Czar.—His Meals.—Invited by the Regent.—His Interview with the King.—He Returns the Visit.—Excursion in Paris.—Visits Madame.—Drinks Beer at the Opera.—At the Invalides.—Meudon.—Issy.—The Tuileries.—Versailles.—Hunt at Fontainebleau.—Saint-Cyr.—Extraordinary Interview with Madame de Maintenon.—My Meeting with the Czar at D'Antin's.—The Ladies Crowd to See Him.—Interchange of Presents.—A Review.—Party Visits.—Desire of the Czar to Be United to France 1017

CHAPTER LXXXVII

Courson in Languedoc.—Complaints of Perigueux.—Deputies to Paris.—Disunion at the Council.—Intrigues of the Duc de Noailles.—Scene.—I Support the Perigueux People.—Triumph.—My Quarrel with Noailles.—The Order of the Pavilion 1027

CHAPTER LXXXVIII

Policy and Schemes of Alberoni.—He is Made a Cardinal.—Other Rewards Bestowed on Him.—Dispute with the Majordomo.—An Irruption into the Royal Apartment.—The Cardinal Thrashed.—Extraordinary Scene . . 1035

CHAPTER LXXXIX

Anecdote of the Duc d'Orléans.—He Pretends to Reform—Trick Played upon Me.—His Hoaxes.—His Panegyric of Me.—Madame de Sabran.—How the Regent Treated His Mistresses 1041

CONTENTS

CHAPTER XC

Encroachments of the Parliament.—The Money Edict.—Conflict of Powers.—Vigorous Conduct of the Parliament.—Opposed with Equal Vigour by the Regent.—Anecdote of the Duchesse du Maine.—Further Proceedings of the Parliament.—Influence of the Reading of Memoirs.—Conduct of the Regent.—My Political Attitude.—Conversation with the Regent on the Subject of the Parliament.—Proposal to Hang Law.—Meeting at My House.—Law Takes Refuge in the Palais Royal . 1046

CHAPTER XCI

Proposed Bed of Justice.—My Scheme.—Interview with the Regent.—The Necessary Seats for the Assembly.—I Go in Search of Fontanieu.—My Interview with Him.—I Return to the Palace.—Preparations.—Proposals of M. le Duc to Degrade M. du Maine.—My Opposition.—My Joy and Delight.—The Bed of Justice Finally Determined On.—A Charming Messenger.—Final Preparations.—Illness of the Regent.—News Given to M. du Maine.—Resolution of the Parliament.—Military Arrangements.—I Am Summoned to the Council.—My Message to the Comte de Toulouse 1057

CHAPTER XCII

The Material Preparations for the Bed of Justice.—Arrival of the Duc d'Orléans.—The Council Chamber.—Attitude of the Various Actors.—The Duc du Maine.—Various Movements.—Arrival of the Duc de Toulouse.—Anxiety of the Two Bastards.—They Leave the Room.—Subsequent Proceedings. — Arrangement of the Council Chamber.—Speech of the Regent.—Countenances of the Members of Council.—The Regent Explains the Object of the Bed of Justice.—Speech of the Keeper of the Seals.—Taking the Votes.—Incidents That Followed.—New Speech of the Duc d'Orléans.—Against the Bastards.—My Joy.—I Express My Opinion Modestly.—Exception in Favour of the Comte de Toulouse.—New Proposal of M. le Duc.—Its Effect.—Threatened Disobedience of the Parliament.—Proper Measures.—The Parliament Sets Out 1070

CHAPTER XCIII

Continuation of the Scene in the Council Chamber.—Slowness of the Parliament.—They Arrive at Last.—The King

Fetched.—Commencement of the Bed of Justice.—My
Arrival.—Its Effect.—What I Observed.—Absence of the
Bastards Noticed.—Appearance of the King.—The
Keeper of the Seals.—The Proceedings Opened.—Humiliation of the Parliament.—Speech of the Chief-President.—New Announcement.—Fall of the Duc du Maine
Announced.—Rage of the Chief-President.—My Extreme
Joy.—M. le Duc Substituted for M. du Maine.—Indifference of the King.—Registration of the Decrees . . 1092

CHAPTER XCIV

My Return Home.—Wanted for a New Commission.—Go
to the Palais Royal.—A Cunning Page.—My Journey to
Saint-Cloud.—My Reception.—Interview with the Duchesse d'Orléans.—Her Grief.—My Embarrassment.—Interview with Madame.—Her Triumph.—Letter of the
Duchesse d'Orléans.—She Comes to Paris.—Quarrels
with the Regent 1107

CHAPTER XCV

Intrigues of M. du Maine.—And of Cellamare, the Spanish
Ambassador.—Montéléon and Portocarrero.—Their Despatches.—How Signed.—The Conspiracy Revealed.—
Conduct of the Regent.—Arrest of Cellamare.—His
House Searched.—The Regency Council.—Speech of
the Duc d'Orléans.—Resolutions Come To.—Arrests.—
Relations with Spain.—Alberoni and Saint-Aignan.—
Their Quarrel.—Escape of Saint-Aignan 1115

CHAPTER XCVI

The Regent Sends for Me.—Guilt of the Duc de Maine.—
Proposed Arrest.—Discussion on the Prison to Be Chosen.
—The Arrest.—His Dejection.—Arrest of the Duchess.
—Her Rage.—Taken to Dijon.—Other Arrests.—Conduct
of the Comte de Toulouse.—The *Faux Sauniers.*—Imprisonment of the Duc and Duchesse du Maine.—Their
Sham Disagreement.—Their Liberation.—Their Reconciliation 1124

CHAPTER XCVII

Anecdote of Madame de Charlus.—The *Phillippiques.*—La
Grange.—Père Tellier.—The Jesuits.—Anecdote.—Tellier's

CONTENTS

Banishment.—Death of Madame de Maintenon.—Her Life at Saint-Cyr 1134

CHAPTER XCVIII

Mode of Life of the Duchesse de Berry.—Her Illness.—Her Degrading Amours.—Her Danger Increases.—The Sacraments Refused.—The Curé Is Supported by the Cardinal de Noailles.—Curious Scene.—The Duchess Refuses to Give Way.—She Recovers, and Is Delivered.—Ambition of Rion.—He Marries the Duchess.—She Determines to Go to Meudon.—Rion Sent to the Army.—Quarrels of Father and Daughter.—Supper on the Terrace of Meudon.—The Duchess Again Ill.—Moves to La Muette.—Great Danger.—Receives the Sacrament.—Garus and Chirac.—Rival Doctors.—Increased Illness.—Death of the Duchess.—Sentiments on the Occasion.—Funeral Ceremonies.—Madame de Saint-Simon Falls Ill.—Her Recovery.—We Move to Meudon.—Character of the Duchesse de Berry 1142

CHAPTER XCIX

The Mississippi Scheme.—Law Offers Me Shares.—Compensation for Blaye.—The Rue Quincampoix.—Excitement of the Public.—Increased Popularity of the Scheme.—Conniving of Law.—Plot against His Life.—Disagreement with Argenson.—Their Quarrel.—Avarice of the Prince de Conti.—His Audacity.—Anger of the Regent.—Comparison with the Period of Louis XIV.—A Ballet Proposed.—The Maréchal de Villeroy.—The Young King Is to Dance.—Young Law Proposed.—Excitement.—The Young King's Disgust.—Extravagant Presents of the Duc d'Orléans 1159

CHAPTER C

System of Law in Danger.—Prodigality of the Duc d'Orléans.—Admissions of Law.—Fall of His Notes.—Violent Measures Taken to Support Them.—Their Failure.—Increased Extravagance of the Regent.—Reduction of the Fervour.—Proposed Colonies.—Forced Emigration.—Decree on the Indian Company.—Scheming of Argenson.—Attitude of the Parliament.—Their Remonstrance.—Dismissal of Law.—His Coolness.—Extraordinary Decree of the Council of State.—Prohibition of Jewellery.—New Schemes 1170

CONTENTS

CHAPTER CI

PAGE

The New Edict.—The Commercial Company.—New Edict.
—Rush on the Bank.—People Stifled in the Crowd.—
Excitement against Law.—Money of the Bank.—Exile
of the Parliament to Pontoise.—New Operation.—The
Place Vendôme.—The Maréchal de Villeroy.—Marseilles.
—Flight of Law.—Character of Him and His Wife.—
Observations on His Schemes.—Decrees of the Finance   1180

CHAPTER CII

Council on the Finances.—Departure of Law.—A Strange
Dialogue.—M. le Duc and the Regent.—Crimes Imputed
to Law during His Absence.—Schemes Proposed.—End
of the Council 1190

CHAPTER CIII

Character of Alberoni.—His Grand Projects.—Plots against
Him.—The Queen's Nurse.—The Scheme against the
Cardinal.—His Fall.—Theft of a Will.—Reception in
Italy.—His Adventures There 1196

CHAPTER CIV

Meetings of the Council.—A Kitten.—The Archbishopric of
Cambrai.—Scandalous Conduct of Dubois.—The Consecration.—I Persuade the Regent Not to Go.—He
Promises Not.—Breaks His Word.—Madame de Parabère.—The Ceremony.—Story of the Comte de Horn . 1204

CHAPTER CV

Quarrel of the King of England with His Son.—Schemes
of Dubois.—Marriage of Brissac.—His Death.—Birth of
the Young Pretender.—Cardinalate of Dubois.—Illness
of the King.—His Convalescence.—A Wonderful Lesson.
—Prudence of the Regent.—Insinuations against Him . 1217

CHAPTER CVI

Projected Marriages of the King and of the Daughter of
the Duc d'Orléans.—How It Was Communicated to Me.
—I Ask for the Embassy to Spain.—It Is Granted to
Me.—Jealousy of Dubois.—His Petty Interference.—Announcement of the Marriages 1227

CONTENTS

CHAPTER CVII

Interview with Dubois.—His Singular Instructions to Me.—His Insidious Object.—Various Tricks and Manœuvres.—My Departure for Spain.—Journey by Way of Bordeaux and Bayonne.—Reception in Spain.—Arrival at Madrid 1235

CHAPTER CVIII

Interview in the Hall of Mirrors.—Preliminaries of the Marriages.—Grimaldo.—How the Question of Precedence Was Settled.—I Ask for an Audience.—Splendid Illuminations.—A Ball.—I Am Forced to Dance . . 1246

CHAPTER CIX

Mademoiselle de Montpensier Sets out for Spain.—I Carry the News to the King.—Set out for Lerma.—Stay at the Escurial.—Take the Small-pox.—Convalescence . . 1256

CHAPTER CX

Mode of Life of Their Catholic Majesties.—Their Night.—Morning.—Toilette.—Character of Philippe V.—And of His Queen.—How She Governed Him 1265

CHAPTER CXI

The King's Taste for Hunting.—Preparations for a Battue.—Dull Work.—My Plans to Obtain the Grandesse.—Treachery of Dubois.—Friendship of Grimaldo.—My Success 1276

CHAPTER CXII

Marriage of the Prince of the Asturias.—An Ignorant Cardinal.—I Am Made Grandee of Spain.—The Vidâme de Chartres Named Chevalier of the Golden Fleece.—His Reception.—My Adieux.—A Belching Princess.—Return to France 1285

CHAPTER CXIII

Attempted Reconciliation between Dubois and Villeroy.—

Violent Scene.—Trap Laid for the Maréchal.—Its Success.—His Arrest 1301

CHAPTER CXIV

I Am Sent for by Cardinal Dubois.—Flight of Fréjus.—He Is Sought and Found.—Behaviour of Villeroy in His Exile at Lyons.—His Rage and Reproaches against Fréjus.—Rise of the Latter in the King's Confidence . . . 1316

CHAPTER CXV

I Retire from Public Life.—Illness and Death of Dubois.—Account of His Riches.—His Wife.—His Character.—Anecdotes.—Madame de Conflans.—Relief of the Regent and the King 1325

CHAPTER CXVI

Death of Lauzun.—His Extraordinary Adventures.—His Success at Court.—Appointment to the Artillery.—Counter-worked by Louvois.—Lauzun and Madame de Montespan.—Scene with the King.—Mademoiselle and Madame de Monaco 1344

CHAPTER CXVII

Lauzun's Magnificence.—Louvois Conspires against Him.—He Is Imprisoned.—His Adventures at Pignerol.—On What Terms He Is Released.—His Life Afterwards.—Return to Court 1353

CHAPTER CXVIII

Lauzun Regrets His Former Favour.—Means Taken to Recover It.—Failure.—Anecdotes.—Biting Sayings.—My Intimacy with Lauzun.—His Illness, Death, and Character 1362

CHAPTER CXIX

Ill-Health of the Regent.—My Fears.—He Desires a Sudden Death.—Apoplectic Fit.—Death.—His Successor as Prime Minister.—The Duc de Chartres.—End of the Memoirs 1376

INTRODUCTION

No library of Court documents could pretend to be representative which ignored the famous "Memoirs" of the Duc de Saint-Simon. They stand, by universal consent, at the head of French historical papers, and are the one great source from which all historians derive their insight into the closing years of the reign of the "Grand Monarch," Louis XIV.—whom the author shows to be anything but grand—and of the Regency. The opinion of the French critic, Sainte-Beuve, is fairly typical: "With the Memoirs of De Retz, it seemed that perfection had been attained, in interest, in movement, in moral analysis, in pictorial vivacity, and that there was no reason for expecting they could be surpassed. But the 'Memoirs' of Saint-Simon came; and they offer merits . . . which make them the most precious body of Memoirs that as yet exist."

Villemain declared their author to be "the most original of geniuses in French literature, the foremost of prose satirists; inexhaustible in details of manners and customs, a word-painter like Tacitus; the author of a language of his own, lacking in accuracy, system, and art, yet an admirable writer." Leon Vallée reinforces this by saying: "Saint-Simon can not be compared to any of his contemporaries. He has an individuality, a style, and a language solely his own. . . . Language he treated like an abject slave. When he had gone to its farthest limit, when it failed to express his ideas or feelings, he forced it—the result was a new term, or a change in the ordinary meaning of words sprang forth from his pen. With this was joined a vigour and breadth of style, very pronounced, which makes up the originality of the works of Saint-Simon and contributes toward placing their author in the foremost rank of French writers."

Louis de Rouvroy, who later became the Duc de Saint-Simon, was born in Paris, January 16, 1675. He claimed descent from Charlemagne, but the story goes that his father, as a young page of Louis XIII., gained favour with his royal master by his skill in holding the stirrup, and was finally made a duke and peer of France. The boy Louis had no lesser persons than the King and Queen Marie Thérèse as godparents, and made his first formal appearance at Court when seventeen. He tells us that he was not a studious boy, but was fond of reading history; and that if he had been given rein to read all he desired of it, he might have made "some figure in the world." At nineteen, like D'Artagnan, he entered the King's Musketeers. At twenty he was made a captain in the cavalry; and the same year he married the beautiful daughter of the Maréchal de Lorges. This marriage, which was purely political in its inception, finally turned into a genuine love match—a pleasant exception to the majority of such affairs. He became devoted to his wife, saying: "She exceeded all that was promised of her, and all that I myself had hoped." Partly because of this marriage, and also because he felt himself slighted in certain army appointments, he resigned his commission, after five years' service, and retired for a time to private life.

Upon his return to Court, taking up apartments which the royal favour had reserved for him at Versailles, Saint-Simon secretly entered upon the self-appointed task for which he is now known to fame—

INTRODUCTION 29

a task which the proud King of a vainglorious Court would have lost no time in terminating had it been discovered—the task of judge, spy, critic, portraitist, and historian, rolled into one. Day by day, henceforth for many years, he was to set down upon his private "Memoirs" the results of his personal observations, supplemented by the gossip brought to him by his unsuspecting friends; for neither courtier, statesman, minister, nor friend ever looked upon those notes which this "little Duke with his cruel, piercing, unsatisfied eyes" was so busily penning. Says Vallée: "He filled a unique position at Court, being accepted by all, even by the King himself, as a cynic, personally liked for his disposition, enjoying consideration on account of the prestige of his social connections, inspiring fear in the more timid by the severity and fearlessness of his criticism." Yet Louis XIV. never seems to have liked him, and Saint-Simon owed his influence chiefly to his friendly relations with the Dauphin's family. During the Regency, he tried to restrain the profligate Duke of Orleans, and in return was offered the position of governor of the boy, Louis XV., which he refused. Soon after, he retired to private life, and devoted his remaining years largely to revising his beloved "Memoirs." The autograph manuscript, still in existence, reveals the immense labour which he put into it. The writing is remarkable for its legibility and freedom from erasure. It comprises no less than 2,300 pages in folio.

After the author's death, in 1755, the secret of his lifelong labour was revealed; and the Duc de Choiseul, fearing the result of these frank revelations, confiscated them and placed them among the state archives. For sixty years they remained under lock and key, being seen by only a few privileged persons, among them Marmontel, Duclos, and Voltaire. A garbled version of extracts appeared in 1789, possibly being used as a

Revolutionary text. Finally, in 1819, a descendant of the analyst, bearing the same name, obtained permission from Louis XVIII. to set this "prisoner of the Bastille" at liberty; and in 1829 an authoritative edition, revised and arranged by chapters, appeared. It created a tremendous stir. Saint-Simon had been merciless, from King down to lady's maid, in depicting the daily life of a famous Court. He had stripped it of all its tinsel and pretension, and laid the ragged framework bare. "He wrote like the Devil for posterity!" exclaimed Chateaubriand. But the work at once became universally read and quoted, both in France and England. Macaulay made frequent use of it in his historical essays. It was, in a word, recognised as the chief authority upon an important period of thirty years (1694-1723).

Since then it has passed through many editions, finally receiving an adequate English translation at the hands of Bayle St. John, who has been careful to adhere to the peculiarities of Saint-Simon's style. It is this version which is now presented in full, giving us not only many vivid pictures of the author's time, but of the author himself. "I do not pride myself upon my freedom from prejudice—impartiality," he confesses—"it would be useless to attempt it. But I have tried at all times to tell the truth."

THE MEMOIRS OF THE DUKE OF SAINT-SIMON

CHAPTER I

I WAS born on the night of the 15th of January, 1675, of Claude Duc de Saint-Simon, Peer of France; and of his second wife Charlotte de l'Aubepine. I was the only child of that marriage. By his first wife, Diana de Budos, my father had had only a daughter. He married her to the Duc de Brissac, Peer of France, only brother of the Duchesse de Villeroy. She died in 1684, without children,—having been long before separated from a husband who was unworthy of her—leaving me heir of all her property.

I bore the name of the Vidame de Chartres; and was educated with great care and attention. My mother, who was remarkable for virtue, perseverance, and sense, busied herself continually in forming my mind and body. She feared for me the usual fate of young men, who believe their fortunes made, and who find themselves their own masters early in life. It was not likely that my father, born in 1606, would live long enough to ward off from me this danger; and my mother repeatedly impressed on me how necessary it was for a young man, the son of the favourite of a King long dead,—with no new friends at Court,—to acquire some personal value of his own. She succeeded in stimulating my courage; and in exciting in me the desire to make the acquisitions she laid stress on; but my aptitude for study and the sciences did not come up to my desire to succeed in them. However, I had an innate inclination for reading, especially works of history; and thus was inspired with ambition to emulate the examples presented to my imagination,—to do something and become somebody, which partly made amends for my coldness for letters. In fact, I have always thought that if I had been allowed to read history more constantly, instead of losing my time in studies for which I had no aptness, I might have made some figure in the world.

What I read of my own accord, of history, and, above all, of the personal memoirs of the times since Francis I., bred in me the desire to write down what I might myself see. The hope of advancement, and of becoming familiar with the affairs of my time, stirred me. The annoyances I might thus bring upon myself did not fail to present themselves to my mind; but the firm resolution I made to keep my writings secret from everybody, appeared to me to remedy all evils. I commenced my memoirs then in July, 1694, being at that time colonel of a cavalry regiment bearing my name, in the camp of Guinsheim, upon the old Rhine, in the army commanded by the Maréchal Duc de Lorges.

In 1691 I was studying my philosophy and beginning to learn to ride at an academy at Rochefort,—getting mightily tired of masters and books, and anxious to join the army. The siege of Mons, formed by the King in person, at the commencement of the spring, had drawn away all the young men of my age to commence their first campaign; and, what piqued me most, the Duc de Chartres was there, too. I had been, as it were, educated with him. I was younger than he by eight months; and if the expression be allowed in speaking of young people, so unequal in position, friendship had united us. I made up my mind, therefore, to escape from my leading-strings; but pass lightly over the artifices I used in order to attain success. I addressed myself to my mother. I soon saw that she trifled with me. I had recourse to my father, whom I made believe that the King, having led a great siege this year, would rest the next. I said nothing of this to my mother, who did not discover my plot until it was just upon the point of execution.

The King had determined rigidly to adhere to a rule he had laid down—namely, that none who entered the service, except his illegitimate children, and the Princes of the blood royal, should be exempt from serving for a year in one of his two companies of musketeers; and passing afterwards through the ordeal of being private or subaltern in one of the regiments of cavalry or infantry,—before receiving permission to purchase a regiment. My father took me, therefore, to Versailles, where he had not been for many years, and begged of the King admission for me into the Musketeers. It was on the day of *St. Simon* and *St. Jude,* at half-past twelve, and just as his Majesty came out of the council.

The King did my father the honour of embracing him three times, and then turned towards me. Finding that I was little and of delicate appearance, he said I was still very young; to which my father replied, that I should be able in consequence to serve longer. Thereupon the King demanded in which of the two companies he wished to put me; and my father named that commanded by Maupertuis, who was one of his friends. The King relied much upon the information given him by the captains of the two companies of Musketeers, as to the young men who served in them.

I have reason for believing, that I owe to Maupertuis the first good opinion that his Majesty had of me.

Three months after entering the Musketeers, that is to say, in the March of the following year, the King held a review of his guards, and of the gendarmerie, at Compiègne, and I mounted guard once at the palace. During this little journey there was talk of a much more important one. My joy was extreme; but my father, who had not counted upon this, repented of having believed me, when I told him that the King would no doubt rest at Paris this year. My mother, after a little vexation and pouting at finding me enrolled by my father against her will, did not fail to bring him to reason, and to make him provide me with an equipment of thirty-five horses or mules, and means to live honourably.

A grievous annoyance happened in our house about three weeks before my departure. A steward of my father named Tessé, who had been with him many years, disappeared all at once with fifty thousand francs due to various tradesfolk. He had written out false receipts from these people, and put them in his accounts. He was a little man, gentle, affable, and clever; who had shown some probity, and who had many friends.

The King set out on the 10th of May, 1692, with the ladies; and I performed the journey on horseback with the soldiers and all the attendants, like the other Musketeers, and continued to do so through the whole campaign. I was accompanied by two gentlemen; the one had been my tutor, the other was my mother's squire. The King's army was formed at the camp of Gevries; that of M. de Luxembourg almost joined it. The ladies were at Mons, two leagues distant. The King made them come into his camp, where he entertained them; and then showed them, perhaps, the most superb review which had ever been seen. The two armies were ranged in two lines, the right of M. de Luxembourg's touching the left of the King's,—the whole extending over three leagues of ground.

After stopping ten days at Gevries, the two armies separated and marched. Two days afterwards the siege of Namur was declared. The King arrived there in five days. Monsiegneur (son of the King); Monsieur (Duc d'Orléans, brother of the King); M. le Prince (de Condé) and Maréchal d'Humières; all four, the one under the other, commanded in the King's army under the King himself. The Duc de Luxembourg, sole general of his own army, covered the siege operations, and observed the enemy. The ladies went away to Dinant. On the third day of the march M. le Prince went forward to invest the place.

The celebrated Vauban, the life and soul of all the sieges the King made, was of opinion that the town should be attacked separately from the castle; and his advice was acted upon. The Baron de Bressé, however, who had fortified the place, was for attacking town and castle together. He was a humble downlooking man, whose physiognomy promised nothing, but who soon acquired the confidence of the King, and the esteem of the army.

The Prince de Condé, Maréchal d'Humières, and the Marquis de Boufflers each led an attack. There was nothing worthy of note during the ten days the siege lasted. On the eleventh day, after the trenches had been opened, a parley was beaten and a capitulation made almost as the besieged desired it. They withdrew to the castle; and it was agreed that it should not be attacked from the town-side, and that the town was not to be battered by it. During the siege the King was almost always in his tent; and the weather remained constantly warm and serene. We lost scarcely anybody of consequence. The Comte de Toulouse received a slight wound in the arm while quite close to the King, who from a prominent place was witnessing the attack of a half-moon, which was carried in broad daylight by a detachment of the oldest of the two companies of Musketeers.

The siege of the castle next commenced. The position of the camp was changed. The King's tents and those of all the Court were pitched in a beautiful meadow about five hundred paces from the monastery of Marlaigne. The fine weather changed to rain, which fell with an abundance and perseverance never before known by any one in the army. This circumstance increased the reputation of Saint Médard, whose fête falls on the 8th of June. It rained in torrents that day, and it is said that when such is the case it will rain for forty days afterwards. By chance it happened so this year. The soldiers in despair at this deluge uttered many imprecations against the Saint; and looked for images of him, burning and breaking as many as they could find. The rains sadly interfered with the progress of the siege. The tents of the King could only be communicated with by paths laid with fascines which required to be renewed every day, as they sank down into the soil. The camps and quarters were no longer accessible; the trenches were full of mud and water, and it took often three days to remove cannon from one battery to another. The waggons became useless, too, so that the transport of bombs, shot, and so forth, could not be performed except upon the backs of mules and of horses taken from the equipages of the Court and the army. The state of the roads deprived the Duc de Luxembourg of the use of waggons and other vehicles. His army was perishing for want of grain. To remedy this inconvenience the King ordered all his household troops to mount every day on horseback by detachments, and to take sacks of grain upon their cruppers to a village where they were to be received and counted by the officers of the Duc de Luxembourg. Although the household of the King had scarcely any repose during this siege, what with carrying fascines, furnishing guards, and other daily services, this increase of duty was given to it because the cavalry served continually also, and was reduced almost entirely to leaves of trees for provender.

The household of the King, accustomed to all sorts of distinctions, complained bitterly of this task. But the King turned a deaf ear to them, and would be obeyed. On the first day some of the Gendarmes and of the light horse of the guard arrived early in the morning at the depôt of the sacks, and commenced murmuring and exciting each other by their discourses. They threw down the sacks at last and flatly refused to carry them. I had been asked very politely if I would be of the detachment for the sacks or of some other. I decided for the sacks, because I felt that I might thereby advance myself, the subject having already made much noise. I arrived with the detachment of the Musketeers at the moment of the refusal of the others; and I loaded my sack before their eyes. Marin, a brigadier of cavalry and lieutenant of the body guards, who was there to superintend the operation, noticed me, and full of anger at the refusal he had just met with, exclaimed that as I did not think such work beneath me, the rest would do well to imitate my example. Without a word being spoken each took up his sack; and from that time forward no further difficulty occurred in the matter. As soon as the detachment had gone, Marin went straight to the King and told him what had occurred. This was a service which procured for me several obliging discourses from his Majesty, who during the rest of the siege always sought to say something agreeable every time he met me.

The twenty-seventh day after opening the trenches, that is, the first of July, 1692, a parley was sounded by the Prince de Barbançon, governor of the place,—a fortunate circumstance for the besiegers, who were worn out with fatigue, and destitute of means, on account of the wretched weather which still continued, and which had turned the whole country round into a quagmire. Even the horses of the King lived upon leaves, and not a horse of all our numerous cavalry ever thoroughly recovered from the effects of such sorry fare. It is certain that without the presence of the King the siege might never have been successful; but he being there, everybody was stimulated. Yet had the place held out ten days longer, there is no saying what might have happened. Before the end of the siege the King was so much fatigued with his exertions, that a new attack of gout came on, with more pain than ever, and compelled him to keep his bed, where, however, he thought of everything, and laid out his plans as though he had been at Versailles.

During the entire siege, the Prince of Orange (William III. of England) had unavailingly used all his science to dislodge the Duc de Luxembourg; but he had to do with a man who in matters of war was his superior, and who continued so all his life. Namur, which, by the surrender of the castle, was now entirely in our power, was one of the strongest places in the Low Countries, and had hitherto boasted of having never changed masters. The inhabitants could not restrain their tears of sorrow. Even the monks of Marlaigne were profoundly moved, so much so, that they could not disguise their grief. The King, feeling for the loss of their corn that they had sent for safety into

Namur, gave them double the quantity, and abundant alms. He incommoded them as little as possible, and would not permit the passage of cannon across their park, until it was found impossible to transport it by any other road. Notwithstanding these acts of goodness, they could scarcely look upon a Frenchman after the taking of the place; and one actually refused to give a bottle of beer to an usher of the King's antechamber, although offered a bottle of champagne in exchange for it!

A circumstance happened just after the taking of Namur, which might have led to the saddest results, under any other prince than the King. Before he entered the town, a strict examination of every place was made, although by the capitulation all the mines, magazines, &c., had to be shown. At a visit paid to the Jesuits, they pretended to show everything, expressing, however, surprise and something more, that their bare word was not enough. But on examining here and there, where they did not expect search would be made, their cellars were found to be stored with gunpowder, of which they had taken good care to say no word. What they meant to do with it is uncertain. It was carried away, and as they were Jesuits nothing was done.

During the course of this siege, the King suffered a cruel disappointment. James II. of England, then a refugee in France, had advised the King to give battle to the English fleet. Joined to that of Holland it was very superior to the sea forces of France. Tourville, our admiral, so famous for his valour and skill, pointed this circumstance out to the King. But it was all to no effect. He was ordered to attack the enemy. He did so. Many of his ships were burnt, and the victory was won by the English. A courier entrusted with this sad intelligence was despatched to the King. On his way he was joined by another courier, who pressed him for his news. The first courier knew that if he gave up his news, the other, who was better mounted, would outstrip him, and be the first to carry it to the King. He told his companion, therefore, an idle tale, very different indeed from the truth, for he changed the defeat into a great victory. Having gained this wonderful intelligence, the second courier put spurs to his horse, and hurried away to the King's camp, eager to be the bearer of good tidings. He reached the camp first, and was received with delight. While his Majesty was still in great joy at his happy victory, the other courier arrived with the real details. The Court appeared prostrated. The King was much afflicted. Nevertheless he found means to appear to retain his self-possession, and I saw, for the first time, that Courts are not long in affliction or occupied with sadness. I must mention that the (exiled) King of England looked on at this naval battle from the shore; and was accused of allowing expressions of partiality to escape him in favour of his countrymen, although none had kept their promises to him.

Two days after the defeated garrison had marched out, the King went to Dinant, to join the ladies, with whom he returned to Versailles. I had hoped that Monseigneur would finish the campaign, and that I should be with him, and it was not without regret that I returned towards Paris. On the way a little circumstance happened. One of our halting-places was Marienburgh, where we camped for the night. I had become united in friendship with Comte de Coetquen, who was in the same company with myself. He was well instructed and full of wit; was exceedingly rich, and even more idle than rich. That evening he had invited several of us to supper in his tent. I went there early, and found him stretched out upon his bed, from which I dislodged him playfully and laid myself down in his place, several of our officers standing by. Coetquen, sporting with me in return, took his gun, which he thought to be unloaded, and pointed it at me. But to our great surprise the weapon went off. Fortunately for me, I was at that moment lying flat upon the bed. Three balls passed just above my head, and then just above the heads of our two tutors, who were walking outside the tent. Coetquen fainted at thought of the mischief he might have done, and we had all the pains in the world to bring him to himself again; indeed, he did not thoroughly recover for several days. I relate this as a lesson which ought to teach us never to play with fire-arms.

The poor lad,—to finish at once all that concerns him,—did not long survive this incident. He entered the King's regiment, and when just upon the point of joining it in the following spring, came to me and said he had had his fortune told by a woman named Du Perchoir, who practised her trade secretly at Paris, and that she had predicted he would be soon drowned. I rated him soundly for indulging a curiosity so dangerous and so foolish. A few days after he set out for Amiens. He found another fortune-teller there, a man, who made the same prediction. In marching afterwards with the regiment of the King to join the army, he wished to water his horse in the *Escaut*, and was drowned there, in the presence of the whole regiment, without it being possible to give him any aid. I felt extreme regret for his loss, which for his friends and his family was irreparable.

But I must go back a little, and speak of two marriages that took place at the commencement of this year, the first (most extraordinary) on the 18th February, the other a month after.

CHAPTER II

THE King was very anxious to establish his illegitimate children, whom he advanced day by day; and had married two of them, daughters, to Princes of the blood. One of these, the Princesse de Conti, only daughter of the King and Madame de la Vallière, was a widow without children; the other, eldest daughter of the King and Madame de Montespan, had married Monsieur le Duc (Louis de Bourbon, eldest son of the Prince de Condé). For some time past Madame de Maintenon, even more than the King, had thought of nothing else than how to raise the remaining illegitimate children, and wished to marry Mademoiselle de Blois (second daughter of the King and of Madame de Montespan) to Monsieur the Duc de Chartres. The Duc de Chartres was the sole nephew of the King, and was much above the Princes of the blood by his rank of *Grandson* of France, and by the Court that Monsieur his father kept up.

The marriages of the two Princes of the blood, of which I have just spoken, had scandalised all the world. The King was not ignorant of this; and he could thus judge of the effect of a marriage even more startling; such as was this proposed one. But for four years he had turned it over in his mind and had even taken the first steps to bring it about. It was the more difficult because the father of the Duc de Chartres was infinitely proud of his rank, and the mother belonged to a nation which abhorred illegitimacy and misalliances, and was indeed of a character to forbid all hope of her ever relishing this marriage.

In order to vanquish all these obstacles, the King applied to M. le Grand (Louis de Lorraine). This person was brother of the Chevalier de Lorraine, the favourite, by disgraceful means, of Monsieur, father of the Duc de Chartres. The two brothers, unscrupulous and corrupt, entered willingly into the scheme, but demanded as a reward, paid in advance, to be made "Chevaliers of the Order." This was done, although somewhat against the inclination of the King, and success was promised.

The young Duc de Chartres had at that time for teacher Dubois (afterwards the famous Cardinal Dubois), whose history was singular. He had formerly been a valet; but displaying unusual aptitude for learning, had been instructed by his master in literature and history, and in due time passed into the service of Saint Laurent, who was the Duc de Chartres' first instructor. He became so useful and showed so much skill, that Saint Laurent made him become an abbé. Thus raised in position, he passed much time with the Duc de Chartres, assisting him to prepare his lessons, to write his exercises, and to look out words in the dictionary. I have seen him thus engaged over and over again, when I used to go and play with the Duc de Chartres. As Saint Laurent grew infirm, Dubois little by little supplied his place; supplied it well too, and yet pleased the young Duke. When Saint Laurent died Dubois aspired to succeed him. He had paid his court to the Chevalier de Lorraine, by whose influence he was much aided in obtaining his wish. When at last appointed successor to Saint Laurent, I never saw a man so glad, nor with more reason. The extreme obligation he was under to the Chevalier de Lorraine, and still more the difficulty of maintaining himself in his new position, attached him more and more to his protector.

It was, then, Dubois that the Chevalier de Lorraine made use of to gain the consent of the young Duc de Chartres to the marriage proposed by the King. Dubois had, in fact, gained the Duke's confidence, which it was easy to do at that age; had made him afraid of his father and of the King; and, on the other hand, had filled him with fine hopes and expectations. All that Dubois could do, however, when he broke the matter of the marriage to the young Duke, was to ward off a direct refusal; but that was sufficient for the success of the enterprise. Monsieur was already gained, and as soon as the King had a reply from Dubois he hastened to broach the affair. A day or two before this, however, Madame (mother of the Duc de Chartres) had scent of what was going on. She spoke to her son of the indignity of this marriage with that force in which she was never wanting, and drew from him a promise that he would not consent to it. Thus, he was feeble towards his teacher, feeble towards his mother, and there was aversion on the one hand and fear on the other, and great embarrassment on all sides.

One day early after dinner I saw M. de Chartres, with a very sad air, come out of his apartment and enter the closet of the King. He found his Majesty alone with Monsieur. The King spoke very obligingly to the Duc de Chartres, said that he wished to see him married; that he offered him his daughter, but that he did not intend to constrain him in the matter, but left him quite at liberty. This discourse, however, pronounced with that terrifying majesty so natural to the King, and addressed to a timid young prince, took away his voice, and quite unnerved him. He thought to escape from his slippery position by throwing himself upon Monsieur and Madame, and stammeringly replied that the King was master, but that a son's will depended upon that of his parents. "What you say is very proper," replied the King; "but as soon as you consent to my proposition your father and mother will not oppose it." And then turning to Monsieur he said, "Is this not true, my brother?" Monsieur consented, as he had already done, and the only person remaining to consult was Madame, who was immediately sent for.

As soon as she came, the King, making her acquainted with his project, said that he reckoned she would not oppose what her husband and her son had already agreed to. Madame, who had counted upon the refusal of her son, was tongue-tied. She threw two furious glances upon Monsieur and upon the Duc de Chartres, and then said that, as they wished it, she had nothing to say, made a slight reverence, and went away. Her son immediately followed her to explain his conduct; but railing against him, with tears in her eyes, she would not listen, and drove him from her room. Her husband, who shortly afterwards joined her, met with almost the same treatment.

That evening an "Apartment" was held at the palace, as was customary three times a week during the winter; the other three evenings being set apart for comedy, and the Sunday being free. An Apartment, as it was called, was an assemblage of all the Court in the grand saloon, from seven o'clock in the evening until ten, when the King sat down to table; and, after ten, in one of the saloons at the end of the grand gallery towards the tribune of the chapel. In the first place there was some music; then tables were placed all about for all kinds of gambling; there was a *lansquenet*, at which Monsieur and Monseigneur always played; also a billiard-table; in a word, every one was free to play with every one, and allowed to ask for fresh tables if all the others were occupied. Beyond the billiards was a refreshment-room. All was perfectly lighted. At the outset, the King went to the "apartments" very often and played, but lately he had ceased to do so. He spent the evening with Madame de Maintenon, working with different ministers one after the other. But still he wished his courtiers to attend assiduously.

This evening, directly after the music had finished, the King sent for Monseigneur and Monsieur, who were already playing at *lansquenet;* Madame, who scarcely looked at a party of *hombre* at which she had seated herself; the Duc de Chartres, who, with a rueful visage, was playing at chess; and Mademoiselle de Blois, who had scarcely begun to appear in society, but who this evening was extraordinarily decked out, and who, as yet, knew nothing and suspected nothing; and therefore, being naturally very timid, and horribly afraid of the King, believed herself sent for in order to be reprimanded, and trembled so that Madame de Maintenon took her upon her knees, where she held her, but was scarcely able to reassure her. The fact of these royal persons being sent for by the King at once made people think that a marriage was in contemplation. In a few minutes they returned, and then the announcement was made public. I arrived at that moment. I found everybody in clusters, and great astonishment expressed upon every face. Madame was walking in the gallery with Châteauthiers—her favourite, and worthy of being so. She took long strides, her handkerchief in her hand, weeping without constraint, speaking pretty loudly, gesticulating, and looking like Ceres after the rape of her daughter Proserpine, seeking her in fury, and demanding her back from Jupiter. Every one respectfully made way to let her pass. Monsieur, who had returned to *lansquenet*, seemed overwhelmed with shame, and his son appeared in despair; and the bride-elect was marvellously embarrassed and sad. Though very young, and likely to be dazzled by such a marriage, she understood what was passing, and feared the consequences. Most people appeared full of consternation.

The Apartment, which, however heavy in appearance, was full of interest to me, seemed quite short. It finished by the supper of the King. His Majesty appeared quite at ease. Madame's eyes were full of tears, which fell from time to time as she looked into every face around, as if in search of all our thoughts. Her son, whose eyes too were red, she would not give a glance to; nor to Monsieur: all three ate scarcely anything. I remarked that the King offered Madame nearly all the dishes that were before him, and that she refused with an air of rudeness which did not, however, check his politeness. It was furthermore noticeable that, after leaving the table, he made to Madame a very marked and very low reverence, during which she performed so complete a pirouette, that the King on raising his head found nothing but her back before him, removed about a step further towards the door.

On the morrow we went as usual to wait in the gallery for the breaking-up of the council, and for the King's Mass. Madame came there. Her son approached her, as he did every day, to kiss her hand. At that very moment she gave him a box on the ear, so sonorous that it was heard several steps distant. Such treatment in presence of all the Court covered with confusion this unfortunate prince, and overwhelmed the infinite number of spectators, of whom I was one, with prodigious astonishment.

That day the immense dowry was declared; and on Sunday there was a grand ball, that is, a ball opened by a *branle*, which settled the order of the dancing throughout the evening. Monseigneur the Duc de Bourgogne danced on this occasion for the first time; and led off the *branle* with Mademoiselle. I danced also for the first time at Court. My partner was Mademoiselle de Sourches, daughter of the Grand Prévôt; she danced excellently. I had been that morning to wait on Madame, who could not refrain from saying, in a sharp and angry voice, that I was doubtless very glad of the promise of so many balls—that this was natural at my age; but that, for her part, she was old, and wished they were well over. A few days after, the contract of marriage was signed in the closet of the King, and in the presence of all the Court. The same day the household of the future Duchesse de Chartres was declared. The King gave her a first gentleman usher and a Dame d'Atours, until then reserved to the daughters of France, and a lady of honour, in order to carry out completely so strange a novelty. I must say something about the persons who composed this household.

M. de Villars was gentleman usher; he was grandson of a recorder of Coindrieu, and one of the best made men in France. There was a great deal of fighting in his young days, and he had acquired a reputation for courage and skill. To these qualities he owed his fortune. M. de Nemours was his first patron, and, in a duel which he had with M. de Beaufort, took Villars for second. M. de Nemours was killed; but Villars was victorious against his adversary, and passed into the service of the Prince de Conti as one of his gentlemen. He succeeded in gaining confidence in his new employment; so much so, that the marriage which afterwards took place between the Prince de Conti and the niece of Cardinal Mazarin was brought about in part by his assistance. He became the confidant of the married pair, and their bond of union with the Cardinal. His position gave him an opportunity of mixing in society much above him; but on this he never presumed. His face was his passport with the ladies: he was gallant, even discreet; and this means was not unuseful to him. He pleased Madame Scarron, who upon the throne never forgot the friendships of this kind, so freely intimate, which she had formed as a private person. Villars was employed in diplomacy; and from honour to honour, at last reached the order of the Saint Esprit, in 1698. His wife was full of wit, and scandalously inclined. Both were very poor—and always dangled about the Court, where they had many powerful friends.

The Maréchale de Rochefort was lady of honour. She was of the house of Montmorency—a widow—handsome—sprightly; formed by nature to live at Court—apt for gallantry and intrigues; full of worldly cleverness, from living much in the world, with little cleverness of any other kind, nearly enough for any post and any business. M. de Louvois found her suited to his taste, and she accommodated herself very well to his purse, and to the display she made by this intimacy. She always became the friend of every new mistress of the King; and when he favoured Madame de Soubise, it was at the Maréchale's house that she waited, with closed doors, for Bontems, the King's valet, who led her by private ways to his Majesty. The Maréchale herself has related to me how one day she was embarrassed to get rid of the people that Madame de Soubise (who had not had time to announce her arrival) found at her house; and how she almost died of fright lest Bontems should return and the interview be broken off if he arrived before the company had departed. The Maréchale de Rochefort was in this way the friend of Mesdames de la Vallière, de Montespan, and de Soubise; and she became the friend of Madame de Maintenon, to whom she attached herself in proportion as she saw her favour increase. She had, at the marriage of Monseigneur, been made Dame d'Atours to the new Dauphiness; and, if people were astonished at that, they were also astonished to see her lady of honour to an "illegitimate grand-daughter of France."

The Comtesse de Mailly was Dame d'Atours. She was related to Madame de Maintenon, to whose favour she owed her marriage with the Comte de Mailly. She had come to Paris with all her provincial awkwardness, and, from want of wit, had never been able to get rid of it. On the contrary, she grafted thereon an immense conceit, caused by the favour of Madame de Maintenon. To complete the household, came M. de Fontaine-Martel, poor and gouty, who was first master of the horse.

On the Monday before Shrove Tuesday, all the marriage party and the bride and bridegroom, superbly dressed, repaired, a little before mid-day, to the closet of the King, and afterwards to the chapel. It was arranged, as usual, for the Mass of the King, excepting that between his place and the altar were two cushions for the bride and bridegroom, who turned their backs to the King. Cardinal de Bouillon, in full robes, married them, and said Mass. From the chapel all the company went to table: it was of horse-shoe shape. The Princes and Princesses of the blood were placed at the right and at the left, according to their rank, terminated by the two illegitimate children of the King, and, for the first time, after them, the Duchesse de Verneuil; so that M. de Verneuil, illegitimate son of Henry IV., became thus "Prince of the blood" so many years after his death, without having ever suspected it. The Duc d'Uzês thought this so amusing that he marched in front of the Duchess, crying out, as loud as he could—"Place, place for Madame Charlotte Séguier!" In the afternoon the King and Queen of England came to Versailles with their Court. There was a great concert; and the play-tables were set out. The supper was similar to the dinner. Afterwards the married couple were led into the apartment of the new Duchesse de Chartres. The Queen of England gave the Duchess her chemise; and the shirt of the Duke was given to him by the King, who had at first refused on the plea that he was in too unhappy circumstances. The benediction of the bed was pronounced by the Cardinal de Bouillon, who kept us all waiting for a quarter of an hour; which made people say that such airs little became a man returned as he was from a long exile, to which he had been sent because he had had the madness to refuse the nuptial benediction to Madame la Duchesse unless admitted to the royal banquet.

On Shrove Tuesday, there was a grand toilette of the Duchesse de Chartres, to which the King and all the Court came; and in the evening a grand ball, similar to that which had just taken place, except that the new Duchesse de Chartres was led out by the Duc de Bourgogne. Every one wore the same dress, and had the same partner as before.

I cannot pass over in silence a very ridiculous adventure which occurred at both of these balls. A son of Montbron, no more made to dance at Court than his father was to be chevalier of the order (to which however, he was promoted in 1688), was among the company. He had been asked if he danced well; and he had replied with a confidence which made every one hope that the contrary was the case. Every one was satisfied. From the very first bow, he became confused, and he lost step at once. He tried to divert attention from his mistake by affected attitudes, and carrying his arms high; but this made him only more ridiculous, and excited bursts of laughter, which, in despite of the respect due to the person of the King (who likewise had great difficulty to hinder himself from laughing), degenerated at length into regular hooting. On the morrow, instead of flying the Court or holding his tongue, he excused himself by saying that the presence of the King had disconcerted him, and promised marvels for the ball which was to follow. He was one of my friends, and I felt for him. I should even have warned him against a second attempt, if the very indifferent success I had met with had not made me fear that my advice would be taken in ill part. As soon as he began to dance at the second ball, those who were near stood up, those who were far off climbed wherever they could get a sight; and the shouts of laughter were mingled with clapping of hands. Every one, even the King himself, laughed heartily, and most of us quite loud, so that I do not think any one was ever treated so before. Montbron disappeared immediately afterwards, and did not show himself again for a long time. It was a pity he exposed himself to this defeat, for he was an honourable and brave man.

Ash Wednesday put an end to all these sad rejoicings by command, and only the expected rejoicings were spoken of. M. du Maine wished to marry. The King tried to turn him from it, and said frankly to him, that it was not for such as he to make a lineage. But pressed by Madame de Maintenon, who had educated M. du Maine, and who felt for him as a nurse, the King resolved to marry him to a daughter of the Prince de Condé. The Prince was greatly pleased at the project. He had three daughters for M. du Maine to choose from: all three were extremely little. An inch of height, that the second had above the others, procured for her the preference, much to the grief of the eldest, who was beautiful and clever, and who dearly wished to escape from the slavery in which her father kept her. The dignity with which she bore her disappointment was admired by every one, but it cost her an effort that ruined her health. The marriage once arranged, was celebrated on the 19th of March, much in the same manner as had been that of the Duc de Chartres. Madame de Saint-Vallery was appointed lady of honour to Madame du Maine, and M. de Montchevreuil gentleman of the chamber. This last had been one of the friends of Madame de Maintenon when she was Madame Scarron. Montchevreuil was a very honest man, modest, brave, but thick-headed. His wife was a tall creature, meagre, and yellow, who laughed sillily, and showed long and ugly teeth; who was extremely devout, of a compassed mien, and who only wanted a broomstick to be a perfect witch. Without possessing any wit, she had so captivated Madame de Maintenon, that the latter saw only with her eyes. All the ladies of the Court were under her surveillance: they depended upon her for their distinctions, and often for their fortunes. Everybody, from the ministers to the daughters of the King, trembled before her. The King himself showed her the most marked consideration. She was of all the Court journeys, and always with Madame de Maintenon.

The marriage of M. du Maine caused a rupture between the Princess de Condé and the Duchess of Hanover her sister, who had strongly desired M. du Maine for one of her daughters, and who pretended that the Prince de Condé had cut the grass from under her feet. She lived in Paris, making a display quite unsuited to her rank, and had even carried it so far as to go about with two coaches and many liveried servants. With this state one day she met in the streets the coach of Madame de Bouillon, which the servants of the German woman forced to give way to their mistress's. The Bouillons, piqued to excess, resolved to be revenged. One day, when they knew the Duchess was going to the play, they went there attended by a numerous livery. Their servants had orders to pick a quarrel with those of the Duchess. They executed these orders completely; the servants of the Duchess were thoroughly thrashed—the harness of her horses cut—her coaches maltreated. The Duchess made a great fuss, and complained to the King, but he would not mix himself in the matter. She was so outraged, that she resolved to retire into Germany, and in a very few months did so.

My year of service in the Musketeers being over, the King, after a time, gave me, without purchase, a company of cavalry in the Royal Roussillon, in garrison at Mons, and just then very incomplete. I thanked the King, who replied to me very obligingly. The company was entirely made up in a fortnight. This was towards the middle of April.

A little before, that is, on the 27th of March, the King made seven new maréchals of France. They were the Comte de Choiseul, the Duc de Villeroy, the Marquis de Joyeuse, Tourville, the Duc de Noailles, the Marquis de Boufflers, and Catinat. These promotions caused very great discontent. Complaint was more especially made that the Duc de Choiseul had not been named. The cause of his exclusion is curious. His wife, beautiful, with the form of a goddess—notorious for the number of her gallantries—was very intimate with the Princess de Conti. The King, not liking such a companion for his daughter, gave the Duc de Choiseul to understand that the public disorders of the Duchess offended him. If the Duke would send her into a convent, the Maréchal's bâton would be his. The Duc de Choiseul, indignant that the reward of his services in the war was attached to a domestic affair which concerned himself alone, refused promotion on such terms. He thus lost the bâton; and, what was worse for him, the Duchess soon after was driven from Court, and so misbehaved herself, that at last he could endure her no longer, drove her away himself, and separated from her for ever.

Mademoiselle—la grande Mademoiselle, as she was called, to distinguish her from the daughter of Monsieur—or to call her by her name, Mademoiselle de Montpensier,—died on Sunday the 5th of April, at her palace in the Luxembourg, sixty-three years of age, and the richest private princess in Europe. She interested herself much in those who were related to her, even to the lowest degree, and wore mourning for them, however far removed. It is well known, from all the memoirs of the time, that she was greatly in love with M. de Lauzun, and that she suffered much when the King withheld his permission to their marriage. M. de Lauzun was so enraged, that he could not contain himself, and at last went so far beyond bounds, that he was sent prisoner to Pignerol, where he remained, extremely ill-treated, for ten years. The affection of Mademoiselle did not grow cold by separation. The King profited by it, to make M. de Lauzun buy his liberty at her expense, and thus enriched M. du Maine. He always gave out that he had married Mademoiselle, and appeared before the King, after her death, in a long cloak, which gave great displeasure. He also assumed ever afterwards a dark brown livery, as an external expression of his grief for Mademoiselle, of whom he had portraits everywhere. As for Mademoiselle, the King never quite forgave her the day of Saint Antoine; and I heard him once at supper reproach her in jest, for having fired the cannons of the Bastille upon his troops. She was a little embarrassed, but she got out of the difficulty very well.

Her body was laid out with great state, watched for several days, two hours at a time, by a duchess or a princess, and by two ladies of quality. The Comtesse de Soissons refused to take part in this watching, and would not obey until the King threatened to dismiss her from the Court. A very ridiculous accident happened in the midst of this ceremony. The urn containing the entrails fell over, with a frightful noise and a stink sudden and intolerable. The ladies, the heralds, the psalmodists, everybody present fled, in confusion. Every one tried to gain the door first. The entrails had been badly embalmed, and it was their fermentation which caused the accident. They were soon perfumed and put in order, and everybody laughed at this mishap. These entrails were in the end carried to the Célestins, the heart to Val de Grâce, and the body to the Cathedral of Saint Denis, followed by a numerous company.

CHAPTER III

ON May 3d, 1693, the King announced his intention of placing himself at the head of his army in Flanders, and, having made certain alterations in the rule of precedence of the maréchale of France, soon after began the campaign. I have here, however, to draw attention to my private affairs, for on the above-mentioned day, at ten o'clock in the morning, I had the misfortune to lose my father. He was eighty-seven years of age, and had been in bad health for some time, with a touch of gout during the last three weeks. On the day in question he had dined as usual with his friends, had retired to bed, and, while talking to those around him there, all at once gave three violent sighs. He was dead almost before it was perceived that he was ill; there was no more oil in the lamp.

I learned this sad news after seeing the King to bed; his Majesty was to purge himself on the morrow. The night was given to the just sentiments of nature; but the next day I went early to visit Bontems, and then the Duc de Beauvilliers, who promised to ask the King, as soon as his curtains were opened, to grant me the offices my father had held. The King very graciously complied with his request, and in the afternoon said many obliging things to me, particularly expressing his regret that my father had not been able to receive the last sacraments. I was able to say that a very short time before, my father had retired for several days to Saint Lazare, where was his confessor, and added something on the piety of his life. The

King exhorted me to behave well, and promised to take care of me. When my father was first taken ill, several persons, amongst others, D'Aubigné, brother of Madame de Maintenon, had asked for the governorship of Blaye. But the King refused them all, and said very bluntly to D'Aubigné, "Is there not a son?" He had, in fact, always given my father to understand I should succeed him, although generally he did not allow offices to descend from father to son.

Let me say a few words about my father. Our family in my grandfather's time had become impoverished; and my father was early sent to the Court as page to Louis XIII. It was very customary then for the sons of reduced gentlemen to accept this occupation. The King was passionately fond of hunting, an amusement that was carried on with far less state, without that abundance of dogs, and followers, and convenience of all kinds which his successor introduced, and especially without roads through the forests. My father, who noticed the impatience of the King at the delays that occurred in changing horses, thought of turning the head of the horse he brought towards the crupper of that which the King quitted. By this means, without putting his feet to the ground, his Majesty, who was active, jumped from one horse to another. He was so pleased that whenever he changed horses he asked for this same page. From that time my father grew day by day in favour. The King made him Chief Écuyer, and in course of years bestowed other rewards upon him, created him Duke and peer of France, and gave him the Government of Blaye. My father, much attached to the King, followed him in all his expeditions, several times commanded the cavalry of the army, was commander-in-chief of all the arrièrebans of the kingdom, and acquired great reputation in the field for his valour and skill. With Cardinal Richelieu he was intimate without sympathy, and more than once, but notably on the famous Day of the Dupes, rendered signal service to that minister. My father used often to be startled out of his sleep in the middle of the night by a valet, with a taper in his hand, drawing the curtain—having behind him the Cardinal de Richelieu, who would often take the taper and sit down upon the bed and exclaim that he was a lost man, and ask my father's advice upon news that he had received or on quarrels he had had with the King. When all Paris was in consternation at the success of the Spaniards, who had crossed the frontier, taken Corbie, and seized all the country as far as Compiègne, the King insisted on my father being present at the council which was then held. The Cardinal de Richelieu maintained that the King should retreat beyond the Seine, and all the assembly seemed of that opinion. But the King in a speech which lasted a quarter of an hour opposed this, and said that to retreat at such a moment would be to increase the general disorder. Then turning to my father he ordered him to be prepared to depart for Corbie on the morrow, with as many of his men as he could get ready. The histories and the memoirs of the time show that this bold step saved the state. The Cardinal, great man as he was, trembled, until the first appearance of success, when he grew bold enough to join the King. This is a specimen of the conduct of that weak King governed by that first minister to whom poets and historians have given the glory they have stripped from his master; as, for instance, all the works of the siege of Rochelle, and the invention and unheard-of success of the celebrated dyke, all solely due to the late King!

Louis XIII. loved my father; but he could scold him at times. On two occasions he did so. The first, as my father has related to me, was on account of the Duc de Bellegarde. The Duke was in disgrace, and had been exiled. My father, who was a friend of his, wished to write to him one day, and for want of other leisure, being then much occupied, took the opportunity of the King's momentary absence to carry out his desire. Just as he was finishing his letter, the King came in; my father tried to hide the paper, but the eyes of the King were too quick for him. " What is that paper?" said he. My father, embarrassed, admitted that it was a few words he had written to M. de Bellegarde.

"Let me see it," said the King; and he took the paper and read it. "I don't find fault with you," said he, "for writing to your friends, although in disgrace, for I know you will write nothing improper; but what displeases me is, that you should fail in the respect you owe to a duke and peer, in that, because he is exiled, you should omit to address him as *Monseigneur;*" and then tearing the letter in two, he added, "Write it again after the hunt, and put Monseigneur, as you ought." My father was very glad to be let off so easily.

The other reprimand was upon a more serious subject. The King was really enamoured of Mademoiselle d'Hautefort. My father, young and gallant, could not comprehend why he did not gratify his love. He believed his reserve to arise from timidity, and under this impression proposed one day to the King to be his ambassador and to bring the affair to a satisfactory conclusion. The King allowed him to speak to the end, and then assumed a severe air. "It is true," said he, "that I am enamoured of her, that I feel it, that I seek her, that I speak of her willingly, and think of her still more willingly; it is true also that I act thus in spite of myself, because I am mortal

and have this weakness; but the more facility I have
as King to gratify myself, the more I ought to be on
my guard against sin and scandal. I pardon you this
time, but never address to me a similar discourse again
if you wish that I should continue to love you." This
was a thunderbolt for my father; the scales fell from
his eyes; the idea of the King's timidity in love disappeared before the display of a virtue so pure and
so triumphant.

My father's career was for a long time very successful, but unfortunately he had an enemy who
brought it to an end. This enemy was M. de
Chavigny: he was secretary of state, and had also
the war department. Either from stupidity or malice
he had left all the towns in Picardy badly supported;
a circumstance the Spaniards knew well how to profit
by when they took Corbie in 1636. My father had an
uncle who commanded in one of these towns, La
Capelle, and who had several times asked for ammunition and stores without success. My father spoke
upon this subject to Chavigny, to the Cardinal de
Richelieu, and to the King, but with no good effect.
La Capelle, left without resources, fell like the places
around. As I have said before, Louis XIII. did not
long allow the Spaniards to enjoy the advantages they
had gained. All the towns in Picardy were soon retaken, and the King, urged on by Chavigny, determined to punish the governors of these places for surrendering them so easily. My father's uncle was included with the others. This injustice was not to
be borne. My father represented the real state of the
case and used every effort to save his uncle, but it
was in vain. Stung to the quick he demanded permission to retire, and was allowed to do so. Accordingly, at the commencement of 1637, he left for
Blaye, and remained there until the death of Cardinal

Richelieu. During this retirement the King frequently wrote to him, in a language they had composed so as to speak before people without being understood; and I possess still many of these letters, with much regret that I am ignorant of their contents.

Chavigny served my father another ill turn. At the Cardinal's death my father had returned to the Court and was in greater favour than ever. Just before Louis XIII. died he gave my father the place of first master of the horse, but left his name blank in the paper fixing the appointment. The paper was given into the hands of Chavigny. At the King's death he had the villainy, in concert with the Queen-regent, to fill in the name of Comte d'Harcourt, instead of that the King had instructed him of. The indignation of my father was great, but, as he could obtain no redress, he retired once again to his Government of Blaye. Notwithstanding the manner in which he had been treated by the Queen-regent, he stoutly defended her cause when the civil war broke out, led by M. le Prince. He garrisoned Blaye at his own expense, incurring thereby debts which hung upon him all his life, and which I feel the effects of still, and repulsed all attempts of friends to corrupt his loyalty. The Queen and Mazarin could not close their eyes to his devotion, and offered him, while the war was still going on, a maréchal's bâton, or the title of foreign prince. But he refused both, and the offer was not renewed when the war ended. These disturbances over, and Louis XIV. being married, my father came again to Paris, where he had many friends. He had married in 1644, and had had, as I have said, one only daughter. His wife dying in 1670, and leaving him without male children, he determined, however much he might be afflicted at the loss he had sustained, to marry again, although old. He carried out his resolution in October of the same year, and was very pleased with the choice he had made. He liked his new wife so much, in fact, that when Madame de Montespan obtained for her a place at the Court, he declined it at once. At his age—it was thus he wrote to Madame de Montespan,—he had taken a wife not for the Court, but for himself. My mother, who was absent when the letter announcing the appointment was sent, felt much regret, but never showed it.

Before I finish this account of my father, I will here relate adventures which happened to him, and which I ought to have placed before his second marriage. A disagreement arose between my father and M. de Vardes, and still existed long after everybody thought they were reconciled. It was ultimately agreed that upon an early day, at about twelve o'clock, they should meet at the Porte St. Honoré, then a very deserted spot, and that the coach of M. de Vardes should run against my father's, and a general quarrel arise between masters and servants. Under cover of this quarrel, a duel could easily take place, and would seem simply to arise out of the broil there and then occasioned. On the morning appointed, my father called as usual upon several of his friends, and, taking one of them for second, went to the Porte St. Honoré. There everything fell out just as had been arranged. The coach of M. de Vardes struck against the other. My father leaped out, M. de Vardes did the same, and the duel took place. M. de Vardes fell, and was disarmed. My father wished to make him beg for his life; he would not do this, but confessed himself vanquished. My father's coach being the nearest, M. de Vardes got into it. He fainted on the road. They separated afterwards like brave people, and went their way. Madame de Châtillon, since of Mecklenburg, lodged in one of the last houses near the Porte St.

Honoré, and at the noise made by the coaches, put her head to the window, and coolly looked at the whole of the combat. It soon made a great noise. My father was complimented everywhere. M. de Vardes was sent for ten or twelve days to the Bastille. My father and he afterwards became completely reconciled to each other.

The other adventure was of gentler ending. The Memoirs of M. de la Rochefoucauld appeared. They contained certain atrocious and false statements against my father, who so severely resented the calumny, that he seized a pen, and wrote upon the margin of the book, "The author has told a lie." Not content with this, he went to the bookseller, whom he discovered with some difficulty, for the book was not sold publicly at first. He asked to see all the copies of the work—prayed, promised, threatened, and at last succeeded in obtaining them. Then he took a pen and wrote in all of them the same marginal note. The astonishment of the bookseller may be imagined. He was not long in letting M. de la Rochefoucauld know what had happened to his books: it may well be believed that he also was astonished. This affair made great noise. My father, having truth on his side, wished to obtain public satisfaction from M. de la Rochefoucauld. Friends, however, interposed, and the matter was allowed to drop. But M. de la Rochefoucauld never pardoned my father; so true it is that we less easily forget the injuries we inflict than those that we receive.

My father passed the rest of his long life surrounded by friends, and held in high esteem by the King and his ministers. His advice was often sought for by them, and was always acted upon. He never consoled himself for the loss of Louis XIII., to whom he owed his advancement and his fortune. Every year he kept sacred the day of his death, going to Saint-Denis, or holding solemnities in his own house if at Blaye. Veneration, gratitude, tenderness, ever adorned his lips every time he spoke of that monarch.

CHAPTER IV

AFTER having paid the last duties to my father I betook myself to Mons to join the Royal Roussillon cavalry regiment, in which I was captain. The King, after stopping eight or ten days with the ladies at Quesnoy, sent them to Namur, and put himself at the head of the army of M. de Boufflers, and camped at Gembloux, so that his left was only half a league distant from the right of M. de Luxembourg. The Prince of Orange was encamped at the Abbey of Pure, was unable to receive supplies, and could not leave his position without having the two armies of the King to grapple with: he entrenched himself in haste, and bitterly repented having allowed himself to be thus driven into a corner. We knew afterwards that he wrote several times to his intimate friend the Prince de Vaudemont,—saying that he was lost, and that nothing short of a miracle could save him.

We were in this position, with an army in every way infinitely superior to that of the Prince of Orange, and with four whole months before us to profit by our strength, when the King declared on the 8th of June that he should return to Versailles, and sent off a large detachment of the army into Germany. The surprise of the Maréchal de Luxembourg was without bounds. He represented the facility with which the Prince of Orange might now be beaten with one army and pursued by another; and how important it was to draw off detachments of the Imperial forces from Germany into Flanders, and how, by sending an army into Flanders instead of Germany, the whole of the Low Countries would be in our power. But the King would not change his plans, although M. de Luxembourg went down on his knees and begged him not to allow such a glorious opportunity to escape. Madame de Maintenon, by her tears when she parted from his Majesty, and by her letters since, had brought about this resolution.

The news had not spread on the morrow, June 9th. I chanced to go alone to the quarters of M. de Luxembourg, and was surprised to find not a soul there; every one had gone to the King's army. Pensively bringing my horse to a stand, I was ruminating on a fact so strange, and debating whether I should return to my tent or push on to the royal camp, when up came M. le Prince de Conti with a single page and a groom leading a horse. "What are you doing there?" cried he, laughing at my surprise. Thereupon he told me he was going to say adieu to the King, and advised me to do likewise. "What do you mean by saying Adieu?" answered I. He sent his servants to a little distance, and begged me to do the same, and with shouts of laughter told me about the King's retreat, making tremendous fun of him, despite my youth, for he had confidence in me. I was astonished. We soon after met the whole company coming back; and the great people went aside to talk and sneer. I then proceeded to pay my respects to the King, by whom I was honourably received. Surprise, however, was expressed by all faces, and indignation by some.

The effect of the King's retreat, indeed, was incredible, even amongst the soldiers and the people. The general officers could not keep silent upon it, and the inferior officers spoke loudly, with a license that could not be restrained. All through the army, in the towns, and even at Court, it was talked about openly. The courtiers, generally so glad to find themselves again at Versailles, now declared that they were ashamed to be there; as for the enemy, they could not contain their surprise and joy. The Prince of Orange said that the retreat was a miracle he could not have hoped for; that he could scarcely believe in it, but that it had saved his army, and the whole of the Low Countries. In the midst of all this excitement the King arrived with the ladies, on the 25th of June, at Versailles.

We gained some successes, however, this year. Maréchal de Villeroy took Huy in three days, losing only a sub-engineer and some soldiers. On the 29th of July we attacked at dawn the Prince of Orange at Neerwinden, and after twelve hours of hard fighting, under a blazing sun, entirely routed him. I was of the third squadron of the Royal Roussillon, and made five charges. One of the gold ornaments of my coat was torn away, but I received no wound. During the battle our brigadier, Quoadt, was killed before my eyes. The Duc de Feuillade became thus commander of the brigade. We missed him immediately, and for more than half an hour saw nothing of him; he had gone to make his toilette. When he returned he was powdered and decked out in a fine red surtout, embroidered with silver, and all his trappings and those of his horse were magnificent; he acquitted himself with distinction.

Our cavalry stood so well against the fire from the enemy's guns, that the Prince of Orange lost all patience, and turning away, exclaimed—" Oh, the insolent nation!" He fought until the last, and retired with the Elector of Hanover only when he saw there was no longer any hope. After the battle my people brought us a leg of mutton and a bottle of wine, which they had wisely saved from the previous evening, and we attacked them in good earnest, as may be believed.

The enemy lost about twenty thousand men, including a large number of officers; our loss was not more than half that number. We took all their cannon, eight mortars, many artillery waggons, a quantity of standards, and some pairs of kettle-drums. The victory was complete.

Meanwhile, the army which had been sent to Germany under the command of Monseigneur and of the Maréchal de Lorges, did little or nothing. The Maréchal wished to attack Heilbronn, but Monseigneur was opposed to it; and, to the great regret of the principal generals and of the troops, the attack was not made. Monseigneur returned early to Versailles.

At sea we were more active. The rich merchant fleet of Smyrna was attacked by Tourville; fifty vessels were burnt or sunk, and twenty-seven taken, all richly freighted. This campaign cost the English and Dutch dear. It is believed their loss was more than thirty millions of écus.

The season finished with the taking of Charleroy. On the 16th of September the Maréchal de Villeroy, supported by M. de Luxembourg, laid siege to it, and on the 11th of October, after a good defence, the place capitulated. Our loss was very slight. Charleroy taken, our troops went into winter-quarters, and I returned to Court, like the rest. The roads and the posting service were in great disorder. Amongst other adventures I met with, I was driven by a deaf and dumb postilion, who stuck me fast in the mud when near Quesnoy. At Pont Saint-Maxence all the horses were retained by M. de Luxembourg. Fearing I might be left behind, I told the postmaster that I was a governor (which was true), and that I would put him in jail if he did not give me horses. I should have been sadly puzzled how to do it; but he was simple enough to believe me, and gave the horses. I arrived, however, at last at Paris, and found a change at the Court, which surprised me.

Daquin—first doctor of the King and creature of Madame de Montespan—had lost nothing of his credit by her removal, but had never been able to get on well with Madame de Maintenon, who looked coldly upon all the friends of her predecessor. Daquin had a son, an abbé, and wearied the King with solicitations on his behalf. Madame de Maintenon seized the opportunity, when the King was more than usually angry with Daquin, to obtain his dismissal: it came upon him like a thunderbolt. On the previous evening the King had spoken to him for a long time as usual, and had never treated him better. All the Court was astonished also. Fagon, a very skilful and learned man, was appointed in his place at the instance of Madame de Maintenon.

Another event excited less surprise than interest. On Sunday, the 29th of November, the King learned that La Vauguyon had killed himself in his bed, that morning, by firing twice into his throat. I must say a few words about this Vauguyon. He was one of the pettiest and poorest gentlemen of France: he was well-made, but very swarthy, with Spanish features, had a charming voice, played the guitar and lute very well, and was skilled in the arts of gallantry. By these talents he had succeeded in finding favour with Madame de Beauvais, much regarded at the Court as having been the King's first mistress. I have seen her—old, blear-eyed, and half blind,—at the toilette of the Dauphiness of Bavaria, where everybody courted her, because she was still much considered by the King. Under this protection La Vauguyon succeeded well; was several times sent as ambassador to foreign countries; was made councillor of state, and to the scandal of everybody, was raised to the Order in 1688. Of late years, having no appointments, he had scarcely the means of living, and endeavoured, but without success, to improve his condition.

Poverty by degrees turned his brain; but a long time passed before it was perceived. The first proof that he gave of it was at the house of Madame Pelot, widow of the Chief President of the Rouen parliament. Playing at *brelan* one evening, she offered him a stake, and because he would not accept it bantered him, and playfully called him a poltroon. He said nothing, but waited until all the rest of the company had left the room; and when he found himself alone with Madame Pelot, he bolted the door, clapped his hat on his head, drove her up against the chimney, and holding her head between his two fists, said he knew no reason why he should not pound it into a jelly, in order to teach her to call him poltroon again. The poor woman was horribly frightened, and made perpendicular curtseys between his two fists, and all sorts of excuses. At last he let her go, more dead than alive. She had the generosity to say no syllable of this occurrence until after his death; she even allowed him to come to the house as usual, but took care never to be alone with him.

One day, a long time after this, meeting, in a gallery, at Fontainebleau, M. de Courtenay, La Vauguyon drew his sword, and compelled the other to draw also, although there had never been the slightest quarrel between them. They were soon separated and La Vauguyon immediately fled to the King, who was just then in his private closet, where nobody ever entered unless expressly summoned. But La Vauguyon turned the key, and, in spite of the usher on guard, forced his way in. The King in great emotion asked him what was the matter. La Vauguyon on his knees said he had been insulted by M. de Courtenay and demanded pardon for having drawn his sword in the palace. His Majesty, promising to examine the matter, with great trouble got rid of La Vauguyon. As nothing could be made of it, M. de Courtenay declaring he had been insulted by La Vauguyon and forced to draw his sword, and the other telling the same tale, both were sent to the Bastille. After a short imprisonment they were released, and appeared at the Court as usual.

Another adventure, which succeeded this, threw some light upon the state of affairs. Going to Versailles, one day, La Vauguyon met a groom of the Prince de Condé leading a saddled horse: he stopped the man, descended from his coach, asked whom the horse belonged to, said that the Prince would not object to his riding it, and leaping upon the animal's back, galloped off. The groom, all amazed, followed him. La Vauguyon rode on until he reached the Bastille, descended there, gave a gratuity to the man, and dismissed him: he then went straight to the governor of the prison, said he had had the misfortune to displease the King, and begged to be confined there. The governor, having no orders to do so, refused, and sent off an express for instructions how to act. In reply he was told not to receive La Vauguyon, whom at last, after great difficulty, he prevailed upon to go away. This occurrence made great noise. Yet even afterwards the King continued to receive La Vauguyon at the Court, and to affect to treat him well, although everybody else avoided him and was afraid of him. His poor wife became so affected by these public derangements, that she retired from Paris, and shortly afterwards died. This completed her husband's madness; he survived her only a month, dying by his own hand, as I have mentioned. During the last two years of his life he carried pistols in his carriage, and frequently pointed them at his coachman and postilion. It is certain that without the assistance of M. de Beauvais he would often have been brought to the last extremities. Beauvais frequently spoke of him to the King; and it is inconceivable that having raised this man to such a point, and having always shown him particular kindness, his Majesty should perseveringly have left him to die of hunger and become mad from misery.

The year finished without any remarkable occurrence.

My mother, who had been much disquieted for me during the campaign, desired strongly that I should not make another without being married. Although very young, I had no repugnance to marry, but wished to do so according to my own inclinations. With a large establishment I felt very lonely in a country where credit and consideration do more than all the rest. Without uncle, aunt, cousins-german, or near relatives, I found myself, I say, extremely solitary.

Among my best friends, as he had been the friend of my father, was the Duc de Beauvilliers. He had always shown me much affection, and I felt a great desire to unite myself to his family. My mother approved of my inclination, and gave me an exact account of my estates and possessions. I carried it to Versailles, and sought a private interview with M. de Beauvilliers. At eight o'clock the same evening he received me alone in the cabinet of Madame de Beauvilliers. After making my compliments to him, I told him my wish, showed him the state of my affairs, and said that all I demanded of him was one of his daughters in marriage, and that whatever contract he thought fit to draw up would be signed by my mother and myself without examination.

The Duke, who had fixed his eyes upon me all this

time, replied like a man penetrated with gratitude by the offer I had made. He said, that of his eight daughters the eldest was between fourteen and fifteen years old; the second much deformed, and in no way marriageable; the third between twelve and thirteen years of age, and the rest were children: the eldest wished to enter a convent, and had shown herself firm upon that point. He seemed inclined to make a difficulty of his want of fortune; but, reminding him of the proposition I had made, I said that it was not for fortune I had come to him, not even for his daughter, whom I had never seen; that it was he and Madame de Beauvilliers who had charmed me, and whom I wished to marry!

"But," said he, "if my eldest daughter wishes absolutely to enter a convent?"

"Then," replied I, "I ask the third of you." To this he objected, on the ground that if he gave the dowry of the first to the third daughter, and the first afterwards changed her mind and wished to marry, he should be thrown into an embarrassment. I replied that I would take the third as though the first were to be married, and that if she were not, the difference between what he destined for her and what he destined for the third, should be given to me. The Duke, raising his eyes to heaven, protested that he had never been combated in this manner, and that he was obliged to gather up all his forces in order to prevent himself yielding to me that very instant.

On the next day, at half-past three, I had another interview with M. de Beauvilliers. With much tenderness he declined my proposal, resting his refusal upon the inclination his daughter had displayed for the convent,—upon his little wealth, if, the marriage of the third being made, she should change her mind— and upon other reasons. He spoke to me with much regret and friendship, and I to him in the same manner; and we separated, unable any longer to speak to each other. Two days after, however, I had another interview with him by his appointment. I endeavoured to overcome the objections that he made, but all in vain. He could not give me his third daughter with the first unmarried, and he would not force her, he said, to change her wish of retiring from the world. His words, pious and elevated, augmented my respect for him, and my desire for the marriage. In the evening, at the breaking up of the appointment, I could not prevent myself whispering in his ear that I should never live happily with anybody but his daughter, and without waiting for a reply hastened away. I had the next evening, at eight o'clock, an interview with Madame de Beauvilliers. I argued with her with such prodigious ardour that she was surprised, and, although she did not give way, she said she would be inconsolable for the loss of me, repeating the same tender and flattering things her husband had said before, and with the same effusion of feeling.

I had yet another interview with M. de Beauvilliers. He showed even more affection for me than before, but I could not succeed in putting aside his scruples. He unbosomed himself afterwards to one of our friends, and in his bitterness said he could only console himself by hoping that his children and mine might some day intermarry, and he prayed me to go and pass some days at Paris, in order to allow him to seek a truce to his grief in my absence. We both were in want of it. I have judged it fitting to give these details, for they afford a key to my exceeding intimacy with M. de Beauvilliers, which otherwise, considering the difference in our ages, might appear incomprehensible.

There was nothing left for me but to look out for another marriage. One soon presented itself, but as soon fell to the ground; and I went to La Trappe to console myself for the impossibility of making an alliance with the Duc de Beauvilliers.

La Trappe is a place so celebrated and so well known, and its reformer so famous, that I shall say but little about it. I will, however, mention that this abbey is five leagues from La Ferté-au-Vidame, or Arnault, which is the real distinctive name of this Ferté among so many other Fertés in France, which have preserved the generic name of what they have been, that is to say, forts or fortresses (*firmitas*). My father had been very intimate with M. de la Trappe, and had taken me to him.

Although I was very young then, M. de la Trappe charmed me, and the sanctity of the place enchanted me. Every year I stayed some days there, sometimes a week at a time, and was never tired of admiring this great and distinguished man. He loved me as a son, and I respected him as though he were my father. This intimacy, singular at my age, I kept secret from everybody, and only went to the convent clandestinely.

CHAPTER V

ON my return from La Trappe, I became engaged in an affair which made a great noise, and which had many results for me.

M. de Luxembourg, proud of his successes, and of the applause of the world at his victories, believed himself sufficiently strong to claim precedence over seventeen dukes, myself among the number; to step, in fact, from the eighteenth rank, that he held amongst the peers, to the second. The following are the names and the order in precedence of the dukes he wished to supersede:—

The Duc d'Elbœuf; the Duc de Montbazon; the Duc de Ventadour; the Duc de Vendôme; the Duc de la Trémoille; the Duc de Sully; the Duc de Chevreuse, the son (minor) of the Duchesse de Lesdiguières-Gondi; the Duc de Brissac; Charles d'Albert, called d'Ailly; the Duc de Richelieu; the Duc de Saint-Simon; the Duc de la Rochefoucauld; the Duc de la Force; the Duc de Valentinois; the Duc de Rohan; the Duc de Bouillon.

To explain this pretension of M. de Luxembourg, I must give some details respecting him and the family whose name he bore. He was the only son of M. de Bouteville, and had married a descendant of François de Luxembourg, Duke of Piney, created Peer of France in 1581. It was a peerage which, in default of male successors, went to the female, but this descendant was not heir to it. She was the child of a second marriage, and by a first marriage her mother had given birth to a son and a daughter, who were the inheritors of the peerage, both of whom were still living. The son was, however, an idiot, had been declared incapable of attending to his affairs, and was shut up in Saint Lazare, at Paris. The daughter had taken the veil, and was mistress of the novices at the Abbaye-aux-Bois. The peerage had thus, it might almost be said, become extinct, for it was vested in an idiot, who could not marry (to prevent him doing so, he had been made a deacon, and he was bound in consequence to remain single), and in a nun, who was equally bound by her vows to the same state of celibacy.

When M. de Bouteville, for that was his only title then, married, he took the arms and the name of Luxembourg. He did more. By powerful influence—notably that of his patron the Prince de Condé—he released the idiot deacon from his asylum, and the nun from her convent, and induced them both to surrender to him their possessions and their titles. This done, he commenced proceedings at once in order to obtain legal recognition of his right to the dignities he had thus got possession of. He claimed to be acknowledged Duc de Piney, with all the privileges attached to that title as a creation of 1581. Foremost among these privileges was that of taking precedence of all dukes whose title did not go back so far as that year. Before any decision was given either for or against this claim, he was made Duc de Piney by new letters patent, dating from 1662, with a clause which left his pretensions to the title of 1581 by no means affected by this new creation. M. de Luxembourg, however, seemed satisfied with what he had obtained, and was apparently disposed to pursue his claim no further. He was received as Duke and Peer in the Parliament, took his seat in the last rank after all the other peers, and allowed his suit to drop. Since then he had tried unsuccessfully to gain it by stealth, but for several years nothing more had been heard of it. Now, however, he recommenced it, and with every intention, as we soon found, to stop at no intrigue or baseness in order to carry his point.

Nearly everybody was in his favour. The Court, though not the King, was almost entirely for him; and the town, dazzled by the splendour of his exploits, was devoted to him. The young men regarded him as the protector of their debauches; for, notwithstanding his age, his conduct was as free as theirs. He had captivated the troops and the general officers.

In the Parliament he had a staunch supporter in Harlay, the Chief President, who led that great body at his will, and whose devotion he had acquired to such a degree, that he believed that to undertake and succeed were only the same things, and that this grand affair would scarcely cost him a winter to carry.

Let me say something more of this Harlay.

Descended from two celebrated magistrates, Achille d'Harlay and Christopher De Thou, Harlay imitated their gravity, but carried it to a cynical extent, affected their disinterestedness and modesty, but dishonoured the first by his conduct, and the second by a refined pride which he endeavoured without success to conceal. He piqued himself, above all things, upon his probity and justice, but the mask soon fell. Between Peter and Paul he maintained the strictest fairness, but as soon as he perceived interest or favour to be acquired, he sold himself. This trial will show him stripped of all disguise. He was learned in the law; in letters he was second to no one; he was well acquainted with history, and knew how, above all, to govern his company with an authority which suffered no reply, and which no other chief president had ever attained.

A pharisaical austerity rendered him redoubtable by the license he assumed in his public reprimands, whether to plaintiffs, or defendants, advocates or magistrates; so that there was not a single person who did not tremble to have to do with him. Besides this, sustained in all by the Court (of which he was the slave, and the very humble servant of those who were really in favour), a subtle courtier, a singularly crafty politician, he used all those talents solely to further his ambition, his desire of domination and his thirst of the reputation of a great man. He was without real honour, secretly of corrupt manners, with only outside probity, without humanity even; in one word, a perfect hypocrite; without faith, without law, without a God, and without a soul; a cruel husband, a barbarous father, a tyrannical brother, a friend of himself alone, wicked by nature—taking pleasure in insulting, outraging, and overwhelming others, and never in his life having lost an occasion to do so. His wit was great, but was always subservient to his wickedness. He was small, vigorous, and thin, with a lozenge-shaped face, a long aquiline nose—fine, speaking, keen eyes, that usually looked furtively at you, but which, if fixed on a client or a magistrate, were fit to make him sink into the earth. He wore narrow robes, an almost ecclesiastical collar and wristband to match, a brown wig mixed with white, thickly furnished but short, and with a great cap over it. He affected a bending attitude, and walked so, with a false air, more humble than modest, and always shaved along the walls, to make people make way for him with greater noise; and at Versailles worked his way on by a series of respectful and, as it were, shame-faced bows to the right and left. He held to the King and to Madame de Maintenon by knowing their weak side; and it was he who, being consulted upon the unheard-of legitimation of children without naming the mother, had sanctioned that illegality in favour of the King.

Such was the man whose influence was given entirely to our opponent.

To assist M. de Luxembourg's case as much as possible, the celebrated Racine, so known by his plays, and by the order he had received at that time to write the history of the King, was employed to polish and ornament his pleas. Nothing was left undone by M. de Luxembourg in order to gain this cause.

I cannot give all the details of the case, the statements made on both sides, and the defences; they would occupy entire volumes. We maintained that M. de Luxembourg was in no way entitled to the precedence he claimed, and we had both law and justice on our side. To give instructions to our counsel, and to follow the progress of the case, we met once a week, seven or eight of us at least, those best disposed to give our time to the matter. Among the most punctual was M. de la Rochefoucauld. I had been solicited from the commencement to take part in the proceedings, and I complied most willingly, apologising for so doing to M. de Luxembourg, who replied with all the politeness and gallantry possible, that I could not do less than follow an example my father had set me.

The trial having commenced, we soon saw how badly disposed the Chief President was towards us. He obstructed us in every way, and acted against all rules. There seemed no other means of defeating his evident intention of judging against us than by gaining time, first of all; and to do this we determined to get the case adjourned. There were, however, only two days at our disposal, and that was not enough in order to comply with the forms required for such a step. We were all in the greatest embarrassment,

when it fortunately came into the head of one of our
lawyers to remind us of a privilege we possessed, by
which, without much difficulty, we could obtain what
we required. I was the only one who could, at that
moment, make use of this privilege. I hastened home,
at once, to obtain the necessary papers, deposited them
with the procureur of M. de Luxembourg, and the
adjournment was obtained. The rage of M. de Luxembourg was without bounds. When we met he
would not salute me, and in consequence I discontinued to salute him; by which he lost more than I,
in his position and at his age, and furnished in the
rooms and the galleries of Versailles a sufficiently
ridiculous spectacle. In addition to this he quarrelled
openly with M. de Richelieu, and made a bitter attack
upon him in one of his pleas. But M. de Richelieu,
meeting him soon after in the Salle des Gardes at Versailles, told him to his face that he should soon have
a reply; and said that he feared him neither on horseback nor on foot—neither him nor his crew—neither
in town nor at the Court, nor even in the army, nor
in any place in the world; and without allowing time
for a reply he turned on his heel. In the end, M. de
Luxembourg found himself so closely pressed that he
was glad to apologise to M. de Richelieu.

After a time our cause, sent back again to the Parliament, was argued there with the same vigour, the
same partiality, and the same injustice as before: seeing this, we felt that the only course left open to us
was to get the case sent before the Assembly of all
the Chambers, where the Judges, from their number,
could not be corrupted by M. de Luxembourg, and
where the authority of Harlay was feeble, while over
the Grand Chambre, in which the case was at present,
it was absolute. The difficulty was to obtain an assembly of all the Chambers, for the power of sum-

moning them was vested solely in Harlay. However, we determined to try and gain his consent. M. de Chaulnes undertook to go upon this delicate errand, and acquitted himself well of his mission. He pointed out to Harlay that everybody was convinced of his leaning towards M. de Luxembourg, and that the only way to efface the conviction that had gone abroad was to comply with our request; in fine, he used so many arguments, and with such address, that Harlay, confused and thrown off his guard, and repenting of the manner in which he had acted towards us as being likely to injure his interests, gave a positive assurance to M. de Chaulnes that what we asked should be granted.

We had scarcely finished congratulating ourselves upon this unhoped-for success, when we found that we had to do with a man whose word was a very sorry support to rest upon. M. de Luxembourg, affrighted at the promise Harlay had given, made him resolve to break it. Suspecting this, M. de Chaulnes paid another visit to the Chief President, who admitted, with much confusion, that he had changed his views, and that it was impossible to carry out what he had agreed to. After this we felt that to treat any longer with a man so perfidious would be time lost; and we determined, therefore, to put it out of his power to judge the case at all.

According to the received maxim, *whoever is at law with the son cannot be judged by the father.* Harlay had a son who was Advocate-General. We resolved that one among us should bring an action against him.

After trying in vain to induce the Duc de Rohan, who was the only one of our number who could readily have done it, to commence a suit against Harlay's son, we began to despair of arriving at our aim. Fortunately for us, the vexation of Harlay became so great at this time, in consequence of the disdain with which we treated him, and which we openly published, that he extricated us himself from our difficulty. We had only to supplicate the Duc de Gesvres in the cause (he said to some of our people), and we should obtain what we wanted; for the Duc de Gesvres was his relative. We took him at his word. The Duc de Gesvres received in two days a summons on our part. Harlay, annoyed with himself for the advice he had given, repented of it: but it was too late; he was declared unable to judge the cause, and the case itself was postponed until the next year.

Meanwhile, let me mention a circumstance which should have found a place before, and then state what occurred in the interval which followed until the trial recommenced.

It was while our proceedings were making some little stir that fresh favours were heaped upon the King's illegitimate sons, at the instance of the King himself, and with the connivance of Harlay, who, for the part he took in the affair, was promised the chancellorship when it should become vacant. The rank of these illegitimate sons was placed just below that of the princes of the blood, and just above that of the peers even of the oldest creation. This gave us all exceeding annoyance: it was the greatest injury the peerage could have received, and became its leprosy and sore. All the peers who could, kept themselves aloof from the parliament, when M. du Maine, M. de Vendôme, and the Comte de Toulouse, for whom this arrangement was specially made, were received there.

There were several marriages at the Court this winter and many very fine balls, at which latter I danced. By the spring, preparations were ready for fresh campaigns. My regiment (I had bought one at the close of the last season) was ordered to join the army of M. de Luxembourg; but, as I had no desire to be under him, I wrote to the King, begging to be exchanged. In a short time, to the great vexation, as I know, of M. de Luxembourg, my request was granted. The Chevalier de Sully went to Flanders in my place, and I to Germany in his. I went first to Soissons to see my regiment, and in consequence of the recommendation of the King, was more severe with it than I should otherwise have been. I set out afterwards for Strasbourg, where I was surprised with the magnificence of the town, and with the number, beauty, and grandeur of its fortifications. As from my youth I knew and spoke German perfectly, I sought out one of my early German acquaintances, who gave me much pleasure. I stopped six days at Strasbourg and then went by the Rhine to Philipsburg. On the next day after arriving there, I joined the cavalry, which was encamped at Obersheim.

After several movements—in which we passed and repassed the Rhine—but which led to no effective result, we encamped for forty days at Gaw-Boecklheim, one of the best and most beautiful positions in the world, and where we had charming weather, although a little disposed to cold. It was in the leisure of that long camp that I commenced these memoirs, incited by the pleasure I took in reading those of Marshal Bassompierre, which invited me thus to write what I should see in my own time.

During this season M. de Noailles took Palamos, Girone, and the fortress of Castel-Follit in Catalonia. This last was taken by the daring of a soldier, who led on a small number of his comrades, and carried the place by assault. Nothing was done in Italy; and in Flanders M. de Luxembourg came to no engagement with the Prince of Orange.

CHAPTER VI

AFTER our long rest at the camp of Gaw-Boecklheim we again put ourselves in movement, but without doing much against the enemy, and on the 16th of October I received permission to return to Paris. Upon my arrival there I learnt that many things had occurred since I left. During that time some adventures had happened to the Princesses, as the three illegitimate daughters of the King were called for distinction sake. Monsieur wished that the Duchesse de Chartres should always call the others "sister," but that the others should never address her except as "Madame." The Princesse de Conti submitted to this; but the other (Madame la Duchesse, being the produce of the same love) set herself to call the Duchesse de Chartres "mignonne." But nothing was less *mignonne* than her face and her figure; and Monsieur, feeling the ridicule, complained to the King. The King prohibited very severely this familiarity.

While at Trianon these Princesses took it into their heads to walk out at night and divert themselves with crackers. Either from malice or imprudence they let off some one night under the windows of Monsieur, rousing him thereby out of his sleep. He was so displeased, that he complained to the King, who made him many excuses (scolding the Princesses), but had great trouble to appease him. His anger lasted a long time, and the Duchesse de Chartres felt it. I do not know if the other two were very sorry. Madame la

Duchesse was accused of writing some songs upon the Duchesse de Chartres.

The Princesse de Conti had another adventure, which made considerable noise, and which had great results. She had taken into her favour Clermont, ensign of the gensdarmes and of the Guard. He had pretended to be enamoured of her, and had not been repelled, for she soon became in love with him. Clermont had attached himself to the service of M. de Luxembourg, and was the merest creature in his hands. At the instigation of M. de Luxembourg, he turned away his regards from the Princesse de Conti, and fixed them upon one of her maids of honour—Mademoiselle Choin, a great, ugly, brown, thick-set girl, upon whom Monseigneur had lately bestowed his affection. Monseigneur made no secret of this, nor did she. Such being the case, it occurred to M. de Luxembourg (who knew he was no favourite with the King, and who built all his hopes of the future upon Monseigneur) that Clermont, by marrying La Choin, might thus secure the favour of Monseigneur, whose entire confidence she possessed. Clermont was easily persuaded that this would be for him a royal road to fortune, and he accordingly entered willingly into the scheme, which had just begun to move, when the campaign commenced, and everybody went away to join the armies.

The King, who partly saw this intrigue, soon made himself entirely master of it, by intercepting the letters which passed between the various parties. He read there the project of Clermont and La Choin to marry, and thus govern Monseigneur; he saw how M. de Luxembourg was the soul of this scheme, and the marvels to himself he expected from it. The letters Clermont had received from the Princesse de Conti he now sent to Mademoiselle la Choin, and always spoke to her of Monseigneur as their "fat friend." With this correspondence in his hands, the King one day sent for the Princesse de Conti, said in a severe tone that he knew of her weakness for Clermont; and, to prove to her how badly she had placed her affection, showed her her own letters to Clermont, and letters in which he had spoken most contemptuously of her to La Choin. Then, as a cruel punishment, he made her read aloud to him the whole of those letters. At this she almost died, and threw herself, bathed in tears, at the feet of the King, scarcely able to articulate. Then came sobs, entreaty, despair, and rage, and cries for justice and revenge. This was soon obtained. Mademoiselle la Choin was driven away the next day; and M. de Luxembourg had orders to strip Clermont of his office, and send him to the most distant part of the kingdom. The terror of M. de Luxembourg and the Prince de Conti at this discovery may be imagined. Songs increased the notoriety of this strange adventure between the Princess and her confidant.

M. de Noyon had furnished on my return another subject for the song-writers, and felt it the more sensibly because everybody was diverted at his expense. M. de Noyon was extremely vain, and afforded thereby much amusement to the King. A chair was vacant at the Académie Française. The King wished it to be given to M. de Noyon, and expressed himself to that effect to Dangeau, who was a member. As may be believed, the prelate was elected without difficulty. His Majesty testified to the Prince de Condé, and to the most distinguished persons of the Court, that he should be glad to see them at the reception. Thus M. de Noyon was the first member of the Académie chosen by the King, and the first at whose reception he had taken the trouble to invite his courtiers to attend.

The Abbé de Caumartin was at that time Director of the Académie. He knew the vanity of M. de Noyon, and determined to divert the public at his expense. He had many friends in power, and judged that his pleasantry would be overlooked, and even approved. He composed, therefore, a confused and bombastic discourse in the style of M. de Noyon, full of pompous phrases, turning the prelate into ridicule, while they seemed to praise him. After finishing this work, he was afraid lest it should be thought out of all measure, and, to reassure himself, carried it to M. de Noyon himself, as a scholar might to his master, in order to see whether it fully met with his approval. M. de Noyon, so far from suspecting anything, was charmed by the discourse, and simply made a few corrections in the style. The Abbé de Caumartin rejoiced at the success of the snare he had laid, and felt quite bold enough to deliver his harangue.

The day came. The Académie was crowded. The King and the Court were there, all expecting to be diverted. M. de Noyon, saluting everybody with a satisfaction he did not dissimulate, made his speech with his usual confidence, and in his usual style. The Abbé replied with a modest air, and with a gravity and slowness that gave great effect to his ridiculous discourse. The surprise and pleasure were general, and each person strove to intoxicate M. de Noyon more and more, making him believe that the speech of the Abbé was relished solely because it had so worthily praised him. The prelate was delighted with the Abbé and the public, and conceived not the slightest mistrust.

The noise which this occurrence made may be imagined, and the praises M. de Noyon gave himself in relating everywhere what he had said, and what had been replied to him. M. de Paris, to whose house he went, thus triumphing, did not like him, and endeavoured to open his eyes to the humiliation he had received. For some time M. de Noyon would not be convinced of the truth; it was not until he had consulted with Père la Chaise that he believed it. The excess of rage and vexation succeeded then to the excess of rapture he had felt. In this state he returned to his house, and went the next day to Versailles. There he made the most bitter complaints to the King, of the Abbé de Caumartin, by whose means he had become the sport and laughing-stock of all the world.

The King, who had learned what had passed, was himself displeased. He ordered Pontchartrain (who was related to Caumartin) to rebuke the Abbé, and to send him a *lettre de cachet,* in order that he might go and ripen his brain in his Abbey of Busay, in Brittany, and better learn there how to speak and write. Pontchartrain executed the first part of his commission, but not the second. He pointed out to the King that the speech of the Abbé de Caumartin had been revised and corrected by M. de Noyon, and that, therefore, this latter had only himself to blame in the matter. He declared, too, that the Abbé was very sorry for what he had done, and was most willing to beg pardon of M. de Noyon. The *lettre de cachet* thus fell to the ground, but not the anger of the prelate. He was so outraged that he would not see the Abbé, retired into his diocese to hide his shame, and remained there a long time.

Upon his return to Paris, however, being taken ill, before consenting to receive the sacraments, he sent for the Abbé, embraced him, pardoned him, and gave him a diamond ring, that he drew from his finger, and that he begged him to keep in memory of him. Nay, more, when he was cured, he used all his influence to reinstate the Abbé in the esteem of the King. But the

King could never forgive what had taken place, and M. de Noyon, by this grand action, gained only the favour of God and the honour of the world.

I must finish the account of the war of this year with a strange incident. M. de Noailles, who had been so successful in Catalonia, was on very bad terms with Barbezieux, secretary of state for the war department. Both were in good favour with the King, both high in power, both spoiled. The successes in Catalonia had annoyed Barbezieux. They smoothed the way for the siege of Barcelona, and that place once taken, the very heart of Spain would have been exposed, and M. de Noailles would have gained fresh honours and glory. M. de Noailles felt this so completely that he had pressed upon the King the siege of Barcelona; and when the fitting time came for undertaking it, sent a messenger to him with full information of the forces and supplies he required. Fearing that if he wrote out this information it might fall into the hands of Barbezieux, and never reach the King, he simply gave his messenger instructions by word of mouth, and charged him to deliver them so. But the very means he had taken to ensure success brought about failure. Barbezieux, informed by his spies of the departure of the messenger, waylaid him, bribed him, and induced him to act with the blackest perfidy, by telling the King quite a different story to that he was charged with. In this way, the project for the siege of Barcelona was entirely broken, at the moment for its execution, and with the most reasonable hopes of success; and upon M. de Noailles rested all the blame. What a thunderbolt this was for him may easily be imagined. But the trick had been so well played, that he could not clear himself with the King; and all through this winter he remained out of favour.

At last he thought of a means by which he might

regain his position. He saw the inclination of the King for his illegitimate children, and determined to make a sacrifice in favour of one of them, rightly judging that this would be a sure means to step back into the confidence he had been so craftily driven from. His scheme, which he caused to be placed before the King, was to go into Catalonia at the commencement of the next campaign, to make a semblance of falling ill immediately upon arriving, to send to Versailles a request that he might be recalled, and at the same time a suggestion that M. de Vendôme (who would then be near Nice, under Maréchal Catinat) should succeed him. In order that no time might be lost, nor the army left without a general, he proposed to carry with him the letters patent, appointing M. de Vendôme, and to send them to him at the same time that he sent to be recalled.

It is impossible to express the relief and satisfaction with which this proposition was received. The King was delighted with it, as with everything tending to advance his illegitimate children and to put a slight upon the Princes of the blood. He could not openly have made this promotion without embroiling himself with the latter; but coming as it would from M. de Noailles, he had nothing to fear. M. de Vendôme, once general of an army, could no longer serve in any other quality, and would act as a stepping-stone for M. du Maine.

From this moment M. de Noailles returned more than ever into the good graces of the King. Everything happened as it had been arranged. But the secret was betrayed in the execution. Surprise was felt that at the same moment M. de Noailles sent a request to be recalled, he also sent, and without waiting for a reply, to call M. de Vendôme to the command. What completely raised the veil were the letters patent that he sent immediately after to M. de Vendôme, and that it was known he could not have received from the King in the time that had elapsed. M. de Noailles returned from Catalonia, and was received as his address merited. He feigned being lame with rheumatism, and played the part for a long time, but forgot himself occasionally, and made his company smile. He fixed himself at the Court, and gained there much more favour than he could have gained by the war; to the great vexation of Barbezieux.

M. de Luxembourg very strangely married his daughter at this time to the Chevalier de Soissons (an illegitimate son of the Comte de Soissons), brought out from the greatest obscurity by the Comtesse de Nemours, and adopted by her to spite her family. M. de Luxembourg did not long survive this fine marriage. At sixty-seven years of age he believed himself twenty-five, and lived accordingly. The want of genuine intrigues, from which his age and his face excluded him, he supplied by money-power; and his intimacy, and that of his son, with the Prince de Conti and Albergotti was kept up almost entirely by the community of their habits, and the secret parties of pleasure they concocted together. All the burden of marches, of orders of subsistence, fell upon a subordinate. Nothing could be more exact than the *coup d'œil* of M. de Luxembourg—nobody could be more brilliant, more sagacious, more penetrating than he before the enemy or in battle, and this, too, with an audacity, an ease, and at the same time a coolness, which allowed him to see all and foresee all under the hottest fire, and in the most imminent danger. It was at such times that he was great. For the rest he was idleness itself. He rarely walked unless absolutely obliged,—spent his time in gaming, or in conversation with his familiars; and had every evening a supper with a chosen few (nearly always the same); and if near a town, the other sex were always agreeably mingled with them. When thus occupied, he was inaccessible to everybody, and if anything pressing happened, it was his subordinate who attended to it. Such was at the army the life of this great general, and such it was at Paris, except that the Court and the great world occupied his days, and his pleasures the evenings. At last, age, temperament, and constitution betrayed him. He fell ill at Versailles. Given over by Fagon, the King's physician, Coretti, an Italian, who had secrets of his own, undertook his cure, and relieved him, but only for a short time. His door during this illness was besieged by all the Court. The King sent to inquire after him, but it was more for appearance' sake than from sympathy, for I have already remarked that the King did not like him. The brilliancy of his campaigns, and the difficulty of replacing him, caused all the disquietude. Becoming worse, M. de Luxembourg received the sacraments, showed some religion and firmness, and died on the morning of the 4th of January, 1695, the fifth day of his illness, much regretted by many people, but personally esteemed by none, and loved by very few.

Not one of the Dukes M. de Luxembourg had attacked went to see him during his illness. I neither went nor sent, although at Versailles, and I must admit that I felt my deliverance from such an enemy.

Here, perhaps, I may as well relate the result of the trial in which we were engaged, and which, after the death of M. de Luxembourg, was continued by his son. It was not judged until the following year. I have shown that by our implicating the Duc de Gesvres, the Chief President had been declared incapable of trying the case. The rage he conceived against us cannot be expressed, and, great actor that he was, he could not hide it. All his endeavour afterwards was to do what he could against us; the rest of the mask fell, and the deformity of the judge appeared in the man, stripped of all disguise.

We immediately signified to M. de Luxembourg that he must choose between the letters patent of 1581 and those of 1662. If he abandoned the first the case fell through; in repudiating the last he renounced the certainty of being duke and peer after us; and ran the risk of being reduced to an inferior title previously granted to him. The position was a delicate one; he was affrighted; but after much consultation he resolved to run all risks and maintain his pretensions. It thus simply became a question of his right to the title of Duc de Piney, with the privilege attached to it as a creation of 1581.

In the spring of 1696 the case was at last brought on, before the Assembly of all the Chambers. Myself and the other Dukes seated ourselves in court to hear the proceedings. The trial commenced. All the facts and particulars of the cause were brought forward. Our advocates spoke, and then few doubted but that we should gain the victory. M. de Luxembourg's advocate, Dumont, was next heard. He was very audacious, and spoke so insolently of us, saying, in Scripture phraseology, that we honoured the King with our lips, whilst our hearts were far from him, that I could not contain myself. I was seated between the Duc de la Rochefoucauld and the Duc d'Estrées. I stood up, crying out against the imposture of this knave, and calling for justice on him. M. de la Rochefoucauld pulled me back, made me keep silent, and I plunged down into my seat more from anger against him than against the advocate. My movement excited a murmur. We might on the instant have had justice against Dumont, but the opportunity had passed for us to ask for it, and the Président de Maisons made a slight excuse for him. We complained, however, afterwards to the King, who expressed his surprise that Dumont had not been stopped in the midst of his speech.

The summing up was made by D'Aguesseau, who acquitted himself of the task with much eloquence and impartiality. His speech lasted two days. This being over, the court was cleared, and the judges were left alone to deliberate upon their verdict. Some time after we were called in to hear that verdict given. It was in favour of M. de Luxembourg in so far as the title dating from 1662 was concerned; but the consideration of his claim to the title of 1581 was adjourned indefinitely, so that he remained exactly in the same position as his father.

It was with difficulty we could believe in a decree so unjust and so novel, and which decided a question that was not under dispute. I was outraged, but I endeavoured to contain myself. I spoke to M. de la Rochefoucauld; I tried to make him listen to me, and to agree that we should complain to the King, but I spoke to a man furious, incapable of understanding anything or of doing anything. Returning to my own house, I wrote a letter to the King, in which I complained of the opinion of the judges. I also pointed out, that when everybody had been ordered to retire from the council chamber, Harlay and his secretary had been allowed to remain. On these and other grounds I begged the King to grant a new trial.

I carried this letter to the Duc de la Trémoille, but I could not get him to look at it. I returned home more vexed if possible than when I left. The King, nevertheless, was exceedingly dissatisfied with the judgment. He explained himself to that effect at his dinner, and in a manner but little advantageous to the

Parliament, and prepared himself to receive the complaints he expected would be laid before him. But the obstinacy of M. de la Rochefoucauld, which turned into vexation against himself, rendered it impossible for us to take any steps in the matter, and so overwhelmed me with displeasure, that I retired to La Trappe during Passion Week in order to recover myself.

At my return I learned that the King had spoken of this judgment to the Chief President, and that that magistrate had blamed it, saying the cause was indubitably ours, and that he had always thought so! If he thought so, why oppose us so long? and if he did not think so, what a prevaricator was he to reply with this flattery, so as to be in accord with the King? The judges themselves were ashamed of their verdict, and excused themselves for it on the ground of their compassion for the state in which M. de Luxembourg would have been placed had he lost the title of 1662, and upon its being impossible that he should gain the one of 1581, of which they had left him the chimera. M. de Luxembourg was accordingly received at the Parliament on the 4th of the following May, with the rank of 1662. He came and visited all of us, but we would have no intercourse with him or with his judges. To the Advocate-General, D'Aguesseau, we carried our thanks.

CHAPTER VII

THUS ended this long and important case; and now let me go back again to the events of the previous year.

Towards the end of the summer and the commencement of the winter of 1695, negotiations for peace were set on foot by the King. Harlay, son-in-law of our enemy, was sent to Maestricht to sound the Dutch. But in proportion as they saw peace desired were they less inclined to listen to terms. They had even the impudence to insinuate to Harlay, whose paleness and thinness were extraordinary, that they took him for a sample of the reduced state of France! He, without getting angry, replied pleasantly, that if they would give him the time to send for his wife, they would, perhaps, conceive another opinion of the position of the realm. In effect, she was extremely fat, and of a very high colour. He was rather roughly dismissed, and hastened to regain our frontier.

Two events followed each other very closely this winter. The first was the death of the Princess of Orange, in London, at the end of January. The King of England prayed our King to allow the Court to wear no mourning, and it was even prohibited to M. de Bouillon and M. de Duras, who were both related to the Prince of Orange. The order was obeyed, and no word was said; but this sort of vengeance was thought petty. Hopes were held out of a change in England, but they vanished immediately, and the Prince of Orange appeared more accredited there and stronger than ever. The Princess was much regretted, and the Prince of Orange, who loved her and gave her his entire confidence, and even most marked respect, was for some days ill with grief.

The other event was strange. The Duke of Hanover, who, in consequence of the Revolution, was destined to the throne of England after the Prince and Princess of Orange and the Princess of Denmark, had married his cousin-german, a daughter of the Duke of Zell. She was beautiful, and he lived happily with her for some time. The Count of Koenigsmarck, young and very well made, came to the Court, and gave him some umbrage. The Duke of Hanover became jealous; he watched his wife and the Count, and at length believed himself fully assured of what he would have wished to remain ignorant of all his life. Fury seized him: he had the Count arrested and thrown into a hot oven. Immediately afterwards he sent his wife to her father, who shut her up in one of his castles, where she was strictly guarded by the people of the Duke of Hanover. An assembly of the Consistory was held in order to break off his marriage. It was decided, very singularly, that the marriage was annulled so far as the Duke was concerned, and that he could marry another woman; but that it remained binding on the Duchess, and that she could not marry. The children she had had during her marriage were declared legitimate. The Duke of Hanover did not remain persuaded as to this last article.

The King, entirely occupied with the aggrandisement of his natural children, had heaped upon the Comte de Toulouse every possible favour. He now (in order to evade a promise he had made to his brother, that the first vacant government should be given to the Duc de Chartres) forced M. de Chaulnes to give up the government of Brittany, which he had long held, and conferred it upon the Comte de Toulouse, giving to the friend and heir of the former the successorship to the government of Guyenne, by way of recompense.

M. de Chaulnes was old and fat, but much loved by the people of Brittany. He was overwhelmed by this determination of the King, and his wife, who had long been accustomed to play the little Queen, still more so; yet there was nothing for them but to obey. They did obey, but it was with a sorrow and chagrin they could not hide.

The appointment was announced one morning at the rising of the King. Monsieur, who awoke later, heard of it at the drawing of his curtains, and was extremely piqued. The Comte de Toulouse came shortly afterwards, and announced it himself. Monsieur interrupted him, and before everybody assembled there said, "The King has given you a good present; but I know not if what he has done is good policy." Monsieur went shortly afterwards to the King, and reproached him for giving, under cover of a trick, the government of Brittany to the Comte de Toulouse, having promised it to the Duc de Chartres. The King heard him in silence: he knew well how to appease him. Some money for play and to embellish Saint Cloud, soon effaced Monsieur's chagrin.

All this winter my mother was solely occupied in finding a good match for me. Some attempt was made to marry me to Mademoiselle de Royan. It would have been a noble and rich marriage; but I was alone, Mademoiselle de Royan was an orphan, and I wished a father-in-law and a family upon whom I could lean. During the preceding year there had been some talk of the eldest daughter of Maréchal de Lorges for me. The affair had fallen through, almost as soon as suggested, and now, on both sides, there was a desire to recommence negotiations. The probity, integrity, the freedom of Maréchal de Lorges pleased me infinitely, and everything tended to give me an extreme desire for this marriage. Madame de Lorges by her virtue and good sense was all I could wish for as the mother of my future wife. Mademoiselle de Lorges was a blonde, with a complexion and figure perfect, a very amiable face, an extremely noble and modest deportment, and with I know not what of majesty derived from her air of virtue, and of natural gentleness. The Maréchal had five other daughters, but I liked this one best without comparison, and hoped to find with her that happiness which she since has given me. As she has become my wife, I will abstain here from saying more about her, unless it be that she has exceeded all that was promised of her, and all that I myself had hoped.

My marriage being agreed upon and arranged the Maréchal de Lorges spoke of it to the King, who had the goodness to reply to him that he could not do better, and to speak of me very obligingly. The marriage accordingly took place at the Hôtel de Lorges, on the 8th of April, 1695, which I have always regarded, and with good reason, as the happiest day of my life. My mother treated me like the best mother in the world. On the Thursday before Quasimodo the contract was signed; a grand repast followed; at midnight the curé of Saint Roch said mass, and married us in the chapel of the house. On the eve, my mother had sent forty thousand livres' worth of precious stones to Mademoiselle de Lorges, and I six hundred louis in a corbeille filled with all the knick-knacks that are given on these occasions.

We slept in the grand apartment of the Hôtel des Lorges. On the morrow, after dinner, my wife went to bed, and received a crowd of visitors, who came to pay their respects and to gratify their curiosity. The next evening we went to Versailles, and were received by Madame de Maintenon and the King. On arriving at the supper-table, the King said to the new Duchess:—" Madame, will you be pleased to seat yourself?"

His napkin being unfolded, he saw all the duchesses and princesses still standing; and rising in his chair, he said to Madame de Saint-Simon—" Madame, I have already begged you to be seated;" and all immediately seated themselves. On the morrow, Madame de Saint-Simon received all the Court in her bed—in the apartment of the Duchesse d'Arpajon, as being more handy, being on the ground floor. Our festivities finished by a supper that I gave to the former friends of my father, whose acquaintance I had always cultivated with great care.

Almost immediately after my marriage the second daughter of the Maréchal de Lorges followed in the footsteps of her sister. She was fifteen years of age, and at the reception of Madame de Saint-Simon had attracted the admiration of M. de Lauzun, who was then sixty-three. Since his return to the Court he had been reinstated in the dignity he had previously held. He flattered himself that by marrying the daughter of a General he should re-open a path to himself for command in the army. Full of this idea he spoke to M. de Lorges, who was by no means inclined towards the marriage. M. de Lauzun offered, however, to marry without dowry; and M. de Lorges, moved by this consideration, assented to his wish. The affair concluded, M. de Lorges spoke of it to the King. " You are bold," said his Majesty, " to take Lauzun into your family. I hope you may not repent of it."

The contract was soon after signed. M. de Lorges gave no dowry with his daughter, but she was to inherit something upon the death of M. Frémont. We carried this contract to the King, who smiled and bantered M. de Lauzun. M. de Lauzun replied, that he was only too happy, since it was the first time since his return that he had seen the King smile at him. The marriage took place without delay: there were only seven or eight persons present at the ceremony. M. de Lauzun *would* undress himself alone with his *valet de chambre,* and did not enter the apartment of his wife until after everybody had left it, and she was in bed with the curtains closed, and nobody to meet him on his passage. His wife received company in bed, as mine had done. Nobody was able to understand this marriage; and all foresaw that a rupture would speedily be brought about by the well-known temper of M. de Lauzun. In effect, this is what soon happened. The Maréchal de Lorges, remaining still in weak health, was deemed by the King unable to take the field again, and his army given over to the command of another General. M. de Lauzun thus saw all his hopes of advancement at an end, and, discontented that the Maréchal had done nothing for him, broke off all connection with the family, took away Madame de Lauzun from her mother (to the great grief of the latter, who doted upon this daughter), and established her in a house of his own adjoining the Assumption, in the Faubourg Saint-Honoré. There she had to endure her husband's continual caprices, but little removed in their manifestation from madness. Everybody cast blame upon him, and strongly pitied her and her father and mother; but nobody was surprised.

A few days after the marriage of M. de Lauzun, as the King was being wheeled in his easy chair in the gardens at Versailles, he asked me for many minute particulars concerning the family of the Maréchal de Lorges. He then set himself to joke with me upon the marriage of M. de Lauzun—and upon mine. He said to me, in spite of that gravity which never quitted him, that he had learnt from the Maréchal I had well acquitted myself, but that he believed the Maréchale had still better news.

The loss of two illustrious men about this time, made more noise than that of two of our grand ladies. The first of these men was La Fontaine, so well known by his "Fables" and stories, and who, nevertheless, was so heavy in conversation. The other was Mignard—so illustrious by his pencil: he had an only daughter—perfectly beautiful: she is repeated in several of those magnificent historical pictures which adorn the grand gallery of Versailles and its two salons, and which have had no slight share in irritating all Europe against the King, and in leaguing it still more against his person than his realm.

At the usual time the armies were got ready for active service, and everybody set out to join them. That of the Rhine, in which I was, was commanded by the Maréchal de Lorges. No sooner had we crossed the river and come upon the enemy, than the Maréchal fell ill. Although we were in want of forage and were badly encamped, nobody complained—nobody wished to move. Never did an army show so much interest in the life of its chief, or so much love for him. M. de Lorges was, in truth, at the last extremity, and the doctors that had been sent for from Strasbourg gave him up entirely. I took upon myself to administer to him some "English Drops." One hundred and thirty were given him in three doses: the effect was astonishing; an eruption burst out upon the Maréchal's body, and saved his life. His illness was not, however, at an end; and the army, although suffering considerably, would not hear of moving until he was quite ready to move also. There was no extremity it would not undergo rather than endanger the life of its chief.

Prince Louis of Baden offered by trumpets all sorts of assistance—doctors and remedies, and gave his word that if the army removed from its General, he and those who remained with him should be provided with forage and provisions—should be unmolested and allowed to rejoin the main body in perfect safety, or go whithersoever they pleased. He was thanked, as he merited, for those very kind offers, which we did not wish, however, to profit by.

Little by little the health of the General was reestablished, and the army demonstrated its joy by bonfires all over the camp, and by salvos, which it was impossible to prevent. Never was seen testimony of love so universal or so flattering. The King was much concerned at the illness of the Maréchal; all the Court was infinitely touched by it. M. de Lorges was not less loved by it than by the troops. When able to support the fatigues of the journey, he was removed in a coach to Philipsburg, where he was joined by the Maréchal, who had come there to meet him. The next day he went to Landau, and I, who formed one of his numerous and distinguished escort, accompanied him there, and then returned to the army, which was placed under the command of the Maréchal de Joyeuse.

We found it at about three leagues from Ketsch, its right at Roth, and its left at Waldsdorff. We learned that the Maréchal de Joyeuse had lost a good occasion of fighting the enemy; but as I was not in camp at the time, I will say no more of the matter. Our position was not good: Schwartz was on our left, and the Prince of Baden on our right, hemming us in, as it were, between them. We had no forage, whilst they had abundance of everything, and were able to procure all they wanted. There was a contest who should de-camp the last. All our communications were cut off with Philipsburg, so that we could not repass the Rhine under the protection of that place. To get out of our position, it was necessary to defile before our enemies into the plain of Hockenun, and this was a delicate operation. The most annoying circumstance was, that M. de Joyeuse would communicate with nobody, and was so ill-tempered that none dared to speak to him. At last he determined upon his plans, and I was of the detachment by which they were to be carried out. We were sent to Manheim to see if out of the ruins of that place (burned in 1688 by M. de Louvois) sufficient materials could be found to construct bridges, by which we might cross the Rhine there. We found that the bridges could be made, and returned to announce this to M. de Joyeuse. Accordingly, on the 20th of July, the army put itself in movement. The march was made in the utmost confusion. Everything was in disorder; the infantry and cavalry were huddled together pell-mell; no commands could be acted upon, and indeed the whole army was so disorganised that it could have been easily beaten by a handful of men. In effect, the enemy at last tried to take advantage of our confusion, by sending a few troops to harass us. But it was too late; we had sufficiently rallied to be able to turn upon them, and they narrowly escaped falling into our hands. We encamped that night in the plain on the banks of the Necker—our rear at Manheim, and our left at Seckenheim, while waiting for the remainder of the army, still very distant. Indeed, so great had been the confusion, that the first troops arrived at one o'clock at night, and the last late in the morning of the next day.

I thought that our headquarters were to be in this village of Seckenheim, and, in company with several officers took possession of a large house and prepared to pass the night there. While we were resting from the fatigues of the day we heard a great noise, and soon after a frightful uproar. It was caused by a body of our men, who, searching for water, had discovered this village, and after having quenched their thirst had, under the cover of thick darkness, set themselves to pillage, to violate, to massacre, and to commit all the horrors inspired by the most unbridled licence. La Bretesche, a lieutenant-general, declared to me that he had never seen anything like it, although he had several times been at pillages and sackings. He was very grateful that he had not yielded to my advice, and taken off his wooden leg to be more at ease; for in a short time we ourselves were invaded, and had some trouble to defend ourselves. As we bore the livery of M. de Lorges, we were respected, but those who bore that of M. de Joyeuse were in some cases severely maltreated. We passed the rest of the night as well as we could in this unhappy place, which was not abandoned by our soldiers until long after there was nothing more to find. At daylight we went to the camp.

We found the army beginning to move: it had passed the night as well as it could without order, the troops constantly arriving, and the last comers simply joining themselves on to the rest. Our camp was soon, however, properly formed, and on the 24th July, the bridges being ready, all the army crossed the Rhine, without any attempt being made by the enemy to follow us. On the day after, the Maréchal de Joyeuse permitted me to go to Landau, where I remained with the Maréchal and the Maréchale de Lorges until the General was again able to place himself at the head of his army.

Nothing of importance was done by our other armies; but in Flanders an interesting adventure occurred. The Prince of Orange, after playing a fine game of chess with our army, suddenly invested Namur with a large force, leaving the rest of his troops under the command of M. de Vaudemont. The Maréchal de Villeroy, who had the command of our army in Flanders, at once pressed upon M. de Vaudemont, who, being much the weaker of the two, tried hard to escape. Both felt that everything was in their hands: Vaudemont, that upon his safety depended the success of the siege of Namur; and Villeroy, that to his victory was attached the fate of the Low Countries, and very likely a glorious peace, with all the personal results of such an event. He took his measures so well that on the evening of the 13th of July it was impossible for M. de Vaudemont to escape falling into his hands on the 14th, and he wrote thus to the King. At daybreak on the 14th M. de Villeroy sent word to M. du Maine to commence the action. Impatient that his orders were not obeyed, he sent again five or six times. M. du Maine wished in the first instance to reconnoitre, then to confess himself, and delayed in effect so long that M. de Vaudemont was able to commence his retreat. The general officers cried out at this. One of them came to M. du Maine and reminded him of the repeated orders of the Maréchal de Villeroy, represented the importance of victory, and the ease with which it could be obtained: with tears in his eyes he begged M. du Maine to commence the attack. It was all in vain; M. du Maine stammered, and could not be prevailed upon to charge, and so allowed M. de Vaudemont's army to escape, when by a single movement it might have been entirely defeated.

All our army was in despair, and officers and soldiers made no scruple of expressing their anger and contempt. M. de Villeroy, more outraged than anybody else, was yet too good a courtier to excuse himself at the expense of M. du Maine. He simply wrote to the King, that he had been deceived in those hopes of success which appeared certain the day before, entered into no further details, and resigned himself to all that might happen. The King, who had counted the hours until news of a great and decisive victory should reach him, was very much surprised when this letter came: he saw at once that something strange had happened of which no intelligence had been sent: he searched the gazettes of Holland; in one he read of a great action said to have been fought, and in which M. du Maine had been grievously wounded; in the next the news of the action was contradicted, and M. du Maine was declared to have received no wounds at all. In order to learn what had really taken place, the King sent for Lavienne, a man he was in the habit of consulting when he wanted to learn things no one else dared to tell him.

This Lavienne had been a bath-keeper much in vogue in Paris, and had become bath-keeper to the King at the time of his amours. He had pleased by his drugs, which had frequently put the King in a state to enjoy himself more, and this road had led Lavienne to become one of the four chief *valets de chambre*. He was a very honest man, but coarse, rough, and free-spoken; it was this last quality which made him useful in the manner I have before mentioned. From Lavienne the King, but not without difficulty, learned the truth: it threw him into despair. The other illegitimate children were favourites with him, but it was upon M. du Maine that all his hopes were placed. They now fell to the ground, and the grief of the King was insupportable: he felt deeply for that dear son whose troops had become the laughing stock of the army; he felt the railleries that, as the gazettes showed him, foreigners were heaping upon his forces; and his vexation was inconceivable.

This Prince, so equal in his manners, so thoroughly master of his lightest movements, even upon the gravest occasions, succumbed under this event. On rising from the table at Marly he saw a servant who, while taking away the dessert, helped himself to a biscuit, which he put in his pocket. On the instant, the King forgets his dignity, and cane in hand runs to this valet (who little suspected what was in store for him), strikes him, abuses him, and breaks the cane upon his body! The truth is, 'twas only a reed, and snapped easily. However, the stump in his hand, he walked away like a man quite beside himself, continuing to abuse this valet, and entered Madame de Maintenon's room, where he remained nearly an hour. Upon coming out he met Father la Chaise. "My father," said the King to him, in a very loud voice, "I have beaten a knave and broken my cane over his shoulders, but I do not think I have offended God." Everybody around trembled at this public confession, and the poor priest muttered a semblance of approval between his teeth, to avoid irritating the King more. The noise that the affair made and the terror it inspired may be imagined; for nobody could divine for some time the cause; and everybody easily understood that that which had appeared could not be the real one. To finish with this matter, once for all, let us add here the saying of M. d'Elbœuf. Courtier though he was, the upward flight of the illegitimate children weighed upon his heart. As the campaign was at its close and the Princes were about to depart, he begged M. du Maine before everybody to say where he expected to serve during the next campaign, because wherever it might be he should like to be there also.

After being pressed to say why, he replied that "with him one's life was safe." This pointed remark made much noise. M. du Maine lowered his eyes, and did not reply one word. As for the Maréchal de Villeroy he grew more and more in favour with the King and with Madame de Maintenon. The bitter fruit of M. du Maine's act was the taking of Namur, which capitulated on August 4th (1695). The Maréchal de Villeroy in turn bombarded Brussels, which was sorely maltreated. The Maréchal de Boufflers, who had defended Namur, was made Duke, and those who had served under him were variously rewarded. This gave occasion for the Prince of Orange to say, that the King recompensed more liberally the loss of a place than *he* could the conquest of one. The army retired into winter-quarters at the end of October, and the Generals went to Paris.

As for me, I remained six weeks at Landau with M. and Madame de Lorges. At the end of that time, the Maréchal, having regained his health, returned to the army, where he was welcomed with the utmost joy: he soon after had an attack of apoplexy, and, by not attending to his malady in time, became seriously ill again. When a little recovered, he and Madame de Lorges set out for Vichy, and I went to Paris.

CHAPTER VIII

BEFORE speaking of what happened at Court after my return, it will be necessary to record what had occurred there during the campaign.

M. de Brias, Archbishop of Cambrai, had died, and the King had given that valuable preferment to the Abbé de Fénelon, preceptor of the children of France. Fénelon was a man of quality, without fortune,—whom the consciousness of wit—of the insinuating and captivating kind—united with much ability, gracefulness of intellect, and learning, inspired with ambition. He had been long going about from door to door, knocking for admission, but without success. Piqued against the Jesuits, to whom he had addressed himself at first, as holding all favours in their hands, and discouraged because unable to succeed in that quarter, he turned next to the Jansenists, to console himself by the reputation he hoped he should derive from them, for the loss of those gifts of fortune which hitherto had despised him.

He remained a considerable time undergoing the process of initiation, and succeeded at last in being of the private parties that some of the important Jansenists then held once or twice a week at the house of the Duchesse de Brancas. I know not if he appeared too clever for them, or if he hoped elsewhere for better things than he could get among people who had only sores to share; but little by little his intimacy with them cooled; and by dint of turning around Saint Sulpice, he succeeded in forming another connection there, upon which he built greater expectations. This society of priests was beginning to distinguish itself, and from a seminary of a Paris parish to extend abroad. Ignorance, the minuteness of their practices, the absence of all patrons and of members at all distinguished in any way, inspired them with a blind obedience to Rome and to all its maxims; with a great aversion for everything that passed for Jansenism, and made them so dependent upon the bishops that they began to be considered an acquisition in many dioceses. They appeared a middle party, very useful to the prelates; who equally feared the Court, on account of suspicions of doctrine, and the Jesuits: for as soon as the latter had insinuated themselves into the good graces of the prelates, they imposed their yoke upon them, or ruined them hopelessly; thus the Sulpicians grew apace. None amongst them could compare in any way with the Abbé de Fénelon; so that he was able easily to play first fiddle, and to make for himself protectors who were interested in advancing him, in order that they might be protected in turn. His piety, which was all things to all men, and his doctrine that he formed upon theirs (abjuring, as it were, in whispers, the impurities he might have contracted amongst those he had abandoned)—the charms, the graces, the sweetness, the insinuation of his mind, rendered him a dear friend to this new congregation, and procured for him what he had long sought,—people upon whom he could lean, and who could and would serve. Whilst waiting opportunities, he carefully courted these people, without thinking, however, of positively joining them, his views being more ambitious; so that he ever sought to make new acquaintances and friends. His was a coquettish mind, which from people the most influential down to the workman and the lackey sought appreciation and was determined to please; and his talents for this work perfectly seconded his desires.

At this time, and while still obscure, he heard speak of Madame Guyon, who has since made so much noise in the world, and who is too well known to need that I should dwell upon her here. He saw her. There was an interchange of pleasure between their minds. Their *sublimes* amalgamated. I know not if they understood each other very clearly in that system, and that new tongue which they hatched subsequently, but they persuaded themselves they did, and friendship grew up between them. Although more known than he, Madame Guyon was nevertheless not much known, and their intimacy was not perceived, because nobody thought of them; Saint Sulpice even was ignorant of what was going on.

The Duc de Beauvilliers became Governor of the children of France almost in spite of himself, without having thought of it. He had to choose a preceptor for Monseigneur le Duc de Bourgogne. He addressed himself to Saint Sulpice, where for a long time he had confessed, for he liked and protected it. He had heard speak of Fénelon with eulogy: the Sulpicians vaunted his piety, his intelligence, his knowledge, his talents; at last they proposed him for preceptor. The Duc de Beauvilliers saw him, was charmed with him, and appointed him to the office.

As soon as installed, Fénelon saw of what importance it would be to gain the entire favour of the Duc de Beauvilliers, and of his brother-in-law the Duc de Chevreuse, both very intimate friends, and both in the highest confidence of the King and Madame de Maintenon. This was his first care, and he succeeded beyond his hopes, becoming the master of their hearts and minds, and the director of their consciences.

Madame de Maintenon dined regularly once a week at the house of one or other of the two Dukes,—fifth of a little party, composed of the two sisters and the two husbands,—with a bell upon the table, in order to dispense with servants in waiting, and to be able to talk without restraint. Fénelon was at last admitted to this sanctuary, at foot of which all the Court was prostrated. He was almost as successful with Madame de Maintenon as he had been with the two Dukes. His spirituality enchanted her: the Court soon perceived the giant strides of the fortunate Abbé, and eagerly courted him. But, desiring to be free and entirely devoted to his great object, he kept himself aloof from their flatteries—made for himself a shield with his modesty and his duties of preceptor—and thus rendered himself still more dear to the persons he had captivated, and that he had so much interest in retaining in that attachment.

Among these cares he forgot not his dear Madame Guyon; he had already vaunted her to the two Dukes and to Madame de Maintenon. He had even introduced her to them, but as though with difficulty and for a few moments, as a woman all in God, whose humility and whose love of contemplation and solitude kept her within the strictest limits, and whose fear, above all, was that she should become known. The tone of her mind pleased Madame de Maintenon extremely; her reserve, mixed with delicate flatteries, won upon her. Madame de Maintenon wished to hear her talk upon matters of piety; with difficulty she consented to speak. She seemed to surrender herself to the charms and to the virtue of Madame de Maintenon, and Madame de Maintenon fell into the nets so skilfully prepared for her.

Such was the situation of Fénelon when he became Archbishop of Cambrai; increasing the admiration in which he was held by taking no step to gain that great benefice. He had taken care not to seek to procure himself Cambrai; the least spark of ambition would have destroyed all his edifice; and, moreover, it was not Cambrai that he coveted.

Little by little he appropriated to himself some distinguished sheep of the small flock Madame Guyon had gathered together. He only conducted them, however, under the direction of that prophetess, and everything passed with a secrecy and mystery that gave additional relish to the manna distributed.

Cambrai was a thunderbolt for this little flock. It was the archbishopric of Paris they wished. Cambrai they looked upon with disdain as a country diocese, the residence in which (impossible to avoid from time to time) would deprive them of their pastor. Their grief was then profound at what the rest of the world took for a piece of amazing luck, and the Countess of Guiche was so affected as to be unable to hide her tears. The new prelate had not neglected such of his brethren as made the most figure; they, in turn, considered it a distinction to command his regard. Saint Cyr, that spot so valuable and so inaccessible, was the place chosen for his consecration; and M. de Meaux, dictator then of the episcopacy and of doctrine, consecrated him. The children of France were among the spectators, and Madame de Maintenon was present with her little court of familiars. No others were invited; the doors were closed to those who sought to pay their court.

The new Archbishop of Cambrai, gratified with his influence over Madame de Maintenon and with the advantages it had brought him, felt that unless he became completely master of her, the hopes he still entertained could not be satisfied. But there was a rival in his way—Godet, Bishop of Chartres, who was much in the confidence of Madame de Maintenon, and had long discourses with her at Saint Cyr. As he was, however, of a very ill figure, had but little support at Court, and appeared exceedingly simple, M. de Cambrai believed he could easily overthrow him. To do this, he determined to make use of Madame Guyon, whose new spirituality had already been so highly relished by Madame de Maintenon. He persuaded this latter to allow Madame Guyon to enter Saint Cyr, where they could discourse together much more at their ease than at the Hôtel de Chevreuse or Beauvilliers. Madame Guyon went accordingly to Saint Cyr two or three times. Soon after, Madame de Maintenon, who relished her more and more, made her sleep there, and their meetings grew longer. Madame Guyon admitted that she sought persons proper to become her disciples, and in a short time she formed a little flock, whose maxims and language appeared very strange to all the rest of the house, and, above all, to M. de Chartres. That prelate was not so simple as M. de Cambrai imagined. Profound theologian and scholar, pious, disinterested, and of rare probity, he could be, if necessary, a most skilful courtier; but he rarely exerted this power, for the favour of Madame de Maintenon sufficed him of itself. As soon as he got scent of this strange doctrine, he caused two ladies, upon whom he could count, to be admitted to Saint Cyr, as if to become disciples of Madame Guyon. He gave them full instructions, and they played their parts to perfection. In the first place they appeared to be ravished, and by degrees enchanted, with the new doctrine. Madame Guyon, pleased with this fresh conquest, took the ladies into her most intimate confidence in order to gain them entirely. They communicated everything to M. de Chartres, who quietly looked on, allowed things to take their course, and, when he believed the right moment had arrived, disclosed all he had learnt to Madame de Maintenon. She was strangely surprised when she saw the extraordinary drift of the new doctrine. Troubled and uncertain, she consulted with M. de Cambrai, who, not suspecting she had been so well instructed, became, when he discovered it, embarrassed, and thus augmented her suspicions.

Suddenly Madame Guyon was driven away from Saint Cyr, and prohibited from spreading her doctrine elsewhere. But the admiring disciples she had made still gathered round her in secret, and this becoming known, she was ordered to leave Paris. She feigned obedience, but in effect went no further than the Faubourg Saint Antoine, where, with great secrecy, she continued to receive her flock. But being again detected, she was sent, without further parley, to the Bastille, well treated there, but allowed to see nobody, not even to write. Before being arrested, however, she had been put into the hands of M. de Meaux, who used all his endeavours to change her sentiments. Tired at last of his sermons, she feigned conviction, signed a recantation of her opinions, and was set at liberty. Yet, directly after, she held her secret assemblies in the Faubourg Saint Antoine, and it was in consequence of this abuse of freedom that she was arrested. These adventures bring me far into the year 1696, and the sequel extends into the following year. Let us finish this history at once, and return afterwards to what happened meanwhile.

Monsieur de Cambrai, stunned but not overpowered by the reverse he had sustained, and by his loss of favour with Madame de Maintenon, stood firm in his stirrups. After Madame Guyon's abuse of her liberty, and the conferences of Issy, he bethought himself of confessing to M. de Meaux, by which celebrated trick he hoped to close that prelate's mouth. These circumstances induced M. de Meaux to take pen in hand, in order to expose to the public the full account of this affair, and of Madame Guyon's doctrine; and he did so in a work under the title of *Instruction sur les Etats d'Oraison.*

While the book was yet unpublished, M. de Cambrai was shown a copy. He saw at once the necessity of writing another to ward off the effect of such a blow. He must have had a great deal of matter already prepared, otherwise the diligence he used would be incredible. Before M. de Meaux's book was ready, M. de Cambrai's, entitled *Maximes des Saints,* was published and distributed. M. de Chevreuse, who corrected the proofs, installed himself at the printer's, so as to see every sheet as soon as printed.

This book, written in the strangest manner, did M. de Cambrai little service. If people were offended to find it supported upon no authority, they were much more so with its confused and embarrassed style, its precision so restrained and so decided, its barbarous terms which seemed as though taken from a foreign tongue,—above all, its high-flown and far-fetched thoughts, which took one's breath away, as in the too subtle air of the middle region. Nobody, except the theologians, understood it, and even they not without reading it three or four times. Connoisseurs found in it a pure Quietism, which, although wrapped up in fine language, was clearly visible. I do not give my own judgment of things so much beyond me, but repeat what was said everywhere. Nothing else was talked about, even by the ladies; and *à propos* of this, the saying of Madame de Sévigné was revived: " Make religion a little more palpable; it evaporates by dint of being over-refined."

Not a word was heard in praise of the book; everybody was opposed to it, and it was the means of making Madame de Maintenon more unfavourable to M. de Cambrai than ever. He sent the King a copy, without informing her. This completed her annoyance against him. M. de Cambrai, finding his book so ill-received by the Court and by the prelates, determined to try and support it on the authority of Rome, a step quite opposed to our manners. In the mean time, M. de Meaux's book appeared in two volumes octavo, well written, clear, modest, and supported upon the authority of the Scriptures. It was received with avidity, and absolutely devoured. There was not a person at the Court who did not take a pleasure in reading it, so that for a long time it was the common subject of conversation of the Court and of the town.

These two books, so opposed in doctrine and in style, made such a stir on every side that the King interposed, and forced M. de Cambrai to submit his work to an examination by a council of prelates, whom he named. M. de Cambrai asked permission to go to Rome to defend his cause in person, but this the King refused. He sent his book, therefore, to the Pope, and had the annoyance to receive a dry, cold reply, and to see M. de Meaux's book triumph. His good fortune was in effect at an end. He remained at Court some little time, but the King was soon irritated against him, sent him off post-haste to Paris, and from there to his diocese, whence he has never returned. He left behind him a letter for one of his friends, M. de Chevreuse it was generally believed, which immediately after became public. It appeared like the manifesto of a man who disgorges his bile and restrains himself no more, because he has nothing more to hope. The letter, bold and bitter in style, was besides so full of ability and artifice, that it was extremely pleasant to read, without finding approvers; so true it is that a wise and disdainful silence is difficult to keep under reverses.

CHAPTER IX

TO return now to the date from which I started. On the 6th of August, 1695, Harlay, Archbishop of Paris, died of epilepsy at Conflans. He was a prelate of profound knowledge and ability, very amiable, and of most gallant manners. For some time past he had lost favour with the King and with Madame de Maintenon, for opposing the declaration of her marriage—of which marriage he had been one of the three witnesses. The clergy, who perceived his fall, and to whom envy is not unfamiliar, took pleasure in revenging themselves upon M. de Paris, for the domination, although gentle and kindly, he had exercised. Unaccustomed to this decay of his power, all the graces of his mind and body withered. He could find no resource but to shut himself up with his *dear* friend the Duchesse de Lesdiguières, whom he saw every day of his life, either at her own house or at Conflans, where he had laid out a delicious garden, kept so strictly clean, that as the two walked, gardeners followed at a distance, and effaced their footprints with rakes. The vapours seized the Archbishop, and turned themselves into slight attacks of epilepsy. He felt this, but prohibited his servants to send for help, when they should see him attacked; and he was only too well obeyed. The Duchesse de Lesdiguières never slept at Conflans, but she went there every afternoon, and was always alone with him. On the 6th of August, he passed the morning, as usual, until dinner-time; his steward came there to him, and found him in his cabinet, fallen back upon a sofa; he was dead. The celebrated Jesuit-Father Gaillard preached his funeral sermon, and carefully eluded pointing the moral of the event. The King and Madame de Maintenon were much relieved by the loss of M. de Paris. Various places he had held were at once distributed. His archbishopric and his nomination to the cardinalship required more discussion. The King learnt the news of the death of M. de Paris on the 6th. On the 8th, in going as usual to his cabinet, he went straight up to the Bishop of Orleans, led him to the Cardinals de Bouillon and de Fursternberg, and said to them:—" Gentlemen, I think you will thank me for giving you an associate like M. d'Orléans, to whom I give my nomination to the cardinalship." At this word the Bishop, who little expected such a scene, fell at the King's feet and embraced his knees. He was a man whose face spoke at once of the virtue and benignity he possessed. In youth he was so pious, that young and old were afraid to say a foul word in his presence. Although very rich, he appropriated scarcely any of his wealth to himself, but gave it away for good works. The modesty and the simplicity with which M. d'Orléans sustained his nomination, increased the universal esteem in which he was held.

The archbishopric of Paris was given to a brother of the Duc de Noailles—the Bishop of Châlons-sur-Marne—M. de Noailles thus reaping the fruit of his wise sacrifice to M. de Vendôme, before related. M. de Châlons was of singular goodness and modesty. He did not wish for this preferment, and seeing from far the prospect of its being given to him, hastened to declare himself against the Jesuits, in the expectation that Père la Chaise, who was of them, and who was always consulted upon these occasions, might oppose him. But it happened, perhaps for the first time, that

Madame de Maintenon, who felt restrained by the Jesuits, did not consult Père la Chaise, and the preferment was made without his knowledge, and without that of M. de Châlons. The affront was a violent one, and the Jesuits never forgave the new Archbishop: he was, however, so little anxious for the office, that it was only after repeated orders he could be made to accept it.

The Bishop of Langres also died about this time. He was a true gentleman, much liked, and called " the good Langres." There was nothing bad about him, except his manners; he was not made for a bishop—gambled very much, and staked high. M. de Vendôme and others won largely at billiards of him, two or three times. He said no word, but, on returning to Langres, did nothing but practise billiards in secret for six months. When next in Paris, he was again asked to play, and his adversaries, who thought him as unskilful as before, expected an easy victory: but, to their astonishment, he gained almost every game, won back much more than he had lost, and then laughed in the faces of his companions.

I paid about this time, my first journey to Marly, and a singular scene happened there. The King at dinner, setting aside his usual gravity, laughed and joked very much with Madame la Duchesse, eating olives with her in sport, and thereby causing her to drink more than usual—which he also pretended to do. Upon rising from the table the King, seeing the Princesse de Conti look extremely serious, said, dryly, that her gravity did not accommodate itself to their drunkenness. The Princess, piqued, allowed the King to pass without saying anything; and then, turning to Madame de Chatillon, said, in the midst of the noise, whilst everybody was washing his mouth, that she " would rather be grave than be a wine-sack " (alluding to some bouts a little prolonged that her sister had recently had).

The saying was heard by the Duchesse de Chartres, who replied, loud enough to be heard, in her slow and trembling voice, that she preferred to be a "wine-sack" rather than a "rag-sack" (*sac à guenilles*)— by which she alluded to the Clermont and La Choin adventure I have related before.

This remark was so cruel that it met with no reply; it spread through Marly, and thence to Paris; and Madame la Duchesse, who had the art of writing witty songs, made one upon this theme. The Princesse de Conti was in despair, for she had not the same weapon at her disposal. Monsieur tried to reconcile them— gave them a dinner at Meudon—but they returned from it as they went.

The end of the year was stormy at Marly. One evening, after the King had gone to bed, and while Monseigneur was playing in the saloon, the Duchesse de Chartres and Madame la Duchesse (who were bound together by their mutual aversion to the Princesse de Conti) sat down to a supper in the chamber of the first-named. Monseigneur, upon retiring late to his own room, found them smoking with pipes, which they had sent for from the Swiss Guards! Knowing what would happen if the smell were discovered, he made them leave off, but the smoke had betrayed them. The King next day severely scolded them, at which the Princesse de Conti triumphed. Nevertheless, these broils multiplied, and the King at last grew so weary of them that one evening he called the Princesses before him, and threatened that if they did not improve he would banish them all from the Court. The measure had its effect; calm and decorum returned, and supplied the place of friendship.

There were many marriages this winter, and

amongst them one very strange—a marriage of love, between a brother of Feuquière's, who had never done much, and the daughter of the celebrated Mignard, first painter of his time. This daughter was still so beautiful, that Bloin, chief valet of the King, had kept her for some time, with the knowledge of every one, and used his influence to make the King sign the marriage-contract.

There are in all Courts persons who, without wit and without distinguished birth, without patrons, or service rendered, pierce into the intimacy of the most brilliant, and succeed at last, I know not how, in forcing the world to look upon them as somebody. Such a person was Cavoye. Rising from nothing, he became Grand Maréchal des Logis in the royal household: he arrived at that office by a perfect romance. He was one of the best made men in France, and was much in favour with the ladies. He first appeared at the Court at a time when much duelling was taking place, in spite of the edicts. Cavoye, brave and skilful, acquired so much reputation in this particular, that the name of "Brave Cavoye" has stuck to him ever since. An ugly but very good creature, Mademoiselle de Coetlogon, one of the Queen's waiting-women, fell in love with him, even to madness. She made all the advances; but Cavoye treated her so cruelly, nay, sometimes so brutally, that (wonderful to say) everybody pitied her, and the King at last interfered, and commanded him to be more humane. Cavoye went to the army; the poor Coetlogon was in tears until his return. In the winter, for being second in a duel, he was sent to the Bastille. Then the grief of Coetlogon knew no bounds: she threw aside all ornaments, and clad herself as meanly as possible; she begged the King to grant Cavoye his liberty, and, upon the King's refusing, quarrelled with him violently, and when in return he laughed at her, became so furious, that she would have used her nails, had he not been too wise to expose himself to them. Then she refused to attend to her duties, would not serve the King, saying, that he did not deserve it, and grew so yellow and ill, that at last she was allowed to visit her lover at the Bastille. When he was liberated, her joy was extreme, she decked herself out anon, but it was with difficulty that she consented to be reconciled to the King.

Cavoye had many times been promised an appointment, but had never received one such as he wished. The office of Grand Maréchal des Logis had just become vacant: the King offered it to Cavoye, but on condition that he should marry Mademoiselle Coetlogon. Cavoye sniffed a little longer, but was obliged to submit to this condition at last. They were married, and she has still the same admiration for him, and it is sometimes fine fun to see the caresses she gives him before all the world, and the constrained gravity with which he receives them. The history of Cavoye would fill a volume, but this I have selected suffices for its singularity, which assuredly is without example.

About this time the King of England thought matters were ripe for an attempt to reinstate himself upon the throne. The Duke of Berwick had been secretly into England, where he narrowly escaped being arrested, and upon his report these hopes were built. Great preparations were made, but they came to nothing, as was always the case with the projects of this unhappy prince.

Madame de Guise died at this time. Her father was the brother of Louis XIII., and she, humpbacked and deformed to excess, had married the last Duc de Guise, rather than not marry at all. During all their lives, she compelled him to pay her all the deference due to her rank. At table he stood while she unfolded her napkin and seated herself, and did not sit until she told him to do so, and then at the end of the table. This form was observed every day of their lives. She was equally severe in such matters of etiquette with all the rest of the world. She would keep her diocesan, the Bishop of Séez, standing for entire hours, while she was seated in her arm-chair and never once offered him a seat even in the corner. She was in other things an entirely good and sensible woman. Not until after her death was it discovered that she had been afflicted for a long time with a cancer, which appeared as though about to burst. God spared her this pain.

We lost, in the month of March, Madame de Miramion, aged sixty-six. She was a bourgeoise, married, and in the same year became a widow—very rich, young, and beautiful. Bussy Rabutin, so known by his *Histoire Amoureuse des Gaules,* and by the profound disgrace it drew upon him, and still more by the vanity of his mind and the baseness of his heart, wished absolutely to marry her, and actually carried her off to a château. Upon arriving at the place, she pronounced before everybody assembled there a vow of chastity, and then dared Bussy to do his worst. He, strangely discomfited by this action, at once set her at liberty, and tried to accommodate the affair. From that moment she devoted herself entirely to works of piety, and was much esteemed by the King. She was the first woman of her condition who wrote above her door, " Hôtel de Nesmond." Everybody cried out, and was scandalised, but the writing remained, and became the example and the father of those of all kinds which little by little have inundated Paris.

Madame de Sévigné, so amiable and of such excellent company, died some time after at Grignan, at the house of her daughter, her idol, but who merited little to be so. I was very intimate with the young Marquis de Grignan, her grandson. This woman, by her natural graces, the sweetness of her wit, communicated these qualities to those who had them not; she was besides extremely good, and knew thoroughly many things without ever wishing to appear as though she knew anything.

Father Seraphin preached during Lent this year at the Court. His sermons, in which he often repeated twice running the same phrase, were much in vogue. It was from him that came the saying, " Without God there is no wit." The King was much pleased with him, and reproached M. de Vendôme and M. de la Rochefoucauld because they never went to hear his sermons. M. de Vendôme replied off-hand, that he did not care to go to hear a man who said whatever he pleased without allowing anybody to reply to him, and made the King smile by this sally. But M. de la Rochefoucauld treated the matter in another manner: he said that he could not induce himself to go like the merest hanger-on about the Court, and beg a seat of the officer who distributed them, and then betake himself early to church in order to have a good one, and wait about in order to put himself where it might please that officer to place him. Whereupon the King immediately gave him a fourth seat behind him, by the side of the Grand Chamberlain, so that everywhere he is thus placed. M. d'Orléans had been in the habit of seating himself there (although his right place was on the *prie-Dieu*), and little by little had accustomed himself to consider it as his proper place. When he found himself driven away, he made a great ado, and, not daring to complain to the King, quarrelled with M. de la Rochefoucauld, who, until then, had been one of his particular friends. The affair soon made a great stir; the friends of both parties mixed themselves up in it. The King tried in vain to make M. d'Orléans listen to reason; the prelate was inflexible, and when he found he could gain nothing by clamour and complaint, he retired in high dudgeon into his diocese: he remained there some time, and upon his return resumed his complaints with more determination than ever; he fell at the feet of the King, protesting that he would rather die than see his office degraded. M. de la Rochefoucauld entreated the King to be allowed to surrender the seat in favour of M. d'Orléans. But the King would not change his decision; he said that if the matter were to be decided between M. d'Orléans and a lackey, he would give the seat to the lackey rather than to M. d'Orléans. Upon this the prelate returned to his diocese, which he would have been wiser never to have quitted in order to obtain a place which did not belong to him.

As the King really esteemed M. d'Orléans, he determined to appease his anger; and to put an end to this dispute he gave therefore the bishopric of Metz to the nephew of M. d'Orléans; and by this means a reconciliation was established. M. d'Orléans and M. de la Rochefoucauld joined hands again, and the King looked on delighted.

The public lost soon after a man illustrious by his genius, by his style, and by his knowledge of men,— I mean La Bruyère, who died of apoplexy at Versailles, after having surpassed Theophrastus in his own manner, and after painting, in the new characters, the men of our days in a manner inimitable. He was besides a very honest man, of excellent breeding, simple, very disinterested, and without anything of the pedant. I had sufficiently known him to regret his death, and the works that might have been hoped from him.

The command of the armies was distributed in the same manner as before, with the exception that M. de Choiseul had the army of the Rhine in place of M. de Lorges. Every one set out to take the field. The Duc de la Feuillade in passing by Metz, to join the army in Germany, called upon his uncle, who was very rich and in his second childhood. La Feuillade thought fit to make sure of his uncle's money beforehand, demanded the key of the cabinet and of the coffers, broke them open upon being refused by the servants, and took away thirty thousand crowns in gold, and many jewels, leaving untouched the silver. The King, who for a long time had been much discontented with La Feuillade for his debauches and his negligence, spoke very strongly and very openly upon this strange forestalling of inheritance. It was only with great difficulty he could be persuaded not to strip La Feuillade of his rank.

Our campaign was undistinguished by any striking event. From June to September of this year (1696), we did little but subsist and observe, after which we recrossed the Rhine at Philipsburg, where our rear guard was slightly inconvenienced by the enemy. In Italy there was more movement. The King sought to bring about peace by dividing the forces of his enemies, and secretly entered into a treaty with Savoy. The conditions were, that every place belonging to Savoy which had been taken by our troops should be restored, and that a marriage should take place between Monseigneur the Duc de Bourgogne and the daughter of the Duke of Savoy, when she became twelve years of age. In the mean time she was to be sent to the Court of France, and preparations were at once made there to provide her with a suitable establishment.

The King was ill with an anthrax in the throat. The eyes of all Europe were turned towards him, for his malady was not without danger; nevertheless in his bed he affected to attend to affairs as usual; and he arranged there with Madame de Maintenon, who scarcely ever quitted his side, the household of the Savoy Princess. The persons selected for the offices in that household were either entirely devoted to Madame de Maintenon, or possessed of so little wit that she had nothing to fear from them. A selection which excited much envy and great surprise was that of the Duchesse de Lude to be lady of honour. The day before she was appointed, Monsieur had mentioned her name in sport to the King. "Yes," said the King, "she would be the best woman in the world to teach the Princess to put rouge and patches on her cheek;" and then, being more devout than usual, he said other things as bitter and marking strong aversion on his part to the Duchess. In fact, she was no favourite of his nor of Madame de Maintenon; and this was so well understood that the surprise of Monsieur and of everybody else was great, upon finding, the day after this discourse, that she had been appointed to the place.

The cause of this was soon learnt. The Duchesse de Lude coveted much to be made lady of honour to the Princess, but knew she had but little chance, so many others more in favour than herself being in the field. Madame de Maintenon had an old servant named Nanon, who had been with her from the time of her early days of misery, and who had such influence with her, that this servant was made much of by everybody at Court, even by the ministers and the daughters of the King. The Duchesse de Lude had also an old servant who was on good terms with the other. The affair therefore was not difficult. The

Duchesse de Lude sent twenty thousand crowns to Nanon, and on the very evening of the day on which the King had spoken to Monsieur, she had the place. Thus it is! A Nanon sells the most important and the most brilliant offices, and a Duchess of high birth is silly enough to buy herself into servitude!

This appointment excited much envy. The Maréchale de Rochefort, who had expected to be named, made a great ado. Madame de Maintenon, who despised her, was piqued, and said that she should have had it but for the conduct of her daughter. This was a mere artifice; but the daughter was, in truth, no sample of purity. She had acted in such a manner with Blansac that he was sent for from the army to marry her, and on the very night of their wedding she gave birth to a daughter. She was full of wit, vivacity, intrigue, and sweetness; yet most wicked, false, and artificial, and all this with a simplicity of manner that imposed even upon those who knew her best. More than gallant while her face lasted, she afterwards was easier of access, and at last ruined herself for the meanest valets. Yet, notwithstanding her vices, she was the prettiest flower of the Court bunch, and had her chamber always full of the best company: she was also much sought after by the three daughters of the King. Driven away from the Court, she was after much supplication recalled, and pleased the King so much that Madame de Maintenon, in fear of her, sent her away again. But to go back again to the household of the Princess of Savoy.

Dangeau was made chevalier d'honneur. He owed his success to his good looks, to the court he paid to the King's mistresses, to his skilfulness at play, and to a lucky stroke of fortune. The King had oftentimes been importuned to give him a lodging, and one day, joking with him upon his fancy of versifying, proposed to him some very hard rhymes, and promised him a lodging if he filled them up upon the spot. Dangeau accepted, thought but for a moment, performed the task, and thus gained his lodging. He was an old friend of Madame de Maintenon, and it was to her he was indebted for his post of chevalier d'honneur in the new household.

Madame d'O was appointed lady of the palace. Her father, named Guilleragues, a gluttonous Gascon, had been one of the intimate friends of Madame Scarron, who, as Madame de Maintenon, did not forget her old acquaintance, but procured him the embassy to Constantinople. Dying there, he left an only daughter, who, on the voyage home to France, gained the heart of Villers, lieutenant of the vessel, and became his wife in Asia-Minor, near the ruins of Troy. Villers claimed to be of the house of d'O; hence the name his wife bore.

Established at the Court, the newly-married couple quickly worked themselves into the favour of Madame de Maintenon, both being very clever in intrigue. M. d'O was made governor of the Comte de Toulouse, and soon gained his entire confidence. Madame d'O, too, infinitely pleased the young Count, just then entering upon manhood, by her gallantry, her wit, and the facilities she allowed him. Both, in consequence, grew in great esteem with the King. Had they been attendants upon Princes of the blood, he would assuredly have slighted them. But he always showed great indulgence to those who served his illegitimate children. Hence the appointment of Madame d'O to be lady of the palace.

The household of the Princess of Savoy being completed, the members of it were sent to the Pont Beauvosin to meet their young mistress. She arrived early on the 16th of October, slept at the Pont Beauvosin that night, and on the morrow parted with her Italian attendants without shedding a single tear. On the 4th of November she arrived at Montargis, and was received by the King, Monseigneur, and Monsieur. The King handed her down from her coach, and conducted her to the apartment he had prepared for her. Her respectful and flattering manners pleased him highly. Her cajoleries, too, soon bewitched Madame de Maintenon, whom she never addressed except as "Aunt;" whom she treated with a respect, and yet with a freedom, that ravished everybody. She became the doll of Madame de Maintenon and the King, pleased them infinitely by her insinuating spirit, and took greater liberties with them than the children of the King had ever dared to attempt.

CHAPTER X

MEANWHILE our campaign upon the Rhine proceeded, and the enemy, having had all their grand projects of victory defeated by the firmness and the capacity of the Maréchal de Choiseul, retired into winter-quarters, and we prepared to do the same. The month of October was almost over when Madame de Saint-Simon lost M. Frémont, father of the Maréchal de Lorges. She had happily given birth to a daughter on the 8th of September. I was desirous accordingly to go to Paris, and having obtained permission from the Maréchal de Choiseul, who had treated me throughout the campaign with much politeness and attention, I set out. Upon arriving at Paris I found the Court at Fontainebleau. I had arrived from the army a little before the rest, and did not wish that the King should know it without seeing me, lest he might think I had returned in secret. I hastened at once therefore to Fontainebleau, where the King received me with his usual goodness,—saying, nevertheless, that I had returned a little too early, but that it was of no consequence.

I had not long left his presence when I learned a report that made my face burn again. It was affirmed that when the King remarked upon my arriving a little early, I had replied that I preferred arriving at once to see him, as my sole mistress, than to remain some days in Paris, as did the other young men with their mistresses. I went at once to the King, who had a numerous company around him; and I openly denied what had been reported, offering a reward for the discovery of the knave who had thus calumniated me, in order that I might give him a sound thrashing. All day I sought to discover the scoundrel. My speech to the King and my choler were the topic of the day, and I was blamed for having spoken so loudly and in such terms. But of two evils I had chosen the least,—a reprimand from the King, or a few days in the Bastille; and I had avoided the greatest, which was to allow myself to be believed an infamous libeller of our young men, in order to basely and miserably curry favour at the Court. The course I took succeeded. The King said nothing of the matter, and I went upon a little journey I wished particularly to take, for reasons I will now relate.

I had, as I have already mentioned, conceived a strong attachment and admiration for M. de La Trappe. I wished to secure a portrait of him, but such was his modesty and humility that I feared to ask him to allow himself to be painted. I went therefore to Rigault, then the first portrait-painter in Europe. In consideration of a sum of a thousand crowns, and all his expenses paid, he agreed to accompany me to La Trappe, and to make a portrait of him from memory. The whole affair was to be kept a profound secret, and only one copy of the picture was to be made, and that for the artist himself.

My plan being fully arranged, I and Rigault set out. As soon as we arrived at our journey's end, I sought M. de La Trappe, and begged to be allowed to introduce to him a friend of mine, an officer, who much wished to see him: I added, that my friend was a stammerer, and that therefore he would be importuned merely with looks and not words. M. de La Trappe smiled with goodness, thought the officer curious about little, and consented to see him. The interview took place. Rigault excusing himself on the ground of his infirmity, did little during three-quarters of an hour but keep his eyes upon M. de La Trappe, and at the end went into a room where materials were already provided for him, and covered his canvas with the images and the ideas he had filled himself with. On the morrow the same thing was repeated, although M. de La Trappe, thinking that a man whom he knew not, and who could take no part in conversation, had sufficiently seen him, agreed to the interview only out of complaisance to me. Another sitting was needed in order to finish the work; but it was with great difficulty M. de La Trappe could be persuaded to consent to it. When the third and last interview was at an end, M. de La Trappe testified to me his surprise at having been so much and so long looked at by a species of mute. I made the best excuses I could, and hastened to turn the conversation.

The portrait was at length finished, and was a most perfect likeness of my venerable friend. Rigault admitted to me that he had worked so hard to produce it from memory, that for several months afterwards he had been unable to do anything to his other portraits. Notwithstanding the thousand crowns I had paid him, he broke the engagement he had made by showing the portrait before giving it up to me. Then, solicited for copies, he made several, gaining thereby, according to his own admission, more than twenty-five thousand francs, and thus gave publicity to the affair.

I was very much annoyed at this, and with the noise it made in the world; and I wrote to M. de La Trappe, relating the deception I had practised upon him, and sued for pardon. He was pained to excess, hurt, and afflicted; nevertheless he showed no anger. He wrote in return to me, and said, I was not ignorant that a Roman Emperor had said, "I love treason but not traitors;" but that, as for himself, he felt on the contrary that he loved the traitor but could only hate his treason. I made presents of three copies of the picture to the monastery of La Trappe. On the back of the original I described the circumstance under which the portrait had been taken, in order to show that M. de La Trappe had not consented to it, and I pointed out that for some years he had been unable to use his right hand, to acknowledge thus the error which had been made in representing him as writing.

The King, about this time, set on foot negotiations for peace in Holland, sending there two plenipotentiaries, Courtin and Harlay, and acknowledging one of his agents, Caillières, who had been for some little time secretly in that country.

The year finished with the disgrace of Madame de Saint Géran. She was on the best of terms with the Princesses, and as much a lover of good cheer as Madame de Chartres and Madame la Duchesse. This latter had in the park of Versailles a little house that she called the "Desert." There she had received very doubtful company, giving such gay repasts that the King, informed of her doings, was angry, and forbade her to continue these parties or to receive certain guests. Madame de Saint Géran was then in the first year of her mourning, so that the King did not think it necessary to include her among the interdicted; but he intimated that he did not approve of her. In spite of this, Madame la Duchesse invited her to an early supper at the Desert a short time after, and the meal was prolonged so far into the night, and with so much gaiety, that it came to the ears of the King. He was in great anger, and learning that Madame de Saint Géran had been of the party, sentenced her to be banished twenty leagues from the Court. Like a clever woman, she retired into a convent at Rouen, saying that as she had been unfortunate enough to displease the King, a convent was the only place for her; and this was much approved.

At the commencement of the next year (1697) the eldest son of the Comte d'Auvergne completed his dishonour by a duel he fought with the Chevalier de Caylus, on account of a tavern broil, and a dispute about some wenches. Caylus, who had fought well, fled from the kingdom; the other, who had used his sword like a poltroon, and had run away dismayed into the streets, was disinherited by his father, sent out of the country, and returned no more. He was in every respect a wretch, who, on account of his disgraceful adventures, was forced to allow himself to be disinherited and to take the cross of Malta; he was hanged in effigy at the Grève, to the great regret of his family, not on account of the sentence, but because, in spite of every entreaty, he had been proceeded against like the most obscure gentleman. The exile of Caylus afterwards made his fortune.

We had another instance, about this time, of the perfidy of Harlay. He had been entrusted with a valuable deposit by Ruvigny, a Huguenot officer, who, quitting France, had entered the service of the Prince of Orange, and who was, with the exception of Marshal Schomberg, the only Huguenot to whom the King offered the permission of remaining at Court with full liberty to practise his religion in secret. This, Ruvigny, like Marshal Schomberg, refused. He was, nevertheless, allowed to retain the property he possessed in France; but after his death his son, not showing himself at all grateful for this favour, the King at last confiscated the property, and publicly testified his anger. This was the moment that Harlay seized to tell the King of the deposit he had. As a recompense the King gave it to him as confiscated, and this hypocrite of justice, of virtue, of disinterestedness, and of rigorism was not ashamed to appropriate it to himself, and to close his ears and his eyes to the noise this perfidy excited.

M. de Monaco, who had obtained for himself the title of foreign prince by the marriage of his son with the Duchesse de Valentinois, daughter of M. le Grand, and who enjoyed, as it were, the sovereignty of a rock —beyond whose narrow limits anybody might spit, so to speak, whilst standing in the middle—soon found, and his son still more so, that they had bought the title very dearly. The Duchess was charming, gallant, and was spoiled by the homage of the Court, in a house open night and day, and to which her beauty attracted all that was young and brilliant. Her husband, with much intelligence, was diffident; his face and figure had acquired for him the name of Goliath; he suffered for a long time the haughtiness and the disdain of his wife and her family. At last he and his father grew tired and took away Madame de Valentinois to Monaco. She grieved, and her parents also, as though she had been carried off to the Indies. After two years of absence and repentance, she promised marvels, and was allowed to return to Paris. I know not who counselled her, but, without changing her conduct, she thought only how to prevent a return to Monaco; and to insure herself against this, she accused her father-in-law of having made vile proposals to her, and of attempting to take her by force. This charge made a most scandalous uproar, but was believed by nobody. M. de Monaco was no longer young; he was a very honest man, and had always passed for such; besides, he was almost blind in both eyes, and had a huge pointed belly, which absolutely excited fear, it jutted out so far!

After some time, as Madame de Valentinois still

continued to swim in the pleasures of the Court under the shelter of her family, her husband redemanded her; and though he was laughed at at first, she was at last given up to him.

A marriage took place at this time between the son of Pontchartrain and the daughter of the Comte de Roye. The Comte de Roye was a Huguenot, and, at the revocation of the edict of Nantes, had taken refuge, with his wife, in Denmark, where he had been made grand marshal and commander of all the troops. One day, as the Comte de Roye was dining with his wife and daughter at the King's table, the Comtesse de Roye asked her daughter if she did not think the Queen of Denmark and Madame Panache resembled each other like two drops of water? Although she spoke in French and in a low tone, the Queen both heard and understood her, and inquired at once who was Madame Panache. The Countess in her surprise replied, that she was a very amiable woman at the French Court. The Queen, who had noticed the surprise of the Countess, was not satisfied with this reply. She wrote to the Danish minister at Paris, desiring to be informed of every particular respecting Madame Panache, her face, her age, her condition, and upon what footing she was at the French Court. The minister, all astonished that the Queen should have heard of Madame Panache, wrote word that she was a little and very old creature, with lips and eyes so disfigured that they were painful to look upon; a species of beggar who had obtained a footing at Court from being half-witted, who was now at the supper of the King, now at the dinner of Monseigneur, or at other places, where everybody amused themselves by tormenting her. She in turn abused the company at these parties, in order to cause diversion, but sometimes rated them very seriously and with strong words, which delighted still more those princes and princesses, who emptied into her pockets meat and ragôuts, the sauces of which ran all down her petticoats: at these parties some gave her a pistole or a crown, and others a filip or a smack in the face, which put her in a fury, because with her bleared eyes not being able to see the end of her nose, she could not tell who had struck her;—she was, in a word, the pastime of the Court!

Upon learning this, the Queen of Denmark was so piqued, that she could no longer suffer the Comtesse de Roye near her; she complained to the King: he was much offended that foreigners, whom he had loaded with favour, should so repay him. The Comte de Roye was unable to stand up against the storm, and withdrew to England, where he died a few years after.

The King at this time drove away the company of Italian actors, and would not permit another in its place. So long as the Italians had simply allowed their stage to overflow with filth or impiety they only caused laughter; but they set about playing a piece called " The False Prude," in which Madame de Maintenon was easily recognised. Everybody ran to see the piece; but after three or four representations, given consecutively on account of the gain it brought, the Italians received orders to close their theatre and to quit the realm in a month. This affair made a great noise; and if the comedians lost an establishment by their boldness and folly, they who drove them away gained nothing—such was the licence with which this ridiculous event was spoken of!

CHAPTER XI

THE disposition of the armies was the same this year as last, except that the Princes did not serve. Towards the end of May I joined the army of the Rhine, under the Maréchal de Choiseul, as before. We made some skilful manœuvres, but did little in the way of fighting. For sixteen days we encamped at Nieder-buhl, where we obtained a good supply of forage. At the end of that time the Maréchal de Choiseul determined to change his position. Our army was so placed, that the enemy could see almost all of it quite distinctly; yet, nevertheless, we succeeded in decamping so quickly, that we disappeared from under their very eyes in open daylight, and in a moment as it were. Such of the Imperial Generals as were out riding ran from all parts to the banks of the Murg, to see our retreat, but it was so promptly executed that there was no time for them to attempt to hinder us. When the Prince of Baden was told of our departure he could not credit it. He had seen us so lately, quietly resting in our position, that it seemed impossible to him we had left it in such a short space of time. When his own eyes assured him of the fact, he was filled with such astonishment and admiration, that he asked those around him if they had ever seen such a retreat,— adding, that he could not have believed, until then, that an army so numerous and so considerable should have been able to disappear thus in an instant.

This honourable and bold retreat was attended by a sad accident. One of our officers, named Blansac, while leading a column of infantry through the woods, was overtaken by night. A small party of his men heard some cavalry near them. The cavalry belonged to the enemy, and had lost their way. Instead of replying when challenged, they said to each other in German, "Let us run for it." Nothing more was wanting to draw upon them a discharge from the small body of our men, by whom they had been heard. To this they replied with their pistols. Immediately, and without orders, the whole column of infantry fired in that direction, and, before Blansac could inquire the cause, fired again. Fortunately he was not wounded; but five unhappy captains were killed, and some subalterns wounded.

Our campaign was brought to an end by the peace of Ryswick. The first news of that event arrived at Fontainebleau on the 22nd of September. Celi, son of Harlay, had been despatched with the intelligence; but he did not arrive until five o'clock in the morning of the 26th of September. He had amused himself by the way with a young girl who had struck his fancy, and with some wine that he equally relished. He had committed all the absurdities and impertinences which might be expected of a debauched, hare-brained young fellow, completely spoiled by his father, and he crowned all by this fine delay.

A little time before the signing of peace, the Prince de Conti, having been elected King of Poland, set out to take possession of his throne. The King, ravished with joy to see himself delivered from a Prince whom he disliked, could not hide his satisfaction—his eagerness—to get rid of a Prince whose only faults were that he had no bastard blood in his veins, and that he was so much liked by all the nation that they wished him at the head of the army, and murmured at the little favour he received, as compared with that showered down upon the illegitimate children.

The King made all haste to treat the Prince to royal honours. After an interview in the cabinet of Madame de Maintenon, he presented him to a number of ladies, saying, "I bring you a king." The Prince was all along doubtful of the validity of his election, and begged that the Princess might not be treated as a queen, until he should have been crowned. He received two millions in cash from the King, and other assistances. Samuel Bernard undertook to make the necessary payments in Poland. The Prince started by way of Dunkerque, and went to that place at such speed, that an ill-closed chest opened, and two thousand louis were scattered on the road, a portion only of which was brought back to the Hôtel Conti. The celebrated Jean Bart pledged himself to take him safely, despite the enemy's fleet; and kept his word. The convoy was of five frigates. The Chevalier de Sillery, before starting, married Mademoiselle Bigot, rich and witty, with whom he had been living for some time. Meanwhile the best news arrived from our ambassador, the Abbé de Polignac, to the King; but all answers were intercepted at Dantzic by the retired Queen of Poland, who sent on only the envelopes! However, the Prince de Conti passed up the Sound; and the King and Queen of Denmark watched them from the windows of the Château de Cronenbourg. Jean Bart, against custom, ordered a salute to be fired. It was returned; and as some light vessels passing near the frigates said that the King and Queen were looking on, the Prince ordered another salvo.

There was, however, another claimant to the throne of Poland; I mean the Elector of Saxony, who had also been elected, and who had many partisans; so many, indeed, that when the Prince de Conti arrived at Dantzic, he found himself almost entirely unsupported. The people even refused provision to his frigates. However, the Prince's partisans at length arrived to salute him. The Bishop of Plosko gave him a grand repast, near the Abbey of Oliva. Marège, a Gascon gentleman of the Prince's suite, was present, but had been ill. There was drinking in the Polish fashion, and he tried to be let off. The Prince pleaded for him; but these Poles, who, in order to make themselves understood, spoke Latin—and very bad Latin indeed—would not accept such an excuse, and forcing him to drink, howled furiously *Bibat et Moriatur!* Marège, who was very jocular and yet very choleric, used to tell this story in the same spirit, and made everyone who heard it laugh.

However, the party of the Prince de Conti made no way, and at length he was fain to make his way back to France with all speed. The King received him very graciously, although at heart exceeding sorry to see him again. A short time after, the Elector of Saxony mounted the throne of Poland without opposition, and was publicly recognised by the King, towards the commencement of August.

By the above-mentioned peace of Ryswick, the King acknowledged the Prince of Orange as King of England. It was, however, a bitter draught for him to swallow, and for these reasons: Some years before, the King had offered his illegitimate daughter, the Princesse de Conti, in marriage to the Prince of Orange, believing he did that Prince great honour by the proposal. The Prince did not think in the same manner, and flatly refused; saying, that the House of Orange was accustomed to marry the legitimate daughters of great kings, and not their bastards. These words sank so deeply into the heart of the King, that he never forgot them; and often, against even his most palpable interest, showed how firmly the indignation he felt at them had taken possession of his mind. Since then, the Prince of Orange had done all in his power to efface the effect his words had made, but every attempt was rejected with disdain. The King's ministers in Holland had orders to do all they could to thwart the projects of the Prince of Orange, to excite people against him, to protect openly those opposed to him, and to be in no way niggard of money in order to secure the election of magistrates unfavourable to him. The Prince never ceased, until the breaking-out of this war, to use every effort to appease the anger of the King. At last, growing tired, and hoping soon to make his invasion into England, he said publicly, that he had uselessly laboured all his life to gain the favours of the King, but that he hoped to be more fortunate in meriting his esteem. It may be imagined, therefore, what a triumph it was for him when he forced the King to recognise him as monarch of England, and what that recognition cost the King.

M. le Duc presided this year over the Assembly of the States of Burgundy, in place of his father M. le Prince, who did not wish to go there. The Duke gave on that occasion a striking example of the friendship of princes, and a fine lesson to those who seek it. Santeuil, Canon of Saint Victor, and the greatest Latin poet who has appeared for many centuries, accompanied him. Santeuil was an excellent fellow, full of wit and of life, and of pleasantries, which rendered him an admirable boon-companion. Fond of wine and of good cheer, he was not debauched; and with a disposition and talents so little fitted for the cloister, was nevertheless, at bottom, as good a churchman as with such a character he could be. He was a great favourite with all the house of Condé, and was invited to

DUKE OF SAINT-SIMON 149

their parties, where his witticisms, his verses, and his pleasantries had afforded infinite amusement for many years.

M. le Duc wished to take him to Dijon. Santeuil tried to excuse himself, but without effect; he was obliged to go, and was established at the house of the Duke while the States were held. Every evening there was a supper, and Santeuil was always the life of the company. One evening M. le Duc diverted himself by forcing Santeuil to drink champagne, and passing from pleasantry to pleasantry, thought it would be a good joke to empty his snuff-box, full of Spanish snuff, into a large glass of wine, and to make Santeuil drink it, in order to see what would happen. It was not long before he was enlightened upon this point. Santeuil was seized with vomiting and with fever, and in twice twenty-four hours the unhappy man died—suffering the tortures of the damned, but with sentiments of extreme penitence, in which he received the sacrament, and edified a company little disposed towards edification, but who detested such a cruel joke.

In consequence of the peace just concluded at Ryswick, many fresh arrangements were made about this time in our embassies abroad. This allusion to our foreign appointments brings to my mind an anecdote which deserves to be remembered. When M. de Vendôme took Barcelona, the Montjoui (which is as it were its citadel) was commanded by the Prince of Darmstadt. He was of the house of Hesse, and had gone into Spain to seek employment; he was a relative of the Queen of Spain, and, being a very well-made man, had not, it was said, displeased her. It was said also, and by people whose word was not without weight, that the same council of Vienna which for reasons of state had made no scruple of poisoning the late Queen of Spain (daughter of Monsieur), because she had no children, and because she had, also, too much ascendancy over the heart of her husband; it was said, I say, that this same council had no scruples upon another point. After poisoning the first Queen, it had remarried the King of Spain to a sister of the Empress. She was tall, majestic, not without beauty and capacity, and, guided by the ministers of the Emperor, soon acquired much influence over the King— her husband. So far all was well, but the most important thing was wanting—she had no children. The council had hoped some from this second marriage, because it had lured itself into the belief that previously the fault rested with the late Queen. After some years, this same council, being no longer able to disguise the fact that the King could have no children, sent the Prince of Darmstadt into Spain, for the purpose of establishing himself there, and of ingratiating himself into the favour of the Queen to such an extent that this defect might be remedied. The Prince of Darmstadt was well received; he obtained command in the army; defended, as I have said, Barcelona; and obtained a good footing at the Court. But the object for which he had been more especially sent he could not accomplish. I will not say whether the Queen was inaccessible from her own fault or that of others. Nor will I say, although I have been assured, but I believe by persons without good knowledge of the subject, that naturally it was impossible for her to become a mother. I will simply say that the Prince of Darmstadt was on the best terms with the King and the Queen, and had opportunities very rare in that country, without any fruit which could put the succession of the monarchy in safety against the different pretensions afloat, or reassure on that head the politic council of Vienna.

But to return to France.

Madame de Maintenon, despite the height to which her insignificance had risen, had yet her troubles. Her brother, who was called the Comte d'Aubigné, was of but little worth, yet always spoke as though no man were his equal, complained that he had not been made Maréchal of France—sometimes said that he had taken his bâton in money, and constantly bullied Madame de Maintenon because she did not make him a duke and a peer. He spent his time running after girls in the Tuileries, always had several on his hands, and lived and spent his money with their families and friends of the same kidney. He was just fit for a strait-waistcoat, but comical, full of wit and unexpected repartees. A good, humorous fellow, and honest—polite, and not too impertinent on account of his sister's fortune. Yet it was a pleasure to hear him talk of the time of Scarron and the Hôtel d'Albret, and of the gallantries and adventures of his sister, which he contrasted with her present position and devotion. He would talk in this manner, not before one or two, but in a compromising manner, quite openly in the Tuileries gardens, or in the galleries of Versailles, before everybody, and would often drolly speak of the King as "the brother-in-law." I have frequently heard him talk in this manner; above all, when he came (more often than was desired) to dine with my father and mother, who were much embarrassed with him; at which I used to laugh in my sleeve.

A brother like this was a great annoyance to Madame de Maintenon. His wife, an obscure creature,—more obscure, if possible, than her birth,—foolish to the last degree, and of humble mien, was almost equally so. Madame de Maintenon determined to rid herself of both. She persuaded her brother to enter a society that had been established by a M. Doyen, at

St. Sulpice, for decayed gentlemen. His wife at the same time was induced to retire into another community, where, however, she did not fail to say to her companions that her fate was very hard, and that she wished to be free. As for d'Aubigné he concealed from nobody that his sister was putting a joke on him by trying to persuade him that he was devout,—declared that he was pestered by priests, and that he should give up the ghost in M. Doyen's house. He could not stand it long, and went back to his girls and to the Tuileries, and wherever he could; but they caught him again, and placed him under the guardianship of one of the stupidest priests of St. Sulpice, who followed him everywhere like his shadow, and made him miserable. The fellow's name was Madot: he was good for no other employment, but gained his pay in this one by an assiduity of which perhaps no one else would have been capable. The only child of this Comte d'Aubigné was a daughter, taken care of by Madame de Maintenon, and educated under her eyes as though her own child.

Towards the end of the year, and not long after my return from the army, the King fixed the day for the marriage of the Duc de Bourgogne to the young Princesse de Savoy. He announced that on that occasion he should be glad to see a magnificent Court; and he himself, who for a long time had worn only the most simple habits, ordered the most superb. This was enough; no one thought of consulting his purse or his state; everyone tried to surpass his neighbour in richness and invention. Gold and silver scarcely sufficed: the shops of the dealers were emptied in a few days; in a word luxury the most unbridled reigned over Court and city, for the fête had a huge crowd of spectators. Things went to such a point, that the King almost repented of what he had said, and remarked, that he could not understand how husbands could be such fools as to ruin themselves by dresses for their wives; he might have added, by dresses for themselves. But the impulse had been given; there was now no time to remedy it, and I believe the King at heart was glad; for it pleased him during the fêtes to look at all the dresses. He loved passionately all kinds of sumptuosity at his Court, and he who should have held only to what had been said, as to the folly of expense, would have grown little in favour. There was no means, therefore, of being wise among so many fools. Several dresses were necessary. Those for Madame Saint-Simon and myself cost us twenty thousand francs. Workmen were wanting to make up so many rich habits. Madame la Duchesse actually sent her people to take some by force who were working at the Duc de Rohan's! The King heard of it, did not like it, and had the workmen sent back immediately to the Hôtel de Rohan, although the Duc de Rohan was one of the men he liked the least in all France. The King did another thing, which showed that he desired everybody to be magnificent: he himself chose the design for the embroidery of the Princess. The embroiderer said he would leave all his other designs for that. The King would not permit this, but caused him to finish the work he had in hand, and to set himself afterwards at the other; adding, that if it was not ready in time, the Princess could do without it.

The marriage was fixed for Saturday, the 7th of December; and, to avoid disputes and difficulties, the King suppressed all ceremonies. The day arrived. At an early hour all the Court went to Monseigneur the Duc de Bourgogne, who went afterwards to the Princess. A little before mid-day the procession started from the *salon*, and proceeded to the chapel.

Cardinal de Coislin performed the marriage service. As soon as the ceremony was finished, a courier, ready at the door of the chapel, started for Turin. The day passed wearily. The King and Queen of England came about seven o'clock in the evening, and some time afterwards supper was served. Upon rising from the table, the Princess was shown to her bed, none but ladies being allowed to remain in the chamber. Her chemise was given her by the Queen of England through the Duchesse de Lude. The Duc de Bourgogne undressed in another room, in the midst of all the Court, and seated upon a folding-chair. The King of England gave him his shirt, which was presented by the Duc de Beauvilliers. As soon as the Duchesse de Bourgogne was in bed, the Duc de Bourgogne entered, and placed himself at her side, in the presence of all the Court. Immediately afterwards everybody went away from the nuptial chamber, except Monseigneur, the ladies of the Princess, and the Duc de Beauvilliers, who remained at the pillow by the side of his pupil, with the Duchesse de Lude on the other side. Monseigneur stopped a quarter of an hour talking with the newly-married couple, then he made his son get up, after having told him to kiss the Princess, in spite of the opposition of the Duchesse de Lude. As it proved, too, her opposition was not wrong. The King said he did not wish that his grandson should kiss the end of the Princess's finger until they were completely on the footing of man and wife. Monsieur le Duc de Bourgogne after this re-dressed himself in the ante-chamber, and went to his own bed as usual. The little Duc de Berry, spirited and resolute, did not approve of the docility of his brother, and declared that he would have remained in bed. The young couple were not, indeed, allowed to live together as man and wife until nearly two years afterwards. The first night that this privilege was granted them, the King repaired to their chamber hoping to surprise them as they went to bed; but he found the doors closed, and would not allow them to be opened. The marriage-fêtes spread over several days. On the Sunday there was an assembly in the apartments of the new Duchesse de Bourgogne. It was magnificent by the prodigious number of ladies seated in a circle, or standing behind the stools, gentlemen in turn behind them, and the dresses of all beautiful. It commenced at six o'clock. The King came at the end, and led all the ladies into the saloon near the chapel, where was a fine collation, and the music. At nine o'clock he conducted Monsieur and Madame la Duchesse de Bourgogne to the apartment of the latter, and all was finished for the day. The Princess continued to live just as before, and the ladies had strict orders never to leave her alone with her husband.

On the Wednesday there was a grand ball in the gallery, superbly ornamented for the occasion. There was such a crowd, and such disorder, that even the King was inconvenienced, and Monsieur was pushed and knocked about in the crush. How other people fared may be imagined. No place was kept—strength or chance decided everything—people squeezed in where they could. This spoiled all the fête. About nine o'clock refreshments were handed round, and at half-past ten supper was served. Only the Princesses of the blood and the royal family were admitted to it. On the following Sunday there was another ball, but this time matters were so arranged that no crowding or inconvenience occurred. The ball commenced at seven o'clock and was admirable; everybody appeared in dresses that had not previously been seen. The King found that of Madame de Saint-Simon much to his taste, and gave it the palm over all the others.

Madame de Maintenon did not appear at these balls, at least only for half an hour at each. On the following Tuesday all the Court went at four o'clock in the afternoon to Trianon, where all gambled until the arrival of the King and Queen of England. The King took them into the theatre, where Destouches's opera of *Issé* was very well performed. The opera being finished, everybody went his way, and thus these marriage-fêtes were brought to an end.

Tessé had married his eldest daughter to La Varenne last year, and now married his second daughter to Maulevrier, son of a brother of Colbert. This mention of La Varenne brings to my recollection a very pleasant anecdote of his ancestor, the La Varenne so known in all the memoirs of the time as having risen from the position of scullion to that of cook, and then to that of cloak-bearer to Henry IV., whom he served in his pleasures, and afterwards in his state-affairs. At the death of the King, La Varenne retired, very old and very rich, into the country. Birds were much in vogue at that time, and he often amused himself with falconry. One day a magpie perched on one of his trees, and neither sticks nor stones could dislodge it. La Varenne and a number of sportsmen gathered around the tree and tried to drive away the magpie. Importuned with all this noise, the bird at last began to cry repeatedly with all its might, "Pandar! Pandar!"

Now La Varenne had gained all he possessed by that trade. Hearing the magpie repeat again and again the same word, he took it into his head that by a miracle, like the observation Balaam's ass made to his master, the bird was reproaching him for his sins. He was so troubled that he could not help showing it; then, more and more agitated, he told the cause of his disturbance to the company, who laughed at him in the first place, but, upon finding that he was growing really ill, they endeavoured to convince him that the magpie belonged to a neighbouring village, where it had learned the word. It was all in vain: La Varenne was so ill that he was obliged to be carried home; fever seized him, and in four days he died.

CHAPTER XII

HERE perhaps is the place to speak of Charles IV., Duc de Lorraine, so well known by his genius, and the extremities to which he was urged. He was married in 1621 to the Duchesse Nicole, his cousin-german, but after a time ceased to live with her. Being at Brussels he fell in love with Madame de Cantecroix, a widow. He bribed a courier to bring him news of the death of the Duchesse Nicole; he circulated the report throughout the town, wore mourning, and fourteen days afterwards, in April, 1637, married Madame de Cantecroix. In a short time it was discovered that the Duchesse Nicole was full of life and health, and had not even been ill. Madame de Cantecroix made believe that she had been duped, but still lived with the Duke. They continued to repute the Duchesse Nicole as dead, and lived together in the face of the world as though effectually married, although there had never been any question either before or since of dissolving the first marriage. The Duc Charles had by this fine marriage a daughter and then a son, both perfectly illegitimate, and universally regarded as such. Of these the daughter married Comte de Lislebonne, by whom she had four children. The son, educated under his father's eye as legitimate, was called Prince de Vaudemont, and by that name has ever since been known. He entered the service of Spain, distinguished himself in the army, obtained the support of the Prince of Orange, and ultimately rose to the very highest influence and prosperity.

People were astonished this year, that while the Princess of Savoy was at Fontainebleau, just before her marriage, she was taken several times by Madame de Maintenon to a little unknown convent at Moret, where there was nothing to amuse her, and no nuns who were known. Madame de Maintenon often went there, and Monseigneur with his children sometimes; the late Queen used to go also. This awakened much curiosity and gave rise to many reports. It seems that in this convent there was a woman of colour, a Moorish woman, who had been placed there very young by Bontems, valet of the King. She received the utmost care and attention, but never was shown to anybody. When the late Queen or Madame de Maintenon went, they did not always see her, but always watched over her welfare. She was treated with more consideration than people the most distinguished; and herself made much of the care that was taken of her, and the mystery by which she was surrounded. Although she lived regularly, it was easy to see she was not too contented with her position. Hearing Monseigneur hunt in the forest one day, she forgot herself so far as to exclaim, " My brother is hunting! " It was pretended that she was a daughter of the King and Queen, but that she had been hidden away on account of her colour; and the report was spread that the Queen had had a miscarriage. Many people believed this story; but whether it was true or not has remained an enigma.

The year 1698 commenced by a reconciliation between the Jesuits and the Archbishop of Rheims. That prelate upon the occasion of an ordinance had expressed himself upon matters of doctrine and morality in a manner that displeased the Jesuits. They acted towards him in their usual manner, by writing an attack upon him, which appeared without any author's name. But the Archbishop complained to the King, and altogether stood his ground so firmly, that in the end the Jesuits were glad to give way, disavow the book, and arrange the reconciliation which took place.

The Czar, Peter the Great, Emperor of Russia, had at this time already commenced his voyages; he was in Holland, learning ship-building. Although incognito, he wished to be recognised, but after his own fashion; and was annoyed that, being so near to England, no embassy was sent to him from that country, which he wished to ally himself with for commercial reasons.

At last an embassy arrived; he delayed for some time to give it an audience, but in the end fixed the day and hour at which he would see it. The reception, however, was to take place on board a large Dutch vessel that he was going to examine. There were two ambassadors; they thought the meeting-place rather an odd one, but were obliged to go there. When they arrived on board the Czar sent word that he was in the "top," and that it was there he would see them. The ambassadors, whose feet were unaccustomed to rope-ladders, tried to excuse themselves from mounting; but it was all in vain. The Czar would receive them in the "top" or not at all. At last they were compelled to ascend, and the meeting took place on that narrow place high up in the air. The Czar received them there with as much majesty as though he had been upon his throne, listened to their harangue, replied very graciously, and then laughed at the fear painted upon their faces, and good-humouredly gave them to understand that he had punished them thus for arriving so late.

After this the Czar passed into England, curious to see and learn as much as possible; and, having well fulfilled his views, repaired into Holland. He wished to visit France, but the King civilly declined to receive him. He went, therefore, much mortified, to Vienna instead. Three weeks after his arrival he was informed of a conspiracy that had been formed against him in Moscow. He hastened there at once, and found that it was headed by his own sister; he put her in prison, and hanged her most guilty accomplices to the bars of his windows, as many each day as the bars would hold. I have related at once all that regards the Czar for this year, in order not to leap without ceasing from one matter to another; I shall do this, and for the same reason, with that which follows.

The King of England was, as I have before said, at the height of satisfaction at having been recognised by the King (Louis XIV.), and at finding himself secure upon the throne. But a usurper is never tranquil and content. William was annoyed by the residence of the legitimate King and his family at Saint Germains. It was too close to the King (of France), and too near England to leave him without disquietude. He had tried hard at Ryswick to obtain the dismissal of James II. from the realm, or at least from the Court of France, but without effect. Afterwards he sent the Duke of St. Albans to our King openly, in order to compliment him upon the marriage of the Duc de Bourgogne, but in reality to obtain the dismissal.

The Duke of St. Albans meeting with no success, the Duke of Portland was sent to succeed him. The Duke of Portland came over with a numerous and superb suite; he kept up a magnificent table, and had horses, liveries, furniture, and dresses of the most tasteful and costly kind. He was on his way when a fire destroyed Whitehall, the largest and ugliest palace in Europe, and which has not since been rebuilt;

so that the kings are lodged, and very badly, at St. James's Palace.

Portland had his first audience of the King on the 4th of February, and remained four months in France. His politeness, his courtly and gallant manners, and the good cheer he gave, charmed everybody, and made him universally popular. It became the fashion to give fêtes in his honour; and the astonishing fact is, that the King, who at heart was more offended than ever with William of Orange, treated this ambassador with the most marked distinction. One evening he even gave Portland his bedroom candlestick, a favour only accorded to the most considerable persons, and always regarded as a special mark of the King's bounty.

Notwithstanding all these attentions, Portland was as unsuccessful as his predecessor. The King had firmly resolved to continue his protection to James II., and nothing could shake this determination. Portland was warned from the first, that if he attempted to speak to the King upon the point, his labour would be thrown away; he wisely therefore kept silence, and went home again without in any way having fulfilled the mission upon which he had been sent.

We had another distinguished foreigner arrive in France about this time,—I mean, the Prince of Parma, respecting whom I remember a pleasing adventure. At Fontainebleau more great dancing-parties are given than elsewhere, and Cardinal d'Estrées wished to give one there in honour of this Prince. I and many others were invited to the banquet; but the Prince himself, for whom the invitation was specially provided, was forgotten. The Cardinal had given invitations right and left, but by some omission the Prince had not had one sent to him. On the morning of the dinner this discovery was made. The Prince was at once sent to, but he was engaged, and for several days. The dinner therefore took place without him; the Cardinal was much laughed at for his absence of mind. He was often similarly forgetful.

The Bishop of Poitiers died at the commencement of this year, and his bishopric was given at Easter to the Abbé de Caudelet. The Abbé was a very good man, but made himself an enemy, who circulated the blackest calumnies against him. Amongst other impostures it was said that the Abbé had gambled all Good Friday; the truth being, that in the evening, after all the services were over, he went to see the Maréchale de Créqui, who prevailed upon him to amuse her for an hour by playing at piquet. But the calumny had such effect, that the bishopric of Poitiers was taken from him, and he retired into Brittany, where he passed the rest of his life in solitude and piety. His brother in the mean time fully proved to Père de la Chaise the falsehood of this accusation; and he, who was upright and good, did all he could to bestow some other living upon the Abbé, in recompense for that he had been stripped of. But the King would not consent, although often importuned, and even reproached for his cruelty.

It was known, too, who was the author of the calumny. It was the Abbé de la Châtre, who for a long time had been chaplain to the King, and who was enraged against everyone who was made bishop before him. He was a man not wanting in intelligence, but bitter, disagreeable, punctilious; very ignorant, because he would never study, and so destitute of morality, that I saw him say mass in the chapel on Ash Wednesday, after having passed a night, masked at a ball, where he said and did the most filthy things, as seen and heard by M. de La Vrillière, before whom he unmasked, and who related this to me: half an hour after, I met the Abbé de la Châtre, dressed and going to the altar. Other adventures had already deprived him of all chance of being made bishop by the King.

The old Villars died at this time. I have already mentioned him as having been made chevalier d'honneur to the Duchesse de Chartres at her marriage. I mention him now, because I omitted to say before the origin of his name of Orondat, by which he was generally known, and which did not displease him. This is the circumstance that gave rise to it. Madame de Choisy, a lady of the fashionable world, went one day to see the Comtesse de Fiesque, and found there a large company. The Countess had a young girl living with her, whose name was Mademoiselle d'Outrelaise, but who was called the Divine. Madame de Choisy, wishing to go into the bedroom, said she would go there, and see the Divine. Mounting rapidly, she found in the chamber a young and very pretty girl, Mademoiselle Bellefonds, and a man, who escaped immediately upon seeing her. The face of this man being perfectly well made, so struck her, that, upon coming down again, she said it could only be that of Orondat. Now that romances are happily no longer read, it is necessary to say that Orondat is a character in *Cyrus*, celebrated by his figure and his good looks, and who charmed all the heroines of that romance, which was then much in vogue. The greater part of the company knew that Villars was upstairs to see Mademoiselle de Bellefonds, with whom he was much in love, and whom he soon afterwards married. Everybody therefore smiled at this adventure of Orondat, and the name clung ever afterwards to Villars.

The Prince de Conti lost, before this time, his son, Prince la Roche-sur-Yon, who was only four years old. The King wore mourning for him, although it was the custom not to do so for children under seven years of age. But the King had already departed from this custom for one of the children of M. du Maine, and he dared not afterwards act differently towards the children of a prince of the blood. Just at the end of September, M. du Maine lost another child, his only son. The King wept very much, and, although the child was considerably under seven years of age, wore mourning for it. The marriage of Mademoiselle to M. de Lorraine was then just upon the point of taking place; and Monsieur (father of Mademoiselle) begged that this mourning might be laid aside when the marriage was celebrated. The King agreed, but Madame la Duchesse and the Princesse de Conti believed it apparently beneath them to render this respect to Monsieur, and refused to comply. The King commanded them to do so, but they pushed the matter so far as to say that they had no other clothes. Upon this, the King ordered them to send and get some directly. They were obliged to obey, and admit themselves vanquished; but they did so not without great vexation. M. de Cambrai's affairs still continued to make a great stir among the prelates and at the Court. Madame Guyon was transferred from the Vincennes to the Bastille, and it was believed she would remain there all her life. The Ducs de Chevreuse and Beauvilliers lost all favour with M. de Maintenon, and narrowly escaped losing the favour of the King. An attempt was in fact made, which Madame de Maintenon strongly supported, to get them disgraced; and, but for the Archbishop of Paris, this would have taken place. But this prelate, thoroughly upright and conscientious, counselled the King against such a step, to the great vexation of his relations, who were the chief plotters in the conspiracy to overthrow the two Dukes. As for M. de Cambrai's book, *Les Maximes des*

Saints, it was as little liked as ever, and underwent rather a strong criticism at this time from M. de La Trappe, which did not do much to improve its reputation. At the commencement of the dispute M. de Meaux had sent a copy of *Les Maximes des Saints* to M. de La Trappe, asking as a friend for his opinion of the work. M. de La Trappe read it, and was much scandalized. The more he studied it, the more this sentiment penetrated him. At last, after having well examined the book, he sent his opinion to M. de Meaux, believing it would be considered as private, and not be shown to anybody. He did not measure his words, therefore, but wrote openly, that if M. de Cambrai was right he might burn the Evangelists, and complain of Jesus Christ, who could have come into the world only to deceive us. The frightful force of this phrase was so terrifying, that M. de Meaux thought it worthy of being shown to Madame de Maintenon; and she, seeking only to crush M. de Cambrai with all the authorities possible, would insist upon this opinion of M. de La Trappe being printed.

It may be imagined what triumphing there was on the one side, and what piercing cries on the other. The friends of M. de Cambrai complained most bitterly that M. de La Trappe had mixed himself up in the matter, and had passed such a violent and cruel sentence upon a book then under the consideration of the Pope. M. de La Trappe on his side was much afflicted that his letter had been published. He wrote to M. de Meaux protesting against this breach of confidence; and said that, although he had only expressed what he really thought, he should have been careful to use more measured language, had he supposed his letter would have seen the light. He said all he could to heal the wounds his words had caused, but M. de Cambrai and his friends never forgave him for having written them.

This circumstance caused much discussion; and M. de La Trappe, to whom I was passionately attached, was frequently spoken of in a manner that caused me much annoyance. Riding out one day in a coach with some of my friends, the conversation took this turn. I listened in silence for some time, and then, feeling no longer able to support the discourse, desired to be set down, so that my friends might talk at their ease, without pain to me. They tried to retain me, but I insisted and carried my point. Another time, Charost, one of my friends, spoke so disdainfully of M. de La Trappe, and I replied to him with such warmth, that on the instant he was seized with a fit, tottered, stammered, his throat swelled, his eyes seemed starting from his head, and his tongue from his mouth. Madame de Saint-Simon and the other ladies who were present flew to his assistance; one unfastened his cravat and his shirt-collar, another threw a jug of water over him and made him drink something; but as for me, I was struck motionless at the sudden change brought about by an excess of anger and infatuation. Charost was soon restored, and when he left I was taken to task by the ladies. In reply I simply smiled. I gained this by the occurrence, that Charost never committed himself again upon the subject of M. de La Trappe.

Before quitting this theme, I will relate an anecdote which has found belief. It has been said, that when M. de La Trappe was the Abbé de Rancé he was much in love with the beautiful Madame de Montbazon, and that he was well treated by her. On one occasion after leaving her, in perfect health, in order to go into the country, he learnt that she had fallen ill. He hastened back, entered hurriedly into her chamber, and the first sight he saw there was her head, that the surgeons, in opening her, had separated from her body. It was the first intimation he had had that she was dead, and the surprise and horror of the sight so converted him that immediately afterwards he retired from the world. There is nothing true in all this except the foundation upon which the fiction arose. I have frankly asked M. de La Trappe upon this matter, and from him I have learned that he was one of the friends of Madame de Montbazon, but that so far from being ignorant of the time of her death, he was by her side at the time, administered the sacrament to her, and had never quitted her during the few days she was ill. The truth is, her sudden death so touched him, that it made him carry out his intention of retiring from the world—an intention, however, he had formed for many years.

The affair of M. de Cambrai was not finally settled until the commencement of the following year, 1699, but went on making more noise day by day. At the date I have named the verdict from Rome arrived. Twenty-three propositions of the *Maximes des Saints* were declared rash, dangerous, erroneous,—*in globo*,—and the Pope excommunicated those who read the book or kept it in their houses. The King was much pleased with this condemnation, and openly expressed his satisfaction. Madame de Maintenon appeared at the summit of joy. As for M. de Cambrai, he learnt his fate in a moment which would have overwhelmed a man with less resources in himself. He was on the point of mounting into the pulpit: he was by no means troubled; put aside the sermon he had prepared, and, without delaying a moment, took for subject the submission due to the Church; he treated this theme in a powerful and touching manner; announced the condemnation of his book; retracted the opinions he had professed; and concluded his sermon by a perfect acquiescence and submission to the judgment the Pope had just pronounced. Two days afterwards he published his retraction, condemned his book, prohibited the reading of it, acquiesced and submitted himself anew to his condemnation, and in the clearest terms took away from himself all means of returning to his opinions. A submission so prompt, so clear, so perfect, was generally admired, although there were not wanting censors who wished he had shown less readiness in giving way. His friends believed the submission would be so flattering to the Pope, that M. de Cambrai might rely upon advancement to a cardinalship, and steps were taken, but without any good result, to bring about that event.

CHAPTER XIII

ABOUT this time the King caused Charnacé to be arrested in a province to which he had been banished. He was accused of many wicked things, and, amongst others, of coining. Charnacé was a lad of spirit, who had been page to the King and officer in the body-guard. Having retired to his own house, he often played off many a prank. One of these I will mention, as being full of wit and very laughable.

He had a very long and perfectly beautiful avenue before his house in Anjou, but in the midst of it were the cottage and garden of a peasant; and neither Charnacé, nor his father before him, could prevail upon him to remove, although they offered him large sums. Charnacé at last determined to gain his point by stratagem. The peasant was a tailor, and lived all alone, without wife or child. One day Charnacé sent for him, said he wanted a Court suit in all haste, and, agreeing to lodge and feed him, stipulated that he should not leave the house until it was done. The tailor agreed, and set himself to the work. While he was thus occupied, Charnacé had the dimensions of his house and garden taken with the utmost exactitude; made a plan of the interior, showing the precise position of the furniture and the utensils; and, when all was done, pulled down the house and removed it a short distance off.

Then it was arranged as before with a similar looking garden, and at the same time the spot on which it had previously stood was smoothed and levelled. All this was done before the suit was finished. The work being at length over on both sides, Charnacé amused the tailor until it was quite dark, paid him, and dismissed him content. The man went on his way down the avenue; but, finding the distance longer than usual, looked about, and perceived he had gone too far. Returning, he searched diligently for his house, but without being able to find it. The night passed in this exercise. When the day came, he rubbed his eyes, thinking they might have been in fault; but as he found them as clear as usual, began to believe that the devil had carried away his house, garden and all. By dint of wandering to and fro, and casting his eyes in every direction, he saw at last a house which was as like to his as are two drops of water to each other. Curiosity tempted him to go and examine it. He did so, and became convinced it was his own. He entered, found everything inside as he had left it, and then became quite persuaded he had been tricked by a sorcerer. The day was not, however, very far advanced before he learned the truth through the banter of his neighbours. In fury he talked of going to law, of demanding justice, but was laughed at everywhere. The King when he heard of it laughed also; and Charnacé had his avenue free. If he had never done anything worse than this, he would have preserved his reputation and his liberty.

A strange scene happened at Meudon after supper one evening, towards the end of July. The Prince de Conti and the Grand Prieur were playing, and a dispute arose respecting the game. The Grand Prieur, inflated by pride on account of the favours the King had showered upon him, and rendered audacious by being placed almost on a level with the Princes of the blood, used words which would have been too strong even towards an equal. The Prince de Conti answered by a repartee, in which the other's honesty at play and his courage in war—both, in truth, little to boast about—were attacked. Upon this the Grand Prieur flew into a passion, flung away the cards, and demanded satisfaction, sword in hand. The Prince de Conti, with a smile of contempt, reminded him that he was wanting in respect, and at the same time said he could have the satisfaction he asked for whenever he pleased. The arrival of Monseigneur, in his dressing-gown, put an end to the fray. He ordered the Marquis de Gesvres, who was one of the courtiers present, to report the whole affair to the King, and that every one should go to bed. On the morrow the King was informed of what had taken place, and immediately ordered the Grand Prieur to go to the Bastille. He was obliged to obey, and remained in confinement several days. The affair made a great stir at Court. The Princes of the blood took a very high tone, and the illegitimates were much embarrassed. At last, on the 7th of August, the affair was finally accommodated through the intercession of Monseigneur. The Grand Prieur demanded pardon of the Prince de Conti in the presence of his brother, M. de Vendôme, who was obliged to swallow this bitter draught, although against his will, in order to appease the Princes of the blood, who were extremely excited.

Nearly at the same time, that is to say, on the 29th of May, in the morning Madame de Saint-Simon was happily delivered of a child. God did us the grace to give us a son. He bore, as I had, the name of Vidame of Chartres. I do not know why people have the fancy for these odd names, but they seduce in all nations, and they who feel the triviality of them, imitate them. It is true that the titles of Count and Marquis have fallen into the dust because of the quantity of people without wealth, and even without land, who usurp them; and that they have become so worthless, that people of quality who are Marquises or Counts (if they will permit me to say it) are silly enough to be annoyed if those titles are given to them in conversation. It is certain, however, that these titles emanated from landed creations, and that in their origin they had functions attached to them, which they have since outlived. The *vidames,* on the contrary, were only principal officers of certain bishops, with authority to lead all the rest of their seigneurs' vassals to the field, either to fight against other lords, or in the armies that our kings used to assemble to combat their enemies before the creation of a standing army put an end to the employment of vassals (there being no further need for them), and to all the power and authority of the seigneurs. There is thus no comparison between the title of *Vidame,* which only marks a vassal, and the titles which by fief emanate from the King. Yet because the few Vidames who have been known were illustrious, the name has appeared grand, and for this reason was given to me, and afterwards by me to my son.

Some little time before this, the King resolved to show all Europe, which believed his resources exhausted by a long war, that in the midst of profound peace, he was as fully prepared as ever for arms. He wished at the same time, to present a superb spectacle to Madame de Maintenon, under pretext of teaching the young Duc de Bourgogne his first lesson in war. He gave all the necessary orders, therefore, for forming a camp at Compiègne, to be commanded by the Maréchal de Boufflers under the young Duke. On Thursday, the 28th of August, all the Court set out for the camp. Sixty thousand men were assembled there. The King, as at the marriage of the Duc de Bourgogne, had announced that he counted upon seeing the troops look their best. The consequence of this was to excite the army to an emulation that was repented of afterwards. Not only were the troops in such beautiful order that it was impossible to give the palm to any one corps, but their commanders added the finery and magnificence of the Court to the majestic and warlike beauty of the men, of the arms, and of the horses; and the officers exhausted their means in uniforms which would have graced a fête.

Colonels, and even simple captains, kept open table; but the Maréchal de Boufflers outstripped everybody by his expenditure, by his magnificence, and his good taste. Never was seen a spectacle so transcendent—so dazzling—and (it must be said) so terrifying. At all hours, day or night, the Maréchal's table was open to every comer—whether officer, courtier, or spectator. All were welcomed and invited, with the utmost civility and attention, to partake of the good things provided. There was every kind of hot and cold liquors; everything which can be the most widely and the most splendidly comprehended under the term refreshment: French and foreign wines, and the rarest liqueurs in the utmost abundance. Measures were so well taken that quantities of game and venison arrived from all sides; and the seas of Normandy, of Holland, of England, of Brittany, even the Mediterranean, furnished all they contained—the most unheard-of, extraordinary, and most exquisite—at a given day and hour with inimitable order, and by a prodigious number of horsemen and little express carriages. Even the water was fetched from Sainte Reine, from the Seine, and from sources the most esteemed; and it is impossible to imagine anything of any kind which was not at once ready for the obscurest as for the most distinguished visitor, the guest most expected, and the guest not expected at all. Wooden houses and magnificent tents stretched all around, in number sufficient to form a camp of themselves, and were furnished in the most superb manner, like the houses in Paris. Kitchens and rooms for every purpose were there, and the whole was marked by an order and cleanliness that excited surprise and admiration. The King, wishing that the magnificence of this camp should be seen by the ambassadors, invited them there, and prepared lodgings for them. But the ambassadors claimed a silly distinction, which the King would not grant, and they refused his invitation. This distinction I call silly because it brings no advantage with it of any kind. I am ignorant of its origin, but this is what it consists in. When, as upon such an occasion as this, lodgings are allotted to the Court, the quartermaster writes in chalk, "for Monsieur Such-a-one," upon those intended for Princes of the blood, cardinals, and foreign princes; but for none other. The King would not allow the "for" to be written upon the lodgings of the ambassadors; and the ambassadors, therefore, kept away. The King was much piqued at this, and I heard him say at supper, that if he treated them as they deserved, he should only allow them to come to Court at audience times, as was the custom everywhere else.

The King arrived at the camp on Saturday, the 30th of August, and went with the Duc and Duchesse de Bourgogne and others to the quarters of Maréchal de Boufflers, where a magnificent collation was served up to them—so magnificent that when the King returned, he said it would be useless for the Duc de Bourgogne to attempt anything so splendid; and that whenever he went to the camp he ought to dine with Maréchal de Boufflers. In effect, the King himself soon after dined there, and led to the Maréchal's table the King of England, who was passing three or four days in the camp.

On these occasions the King pressed Maréchal de Boufflers to be seated. He would never comply, but waited upon the King while the Duc de Grammont, his brother-in-law, waited upon Monseigneur.

The King amused himself much in pointing out the disposition of the troops to the ladies of the Court, and in the evening showed them a grand review.

A very pleasant adventure happened at this review to Count Tessé, colonel of dragoons. Two days previously M. de Lauzun, in the course of chit-chat, asked him how he intended to dress at the review; and persuaded him that, it being the custom, he must appear at the head of his troops in a grey hat, or that he would assuredly displease the King. Tessé, grateful for this information, and ashamed of his ignorance, thanked M. de Lauzun, and sent off for a hat in all haste to Paris. The King, as M. de Lauzun well knew, had an aversion to grey, and nobody had worn it for several years. When, therefore, on the day of the review he saw Tessé in a hat of that colour, with a black feather, and a huge cockade dangling and flaunting above, he called to him, and asked him why he wore it. Tessé replied that it was the privilege of the colonel-general to wear that day a grey hat. "A grey hat," replied the King; "where the devil did you learn that?" "From M. de Lauzun, Sire, for whom you created the charge," said Tessé, all embarrassment. On the instant, the good Lauzun vanished, bursting with laughter, and the King assured Tessé that M. de Lauzun had merely been joking with him. I never saw a man so confounded as Tessé at this. He remained with downcast eyes, looking at his hat, with a sadness and confusion that rendered the scene perfect. He was obliged to treat the matter as a joke, but was for a long time much tormented about it, and much ashamed of it.

Nearly every day the Princes dined with Maréchal de Boufflers, whose splendour and abundance knew no end. Everybody who visited him, even the humblest, was served with liberality and attention. All the villages and farms for four leagues round Compiègne were filled with people, French, and foreigners, yet there was no disorder. The gentlemen and valets at the Maréchal's quarters were of themselves quite a world, each more polite than his neighbour, and all incessantly engaged from five o'clock in the morning until ten and eleven o'clock at night, doing the honours to various guests. I return in spite of myself to the Maréchal's liberality; because, who ever saw it, cannot forget, or ever cease to be in a state of astonishment and admiration at its abundance and sumptuousness, or at the order, never deranged for a moment at a single point, that prevailed.

The King wished to show the Court all the manœuvres of war; the siege of Compiègne was therefore undertaken, according to due form, with lines, trenches, batteries, mines, &c. On Saturday, the 13th of September, the assault took place. To witness it, the King, Madame de Maintenon, all the ladies of the Court, and a number of gentlemen, stationed themselves upon an old rampart, from which the plain and all the disposition of the troops could be seen. I was in the half circle very close to the King. It was the most beautiful sight that can be imagined, to see all that army, and the prodigious number of spectators on horse and foot, and that game of attack and defence so cleverly conducted.

But a spectacle of another sort, that I could paint forty years hence as well as to-day, so strongly did it strike me, was that which from the summit of this rampart the King gave to all his army, and to the innumerable crowd of spectators of all kinds in the plain below. Madame de Maintenon faced the plain and the troops in her sedan-chair—alone, between its three windows drawn up—her porters having retired to a distance. On the left pole in front sat Madame la Duchesse de Bourgogne; and on the same side in a semicircle, standing, were Madame la Duchesse, Madame la Princesse de Conti, and all the ladies, and behind them again, many men. At the right window was the King, standing, and a little in the rear, a semicircle of the most distinguished men of the Court. The King was nearly always uncovered; and every now and then stooped to speak to Madame de Maintenon, and explain to her what she saw, and the reason of each movement. Each time that he did so she was obliging enough to open the window four or five inches, but never half way; for I noticed particularly, and I admit that I was more attentive to this spectacle than to that of the troops. Sometimes she opened of her own accord to ask some question of him, but generally it was he who, without waiting for her, stooped down to instruct her of what was passing; and sometimes, if she did not notice him, he tapped at the glass to make her open it. He never spoke, save to her, except when he gave a few brief orders, or just answered Madame la Duchesse de Bourgogne, who wanted to make him speak, and with whom Madame de Maintenon carried on a conversation by signs, without opening the front window, through which the young Princess screamed to her from time to time. I watched the countenance of every one carefully; all expressed surprise tempered with prudence and shame, that was, as it were, ashamed of itself: every one behind the chair and in the semicircle watched this scene more than what was going on in the army. The King often put his hat on the top of the chair in order to get his head in to speak; and this continual exercise tired his loins very much. Monseigneur was on horseback in the plain with the young Princes. It was about five o'clock in the afternoon, and the weather was as brilliant as could be desired.

Opposite the sedan-chair was an opening with some steps cut through the wall, and communicating with the plain below. It had been made for the purpose of fetching orders from the King, should they be necessary. The case happened. Crenan, who commanded, sent Conillac, an officer in one of the defending regiments, to ask for some instructions from the King. Conillac had been stationed at the foot of the rampart, where what was passing above could not be seen. He mounted the steps; and as soon as his head and shoulders were at the top, caught sight of the chair, the King, and all the assembled company. He was not prepared for such a scene, and it struck him with such astonishment, that he stopped short, with mouth and eyes wide open—surprise painted upon every feature. I see him now as distinctly as I did then. The King, as well as all the rest of the company, remarked the agitation of Conillac, and said to him with emotion, " Well, Conillac! come up." Conillac remained motionless, and the King continued, " Come up. What is the matter?" Conillac, thus addressed, finished his ascent, and came towards the King with slow and trembling steps, rolling his eyes from right to left like one deranged. Then he stammered something, but in a tone so low that it could not be heard. " What do you say?" cried the King. " Speak up." But Conillac was unable; and the King, finding he could get nothing out of him, told him to go away. He did not need to be told twice, but disappeared at once. As soon as he was gone, the King, looking round, said, " I don't know what is the matter with Conillac. He has lost his wits; he did not remember what he had to say to me." No one answered.

Towards the moment of the capitulation, Madame de Maintenon apparently asked permission to go away, for the King cried, "The chairmen of Madame!" They came and took her away; in less than a quarter of an hour afterwards the King retired also, and nearly everybody else. There was much interchange of glances, nudging with elbows, and then whisperings in the ear. Everybody was full of what had taken place on the ramparts between the King and Madame de Maintenon. Even the soldiers asked what meant that sedan-chair and the King every moment stooping to put his head inside of it. It became necessary gently to silence these questions of the troops. What effect this sight had upon foreigners present, and what they said of it, may be imagined. All over Europe it was as much talked of as the camp of Compiègne itself, with all its pomp and prodigious splendour.

The last act of this great drama was a sham fight. The execution was perfect; but the commander, Rose, who was supposed to be beaten, would not yield. Maréchal de Boufflers sent and told him more than once that it was time. Rose flew into a passion, and would not obey. The King laughed much at this, and said, "Rose does not like to be beaten." At last he himself sent the order for retreat. Rose was forced then to comply; but he did it with a very bad grace, and abused the bearer of the order.

The King left the camp on Monday the 22d of September, much pleased with the troops. He gave, in parting, six hundred francs to each cavalry captain, and three hundred francs to each captain of infantry. He gave as much to the majors of all the regiments, and distributed some favours to his household. To Maréchal de Boufflers he presented one hundred thousand francs. All these gifts together amounted to something: but separately were as mere drops of water. There was not a single regiment that was not ruined, officers and men, for several years. As for Maréchal de Boufflers, I leave it to be imagined what a hundred thousand francs were to him whose magnificence astounded all Europe, described as it was by foreigners who were witnesses of it, and who day after day could scarcely believe their own eyes.

CHAPTER XIV

HERE I will relate an adventure, which shows that, however wise and enlightened a man may be, he is never infallible. M. de La Trappe had selected from amongst his brethren one who was to be his successor. The name of this monk was D. François Gervaise. He had been in the monastery for some years, had lived regularly during that time, and had gained the confidence of M. de La Trappe. As soon, however, as he received this appointment, his manners began to change. He acted as though he were already master, brought disorder and ill-feeling into the monastery, and sorely grieved M. de La Trappe; who, however, looked upon this affliction as the work of Heaven, and meekly resigned himself to it. At last, François Gervaise was by the merest chance detected openly, under circumstances which blasted his character for ever. His companion in guilt was brought before M. de La Trappe, to leave no doubt upon the matter. D. François Gervaise, utterly prostrated, resigned his office, and left La Trappe. Yet, even after this, he had the hardihood to show himself in the world, and to try and work himself into the favour of Père la Chaise. A discovery that was made, effectually stopped short his hopes in this direction. A letter of his was found, written to a nun with whom he had been intimate, whom he loved, and by whom he was passionately loved. It was a tissue of filthiness and stark indecency, enough to make the most abandoned tremble. The pleasures, the regrets, the desires, the hopes of this precious pair, were all expressed in the boldest language, and with the utmost licence. I believe that so many abominations are not uttered in several days, even in the worst places. For this offence Gervaise might have been confined in a dungeon all his life, but he was allowed to go at large. He wandered from monastery to monastery for five or six years, and always caused so much disorder wherever he stopped, that at last the superiors thought it best to let him live as he liked in a curacy of his brother's. He never ceased troubling La Trappe, to which he wished to return; so that at last I obtained a *lettre de cachet,* which prohibited him from approaching within thirty leagues of the abbey, and within twenty of Paris. It was I who made known to him that his abominations had been discovered. He was in no way disturbed, declared he was glad to be free, and assured me with the hypocrisy which never left him, that in his solitude he was going to occupy himself in studying the Holy Scriptures.

Bonnœil, introducer of the ambassadors, being dead, Breteuil obtained his post. Breteuil was not without intellect, but aped courtly manners, called himself Baron de Breteuil, and was much tormented and laughed at by his friends. One day, dining at the house of Madame de Pontchartrain, and, speaking very authoritatively, Madame de Pontchartrain disputed with him, and, to test his knowledge, offered to make a bet that he did not know who wrote the Lord's Prayer. He defended himself as well as he was able, and succeeded in leaving the table without being called upon to decide the point. Caumartin, who saw his embarrassment, ran to him, and kindly whispered in his ear that Moses was the author of the Lord's Prayer. Thus strengthened, Breteuil returned to the attack, brought, while taking coffee, the conversation back again to the bet; and, after reproaching Madame de Pontchartrain for supposing him ignorant upon such a point, and declaring he was ashamed of being obliged to say such a trivial thing, pronounced emphatically that it was Moses who had written the Lord's Prayer. The burst of laughter that, of course, followed this, overwhelmed him with confusion. Poor Breteuil was for a long time at loggerheads with his friend, and the Lord's Prayer became a standing reproach to him.

He had a friend, the Marquis de Gesvres, who, upon some points, was not much better informed. Talking one day in the cabinet of the King, and admiring in the tone of a connoisseur some fine paintings of the Crucifixion by the first masters, he remarked that they were all by one hand.

He was laughed at, and the different painters were named, as recognized by their style.

"Not at all," said the Marquis, "the painter is called INRI; do you not see his name upon all the pictures?" What followed after such gross stupidity and ignorance may be imagined.

At the end of this year the King resolved to undertake three grand projects, which ought to have been carried out long before: the chapel of Versailles, the Church of the Invalides, and the altar of Notre-Dame de Paris. This last was a vow of Louis XIII., made when he no longer was able to accomplish it, and which he had left to his successor, who had been more than fifty years without thinking of it.

On the 6th of January, upon the reception of the ambassadors at the house of the Duchesse de Bourgogne, an adventure happened which I will here relate. M. de Lorraine belonged to a family which had been noted for its pretensions, and for the disputes of precedency in which it engaged. He was as prone to this absurdity as the rest, and on this occasion incited the Princesse d'Harcourt, one of his relations, to act in a manner that scandalised all the Court. Entering the room in which the ambassadors were to be received and where a large number of ladies were already collected, she glided behind the Duchesse de Rohan, and told her to pass to the left. The Duchesse de Rohan, much surprised, replied that she was very well placed already. Whereupon, the Princesse d'Harcourt, who was tall and strong, made no further ado, but with her two arms seized the Duchesse de Rohan, turned her round, and sat down in her place. All the ladies were strangely scandalised at this, but none dared say a word, not even Madame de Lude, lady in waiting on the Duchesse de Bourgogne, who, for her part also, felt the insolence of the act, but dared not speak, being so young. As for the Duchesse de Rohan, feeling that opposition must lead to fisticuffs, she curtseyed to the Duchess, and quietly retired to another place. A few minutes after this, Madame de Saint-Simon, who was then with child, feeling herself unwell, and tired of standing, seated herself upon the first cushion she could find. It so happened, that in the position she thus occupied, she had taken precedence of Madame d'Armagnac by two degrees. Madame d'Armagnac, perceiving it, spoke to her upon the subject. Madame de Saint-Simon, who had only placed herself there for a moment, did not reply, but went elsewhere.

As soon as I learnt of the first adventure, I thought it important that such an insult should not be borne, and I went and conferred with M. de la Rochefoucauld upon the subject, at the same time that Maréchal de Boufflers spoke of it to M. de Noailles. I called upon other of my friends, and the opinion was that the Duc de Rohan should complain to the King on the morrow of the treatment his wife had received.

In the evening while I was at the King's supper, I was sent for by Madame de Saint-Simon, who informed me that the Lorraines, afraid of the complaints that would probably be addressed to the King upon what had taken place between the Princesse d'Harcourt and the Duchesse de Rohan, had availed themselves of what happened between Madame de Saint-Simon and Madame d'Armagnac, in order to be the first to complain, so that one might balance the other. Here was a specimen of the artifice of these gentlemen, which much enraged me. On the instant I determined to lose no time in speaking to the King; and that very evening I related what had occurred, in so far as Madame de Saint-Simon was concerned, but made no allusion to M. de Rohan's affair, thinking it best to leave that to be settled by itself on the morrow. The King replied to me very graciously, and I retired, after assuring him that all I had said was true from beginning to end.

The next day the Duc de Rohan made his complaint. The King, who had already been fully informed of the matter, received him well, praised the respect and moderation of Madame de Rohan, declared Madame d'Harcourt to have been very impertinent, and said some very hard words upon the Lorraines.

I found afterwards, that Madame de Maintenon, who much favoured Madame d'Harcourt, had all the trouble in the world to persuade the King not to exclude her from the next journey to Marly. She received a severe reprimand from the King, a good scolding from Madame de Maintenon, and was compelled publicly to ask pardon of the Duchesse de Rohan. This she did; but with a crawling baseness equal to her previous audacity. Such was the end of this strange history.

There appeared at this time a book entitled " Problème," but without name of author, and directed against M. de Paris, declaring that he had uttered sentiments favourable to the Jansenists being at Châlons, and unfavourable being at Paris. The book came from the Jesuits, who could not pardon M. de Paris for having become archbishop without their assistance. It was condemned and burnt by decree of the Parliament, and the Jesuits had to swallow all the shame of it. The author was soon after discovered. He was named Boileau; not the friend of Bontems, who so often preached before the King, and still less the celebrated poet and author of the *Flagellants,* but a doctor of much wit and learning whom M. de Paris had taken into his favour and treated like a brother. Who would have believed that "Problème" could spring from such a man? M. de Paris was much hurt; but instead of imprisoning Boileau for the rest of his days, as he might have done, he acted the part of a great bishop, and gave him a good canonical of Saint Honoré, which became vacant a few days afterwards. Boileau, who was quite without means, completed his dishonour by accepting it.

The honest people of the Court regretted a cynic who died at this time, I mean the Chevalier de Coislin. He was a most extraordinary man, very splenetic, and very difficult to deal with. He rarely left Versailles, and never went to see the King. I have seen him get out of the way not to meet him. He lived with Cardinal Coislin, his brother. If anybody displeased him, he would go and sulk in his own room; and if, whilst at table, any one came whom he did not like, he would throw away his plate, go off to sulk, or to finish his dinner all alone. One circumstance will paint him completely. Being on a journey once with his brothers, the Duc de Coislin and the Cardinal de Coislin, the party rested for the night at the house of a vivacious and very pretty bourgeoise. The Duc de Coislin was an exceedingly polite man, and bestowed amiable compliments and civilities upon their hostess, much to the disgust of the Chevalier. At parting, the Duke renewed the politeness he had displayed so abundantly the previous evening, and delayed the others by his long-winded flatteries. When, at last, they left the house, and were two or three leagues away from it, the Chevalier de Coislin said, that, in spite of all this politeness, he had reason to believe that their pretty hostess would not long be pleased with the Duke. The Duke, disturbed, asked his reason for thinking so. "Do you wish to learn it?" said the Chevalier; "well, then, you must know that, disgusted by your compliments, I went up into the bedroom in which you slept, and made a filthy mess on the floor, which the landlady will no doubt attribute to you, despite all your fine speeches."

At this there was loud laughter, but the Duke was in fury, and wished to return in order to clear up his character. Although it rained hard, they had all the pains in the world to hinder him, and still more to bring about a reconciliation. Nothing was more pleasant than to hear the brothers relate this adventure each in his own way.

Two cruel effects of gambling were noticed at this time. Reineville, a lieutenant of the body-guard, a general officer distinguished in war, very well treated by the King, and much esteemed by the captain of the Guards, suddenly disappeared, and could not be found anywhere, although the utmost care was taken to search for him. He loved gaming. He had lost what he could not pay. He was a man of honour, and could not sustain his misfortune. Twelve or fifteen years afterwards he was recognised among the Bavarian troops, in which he was serving in order to gain his bread and to live unknown. The other case was still worse. Permillac, a man of much intelligence and talent, had lost more than he possessed, and blew his brains out one morning in bed. He was much liked throughout the army; had taken a friendship for me, and I for him. Everybody pitied him, and I much regretted him.

Nearly at the same time we lost the celebrated Racine, so known by his beautiful plays. No one possessed a greater talent or a more agreeable mien. There was nothing of the poet in his manners: he had the air of a well-bred and modest man, and at last that of a good man. He had friends, the most illustrious, at the Court as well as among men of letters. I leave it to the latter to speak of him in a better way than I can. He wrote, for the amusement of the King and Madame de Maintenon, and to exercise the young ladies of Saint Cyr, two dramatic masterpieces, *Esther* and *Athalie*. They were very difficult to write, because there could be no love in them, and because they are sacred tragedies, in which, from respect to the Holy Scriptures, it was necessary rigidly to keep to the historical truth. They were several times played at Saint Cyr before a select Court. Racine was charged with the history of the King, conjointly with Despreaux, his friend. This employment, the pieces I have just spoken of, and his friends, gained for Racine some special favours. It sometimes happened that the King had no ministers with him, as on Fridays, and, above all, when the bad weather of winter rendered the sittings very long; then he would send for Racine to amuse him and Madame de Maintenon. Unfortunately the poet was oftentimes very absent. It happened one evening that, talking with Racine upon the theatre, the King asked why comedy was so much out of fashion. Racine gave several reasons, and concluded by naming the principal,—namely, that for want of new pieces the comedians gave old ones, and, amongst others, those of Scarron, which were worth nothing, and which found no favour with anybody. At this the poor widow blushed, not for the reputation of the cripple attacked, but at hearing his name uttered in presence of his successor! The King was also embarrassed, and the unhappy Racine, by the silence which followed, felt what a slip he had made. He remained the most confounded of the three, without daring to raise his eyes or to open his mouth. This silence did not terminate for several moments, so heavy and profound was the surprise. The end was that the King sent away Racine, saying he was going to work. The poet never afterwards recovered his position. Neither the King nor Madame de Maintenon ever spoke to him again, or even looked at him; and he conceived so much sorrow at this, that he fell into a languor, and died two years afterwards. At his death, Valincourt was chosen to work in his place with Despreaux upon the history of the King.

The King, who had just paid the heavy gaming and tradesmen's debts of Madame la Duchesse, paid also those of Monseigneur, which amounted to fifty thousand francs, undertook the payment of the buildings at Meudon, and, in lieu of fifteen hundred pistoles a month which he had allowed Monseigneur, gave him fifty thousand crowns. M. de la Rochefoucauld, always necessitous and pitiful in the midst of riches, a prey to his servants, obtained an increase of forty-two thousand francs a-year upon the salary he received as Grand Veneur, although it was but a short time since the King had paid his debts. The King gave also, but in secret, twenty thousand francs a-year to M. de Chartres, who had spent so much in journeys and building that he feared he should be unable to pay his debts. He had asked for an abbey; but as he had already one, the King did not like to give him another, lest it should be thought too much.

M. de Vendôme began at last to think about his health, which his debauches had thrown into a very bad state. He took public leave of the King and of all the Court before going away, to put himself in the hands of the doctors. It was the first and only example of such impudence. From this time he lost ground. The King said, at parting, that he hoped he would come back in such a state that people might kiss him without danger! His going in triumph, where another would have gone in shame and secrecy, was startling and disgusting. He was nearly three months under the most skilful treatment—and returned to the Court with half his nose, his teeth out, and a physiognomy entirely changed, almost idiotic. The King was so much struck by this change, that he recommended the courtiers not to appear to notice it, for fear of afflicting M. de Vendôme. That was taking much interest in him assuredly. As, moreover, he had departed in triumph upon this medical expedition, so he returned triumphant by the reception of the King, which was imitated by all the Court. He remained only a few days, and then, his mirror telling sad tales, went away to Anet, to see if nose and teeth would come back to him with his hair.

A strange adventure, which happened at this time, terrified everybody, and gave rise to many surmises. Savary was found assassinated in his house at Paris: he kept only a valet and a maid-servant, and they were discovered murdered at the same time, quite dressed, like their master, and in different parts of the house. It appeared by writings found there, that the crime was one of revenge: it was supposed to have been committed in broad daylight. Savary was a citizen of Paris, very rich, without occupation, and lived like an epicurean. He had some friends of the highest rank, and gave parties, of all kinds of pleasure, at his house, politics sometimes being discussed. The cause of this assassination was never known; but so much of it was found out, that no one dared to search for more. Few doubted but that the deed had been done by a very ugly little man, but of a blood so highly respected, that all forms were dispensed with, in the fear lest it should be brought home to him; and, after the first excitement, everybody ceased to speak of this tragic history.

On the night between the 3rd and 4th of June, a daring robbery was effected at the grand stables of Versailles. All the horse-cloths and trappings, worth at least fifty thousand crowns, were carried off, and so cleverly and with such speed, although the night was short, that no traces of them could ever afterwards be found. This theft reminds me of another which took place a little before the commencement of these memoirs. The grand apartment at Versailles, that is to say, from the gallery to the tribune, was hung with crimson velvet, trimmed and fringed with gold. One fine morning the fringe and trimmings were all found to have been cut away. This appeared extraordinary in a place so frequented all day, so well closed at night, and so well guarded at all times. Bontems, the King's valet, was in despair, and did his utmost to discover the thieves, but without success.

Five or six days afterwards, I was at the King's supper, with nobody but Daquin, chief physician, between the King and *me*, and nobody at all between *me* and the table. Suddenly I perceived a large black form in the air, but before I could tell what it was, it fell upon the end of the King's table just before the cover which had been laid for Monseigneur and Madame. By the noise it made in falling, and the weight of the thing itself, it seemed as though the table must be broken. The plates jumped up, but none were upset, and the thing, as luck would have it, did not fall upon any of them, but simply upon the cloth. The King moved his head half round, and without being moved in any way said, "I think that is my fringe!"

It was indeed a bundle, larger than a flat-brimmed priest's hat, about two feet in height, and shaped like a pyramid. It had come from behind me, from towards the middle door of the two ante-chambers, and a piece of fringe getting loose in the air, had fallen upon the King's wig, from which it was removed by Livry, a gentleman-in-waiting. Livry also opened the bundle, and saw that it did indeed contain the fringes all twisted up, and everybody saw likewise. A murmur was heard. Livry wishing to take away the bundle found a paper attached to it. He took the paper and left the bundle. The King stretched out his hand and said, "Let us see." Livry, and with reason, would not give up the paper, but stepped back, read it, and then passed it to Daquin, in whose hands I read it. The writing, counterfeited and long like that of a woman, was in these words:—"Take back your fringes, Bontems; they are not worth the trouble of keeping—my compliments to the King."

The paper was rolled up, not folded: the King wished to take it from Daquin, who, after much hesitation, allowed him to read it, but did not let it out of his hands. "Well, that is very insolent!" said the King, but in quite a placid unmoved tone—as it were, an historical tone. Afterwards he ordered the bundle to be taken away. Livry found it so heavy that he could scarcely lift it from the table, and gave it to an attendant who presented himself. The King spoke no more of this matter, nobody else dared to do so; and the supper finished as though nothing had happened.

Besides the excess of insolence and impudence of this act, it was so perilous as to be scarcely understood. How could any one, without being seconded by accomplices, throw a bundle of this weight and volume in the midst of a crowd such as was always present at the supper of the King, so dense that it could with difficulty be passed through? How, in spite of a circle of accomplices, could a movement of the arms necessary for such a throw escape all eyes? The Duc de Gesvres was in waiting. Neither he nor anybody else thought of closing the doors until the King had left the table. It may be guessed whether the guilty parties remained until then, having had more than three-quarters of an hour to escape, and every issue being free. Only one person was discovered, who was not known, but he proved to be a very honest man, and was dismissed after a short detention. Nothing has since been discovered respecting this theft or its bold restitution.

CHAPTER XV

ON the 12th August, Madame de Saint-Simon was happily delivered of a second son, who bore the name of Marquis de Ruffec. A singular event which happened soon after, made all the world marvel.

There arrived at Versailles a farrier, from the little town of Salon, in Provence, who asked to see the King in private. In spite of the rebuffs he met with, he persisted in his request, so that at last it got to the ears of the King. The King sent word that he was not accustomed to grant such audiences to whoever liked to ask for them. Thereupon the farrier declared that if he was allowed to see the King he would tell him things so secret and so unknown to everybody else that he would be persuaded of their importance, demanding, if the King would not see him, to be sent to a minister of state. Upon this the King allowed him to have an interview with one of his secretaries, Barbezieux. But Barbezieux was not a minister of state, and to the great surprise of everybody, the farrier, who had only just arrived from the country, and who had never before left it or his trade, replied, that not being a minister of state he would not speak with him. Upon this he was allowed to see Pomponne, and converse with him; and this is the story he told:

He said, that returning home late one evening he found himself surrounded by a great light, close against a tree and near Salon. A woman clad in white—but altogether in a royal manner, and beautiful, fair, and very dazzling—called him by his name, commanded him to listen to her, and spake to him more than half-an-hour. She told him she was the Queen, who had been the wife of the King; to whom she ordered him to go and say what she had communicated; assuring him that God would assist him through all the journey, and that upon a secret thing he should say, the King, who alone knew that secret, would recognise the truth of all he uttered. She said that in case he could not see the King he was to speak with a minister of state, telling him certain things, but reserving certain others for the King alone. She told him, moreover, to set out at once, assuring him he would be punished with death if he neglected to acquit himself of his commission. The farrier promised to obey her in everything, and the Queen then disappeared. He found himself in darkness near the tree. He lay down and passed the night there, scarcely knowing whether he was awake or asleep. In the morning he went home, persuaded that what he had seen was a mere delusion and folly, and said nothing about it to a living soul.

Two days afterwards he was passing by the same place when the same vision appeared to him, and he was addressed in the same terms. Fresh threats of punishment were uttered if he did not comply, and he was ordered to go at once to the Intendant of the province, who would assuredly furnish him with money, after saying what he had seen. This time the farrier was convinced there was no delusion in the matter; but, halting between his fears and doubts, knew not what to do, told no one what had passed, and was in great perplexity. He remained thus eight days, and at last had resolved not to make the journey; when, passing by the same spot, he saw and heard the same vision, which bestowed upon him so many dreadful menaces that he no longer thought of anything but setting out immediately. In two days from that time he presented himself, at Aix, to the Intendant of the province, who, without a moment's hesitation, urged him to pursue his journey, and gave him sufficient money to travel by a public conveyance. Nothing more of the story was ever known.

The farrier had three interviews with M. de Pomponne, each of two hours' length. M. de Pomponne rendered, in private, an account of these to the King, who desired him to speak more fully upon the point in a council composed of the Ducs de Beauvilliers, Pontchartrain, Torcy, and Pomponne himself; Monseigneur to be excluded. This council sat very long, perhaps because other things were spoken of. Be that as it may, the King after this wished to converse with the farrier, and did so in his cabinet. Two days afterwards he saw the man again, at each time was nearly an hour with him, and was careful that no one was within hearing.

The day after the first interview, as the King was descending the staircase, to go a-hunting, M. de Duras, who was in waiting, and who was upon such a footing that he said almost what he liked, began to speak of this farrier with contempt, and, quoting the bad proverb, said, " The man was mad, or the King was not noble." At this the King stopped, and, turning round, a thing he scarcely ever did in walking, replied, " If that be so, I am not noble, for I have discoursed with him long, he has spoken to me with much good sense, and I assure you he is far from being mad."

These last words were pronounced with a sustained gravity which greatly surprised those near, and which in the midst of deep silence opened all eyes and ears. After the second interview the King felt persuaded that one circumstance had been related to him by the farrier, which he alone knew, and which had happened more than twenty years before. It was that he had seen a phantom in the forest of Saint Germains. Of this phantom he had never breathed a syllable to anybody.

The King on several other occasions spoke favourably of the farrier; moreover, he paid all the expenses the man had been put to, gave him a gratuity, sent him back free, and wrote to the Intendant of the province to take particular care of him, and never to let him want for anything all his life.

The most surprising thing of all this is, that none of the ministers could be induced to speak a word upon the occurrence. Their most intimate friends continually questioned them, but without being able to draw forth a syllable. The ministers either affected to laugh at the matter or answered evasively. This was the case whenever I questioned M. de Beauvilliers or M. de Pontchartrain, and I knew from their most intimate friends that nothing more could ever be obtained from M. de Pomponne or M. de Torcy. As for the farrier himself, he was equally reserved. He was a simple, honest, and modest man, about fifty years of age. Whenever addressed upon this subject, he cut short all discourse by saying, "I am not allowed to speak," and nothing more could be extracted from him. When he returned to his home he conducted himself just as before, gave himself no airs, and never boasted of the interview he had had with the King and his ministers. He went back to his trade, and worked at it as usual.

Such is the singular story which filled everybody with astonishment, but which nobody could understand. It is true that some people persuaded themselves, and tried to persuade others, that the whole affair was a clever trick, of which the simple farrier had been the dupe. They said that a certain Madame

Arnoul, who passed for a witch, and who, having known Madame de Maintenon when she was Madame Scarron, still kept up a secret intimacy with her, had caused the three visions to appear to the farrier, in order to oblige the King to declare Madame de Maintenon queen. But the truth of the matter was never known.

The King bestowed at this time some more distinctions on his illegitimate children. M. du Maine, as grand-master of the artillery, had to be received at the Chambre des Comptes; and his place ought to have been, according to custom, immediately above that of the senior member. But the King wished him to be put between the first and second presidents; and this was done. The King accorded also to the Princesse de Conti that her two ladies of honour should be allowed to sit at the Duchesse de Bourgogne's table. It was a privilege that no lady of honour to a Princess of the blood had ever been allowed. But the King gave these distinctions to the ladies of his illegitimate children, and refused it to those of the Princesses of the blood.

In thus according honours, the King seemed to merit some new ones himself. But nothing fresh could be thought of. What had been done therefore at his statue in the Place des Victoires, was done over again in the Place Vendôme on the 13th August, after midday. Another statue which had been erected there was uncovered. The Duc de Gesvres, Governor of Paris, was in attendance on horseback, at the head of the city troops, and made turns, and reverences, and other ceremonies, imitated from those in use at the consecration of the Roman Emperors. There were, it is true, no incense and no victims: something more in harmony with the title of Christian King was necessary. In the evening, there was upon the river a fine illumination, which Monsieur and Madame went to see.

A difficulty arose soon after this with Denmark. The Prince Royal had become King, and announced the circumstance to our King, but would not receive the reply sent him because he was not styled in it "Majesty." We had never accorded to the Kings of Denmark this title, and they had always been contented with that of "Serenity." The King in his turn would not wear mourning for the King of Denmark, just dead, although he always did so for any crowned head, whether related to him or not. This state of things lasted some months; until, in the end, the new King of Denmark gave way, received the reply as it had been first sent, and our King wore mourning as if the time for it had not long since passed.

Boucherat, chancellor and keeper of the seals, died on the 2nd of September. Harlay, as I have previously said, had been promised this appointment when it became vacant. But the part he had taken in our case with M. de Luxembourg had made him so lose ground, that the appointment was not given to him. M. de la Rochefoucauld, above all, had undermined him in the favour of the King; and none of us had lost an opportunity of assisting in this work. Our joy, therefore, was extreme when we saw all Harlay's hopes frustrated, and we did not fail to let it burst forth. The vexation that Harlay conceived was so great, that he became absolutely intractable, and often cried out with a bitterness he could not contain, that he should be left to die in the dust of the palace. His weakness was such, that he could not prevent himself six weeks after from complaining to the King at Fontainebleau, where he was playing the valet with his accustomed suppleness and deceit. The King put him off with fine speeches, and by appointing him to take part in a commission then sitting for the purpose of bringing about a reduction in the price of corn in Paris and the suburbs, where it had become very dear. Harlay made a semblance of being contented, but remained not the less annoyed. His health and his head were at last so much attacked that he was forced to quit his post: he then fell into contempt after having excited so much hatred. The chancellorship was given to Pontchartrain, and the office of comptroller-general, which became vacant at the same time, was given to Chamillart, a very honest man, who owed his first advancement to his skill at billiards, of which game the King was formerly very fond. It was while Chamillart was accustomed to play billiards with the King, at least three times a week, that an incident happened which ought not to be forgotten. Chamillart was Counsellor of the Parliament at that time. He had just reported on a case that had been submitted to him. The losing party came to him, and complained that he had omitted to bring forward a document that had been given into his hands, and that would assuredly have turned the verdict. Chamillart searched for the document, found it, and saw that the complainer was right. He said so, and added,—" I do not know how the document escaped me, but it decides in your favour. You claimed twenty thousand francs, and it is my fault you did not get them. Come to-morrow, and I will pay you." Chamillart, although then by no means rich, scraped together all the money he had, borrowing the rest, and paid the man as he had promised, only demanding that the matter should be kept a secret. But after this, feeling that billiards three times a week interfered with his legal duties, he surrendered part of them, and thus left himself more free for other charges he was obliged to attend to.

The Comtesse de Fiesque died very aged, while the

Court was at Fontainebleau this year. She had passed her life with the most frivolous of the great world. Two incidents amongst a thousand will characterise her. She was very straitened in means, because she had frittered away all her substance, or allowed herself to be pillaged by her business people. When those beautiful mirrors were first introduced she obtained one, although they were then very dear and very rare. "Ah, Countess!" said her friends, "where did you find that?"

"Oh!" replied she, "I had a miserable piece of land, which only yielded me corn; I have sold it, and I have this mirror instead. Is not this excellent? Who would hesitate between corn and this beautiful mirror?"

On another occasion she harangued with her son, who was as poor as a rat, for the purpose of persuading him to make a good match and thus enrich himself. Her son, who had no desire to marry, allowed her to talk on, and pretended to listen to her reasons. She was delighted—entered into a description of the wife she destined for him, painting her as young, rich, an only child, beautiful, well-educated, and with parents who would be delighted to agree to the marriage. When she had finished, he pressed her for the name of this charming and desirable person. The Countess said she was the daughter of Jacquier, a man well known to everybody, and who had been a contractor of provisions to the armies of M. de Turenne. Upon this, her son burst out into a hearty laugh, and she in anger demanded why he did so. and what he found so ridiculous in the match.

The truth was, Jacquier had no children, as the Countess soon remembered. At which she said it was a great pity, since no marriage would have better suited all parties. She was full of such oddities, which she persisted in for some time with anger, but at which she was the first to laugh. People said of her that she had never been more than eighteen years old. The memoirs of Mademoiselle paint her well. She lived with Mademoiselle, and passed all her life in quarrels about trifles.

It was immediately after leaving Fontainebleau that the marriage between the Duc and Duchesse de Bourgogne was consummated. It was upon this occasion that the King named four gentlemen to wait upon the Duke,—four who in truth could not have been more badly chosen. One of them, Gamaches, was a gossip, who never knew what he was doing or saying—who knew nothing of the world, or the Court, or of war, although he had always been in the army. D'O was another; but of him I have spoken. Cheverny was the third, and Saumery the fourth. Saumery had been raised out of obscurity by M. de Beauvilliers. Never was man so intriguing, so truckling, so mean, so boastful, so ambitious, so intent upon fortune, and all this without disguise, without veil, without shame! Saumery had been wounded, and no man ever made so much of such a mishap. I used to say of him that he limped audaciously, and it was true. He would speak of personages the most distinguished, whose ante-chambers even he had scarcely seen, as though he spoke of his equals or of his particular friends. He related what he had heard, and was not ashamed to say before people who at least had common sense, "Poor *Mons.* Turenne said to me," M. de Turenne never having probably heard of his existence. With *Monsieur* in full he honoured nobody. It was *Mons.* de Beauvilliers, *Mons.* de Chevreuse, and so on; except with those whose names he clipped off short, as he frequently would even with Princes of the blood. I have heard him say many times, "the Princesse de

Conti," in speaking of the daughter of the King; and "the Prince de Conti," in speaking of Monsieur her brother-in-law! As for the chief nobles of the Court, it was rare for him to give them the *Monsieur* or the *Mons*. It was Maréchal d'Humières, and so on with the others. Fatuity and insolence were united in him, and by dint of mounting a hundred staircases a day, and bowing and scraping everywhere, he had gained the ear of I know not how many people. His wife was a tall creature, as impertinent as he, who wore the breeches, and before whom he dared not breathe. Her effrontery blushed at nothing, and after many gallantries she had linked herself on to M. de Duras, whom she governed, and of whom she was publicly and absolutely the mistress, living at his expense. Children, friends, servants, all were at her mercy; even Madame de Duras herself when she came, which was but seldom, from the country.

Such were the people whom the King placed near M. le Duc de Bourgogne.

The Duc de Gesvres, a malicious old man, a cruel husband and unnatural father, sadly annoyed Maréchal de Villeroy towards the end of this year, having previously treated me very scurvily for some advice I gave him respecting the ceremonies to be observed at the reception by the King of M. de Lorraine as Duc de Bar. M. de Gesvres and M. de Villeroy had both had fathers who made large fortunes and who became secretaries of state. One morning M. de Gesvres was waiting for the King, with a number of other courtiers, when M. de Villeroy arrived, with all that noise and those airs he had long assumed, and which his favour and his appointments rendered more superb. I know not whether this annoyed De Gesvres, more than usual, but as soon as the other had placed himself, he said, "Monsieur le Maréchal, it must be admitted that you and I are very lucky." The Maréchal, surprised at a remark which seemed to be suggested by nothing, assented with a modest air, and, shaking his head and his wig, began to talk to some one else. But M. de Gesvres had not commenced without a purpose. He went on, addressed M. de Villeroy point-blank, admiring their mutual good fortune, but when he came to speak of the father of each, " Let us go no further," said he, " for what did our fathers spring from? From tradesmen; even tradesmen they were themselves. Yours was the son of a dealer in fresh fish at the markets, and mine of a pedlar, or, perhaps, worse. Gentlemen," said he, addressing the company, " have we not reason to think our fortune prodigious—the Maréchal and I?" The Maréchal would have liked to strangle M. de Gesvres, or to see him dead—but what can be done with a man who, in order to say something cutting to you, says it to himself first? Everybody was silent, and all eyes were lowered. Many, however, were not sorry to see M. de Villeroy so pleasantly humiliated. The King came and put an end to the scene, which was the talk of the Court for several days.

Omissions must be repaired as soon as they are perceived. Other matters have carried me away. At the commencement of April, Ticquet, Counsellor at the Parliament, was assassinated in his own house; and if he did not die, it was not the fault of his porter, or of the soldier who had attempted to kill him, and who left him for dead, disturbed by a noise they heard. This councillor, who was a very poor man, had complained to the King, the preceding year, of the conduct of his wife with Montgeorges, captain in the Guards, and much esteemed. The King prohibited Montgeorges from seeing the wife of the councillor again.

Such having been the case, when the crime was attempted, suspicion fell upon Montgeorges and the wife of Ticquet, a beautiful, gallant, and bold woman, who took a very high tone in the matter. She was advised to fly, and one of my friends offered to assist her to do so, maintaining that in all such cases it is safer to be far off than close at hand. The woman would listen to no such advice, and in a few days she was no longer able. The porter and the soldier were arrested and tortured, and Madame Ticquet, who was foolish enough to allow herself to be arrested, also underwent the same examination, and avowed all. She was condemned to lose her head, and her accomplice to be broken on the wheel. Montgeorges managed so well, that he was not legally criminated. When Ticquet heard the sentence, he came with all his family to the King, and sued for mercy. But the King would not listen to him, and the execution took place on Wednesday, the 17th of June, after mid-day, at the Grève. All the windows of the Hôtel de Ville, and of the houses in the Place de Grève, in the streets that lead to it from the Conciergerie of the palace where Madame Ticquet was confined, were filled with spectators, men and women, many of title and distinction. There were even friends of both sexes of this unhappy woman, who felt no shame or horror in going there. In the streets the crowd was so great that it could not be passed through. In general, pity was felt for the culprit; people hoped she would be pardoned, and it was because they hoped so, that they went to see her die. But such is the world; so unreasoning, and so little in accord with itself.

CHAPTER XVI

THE year 1700 commenced by a reform. The King declared that he would no longer bear the expense of the changes that the courtiers introduced into their apartments. It had cost him more than sixty thousand francs since the Court left Fontainebleau. It is believed that Madame de Mailly was the cause of this determination of the King; for during the last two or three years she had made changes in her apartments every year.

A difficulty occurred at this time which much mortified the King. Little by little he had taken all the ambassadors to visit Messieurs du Maine and de Toulouse, as though they were Princes of the blood. The nuncio, Cavallerini, visited them thus, but upon his return to Rome was so taken to task for it, that his successor, Delfini, did not dare to imitate him. The cardinals considered that they had lowered themselves, since Richelieu and Mazarin, by treating even the Princes of the blood on terms of equality, and giving them their hand, which had not been customary in the time of the two first ministers just named. To do so to the illegitimate offspring of the King, and on occasions of ceremony, appeared to them monstrous. Negotiations were carried on for a month, but Delfini would not bend, and although in every other respect he had afforded great satisfaction during his nunciature, no farewell audience was given to him, nor even a secret audience. He was deprived of the gift of a silver vessel worth eighteen hundred francs, that it was customary to present to the cardinal nuncios at their departure: and he went away without saying adieu to anybody.

Some time before, M. de Monaco had been sent as ambassador to Rome. He claimed to be addressed by the title of " Highness," and persisted in it with so much obstinacy that he isolated himself from almost everybody, and brought the affairs of his embassy nearly to a standstill by the fetters he imposed upon them in the most necessary transactions. Tired at last of the resistance he met with, he determined to refuse the title of " Excellence," although it might fairly belong to them, to all who refused to address him as " Highness." This finished his affair; for after that determination no one would see him, and the business of the embassy suffered even more than before. It is difficult to comprehend why the King permitted such a man to remain as his representative at a foreign Court.

Madame de Navailles died on the 14th of February. Her mother, Madame de Neuillant, who became a widow, was avarice itself. I cannot say by what accident or chance it was that Madame de Maintenon in returning young and poor from America, where she had lost her father and mother, fell in landing at Rochelle into the hands of Madame de Neuillant, who lived in Poitou. Madame de Neuillant took home Madame de Maintenon, but could not resolve to feed her without making her do something in return. Madame de Maintenon was charged therefore with the key of the granary, had to measure out the corn and to see that it was given to the horses. It was Madame de Neuillant who brought Madame de Maintenon to Paris, and to get rid of her married her to Scarron, and then retired into Poitou.

Madame de Navailles was the eldest daughter of this Madame de Neuillant, and it was her husband, M. de Navailles, who, serving under M. le Prince in

Flanders, received from that General a strong reprimand for his ignorance. M. le Prince wanted to find the exact position of a little brook which his maps did not mark. To assist him in the search, M. de Navailles brought a map of the world! On another occasion, visiting M. Colbert, at Sceaux, the only thing M. de Navailles could find to praise was the endive of the kitchen garden: and when on the occasion of the Huguenots the difficulty of changing religion was spoken of, he declared that if God had been good enough to make him a Turk, he should have remained so.

Madame de Navailles had been lady of honour to the Queen-mother, and lost that place by a strange adventure.

She was a woman of spirit and of virtue, and the young ladies of honour were put under her charge. The King was at this time young and gallant. So long as he held aloof from the chamber of the young ladies, Madame de Navailles meddled not, but she kept her eye fixed upon all that she controlled. She soon perceived that the King was beginning to amuse himself, and immediately after she found that a door had secretly been made into the chamber of the young ladies; that this door communicated with a staircase by which the King mounted into the room at night, and was hidden during the day by the back of a bed placed against it. Upon this Madame de Navailles held counsel with her husband. On one side was virtue and honour, on the other, the King's anger, disgrace, and exile. The husband and wife did not long hesitate. Madame de Navailles at once took her measures, and so well, that in a few hours one evening the door was entirely closed up. During the same night the King, thinking to enter as usual by the little staircase, was much surprised to no longer find a door. He groped, he searched, he could not comprehend the disappearance of the door, or by what means it had become wall again. Anger seized him; he doubted not that the door had been closed by Madame de Navailles and her husband. He soon found that such was the case, and on the instant stripped them of almost all their offices, and exiled them from the Court. The exile was not long; the Queen-mother on her death-bed implored him to receive back Monsieur and Madame de Navailles, and he could not refuse. They returned, and M. de Navailles nine years afterwards was made Maréchal of France. After this Madame de Navailles rarely appeared at the Court. Madame de Maintenon could not refuse her distinctions and special favours, but they were accorded rarely and by moments. The King always remembered his door; Madame de Maintenon always remembered the hay and barley of Madame de Neuillant, and neither years nor devotion could deaden the bitterness of the recollection.

From just before Candlemas-day to Easter of this year, nothing was heard of but balls and pleasures of the Court. The King gave at Versailles and at Marly several masquerades, by which he was much amused, under pretext of amusing the Duchesse de Bourgogne. At one of these balls at Marly a ridiculous scene occurred. Dancers were wanting and Madame de Luxembourg on account of this obtained an invitation, but with great difficulty, for she lived in such a fashion that no woman would see her. Monsieur de Luxembourg was perhaps the only person in France who was ignorant of Madame de Luxembourg's conduct. He lived with his wife on apparently good terms and as though he had not the slightest mistrust of her. On this occasion, because of the want of dancers, the King made older people dance than was customary, and among others M. de Luxembourg. Everybody was compelled to be masked. M. de Luxembourg spoke on this subject to M. le Prince, who, malicious as any monkey, determined to divert all the Court and himself at the Duke's expense. He invited M. de Luxembourg to supper, and after that meal was over, masked him according to his fancy.

Soon after my arrival at the ball, I saw a figure strangely clad in long flowing muslin, and with a headdress on which was fixed the horns of a stag, so high that they became entangled in the chandelier. Of course everybody was much astonished at so strange a sight, and all thought that that mask must be very sure of his wife to deck himself so. Suddenly the mask turned round and showed us M. de Luxembourg. The burst of laughter at this was scandalous. Good M. de Luxembourg, who never was very remarkable for wit, benignly took all this laughter as having been excited simply by the singularity of his costume, and to the questions addressed him, replied quite simply that his dress had been arranged by M. le Prince; then, turning to the right and to the left, he admired himself and strutted with pleasure at having been masked by M. le Prince. In a moment more the ladies arrived, and the King immediately after them. The laughter commenced anew as loudly as ever, and M. de Luxembourg presented himself to the company with a confidence that was ravishing. His wife had heard nothing of this masquerading, and when she saw it, lost countenance, brazen as she was. Everybody stared at her and her husband, and seemed dying of laughter. M. le Prince looked at the scene from behind the King, and inwardly laughed at his malicious trick. This amusement lasted throughout all the ball, and the King, self-contained as he usually was, laughed also; people were never tired of admiring an invention so cruelly ridiculous, and spoke of it for several days.

No evening passed on which there was not a ball. The chancellor's wife gave one which was a fête the most gallant and the most magnificent possible. There were different rooms for the fancy-dress ball, for the masqueraders, for a superb collation, for shops of all countries, Chinese, Japanese, &c., where many singular and beautiful things were sold, but no money taken; they were presents for the Duchesse de Bourgogne and the ladies. Everybody was especially diverted at this entertainment, which did not finish until eight o'clock in the morning. Madame de Saint-Simon and I passed the last three weeks of this time without ever seeing the day. Certain dancers were only allowed to leave off dancing at the same time as the Duchesse de Bourgogne. One morning, at Marly, wishing to escape too early, the Duchess caused me to be forbidden to pass the doors of the salon; several of us had the same fate. I was delighted when Ash Wednesday arrived; and I remained a day or two dead beat, and Madame de Saint-Simon could not get over Shrove Tuesday.

La Bourlie, brother of Guiscard, after having quitted the service, had retired to his estate near Cévennes, where he led a life of much licence. About this time a robbery was committed in his house; he suspected one of the servants, and on his own authority put the man to the torture. This circumstance could not remain so secret but that complaints spread abroad. The offence was a capital one. La Bourlie fled from the realm, and did many strange things until his death, which was still more strange; but of which it is not yet time to speak.

Madame la Duchesse, whose heavy tradesmen's debts the King had paid not long since, had not dared to speak of her gambling debts, also very heavy. They increased, and, entirely unable to pay them, she found herself in the greatest embarrassment. She feared, above all things, lest M. le Prince or M. le Duc should hear of this. In this extremity she addressed herself to Madame de Maintenon, laying bare the state of her finances, without the slightest disguise. Madame de Maintenon had pity on her situation, and arranged that the King should pay her debts, abstain from scolding her, and keep her secret. Thus, in a few weeks, Madame la Duchesse found herself free of debts, without anybody whom she feared having known even of their existence.

Langlée was entrusted with the payment and arrangement of these debts. He was a singular kind of man at the Court, and deserves a word. Born of obscure parents, who had enriched themselves, he had early been introduced into the great world, and had devoted himself to play, gaining an immense fortune; but without being accused of the least unfairness. With but little or no wit, but much knowledge of the world, he had succeeded in securing many friends, and in making his way at the Court. He joined in all the King's parties, at the time of his mistresses. Similarity of tastes attached Langlée to Monsieur, but he never lost sight of the King. At all the fêtes Langlée was present, he took part in the journeys, he was invited to Marly, was intimate with all the King's mistresses; then with all the daughters of the King, with whom indeed he was so familiar that he often spoke to them with the utmost freedom. He had become such a master of fashions and of fêtes that none of the latter were given, even by Princes of the blood, except under his directions; and no houses were bought, built, furnished, or ornamented, without his taste being consulted. There were no marriages of which the dresses and the presents were not chosen, or at least approved, by him. He was on intimate terms with the most distinguished people of the Court; and often took improper advantage of his position. To the daughters of the King and to a number of female friends he said horribly filthy things, and that too in their own houses, at St. Cloud or at Marly. He was often made a confidant in matters of gallantry, and continued to be made so all his life. For he was a sure man, had nothing disagreeable about him, was obliging, always ready to serve others with his purse or his influence, and was on bad terms with no one.

While everybody, during all this winter, was at balls and amusements, the beautiful Madame de Soubise— for she was so still—employed herself with more serious matters. She had just bought, very cheap, the immense Hôtel de Guise, that the King assisted her to pay for. Assisted also by the King, she took steps to make her bastard son canon of Strasbourg; intrigued so well that his birth was made to pass muster, although among Germans there is a great horror of illegitimacy, and he was received into the chapter. This point gained, she laid her plans for carrying out another, and a higher one, nothing less than that of making her son Archbishop of Strasbourg.

But there was an obstacle in the way. This obstacle was the Abbé d'Auvergne (nephew of Cardinal de Bouillon), who had the highest position in the chapter, that of Grand Prévôt, had been there much longer than the Abbé de Soubise, was older, and of more consequence. His reputation, however, was against him; his habits were publicly known to be those of the Greeks, whilst his intellect resembled theirs in no way. By his stupidity he published his bad conduct, his perfect ignorance, his dissipation, his ambition; and to sustain himself he had only a low, stinking, continual vanity,—which drew upon him as much disdain as did his habits, alienated him from all the world, and constantly subjected him to ridicule.

The Abbé de Soubise had, on the contrary, everything smiling in his favour, even his exterior, which showed that he was born of the tenderest amours. Upon the forms of the Sorbonne he had much distinguished himself. He had been made Prior of Sorbonne, and had shone conspicuously in that position, gaining eulogies of the most flattering kind from everybody, and highly pleasing the King. After this, he entered the seminary of Saint Magloire, then much in vogue, and gained the good graces of the Archbishop of Paris, by whom that seminary was favoured. On every side the Abbé de Soubise was regarded, either as a marvel of learning, or a miracle of piety and purity of manners. He had made himself loved everywhere, and his gentleness, his politeness, his intelligence, his graces, and his talent for securing friends, confirmed more and more the reputation he had established.

The Abbé d'Auvergne had a relative, the Cardinal de Furstenberg, who also had two nephews, canons of Strasbourg, and in a position to become claimants to the bishopric. Madame de Soubise rightly thought that her first step must be to gain over the Cardinal to her side. There was a channel through which this could be done which at once suggested itself to her mind. Cardinal Furstenberg, it was said, had been much enamoured of the Comtesse de La Marck, and had married her to one of his nephews, in order that he might thus see her more easily. It was also said that he had been well treated, and it is certain that nothing was so striking as the resemblance, feature for feature, of the Comte de La Marck to Cardinal de Furstenberg. If the Count was not the son of the Cardinal he was nothing to him. The attachment of

Cardinal Furstenberg for the Comtesse de La Marck did not abate when she became by her marriage Comtesse de Furstenberg; indeed he could not exist without her; she lived and reigned in his house. Her son, the Comte de La Marck, lived there also, and her dominion over the Cardinal was so public, that whoever had affairs with him spoke to the Countess, if he wished to succeed. She had been very beautiful, and at fifty-two years of age, still showed it, although tall, stout, and coarse featured as a Swiss guard in woman's clothes. She was, moreover, bold, audacious, talking loudly and always with authority; was polished, however, and of good manners when she pleased. Being the most imperious woman in the world, the Cardinal was fairly tied to her apron-strings, and scarcely dared to breathe in her presence. In dress and finery she spent like a prodigal, played every night, and lost large sums, oftentimes staking her jewels and her various ornaments. She was a woman who loved herself alone, who wished for everything, and who refused herself nothing,—not even, it was said, certain gallantries which the poor Cardinal was obliged to pay for, as for everything else. Her extravagance was such, that she was obliged to pass six or seven months of the year in the country, in order to have enough to spend in Paris during the remainder of the year.

It was to the Comtesse de Furstenberg, therefore, that Madame de Soubise addressed herself in order to gain over the support of Cardinal de Furstenberg, in behalf of her son. Rumour said, and it was never contradicted, that Madame de Soubise paid much money to the Cardinal through the Countess, in order to carry this point. It is certain that in addition to the prodigious pensions the Cardinal drew from the King, he touched at this time a gratification of forty thousand crowns, that it was pretended had been long promised him.

Madame de Soubise having thus assured herself of the Countess and the Cardinal (and they having been privately thanked by the King), she caused an order to be sent to Cardinal de Bouillon, who was then at Rome, requesting him to ask the Pope in the name of the King, for a bull summoning the Chapter of Strasbourg to meet and elect a coadjutor and a declaration of the eligibility of the Abbé de Soubise.

But here a new obstacle arose in the path of Madame de Soubise. Cardinal de Bouillon, a man of excessive pride and pretension, who upon reaching Rome claimed to be addressed as "Most Eminent Highness," and obtaining this title from nobody except his servants, set himself at loggerheads with all the city— Cardinal de Bouillon, I say, was himself canon of Strasbourg, and uncle of the Abbé d'Auvergne. So anxious was the Cardinal to secure the advancement of the Abbé d'Auvergne, that he had already made a daring and fraudulent attempt to procure for him a cardinalship. But the false representations which he made in order to carry his point, having been seen through, his attempt came to nothing, and he himself lost all favour with the King for his deceit. He, however, hoped to make the Abbé d'Auvergne bishop of Strasbourg, and was overpowered, therefore, when he saw this magnificent prey about to escape him. The news came upon him like a thunderbolt. It was bad enough to see his hopes trampled under foot; it was insupportable to be obliged to aid in crushing them. Vexation so transported and blinded him, that he forgot the relative positions of himself and of Madame de Soubise, and imagined that he should be able to make the King break a resolution he had taken, and an engagement he had entered into. He sent therefore, as though he had been a great man, a letter to the King, telling him that he had not thought sufficiently upon this matter, and raising scruples against it. At the same time he despatched a letter to the canons of Strasbourg, full of gall and compliments, trying to persuade them that the Abbé de Soubise was too young for the honour intended him, and plainly intimating that the Cardinal de Furstenberg had been gained over by a heavy bribe paid to the Comtesse de Furstenberg. These letters made a terrible uproar.

I was at the palace on Tuesday, March 30th, and after supper I saw Madame de Soubise arrive, leading the Comtesse de Furstenberg, both of whom posted themselves at the door of the King's cabinet. It was not that Madame de Soubise had not the privilege of entering if she pleased, but she preferred making her complaint as public as the charges made against her by Cardinal de Bouillon had become. I approached in order to witness the scene. Madame de Soubise appeared scarcely able to contain herself, and the Countess seemed furious. As the King passed, they stopped him. Madame de Soubise said two words in a low tone. The Countess in a louder strain demanded justice against the Cardinal de Bouillon, who, she said, not content in his pride and ambition with disregarding the orders of the King, had calumniated her and Cardinal de Furstenberg in the most atrocious manner, and had not even spared Madame de Soubise herself. The King replied to her with much politeness, assured her she should be contented, and passed on.

Madame de Soubise was so much the more piqued because Cardinal de Bouillon had acquainted the King with the simony she had committed, and assuredly if he had not been ignorant of this he would never have supported her in the affair. She hastened therefore to secure the success of her son, and was so well served by the whispered authority of the King, and the money she had spent, that the Abbé de Soubise was elected by unanimity Coadjutor of Strasbourg.

As for the Cardinal de Bouillon, foiled in all his attempts to prevent the election, he wrote a second letter to the King, more foolish than the first. This filled the cup to overflowing. For reply, he received orders, by a courier, to quit Rome immediately and to retire to Cluni or to Tournus, at his choice, until further orders. This order appeared so cruel to him that he could not make up his mind to obey. He was under-doyen of the sacred college. Cibo, the doyen, was no longer able to leave his bed. To become doyen, it was necessary to be in Rome when the appointment became vacant. Cardinal de Bouillon wrote therefore to the King, begging to be allowed to stay a short time, in order to pray the Pope to set aside this rule, and give him permission to succeed to the doyenship, even although absent from Rome when it became vacant. He knew he should not obtain this permission, but he asked for it in order to gain time, hoping that in the meanwhile Cardinal Cibo might die, or even the Pope himself, whose health had been threatened with ruin for some time. This request of the Cardinal de Bouillon was refused. There seemed nothing for him but to comply with the orders he had received. But he had evaded them so long that he thought he might continue to do so. He wrote to Père la Chaise, begging him to ask the King for permission to remain at Rome until the death of Cardinal Cibo, adding that he would wait for a reply at Caprarole, a magnificent house of the Duke of Parma, at eight leagues from Rome. He addressed himself to Père la Chaise, because M. de Torcy, to whom he had previously written, had been forbidden to open his letters, and had sent him word to that effect. Having, too, been always on the best of terms with the Jesuits, he hoped for good assistance from Père la Chaise. But he found this door closed like that of M. de Torcy. Père la Chaise wrote to Cardinal de Bouillon that he too was prohibited from opening his letters. At the same time a new order was sent to the Cardinal to set out immediately. Just after he had read it Cardinal Cibo died, and the Cardinal de Bouillon hastened at once to Rome to secure the doyenship, writing to the King to say that he had done so, that he would depart in twenty-four hours, and expressing a hope that this delay would not be refused him. This was laughing at the King and his orders, and becoming doyen in spite of him. The King, therefore, displayed his anger immediately he learnt this last act of disobedience. He sent word immediately to M. de Monaco to command the Cardinal de Bouillon to surrender his charge of grand chaplain, to give up his cordon bleu, and to take down the arms of France from the door of his palace; M. de Monaco was also ordered to prohibit all French people in Rome from seeing Cardinal de Bouillon, or from having any communication with him. M. de Monaco, who hated the Cardinal, hastened willingly to obey these instructions. The Cardinal appeared overwhelmed, but he did not even then give in. He pretended that his charge of grand chaplain was a crown office, of which he could not be dispossessed, without resigning. The King, out of all patience with a disobedience so stubborn and so marked, ordered, by a decree in council, on the 12th September, the seizure of all the Cardinal's estates, laical and ecclesiastical, the latter to be confiscated to the state, the former to be divided into three portions, and applied to various uses. The same day the charge of grand chaplain was given to Cardinal Coislin, and that of chief chaplain to the Bishop of Metz. The despair of the Cardinal de Bouillon, on hearing of this decree, was extreme. Pride had hitherto hindered him from believing that matters would be pushed so far against him. He sent in his resignation only when it was no longer needed of him. His order he would not give up. M. de Monaco warned him that, in case of refusal, he had orders to snatch it from his neck. Upon this the Cardinal saw the folly of holding out against the orders of the King. He quitted then the marks of the order, but he was pitiful enough to wear a narrow blue ribbon, with a cross of gold attached, under his cassock, and tried from time to time to show a little of the blue. A short time afterwards, to make the best of a bad bargain, he tried to persuade himself and others, that no cardinal was at liberty to wear the orders of any prince. But it was rather late in the day to think of this, after having worn the order of the King for thirty years, as grand chaplain; and everybody thought so, and laughed at the idea.

CHAPTER XVII

CHATEAUNEUF, Secretary of State, died about this time. He had asked that his son, La Vrillière, might be allowed to succeed him, and was much vexed that the King refused this favour. The news of Chateauneuf's death was brought to La Vrillière by a courier, at five o'clock in the morning. He did not lose his wits at the news, but at once sent and woke up the Princesse d'Harcourt, and begged her to come and see him instantly. Opening his purse, he prayed her to go and see Madame de Maintenon as soon as she got up, and propose his marriage with Mademoiselle de Mailly, whom he would take without dowry, if the King gave him his father's appointments. The Princesse d'Harcourt, whose habit it was to accept any sum, from a crown upwards, willingly undertook this strange business. She went upon her errand immediately, and then repaired to Madame de Mailly, who without property, and burdened with a troop of children—sons and daughters,—was in no way averse to the marriage.

The King, upon getting up, was duly made acquainted with La Vrillière's proposal, and at once agreed to it. There was only one person opposed to the marriage, and that was Mademoiselle de Mailly. She was not quite twelve years of age. She burst out a-crying, and declared she was very unhappy, that she would not mind marrying a poor man, if necessary, provided he was a gentleman, but that to marry a paltry bourgeois, in order to make his fortune, was odious to her. She was furious against her mother and against Madame de Maintenon. She could not be kept quiet or appeased, or hindered from making grimaces at La Vrillière and all his family, who came to see her and her mother. They felt it; but the bargain was made, and was too good to be broken. They thought Mademoiselle de Mailly's annoyance would pass with her youth—but they were mistaken. Mademoiselle de Mailly always was sore at having been made Madame de la Vrillière, and people often observed it.

At the marriage of Monseigneur the Duc de Bourgogne, the King had offered to augment considerably his monthly income. The young Prince, who found it sufficient, replied with thanks, and said that if money failed him at any time he would take the liberty of asking the King for more. Finding himself short just now, he was as good as his word. The King praised him highly, and told him to ask whenever he wanted money, not through a third person, but direct, as he had done in this instance. The King, moreover, told the Duc de Bourgogne to play without fear, for it was of no consequence how much such persons as he might lose. The King was pleased with confidence, but liked not less to see himself feared; and when timid people who spoke to him discovered themselves, and grew embarrassed in their discourse, nothing better made their court, or advanced their interests.

The Archbishop of Rheims presided this year over the assembly of the clergy, which was held every five years. It took place on this occasion at Saint Germains, although the King of England occupied the château. M. de Rheims kept open table there, and had some champagne that was much vaunted. The King of England, who drank scarcely any other wine, heard of this and asked for some. The Archbishop sent him six bottles. Some time after, the King of

England, who had much relished the wine, sent and asked for more. The Archbishop, more sparing of his wine than of his money, bluntly sent word that his wine was not mad, and did not run through the streets; and sent none. However accustomed people might be to the rudeness of the Archbishop, this appeared so strange that it was much spoken of: but that was all.

M. de Vendôme took another public leave of the King, the Princes, and the Princesses, in order to place himself again under the doctor's hands. He perceived at last that he was not cured, and that it would be long before he was; so went to Anet to try and recover his health, but without success better than before. He brought back a face upon which his state was still more plainly printed than at first. Madame d'Uzès, only daughter of the Prince de Monaco, died of this disease. She was a woman of merit—very virtuous and unhappy—who merited a better fate. M. d'Uzès was an obscure man, who frequented the lowest society, and suffered less from its effects than his wife, who was much pitied and regretted. Her children perished of the same disease, and she left none behind her.

Soon after this the King ordered the Comtes d'Uzès and d'Albert to go to the Conciergerie for having fought a duel against the Comtes de Rontzau, a Dane, and Schwartzenberg, an Austrian. Uzès gave himself up, but the Comte d'Albert did not do so for a long time, and was broken for his disobedience. He had been on more than good terms with Madame de Luxembourg—the Comte de Rontzau also: hence the quarrel; the cause of which was known by everybody, and made a great stir. Everybody knew it, at least, except M. de Luxembourg, and said nothing, but was glad of it; and yet in every direction he asked the reason; but, as may be imagined, could find nobody to tell him;

so that he went over and over again to M. le Prince de Conti, his most intimate friend, praying him for information upon the subject. M. de Conti related to me that on one occasion, coming from Meudon, he was so solicited by M. de Luxembourg on this account, that he was completely embarrassed, and never suffered to such an extent in all his life. He contrived to put off M. de Luxembourg, and said nothing, but was glad indeed to get away from him at the end of the journey.

Le Nôtre died about this time, after having been eighty-eight years in perfect health, and with all his faculties and good taste to the very last. He was illustrious, as having been the first designer of those beautiful gardens which adorn France, and which, indeed, have so surpassed the gardens of Italy, that the most famous masters of that country come here to admire and learn. Le Nôtre had a probity, an exactitude, and an uprightness which made him esteemed and loved by everybody. He never forgot his position, and was always perfectly disinterested. He worked for private people as for the King, and with the same application—seeking only to aid nature, and to attain the beautiful by the shortest road. He was of a charming simplicity and truthfulness. The Pope, upon one occasion, begged the King to lend him Le Nôtre for some months. On entering the Pope's chamber, instead of going down upon his knees, Le Nôtre ran to the Holy Father, clasped him round the neck, kissed him on the two cheeks, and said—" Good morning, Reverend Father; how well you look, and how glad I am to see you in such good health."

The Pope, who was Clement X., Altieri, burst out laughing with all his might. He was delighted with this odd salutation, and showed his friendship towards the gardener in a thousand ways. Upon Le Nôtre's return, the King led him into the gardens of Versailles, and showed him what had been done in his absence. About the Colonnade he said nothing. The King pressed him to give his opinion thereupon.

"Why, sire," said Le Nôtre, "what can I say? Of a mason you have made a gardener, and he has given you a sample of his trade."

The King kept silence and everybody laughed; and it was true that this morsel of architecture, which was anything but a fountain, and yet which was intended to be one, was much out of place in a garden. A month before Le Nôtre's death, the King, who liked to see him and to make him talk, led him into the gardens, and on account of his great age, placed him in a wheeled chair, by the side of his own. Upon this Le Nôtre said, "Ah, my poor father, if you were living and could see a simple gardener like me, your son, wheeled along in a chair by the side of the greatest King in the world, nothing would be wanting to my joy!"

Le Nôtre was Overseer of the Public Buildings, and lodged at the Tuileries, the garden of which (his design), together with the Palace, being under his charge. All that he did is still much superior to everything that has been done since, whatever care may have been taken to imitate and follow him as closely as possible. He used to say of flower-beds that they were only good for nurses, who, not being able to quit the children, walked on them with their eyes, and admired them from the second floor. He excelled, nevertheless, in flower-beds, as in everything concerning gardens; but he made little account of them, and he was right, for they are the spots upon which people never walk.

The King of England (William III.) lost the Duke of Gloucester, heir-presumptive to the crown. He was eleven years of age, and was the only son of the Princess of Denmark, sister of the defunct Queen Mary, wife of William. His preceptor was Doctor Burnet, Bishop of Salisbury, who was in the secret of the invasion, and who passed into England with the Prince of Orange at the Revolution, of which Revolution he has left a very fraudulent history, and many other works of as little truth and good faith. The under-preceptor was the famous Vassor, author of the "History of Louis XIII.," which would be read with more pleasure if there were less spite against the Catholic religion, and less passion against the King. With those exceptions it is excellent and true. Vassor must have been singularly well informed of the anecdotes that he relates, and which escape almost all historians. I have found there, for instance, the Day of the Dupes related precisely as my father has related it to me, and several other curious things not less exact. This author has made such a stir that it is worth while to say something about him. He was a priest of the Oratory, and in much estimation as a man whose manners were without reproach. After a time, however, he was found to have disclosed a secret that had been entrusted to him, and to have acted the spy on behalf of the Jesuits. The proofs of his treason were found upon his table, and were so conclusive that there was nothing for him but to leave the Oratory. He did so, and being deserted by his Jesuit employers, threw himself into La Trappe. But he did not enter the place in a proper spirit, and in a few days withdrew. After this he went to the Abbey of Perseigne, hired a lodging there, and remained several months. But he was continually at loggerheads with the monks. Their garden was separate from his only by a thick hedge; their fowls could jump over it. He laid the blame upon the monks, and one day caught as many of their fowls as he could; cut off their beaks and their spurs with a cleaver, and threw them back again over the hedge. This was cruelty so marked that I could not refrain from relating it.

Vassor did not long remain in this retreat, but returned to Paris, and still being unable to gain a living, passed into Holland, from rage and hunger became a Protestant, and set himself to work to live by his pen. His knowledge, talent, and intelligence procured him many friends, and his reputation reached England, into which country he passed, hoping to gain there more fortune than in Holland. Burnet received him with open arms, and obtained for him the post of under-preceptor to the Duke of Gloucester. It would have been difficult to have found two instructors so opposed to the Catholics and to France, or so well suited to the King as teachers of his successor.

Among so many things which paved the way for the greatest events, a very strange one happened, which from its singularity merits a short recital. For many years the Comtesse de Verrue lived at Turin, mistress, publicly, of M. de Savoie. The Comtesse de Verrue was daughter of the Duc de Luynes, and had been married in Piedmont, when she was only fourteen years of age, to the Comte de Verrue, young, handsome, rich, and honest; whose mother was lady of honour to Madame de Savoie.

M. de Savoie often met the Comtesse de Verrue, and soon found her much to his taste. She saw this, and said so to her husband and her mother-in-law. They praised her, but took no further notice of the matter. M. de Savoie redoubled his attentions, and, contrary to his usual custom, gave fêtes, which the Comtesse de Verrue felt were for her. She did all she could not to attend them, but her mother-in-law quarrelled with her, said she wished to play the important, and that it was her vanity which gave her these ideas. Her husband, more gentle, desired her to attend these fêtes, saying that even if M. de Savoie were really in love with her, it would not do to fail in anything towards him. Soon after M. de Savoie spoke to the Comtesse de Verrue. She told her husband and her mother-in-law, and used every entreaty in order to prevail upon them to let her go and pass some time in the country. They would not listen to her, and seeing no other course open, she feigned to be ill, and had herself sent to the waters of Bourbon. She wrote to her father, the Duc de Luynes, to meet her there, and set out under the charge of the Abbé de Verrue, uncle of her husband. As soon as the Duc de Luynes arrived at Bourbon, and became acquainted with the danger which threatened his daughter, he conferred with the Abbé as to the best course to adopt, and agreed with him that the Countess should remain away from Turin some time, in order that M. de Savoie might get cured of his passion. M. de Luynes little thought that he had conferred with a wolf who wished to carry off his lamb. The Abbé de Verrue, it seems, was himself violently in love with the Countess, and directly her father had gone declared the state of his heart. Finding himself only repulsed, the miserable old man turned his love into hate, ill-treated the Countess, and upon her return to Turin, lost no opportunity of injuring her in the eyes of her husband and her mother-in-law.

The Comtesse de Verrue suffered this for some time, but at last her virtue yielded to the bad treatment she received. She listened to M. de Savoie, and delivered herself up to him in order to free herself from persecution. Is not this a real romance? But it happened in our own time, under the eyes and to the knowledge of everybody.

When the truth became known, the Verrues were in

despair, although they had only themselves to blame for what had happened. Soon the new mistress ruled all the Court of Savoy, whose sovereign was at her feet as before a goddess. She disposed of the favours of her lover, and was feared and courted by the ministry. Her haughtiness made her hated; she was poisoned; M. de Savoie gave her a subtle antidote, which fortunately cured her, and without injury to her beauty. Her reign still lasted. After a while she had the small-pox. M. de Savoie tended her during this illness, as though he had been a nurse; and although her face suffered a little by it, he loved her not the less. But he loved her after his own fashion. He kept her shut up from view, and at last she grew so tired of her restraint that she determined to fly. She conferred with her brother, the Chevalier de Luynes, who served with much distinction in the navy, and together they arranged the matter.

They seized an opportunity when M. de Savoie had gone on a tour to Chambéry, and departed furtively. Crossing our frontier, they arrived in Paris, where the Comtesse de Verrue, who had grown very rich, took a house, and by degrees succeeded in getting people to come and see her, though, at first, owing to the scandal of her life, this was difficult. In the end, her opulence gained her a large number of friends, and she availed herself so well of her opportunities, that she became of much importance, and influenced strongly the government. But that time goes beyond my memoirs. She left in Turin a son and a daughter, both recognised by M. de Savoie, after the manner of our King. He loved passionately these illegitimate children, and married the daughter to the Prince de Carignan.

Mademoiselle de Condé died at Paris on October 24th, after a long illness, from a disease in the chest, which consumed her less than the torments she experienced without end from M. le Prince, her father, whose continual caprices were the plague of all those over whom he could exercise them. Almost all the children of M. le Prince were little bigger than dwarfs, which caused M. le Prince, who was tall, to say in pleasantry, that if his race went on always thus diminishing it would come to nothing. People attributed the cause to a dwarf that Madame la Princesse had had for a long time near her.

At the funeral of Mademoiselle de Condé, a very indecorous incident happened. My mother, who was invited to take part in the ceremony, went to the Hôtel de Condé, in a coach and six horses, to join Mademoiselle d'Enghien. When the procession was about to start the Duchesse de Chatillon tried to take precedence of my mother. But my mother called upon Mademoiselle d'Enghien to prevent this, or else to allow her to return. Madame de Chatillon persisted in her attempt, saying that relationship decided the question of precedence on these occasions, and that she was a nearer relative to the deceased than my mother. My mother, in a cold but haughty tone, replied that she could pardon this mistake on account of the youth and ignorance of Madame de Chatillon; but that in all such cases it was rank and not relationship which decided the point. The dispute was at last put to an end by Madame de Chatillon giving way. But when the procession started an attempt was made by her coachman to drive before the coach of my mother, and one of the company had to descend and decide the dispute. On the morrow M. le Prince sent to apologise to my mother for the occurrence that had taken place, and came himself shortly afterwards full of compliments and excuses. I never could understand what induced Madame de Chatillon to take this fancy into her head; but she was much ashamed of it afterwards, and made many excuses to my mother.

I experienced, shortly after this, at Fontainebleau, one of the greatest afflictions I had ever endured. I mean the loss of M. de La Trappe. These Memoirs are too profane to treat slightly of a life so sublimely holy, and of a death so glorious and precious before God. I will content myself with saying here that praises of M. de La Trappe were so much the more great and prolonged because the King eulogised him in public; that he wished to see narrations of his death; and that he spoke more than once of it to his grandsons by way of instruction. In every part of Europe this great loss was severely felt. The Church wept for him, and the world even rendered him justice. His death, so happy for him and so sad for his friends, happened on the 26th of October, towards half-past twelve, in the arms of his bishop, and in presence of his community, at the age of nearly seventy-seven years, and after nearly forty years of the most prodigious penance. I cannot omit, however, the most touching and the most honourable mark of his friendship. Lying upon the ground, on straw and ashes, in order to die like all the brethren of La Trappe, he deigned, of his own accord, to recollect me, and charged the Abbé La Trappe to send word to me, on his part, that as he was quite sure of my affection for him, he reckoned that I should not doubt of his tenderness for me. I check myself at this point; everything I could add would be too much out of place here.

CHAPTER XVIII

FOR the last two or three years the King of Spain had been in very weak health, and in danger of his life several times. He had no children, and no hope of having any. The question, therefore, of the succession to his vast empire began now to agitate every European Court. The King of England (William III.), who since his usurpation had much augmented his credit by the grand alliance he had formed against France, and of which he had been the soul and the chief up to the Peace of Ryswick, undertook to arrange this question in a manner that should prevent war when the King of Spain died. His plan was to give Spain, the Indies, the Low Countries, and the title of King of Spain to the Archduke, second son of the Emperor; Guipuscoa, Naples, Sicily, and Lorraine to France; and the Milanese to M. de Lorraine, as compensation for taking away from him his territory.

The King of England made this proposition first of all to our King; who, tired of war, and anxious for repose, as was natural at his age, made few difficulties, and soon accepted. M. de Lorraine was not in a position to refuse his consent to a change recommended by England, France, and Holland. Thus much being settled, the Emperor was next applied to. But he was not so easy to persuade: he wished to inherit the entire succession, and would not brook the idea of seeing the House of Austria driven from Italy, as it would have been if the King of England's proposal had been carried out. He therefore declared it was altogether unheard of and unnatural to divide a succession under such circumstances, and that he would hear nothing upon the subject until after the death of the King of Spain. The resistance he made caused the whole scheme to come to the ears of the King of Spain, instead of remaining a secret, as was intended.

The King of Spain made a great stir in consequence of what had taken place, as though the project had been formed to strip him, during his lifetime, of his realm. His ambassador in England spoke so insolently that he was ordered to leave the country by William, and retired to Flanders. The Emperor, who did not wish to quarrel with England, intervened at this point, and brought about a reconciliation between the two powers. The Spanish ambassador returned to London.

The Emperor next endeavoured to strengthen his party in Spain. The reigning Queen was his sister-in-law and was all-powerful. Such of the nobility and of the ministers who would not bend before her she caused to be dismissed; and none were favoured by her who were not partisans of the House of Austria. The Emperor had, therefore, a powerful ally at the Court of Madrid to aid him in carrying out his plans; and the King was so much in his favour, that he had made a will bequeathing his succession to the Archduke. Everything therefore seemed to promise success to the Emperor.

But just at this time, a small party arose in Spain, equally opposed to the Emperor, and to the propositions of the King of England. This party consisted at first of only five persons: namely, Villafranca, Medina-Sidonia, Villagarcias, Villena, and San Estevan, all of them nobles, and well instructed in the affairs of government. Their wish was to prevent the dismemberment of the Spanish kingdom by conferring the whole succession upon the son of the only son of the Queen of France, Maria Theresa, sister of the King of Spain. There were, however, two great obstacles in their path. Maria Theresa, upon her marriage with our King, had solemnly renounced all claim to the Spanish throne, and these renunciations had been repeated at the Peace of the Pyrenees. The other obstacle was the affection the King of Spain bore to the House of Austria,—an affection which naturally would render him opposed to any project by which a rival house would be aggrandised at its expense.

As to the first obstacle, these politicians were of opinion that the renunciations made by Maria Theresa held good only as far as they applied to the object for which they were made. That object was to prevent the crowns of France and Spain from being united upon one head, as might have happened in the person of the Dauphin. But now that the Dauphin had three sons, the second of whom could be called to the throne of Spain, the renunciations of the Queen became of no import. As to the second obstacle, it was only to be removed by great perseverance and exertions; but they determined to leave no stone unturned to achieve their ends.

One of the first resolutions of this little party was to bind one another to secrecy. Their next was to admit into their confidence Cardinal Portocarrero, a determined enemy to the Queen. Then they commenced an attack upon the Queen in the council; and being supported by the popular voice, succeeded in driving out of the country Madame Berlips, a German favourite of hers, who was much hated on account of the undue influence she exerted, and the rapacity she displayed. The next measure was of equal importance. Madrid and its environs groaned under the weight of a regiment of Germans commanded by the Prince of Darmstadt. The council decreed that this regiment should be disbanded, and the Prince thanked for his assistance. These two blows following upon each other so closely, frightened the Queen, isolated her, and put it out of her power to act during the rest of the life of the King.

There was yet one of the preliminary steps to take, without which it was thought that success would not be certain. This was to dismiss the King's Confessor, who had been given to him by the Queen, and who was a zealous Austrian.

Cardinal Portocarrero was charged with this duty, and he succeeded so well, that two birds were killed with one stone. The Confessor was dismissed, and another was put in his place, who could be relied upon to do and say exactly as he was requested. Thus, the King of Spain was influenced in his conscience, which had over him so much the more power, because he was beginning to look upon the things of this world by the glare of that terrible flambeau that is lighted for the dying. The Confessor and the Cardinal, after a short time, began unceasingly to attack the King upon the subject of the succession. The King, enfeebled by illness, and by a lifetime of weak health, had little power of resistance. Pressed by the many temporal, and affrighted by the many spiritual reasons which were brought forward by the two ecclesiastics, with no friend near whose opinion he could consult, no Austrian at hand to confer with, and no Spaniard who was not opposed to Austria;—the King fell into a profound perplexity, and in this strait, proposed to consult the Pope, as an authority whose decision would be infallible. The Cardinal, who felt persuaded that the Pope was sufficiently enlightened and sufficiently impartial to declare in favour of France, assented to this step; and the King of Spain accordingly wrote a long letter to Rome, feeling much relieved by the course he had adopted.

The Pope replied at once and in the most decided manner. He said he saw clearly that the children of the Dauphin were the next heirs to the Spanish throne, and that the House of Austria had not the smallest right to it. He recommended therefore the King of Spain to render justice to whom justice was due, and to assign the succession of his monarchy to a son of France. This reply, and the letter which had given rise to it, were kept so profoundly secret that they were not known in Spain until after the King's death.

Directly the Pope's answer had been received the King was pressed to make a fresh will, and to destroy that which he had previously made in favour of the Archduke. The new will accordingly was at once drawn up and signed; and the old one burned in the presence of several witnesses.

Matters having arrived at this point, it was thought opportune to admit others to the knowledge of what had taken place. The council of state, consisting of eight members, four of whom were already in the secret, was made acquainted with the movements of the new party; and, after a little hesitation, were gained over.

The King, meantime, was drawing near to his end. A few days after he had signed the new will he was at the last extremity, and in a few days more he died. In his last moments the Queen had been kept from him as much as possible, and was unable in any way to interfere with the plans that had been so deeply laid. As soon as the King was dead the first thing to be done was to open his will. The council of state assembled for that purpose, and all the grandees of Spain who were in the capital took part in it. The singularity and the importance of such an event, interesting many millions of men, drew all Madrid to the palace, and the rooms adjoining that in which the council assembled were filled to suffocation. All the foreign ministers besieged the door. Every one sought to be the first to know the choice of the King who had just died, in order to be the first to inform his court. Blécourt, our ambassador, was there with the others, without knowing more than they; and Count d'Harrach, ambassador from the Emperor, who counted upon the will in favour of the Archduke, was there also, with a triumphant look, just opposite the door, and close by it.

At last the door opened, and immediately closed again. The Duc d'Abrantes, a man of much wit and humour, but not to be trifled with, came out. He wished to have the pleasure of announcing upon whom the successorship had fallen, and was surrounded as soon as he appeared. Keeping silence, and turning his eyes on all sides, he fixed them for a moment on Blécourt, then looked in another direction, as if seeking some one else. Blécourt interpreted this action as a bad omen. The Duc d'Abrantes feigning at last to discover the Count d'Harrach, assumed a gratified look, flew to him, embraced him, and said aloud in Spanish, " Sir, it is with much pleasure;" then pausing, as though to embrace him better, he added: " Yes, sir, it is with an extreme joy that for all my life,"— here the embraces were redoubled as an excuse for a second pause, after which he went on—" and with the greatest contentment that I part from you, and take leave of the very august House of Austria." So saying he clove the crowd, and every one ran after him to know the name of the real heir.

The astonishment and indignation of Count d'Harrach disabled him from speaking, but showed themselves upon his face in all their extent. He remained motionless some moments, and then went away in the greatest confusion at the manner in which he had been duped.

Blécourt, on the other hand, ran home without asking other information, and at once despatched to the King a courier, who fell ill at Bayonne, and was replaced by one named by Harcourt, then at Bayonne getting ready for the occupation of Guipuscoa. The news arrived at Court (Fontainebleau) in the month of November. The King was going out shooting that day; but, upon learning what had taken place, at once countermanded the sport, announced the death of the King of Spain, and at three o'clock held a council of the ministers in the apartments of Madame de Maintenon. This council lasted until past seven o'clock in the evening. Monseigneur, who had been out wolf-hunting, returned in time to attend it. On the next morning, Wednesday, another council was held, and in the evening a third, in the apartments of Madame de Maintenon. However accustomed persons were at the Court to the favour Madame de Maintenon enjoyed there, they were extremely surprised to see two councils assembled in her rooms for the greatest and most important deliberation that had taken place during this long reign, or indeed during many others.

The King, Monseigneur, the Chancellor, the Duc de Brinvilliers, Torcy, and Madame de Maintenon, were the only persons who deliberated upon this affair. Madame de Maintenon preserved at first a modest silence; but the King forced her to give her opinion after everybody had spoken except herself. The council was divided. Two were for keeping to the treaty that had been signed with King William, two for accepting the will.

Monseigneur, drowned as he was in fat and sloth, appeared in quite another character from his usual one, at these councils. To the great surprise of the King and his assistants, when it was his turn to speak he expressed himself with force in favour of accepting the testament. Then, turning towards the King in a respectful but firm manner, he said that he took the liberty of asking for his inheritance, that the monarchy of Spain belonged to the Queen his mother, and consequently to him; that he surrendered it willingly to his second son for the tranquillity of Europe; but that to none other would he yield an inch of ground. These words, spoken with an inflamed countenance, caused excessive surprise. The King listened very attentively, and then said to Madame de Maintenon, "And you, Madame, what do you think upon all this?" She began by affecting modesty; but pressed, and even commanded to speak, she expressed herself with becoming confusion; briefly sang the praises of Monseigneur, whom she feared and liked but little—sentiments perfectly reciprocated—and at last was for accepting the will.

The King did not yet declare himself. He said that the affair might well be allowed to sleep for four-and-twenty hours, in order that they might ascertain if the Spaniards approved the choice of their King. He dismissed the council, but ordered it to meet again the next evening at the same hour and place. Next day, several couriers arrived from Spain, and the news they brought left no doubt upon the King's mind as to the wishes of the Spanish nobles and people upon the subject of the will. When therefore the council reassembled in the apartments of Madame de Maintenon, the King, after fully discussing the matter, resolved to accept the will.

At the first receipt of the news the King and his

ministers had been overwhelmed with a surprise that they could not recover from for several days. When the news was spread abroad, the Court was equally surprised. The foreign ministers passed whole nights deliberating upon the course the King would adopt. Nothing else was spoken of but this matter. The King one evening, to divert himself, asked the princesses their opinion. They replied that he should send M. le Duc d'Anjou (the second son of Monseigneur) into Spain, and that this was the general sentiment. " I am sure," replied the King, " that whatever course I adopt many people will condemn me."

At last, on Tuesday, the 16th of November, the King publicly declared himself. The Spanish ambassador had received intelligence which proved the eagerness of Spain to welcome the Duc d'Anjou as its King. There seemed to be no doubt of the matter. The King, immediately after getting up, called the ambassador into his cabinet, where M. le Duc d'Anjou had already arrived. Then, pointing to the Duke, he told the ambassador he might salute him as King of Spain. The ambassador threw himself upon his knees after the fashion of his country, and addressed to the Duke a tolerably long compliment in the Spanish language. Immediately afterwards, the King, contrary to all custom, opened the two folding doors of his cabinet, and commanded everybody to enter. It was a very full Court that day. The King, majestically turning his eyes towards the numerous company, and showing them M. le Duc d'Anjou said—" Gentlemen, behold the King of Spain. His birth called him to that crown: the late King also has called him to it by his will; the whole nation wished for him, and has asked me for him eagerly; it is the will of heaven: I have obeyed it with pleasure." And then, turning towards his grandson, he said, " Be a good Spaniard, that is your first duty; but remember that you are a Frenchman born, in order that the union between the two nations may be preserved; it will be the means of rendering both happy, and of preserving the peace of Europe." Pointing afterwards with his finger to the Duc d'Anjou, to indicate him to the ambassador, the King added, " If he follows my counsels you will be a grandee, and soon; he cannot do better than follow your advice."

When the hubbub of the courtiers had subsided, the two other sons of France, brothers of M. d'Anjou, arrived, and all three embraced one another tenderly several times, with tears in their eyes. The ambassador of the Emperor immediately entered, little suspecting what had taken place, and was confounded when he learned the news. The King afterwards went to mass, during which at his right hand was the new King of Spain, who during the rest of his stay in France, was publicly treated in every respect as a sovereign, by the King and all the Court.

The joy of Monseigneur at all this was very great. He seemed beside himself, and continually repeated that no man had ever found himself in a condition to say as he could, " The King my father, and the King my son." If he had known the prophecy which from his birth had been said of him, " A King's son, a King's father, and never a King," which everybody had heard repeated a thousand times, I think he would not have so much rejoiced, however vain may be such prophecies. The King himself was so overcome, that at supper he turned to the Spanish ambassador and said that the whole affair seemed to him like a dream. In public, as I have observed, the new King of Spain was treated in every respect as a sovereign, but in private he was still the Duc d'Anjou. He passed his evenings in the apartments of Madame de Maintenon, where he played at all sorts of children's games, scampering to and fro with Messeigneurs his brothers, with Madame la Duchesse de Bourgogne, and with the few ladies to whom access was permitted.

On Friday, the 19th of November, the new King of Spain put on mourning. Two days after, the King did the same. On Monday, the 22nd, letters were received from the Elector of Bavaria, stating that the King of Spain had been proclaimed at Brussels with much rejoicing and illuminations. On Sunday, the 28th, M. Vaudemont, governor of the Milanese, sent word that he had been proclaimed in that territory, and with the same demonstrations of joy as at Brussels.

On Saturday, the 4th of December, the King of Spain set out for his dominions. The King rode with him in his coach as far as Sceaux, surrounded in pomp by many more guards than usual, gendarmes and light horse, all the road covered with coaches and people; and Sceaux, where they arrived a little after midday, full of ladies and courtiers, guarded by two companies of Musketeers. There was a good deal of leave-taking, and all the family was collected alone in the last room of the apartment; but as the doors were left open, the tears they shed so bitterly could be seen. In presenting the King of Spain to the Princes of the blood, the King said—" Behold the Princes of my blood and of yours; the two nations from this time ought to regard themselves as one nation; they ought to have the same interests; therefore I wish these Princes to be attached to you as to me; you cannot have friends more faithful or more certain." All this lasted a good hour and a half. But the time of separation at last came. The King conducted the King of Spain to the end of the apartment, and embraced him several times, holding him a long while in his arms. Monseigneur did the same. The spectacle was extremely touching.

The King returned into the palace for some time, in order to recover himself. Monseigneur got into a *calèche* alone, and went to Meudon; and the King of Spain, with his brother, M. de Noailles, and a large number of courtiers, set out on his journey. The King gave to his grandson twenty-one purses of a thousand louis each, for pocket-money, and much money besides for presents. Let us leave them on their journey, and admire the Providence which sports with the thoughts of men and disposes of states. What would have said Ferdinand and Isabella, Charles V. and Philip II., who so many times attempted to conquer France, and who have been so frequently accused of aspiring to universal monarchy, and Philip IV., even, with all his precautions at the marriage of the King and at the Peace of the Pyrenees,—what would they have said, to see a son of France become King of Spain, by the will and testament of the last of their blood in Spain, and by the universal wish of all the Spaniards—without plot, without intrigue, without a shot being fired on our part, and without the sanction of our King, nay even to his extreme surprise and that of all his ministers, who had only the trouble of making up their minds and of accepting? What great and wise reflections might be made thereon! But they would be out of place in these Memoirs.

The King of Spain arrived in Madrid on the 19th February. From his first entrance into the country he had everywhere been most warmly welcomed. Acclamations were uttered when he appeared; *fêtes* and bull-fights were given in his honour; the nobles and ladies pressed around him. He had been proclaimed in Madrid some time before, in the midst of demonstrations of joy. Now that he had arrived among his subjects there, that joy burst out anew. There was such a crowd in the streets that sixty people were stifled! All along the line of route were an infinity of coaches filled with ladies richly decked. The streets through which he passed were hung in the Spanish fashion; stands were placed, adorned with fine pictures and a vast number of silver vessels; triumphal arches were built from side to side. It is impossible to conceive a greater or more general demonstration of joy. The Buen-Retiro, where the new King took up his quarters, was filled with the Court and the nobility. The Junta and a number of great men received him at the door, and the Cardinal Portocarrero, who was there, threw himself on his knees, and wished to kiss the King's hand. But the King would not permit this; raised the Cardinal, embraced him, and treated him as his father. The Cardinal wept with joy, and could not take his eyes off the King. He was just then in the flower of his first youth—fair like the late King Charles, and the Queen his grandmother; grave, silent, measured, self-contained, formed exactly to live among Spaniards. With all this, very attentive in his demeanour, and paying everybody the attention due to him, having taken lessons from d'Harcourt on the way. Indeed he took off his hat or raised it to nearly everybody, so that the Spaniards spoke on the subject to the Duc d'Harcourt, who replied to them that the King in all essential things would conform himself to usage, but that in others he must be allowed to act according to French politeness. It cannot be imagined how much these trifling external attentions attached all hearts to this Prince.

He was, indeed, completely triumphant in Spain, and the Austrian party as completely routed. The Queen of Spain was sent away from Madrid, and banished to Toledo, where she remained with but a small suite, and still less consideration. Each day the nobles, the citizens, and the people had given fresh proof of their hatred against the Germans and against the Queen. She had been almost entirely abandoned, and was refused the most ordinary necessaries of her state.

CHAPTER XIX

SHORTLY after his arrival in Madrid, the new King of Spain began to look about him for a wife, and his marriage with the second daughter of M. de Savoie (younger sister of Madame de Bourgogne) was decided upon as an alliance of much honour and importance to M. de Savoie, and, by binding him to her interest, of much utility to France. An extraordinary ambassador (Homodeï, brother of the Cardinal of that name) was sent to Turin to sign the contract of marriage, and bring back the new Queen into Spain. He was also appointed her *Ecuyer,* and the Princesse des Ursins was selected as her *Camarera Mayor,* a very important office. The Princesse des Ursins seemed just adapted for it. A Spanish lady could not have been relied upon: a lady of our court would not have been fit for the post. The Princesse des Ursins was, as it were, both French and Spanish— French by birth, Spanish by marriage. She had passed the greater part of her life in Rome and Italy, and was a widow without children. I shall have more hereafter to say of this celebrated woman, who so long and so publicly governed the Court and Crown of Spain, and who has made so much stir in the world by her reign and by her fall; at present let me finish with the new Queen of Spain.

She was married, then, at Turin, on the 11th of September, with but little display, the King being represented by procuration, and set out on the 13th for Nice, where she was to embark on board the Spanish galleys for Barcelona. The King of Spain, meanwhile, after hearing news that he had been proclaimed with much unanimity and rejoicing in Peru and Mexico, left Madrid on the 5th of September, to journey through Aragon and Catalonia to Barcelona to meet his wife. He was much welcomed on his route, above all by Saragossa, which received him magnificently.

The new Queen of Spain, brought by the French galleys to Nice, was so fatigued with the sea when she arrived there, that she determined to finish the rest of the journey by land, through Provence and Languedoc. Her graces, her presence of mind, the aptness and the politeness of her short replies, and her judicious curiosity, remarkable at her age, surprised everybody, and gave great hopes to the Princesse des Ursins.

When within two days' journey of Barcelona, the Queen was met by a messenger, bearing presents and compliments from the King. All her household joined her at the same time, being sent on in advance for that purpose, and her Piedmontese attendants were dismissed. She appeared more affected by this separation than Madame de Bourgogne had been when parting from her attendants. She wept bitterly, and seemed quite lost in the midst of so many new faces, the most familiar of which (that of Madame des Ursins) was quite fresh to her. Upon arriving at Figueras, the King, impatient to see her, went on before on horseback. In this first embarrassment Madame des Ursins, although completely unknown to the King, and but little known to the Queen, was of great service to both.

Upon arriving at Figueras, the bishop diocesan married them anew, with little ceremony, and soon after they sat down to supper, waited upon by the Princesse des Ursins and the ladies of the palace, half the dishes being French, half Spanish. This mixture displeased the ladies of the palace and several of the Spanish grandees, who plotted with the ladies openly to mark their displeasure; and they did so in a scandalous manner. Under one pretext or another—such as the weight or heat of the dishes—not one of the French dishes arrived upon the table; all were upset; while the Spanish dishes, on the contrary, were served without any accident. The affectation and air of chagrin, to say the least of it, of the ladies of the palace, were too visible not to be perceived. But the King and Queen were wise enough to appear not to notice this; and Madame des Ursins, much astonished, said not a word.

After a long and disagreeable supper, the King and Queen withdrew. Then feelings which had been kept in during supper overflowed. The Queen wept for her Piedmontese women. Like a child, as she was, she thought herself lost in the hands of ladies so insolent; and when it was time to go to bed, she said flatly that she would not go, and that she wished to return home. Everything was done to console her; but the astonishment and embarrassment were great indeed when it was found that all was of no avail. The King had undressed, and was awaiting her. Madame des Ursins was at length obliged to go and tell him the resolution the Queen had taken. He was piqued and annoyed. He had until that time lived with the completest regularity; which had contributed to make him find the Princess more to his taste than he might otherwise have done. He was therefore affected by her *fantaisie,* and by the same reason easily persuaded that she would not keep to it beyond the first night. They did not see each other therefore until the morrow, and after they were dressed. It was lucky that by the Spanish custom no one was permitted to be present when the newly-married pair went to bed; or this affair, which went no further than the young couple,

Madame des Ursins, and one or two domestics, might have made a very unpleasant noise.

Madame des Ursins consulted with two of the courtiers, as to the best measures to be adopted with a child who showed so much force and resolution. The night was passed in exhortations and in promises upon what had occurred at the supper; and the Queen consented at last to remain Queen. The Duke of Medina-Sidonia and Count San Estevan were consulted on the morrow. They were of opinion that in his turn the King, in order to mortify her and reduce her to terms, should not visit the Queen on the following night. This opinion was acted upon. The King and Queen did not see each other in private that day. In the evening the Queen was very sorry. Her pride and her little vanity were wounded; perhaps also she had found the King to her taste.

The ladies and the grand seigneurs who had attended at the supper were lectured for what had occurred there. Excuses, promises, demands for pardon, followed; all was put right; the third day was tranquil, and the third night still more agreeable to the young people. On the fourth day they went to Barcelona, where only *fêtes* and pleasures awaited them. Soon after they set out for Madrid.

At the commencement of the following year (1702), it was resolved, after much debate, at our court, that Philip V. should make a journey to Italy, and on Easter-day he set out. He went to Naples, Leghorn, Milan, and Alessandria. While at the first-named place a conspiracy which had been hatching against his life was discovered, and put down. But other things which previously occurred in Italy ought to have been related before. I must therefore return to them now.

From the moment that Philip V. ascended the Spanish throne it was seen that a war was certain. England maintained for some time an obstinate silence, refusing to acknowledge the new King; the Dutch secretly murmured against him, and the Emperor openly prepared for battle. Italy, it was evident at once, would be the spot on which hostilities would commence, and our King lost no time in taking measures to be ready for events. By land and by sea every preparation was made for the struggle about to take place.

After some time the war, waited for and expected by all Europe, at last broke out, by some Imperialist troops firing upon a handful of men near Albaredo. One Spaniard was killed, and all the rest of the men were taken prisoners. The Imperialists would not give them up until a cartel was arranged. The King, upon hearing this, at once despatched the general officers to Italy. Our troops were to be commanded by Catinat, under M. de Savoie; and the Spanish troops by Vaudemont, who was Governor-General of the Milanese, and to whom, and his dislike to our King, I have before alluded.

Vaudemont at once began to plot to overthrow Catinat, in conjunction with Tessé, who had expected the command, and who was irritated because it had not been given to him. They were in communication with Chamillart, Minister of War, who aided them, as did other friends at Court, to be hereafter named, in carrying out their object. It was all the more easy because they had to do with a man who depended for support solely upon his own talent, and whose virtue and simplicity raised him above all intrigue and scheming; and who, with much ability and intelligence, was severe in command, very laconic, disinterested, and of exceeding pure life.

Prince Eugène commanded the army of the Emperor in Italy. The first two generals under him, in order of rank, were allied with Vaudemont: one, in fact, was his only son; the other was the son of a friend of his. The least reflection ought to have opened all eyes to the conduct of Vaudemont, and to have discerned it to be more than suspicious. Catinat soon found it out. He could plan nothing against the enemy that they did not learn immediately; and he never attempted any movement without finding himself opposed by a force more than double his own; so gross was this treachery.

Catinat often complained of this: he sent word of it to the Court, but without daring to draw any conclusion from what happened. Nobody sustained him at Court, for Vaudemont had everybody in his favour. He captured our general officers by his politeness, his magnificence, and, above all, by presenting them with abundant supplies. All the useful, and the agreeable, came from his side; all the dryness, all the exactitude, came from Catinat. It need not be asked which of the two had all hearts. In fine, Tessé and Vaudemont carried out their schemes so well that Catinat could do nothing.

While these schemes were going on, the Imperialists were enabled to gain time, to strengthen themselves, to cross the rivers without obstacle, to approach us; and, acquainted with everything as they were, to attack a portion of our army on the 9th July, at Capri, with five regiments of cavalry and dragoons. Prince Eugène led this attack without his coming being in the least degree suspected, and fell suddenly upon our troops. Tessé, who was in the immediate neighbourhood with some dragoons, advanced rapidly upon hearing this, but only with a few dragoons. A long resistance was made, but at last retreat became necessary. It was accomplished in excellent order, and without disturbance from the enemy; but our loss was very great, many officers of rank being among the dead.

Such was our first exploit in Italy; all the fault of which was attributed to Catinat. Tessé and Vaudemont did everything in their power to secure his disgrace. The King, indeed, thus prejudiced against Catinat, determined to take from him the command, and appointed the Maréchal de Villeroy as his successor. The surprise of everybody at this was very great, for no one expected that the Maréchal de Villeroy would repair the fault of Catinat. On the evening of his appointment, this general was exposed in a very straightforward and public manner by M. de Duras. He did not like the Maréchal de Villeroy; and, while everybody else was applauding, took the Maréchal by the arm, and said, " Monsieur le Maréchal, everybody is paying you compliments upon your departure to Italy, I keep mine until you return;" and then, bursting out laughing, he looked round upon the company. Villeroy remained confounded, without offering a word. Everybody smiled and looked down. The King took no notice.

Catinat, when the command was taken out of his hands by the Maréchal de Villeroy, made himself admired on every side by the moderation and tranquillity with which he conducted himself. If Vaudemont was satisfied with the success of his schemes, it was far otherwise with Tessé, who had merely intrigued against Catinat for the purpose of obtaining the command of the army. He did all in his power to ingratiate himself into the favour of the Maréchal de Villeroy; but the Maréchal received these advances very coldly. Tessé's schemes against Catinat were beginning to be scented out; he was accused of having wished the Imperialists to succeed at Capri, and of indirectly aiding them by keeping back his troops; his tirades against Catinat, too, made him suspected. The Maréchal de Villeroy would have nothing to do with him. His conduct was contrasted with that of Catinat, who, free after his fall to retire from the army, continued to remain there, with rare modesty, interfering in nothing.

The first campaign passed without notable incident, except an unsuccessful attack upon Chiari, by our troops on the 1st of September. M. de Savoie led the attack; but was so firmly met by Prince Eugène, who was in an excellent position for defence, that he could do nothing, and in the end was compelled to retire disgracefully. We lost five or six colonels and many men, and had a large number wounded. This action much astonished our army, and encouraged that of the enemy, who did almost as they wished during the rest of the campaign.

Towards the end of this campaign, the grand airs of familiarity which the Maréchal de Villeroy gave himself with M. de Savoie drew upon him a cruel rebuke, not to say an affront. M. de Savoie being in the midst of all the generals and of the flower of the army, opened, while talking, his snuff-box, and was about to take a pinch of snuff, when M. de Villeroy, who was standing near, stretched out his hand and put it into the box without saying a word. M. de Savoie flushed up, and instantly threw all the snuff upon the ground, gave the box to one of his attendants, and told him to fill it again. The Maréchal, not knowing what to do with himself, swallowed his shame without daring to say a word, M. de Savoie continuing the conversation that he had not interrupted, except to ask for the fresh snuff.

The campaign passed away, our troops always retreating, the Imperialists always gaining ground; they continually increasing in numbers; we diminishing little by little every day. The Maréchal de Villeroy and Prince Eugène each took up his winter quarters and crossed the frontier: M. de Savoie returned to Turin, and Catinat went to Paris. The King received him well, but spoke of nothing but unimportant matters, and gave him no private audience, nor did he ask for one.

Prince Eugène, who was more knowing than the Maréchal de Villeroy, had obliged him to winter in the midst of the Milanese, and kept him closely pressed there, while his own troops enjoyed perfect liberty, by means of which they much disturbed ours. In this advantageous situation, Prince Eugène conceived the design of surprising the centre of our quarters, and by that blow to make himself master of our positions, and afterwards of Milan, and other places of the country, all in very bad order; thus finishing effectively and suddenly his conquest.

Cremona was our centre, and it was defended by a strong garrison. Prince Eugène ascertained that there was at Cremona an ancient aqueduct which extended far out into the country, and which started from the town in the vault of a house occupied by a priest. He also learnt that this aqueduct had been recently cleaned, but that it carried very little water, and that in former times the town had been surprised by means of it. He caused the entrance of the aqueduct, in the country, to be reconnoitred, he gained over the priest in whose vault it ended, and who lived close to one of the gates of the city, which was walled up and but little guarded; he sent into Cremona as many chosen soldiers as he could, disguised as priests or peasants, and these hiding themselves in the house of the friendly priest, obtained secretly as many axes as they could. Then the Prince despatched five hundred picked men and officers to march by the aqueduct to the priest's vault;

he put Thomas de Vaudemont, son of the Governor-General of the Milanese, at the head of a large detachment of troops, with orders to occupy a redoubt that defended the Po, and to come by the bridge to his assistance, when the struggle commenced in the town; and he charged the soldiers secreted in the priest's house to break down the walled-up gate, so as to admit the troops whom he would lead there.

Everything, thus concerted with exactness, was executed with precision, and with all possible secrecy and success. It was on the 1st of February, 1702, at break of day, that the surprise was attempted. The Maréchal de Villeroy had only arrived in the town on the previous night. The first person who got scent of what was going forward was the cook of the Lieutenant-General Crenan, who going out in the early morning to buy provisions, saw the streets full of soldiers, whose uniforms were unknown to him. He ran back and awakened his master. Neither he nor his valets would believe what the cook said, but nevertheless Crenan hurriedly dressed himself, went out, and was only too soon convinced that it was true.

At the same time, by a piece of good luck, which proved the saving of Cremona, a regiment under the command of D'Entragues, drew up in battle array in one of the public places. D'Entragues was a bold and skilful soldier, with a great desire to distinguish himself. He wished to review this regiment, and had commenced business before the dawn. While the light was still uncertain and feeble, and his battalions were under arms, he indistinctly perceived infantry troops forming at the end of the street, in front of him. He knew by the orders given on the previous evening that no other review was to take place except his own. He immediately feared, therefore, some surprise, marched at once to these troops, whom he found to be Imperialists, charged them, overthrew them, sustained the shock of the fresh troops which arrived, and kept up a defence so obstinate, that he gave time to all the town to awake, and to the majority of the troops to take up arms. Without him, all would have been slaughtered as they slept.

Just at dawn the Maréchal de Villeroy, already up and dressed, was writing in his chamber. He heard a noise, called for a horse, and followed by a single aide-de-camp and a page, threaded his way through the streets to the grand place, which is always the rendezvous in case of alarm. At the turning of one of the streets he fell into the midst of an Imperialist *corps de garde*, who surrounded him and arrested him. Feeling that it was impossible to defend himself, the Maréchal de Villeroy whispered his name to the officer, and promised him ten thousand pistoles, a regiment, and the grandest recompenses from the King, to be allowed to escape. The officer was, however, above all bribes, said he had not served the Emperor so long in order to end by betraying him, and conducted the Maréchal de Villeroy to Prince Eugène, who did not receive him so well as he himself would have been received, under similar circumstances, by the Maréchal. While in the *suite* of Prince Eugène, Villeroy saw Crenan led in prisoner, and wounded to the death, and exclaimed that he should like to be in his place. A moment after they were both sent out of the town, and passed the day, guarded, in the coach of Prince Eugène.

Revel, become commander-in-chief by the capture of the Maréchal de Villeroy, tried to rally the troops. There was a fight in every street; the troops dispersed about, some in detachments, several scarcely armed; some only in their shirts fought with the greatest bravery. They were driven at last to the ramparts, where they had time to look about them, to rally and form themselves. If the enemy had not allowed our troops time to gain the ramparts, or if they had driven them beyond this position, when they reached it, the town could never have held out. But the Imperialists kept themselves entirely towards the centre of the town, and made no effort to fall upon our men, or to drive them from the ramparts.

Praslin, who had the command of our cavalry, put himself at the head of some Irish battalions which under him did wonders. Although continually occupied in defending and attacking, Praslin conceived the idea that the safety of Cremona depended upon the destruction of the bridge of the Po, so that the Imperialists could not receive reinforcements from that point. He repeated this so many times, that Revel was informed of it, and ordered Praslin to do what he thought most advisable in the matter. Thereupon, Praslin instantly commanded the bridge to be broken down. There was not a moment to lose. Thomas de Vaudemont was already approaching the bridge at the head of his troops. But the bridge, nevertheless, was destroyed before his eyes, and with all his musketeers he was not able to prevent it.

It was now three o'clock in the afternoon. Prince Eugène was at the Hôtel de Ville, swearing in the magistrates. Leaving that place, and finding that his troops were giving way, he ascended the cathedral steeple to see what was passing in different parts of the town, and to discover why the troops of Thomas de Vaudemont did not arrive. He had scarcely reached the top of the steeple, when he saw his detachments on the banks of the Po, and the bridge broken, thus rendering their assistance useless. He was not more satisfied with what he discovered in every other direction. Furious at seeing his enterprise in such bad case, after having been so nearly successful, he descended, tearing his hair and yelling. From that time, although superior in force, he thought of nothing but retreat.

Revel, who saw that his troops were overwhelmed by hunger, fatigue, and wounds, for since the break of day they had had no repose or leisure, thought on his side of withdrawing his men into the castle of Cremona, in order, at least, to defend himself under cover, and to obtain a capitulation. So that the two opposing chiefs each thought at one and the same time of retreat.

Towards the evening therefore the combat slackened on both sides, until our troops made a last effort to drive the enemy from one of the gates of the town; so as to have that gate free and open during the night to let in assistance. The Irish seconded so well this attack, that it was at length successful. A tolerably long calm succeeded this last struggle. Revel, nevertheless, thought of withdrawing his troops to the castle, when Mahony, an Irish officer who had fought bravely as a lion all day, proposed to go and see what was passing all around. It was already growing dark; the reconnoiterers profited by this. They saw that everything was tranquil, and understood that the enemy had retreated. This grand news was carried to Revel, who, with many around him, was a long time in believing it. Persuaded at last, he left everything as it was then, until broad daylight, when he found that the enemy had gone, and that the streets and public places were filled with the wounded, the dying, and the dead. He made arrangements for everything, and despatched Mahony to the King.

Prince Eugène retreated all that night with the detachment he had led, and made the Maréchal de Villeroy, disarmed and badly mounted, follow him, very indecently. The Maréchal was afterwards sent to Gratz in Styria. Crenan died in the coach of the Maréchal de Villeroy. D'Entragues, to whose valour the safety of Cremona was owing, did not survive this glorious day. Our loss was great; that of the enemy greater.

The news of this, the most surprising event that has been heard of in recent ages, was brought to the King at Marly on the 9th of February, 1702, by Mahony. Soon after it arrived I heard of it, and at once hastened to the château, where I found a great buzzing and several groups of people talking. Mahony was closeted a long time with the King. At the end of an hour the King came out of his cabinet, and spoke strongly in praise of what had occurred. He took pleasure in dwelling at great length upon Mahony, and declared that he had never heard anybody give such a clear and good account of an occurrence as he. The King kindly added that he should bestow a thousand francs a year upon Mahony, and a brevet of Colonel.

In the evening M. le Prince de Conti told me that the King had decorated Revel, and made Praslin Lieutenant-General. As the latter was one of my particular friends, this intelligence gave me much joy. I asked again to be more sure of the news. The other principal officers were advanced in proportion to their grades, and many received pensions.

As for the Maréchal de Villeroy he was treated as those who excite envy and then become unfortunate are always treated. The King, however, openly took his part; and in truth it was no fault of the Maréchal, who had arrived at Cremona the day before the surprise, that he was taken prisoner directly he set his foot in the street. How could he know of the aqueduct, the barred-up gate, and the concealed soldiers? Nevertheless, his friends were plunged into the greatest grief, and his wife, who had not been duped by the *éclat* which accompanied her husband upon his departure for Italy, but who feared for the result, was completely overwhelmed, and for a long time could not be prevailed upon to see anybody.

M. de Vendôme was appointed successor to M. de Villeroy, in command of the army in Italy.

CHAPTER XX

BUT it is time now for me to go back to other matters, and to start again from the commencement of 1701, from which I have been led by reciting, in a continuous story, the particulars of our first campaign in Italy.

Barbezieux had viewed with discontent the elevation of Chamillart. His pride and presumption rose in arms against it; but as there was no remedy he gave himself up to debauch, to dissipate his annoyance. He had built between Versailles and Vaucresson, at the end of the park of Saint Cloud, a house in the open fields, called l'Etang, which though in the dismallest position in the world had cost him millions. He went there to feast and riot with his friends; and committing excesses above his strength, was seized with a fever, and died in a few days, looking death steadily in the face. He was told of his approaching end by the Archbishop of Rheims; for he would not believe Fagon.

He was thirty-three years of age, with a striking and expressive countenance, and much wit and aptitude for labour. He was remarkable for grace, fine manners, and winning ways; but his pride and ambition were excessive, and when his fits of ill-temper came, nothing could repress them. Resistance always excited and irritated him. He had accustomed the King—whenever he had drunk too much, or when a party of pleasure was toward—to put off work to another time. It was a great question, whether the State gained or lost most by his death?

As soon as he was dead, Saint-Pouange went to Marly to tell the news to the King, who was so prepared for it that two hours before, starting from Versailles, he had left La Vrillière behind to put the seals everywhere. Fagon, who had condemned him at once, had never loved him or his father, and was accused of overbleeding him on purpose. At any rate he allowed, at one of his last visits, expressions of joy to escape him because recovery was impossible. Barbezieux used to annoy people very much by answering aloud when they spoke to him in whispers, and by keeping visitors waiting whilst he was playing with his dogs or some base parasite.

Many people, especially divers beautiful ladies, lost much by his death. Some of the latter looked very disconsolate in the *salon* at Marly; but when they had gone to table, and the cake had been cut (it was Twelfth Night), the King manifested a joy which seemed to command imitation. He was not content with exclaiming " The Queen drinks," but as in a common wine-shop, he clattered his spoon and fork on his plate, and made others do so likewise, which caused a strange din, that lasted at intervals all through the supper. The snivellers made more noise than the others, and uttered louder screams of laughter; and the nearest relatives and best friends were still more riotous. On the morrow all signs of grief had disappeared.

Chamillart was appointed in the place of Barbezieux, as Secretary of State; and wanted to give up the Finance, but the King, remembering the disputes of Louvois and Colbert, insisted on his occupying both posts. Chamillart was a very worthy man, with clean hands and the best intentions, polite, patient, obliging, a good friend, and a moderate enemy, loving his country, but his King better; and on very good terms with him and Madame de Maintenon. His mind was limited and, like all persons of little wit and knowledge, he was obstinate and pig-headed—smiling affectedly with a gentle compassion on whoever opposed reasons to his, but utterly incapable of understanding them—consequently a dupe in friendship, in business, in everything; governed by all who could manage to win his admiration, or on very slight grounds could claim his affection. His capacity was small, and yet he believed he knew everything, which was the more pitiable, as all this came to him with his places, and arose more from stupidity than presumption—not at all from vanity, of which he was divested. The most remarkable thing is that the chief origin of the King's tender regard for him was this very incapacity. He used to confess it to the King at every opportunity; and the King took pleasure in directing and instructing him, so that he was interested in his successes as if they had been his own, and always excused him. The world and the Court excused him also, charmed by the facility with which he received people, the pleasure he felt in granting requests and rendering services, the gentleness and regretfulness of his refusals, and his indefatigable patience as a listener. His memory was so great that he remembered all matters submitted to him, which gave pleasure to people who were afraid of being forgotten. He wrote excellently; and his clear, flowing, and precise style was extremely pleasing to the King and Madame de Maintenon, who were never weary of praising him, encouraging him, and congratulating themselves for having placed upon such weak shoulders two burdens, each of which was sufficient to overwhelm the most sturdy.

Rose, secretary in the King's cabinet, died, aged about eighty-six, at the commencement of the year (1701). For nearly fifty years he had held the office of the "pen," as it is called. To have the "pen," is to be a public forger, and to do what would cost anybody else his life. This office consists in imitating so exactly the handwriting of the King, that the real cannot be distinguished from the counterfeit. In this manner are written all the letters that the King ought or wishes to write with his own hand, but which, nevertheless, he will not take the trouble to write. Sovereigns and people of high rank, even generals and others of importance, employ a secretary of this kind. It is not possible to make a great King speak with more dignity than did Rose; nor with more fitness to each person, and upon every subject. The King signed all the letters Rose wrote, and the characters were so alike it was impossible to find the smallest difference. Many important things had passed through the hands of Rose. He was extremely faithful and secret, and the King put entire trust in him.

Rose was artful, scheming, adroit, and dangerous. There are stories without number of him; and I will relate one or two solely because they characterise him, and those to whom they also relate.

He had, near Chantilly, a nice house and grounds that he much liked, and that he often visited. This little property bordered the estate of M. le Prince, who, not liking so close a neighbour, wished to get rid of him. M. le Prince endeavoured to induce Rose to give up his house and grounds, but all to no effect; and at last tried to annoy him in various ways into acquiescence. Among other of his tricks, he put about four hundred foxes, old and young, into Rose's park. It may be imagined what disorder this company made there, and the surprise of Rose and his servants at an inexhaustible ant-hill of foxes come in one night!

The worthy fellow, who was anger and vehemence itself, knew only too well who had treated him thus scurvily, and straightway went to the King, requesting to be allowed to ask him rather a rough question. The King, quite accustomed to him and to his jokes, for he was pleasant and very witty, demanded what was the matter.

"What is the matter, Sire?" replied Rose, with a face all flushed. "Why, I beg you will tell me if we have two Kings in France?"

"What do you mean?" said the King, surprised, and flushing in his turn.

"What I mean, Sire, is, that if M. le Prince is King like you, folks must weep and lower their heads before that tyrant. If he is only Prince of the blood, I ask justice from you, Sire, for you owe it to all your subjects, and you ought not to suffer them to be the prey of M. le Prince," said Rose; and he related everything that had taken place, concluding with the adventure of the foxes.

The King promised that he would speak to M. le Prince in a manner to insure the future repose of Rose; and, indeed, he ordered all the foxes to be removed from the worthy man's park, all the damages they had made to be repaired, and all the expenses incurred to be paid by M. le Prince. M. le Prince was too good a courtier to fail in obeying this order, and never afterwards troubled Rose in the least thing; but, on the contrary, made all the advances towards a reconciliation. Rose was obliged to receive them, but held himself aloof, nevertheless, and continually let slip some raillery against M. le Prince. I and fifty others were one day witnesses of this.

M. le Prince was accustomed to pay his court to the ministers as they stood waiting to attend the council in the King's chamber; and although he had nothing to say, spoke to them with the mien of a client obliged to fawn. One morning, when there was a large assembly of the Court in this chamber, and M. le Prince had been cajoling the ministers with much suppleness and flattery, Secretary Rose, who saw what had been going on, went up to him on a sudden, and said aloud, putting one finger under his closed eye, as was sometimes his habit, " Sir, I have seen your scheming here with all these gentlemen, and for several days; it is not for nothing. I have known the Court and mankind many years; and am not to be imposed upon: I see clearly where matters point:" and this with turns and inflections of voice which thoroughly embarrassed M. le Prince, who defended himself as he could. Every one crowded to hear what was going on; and at last Rose, taking M. le Prince respectfully by his arm, said, with a cunning and meaning smile, " Is it not that you wish to be made first Prince of the blood royal?" Then he turned on his heel, and slipped off. The Prince was stupefied; and all present tried in vain to restrain their laughter.

Rose had never pardoned M. de Duras an ill turn the latter had served him. During one of the Court journeys, the carriage in which Rose was riding broke down. He took a horse; but, not being a good equestrian, was very soon pitched into a hole full of mud. While there M. de Duras passed, and Rose from the midst of the mire cried for help. But M. de Duras, instead of giving assistance, looked from his coach-window, burst out laughing, and cried out: " What a luxurious horse thus to roll upon *Roses!*"—and with this witticism passed gently on through the mud. The next comer, the Duc de Coislin, was more charitable; he picked up the worthy man, who was so furious, so carried away by anger, that it was some time before he could say who he was. But the worst was to come; for M. de Duras, who feared nobody, and whose tongue was accustomed to wag as freely as that of

Rose, told the story to the King and to all the Court, who much laughed at it. This outraged Rose to such a point, that he never afterwards approached M. de Duras, and only spoke of him in fury. Whenever he hazarded some joke upon M. de Duras, the King began to laugh, and reminded him of the mud-ducking he had received.

Towards the end of his life, Rose married his granddaughter, who was to be his heiress, to Portail, since Chief President of the Parliament. The marriage was not a happy one; the young spouse despised her husband; and said that instead of entering into a good house, she had remained at the *portal*. At last her husband and his father complained to Rose. He paid no attention at first; but, tired out at last, said if his granddaughter persisted in her bad conduct, he would disinherit her. There were no complaints after this.

Rose was a little man, neither fat nor lean, with a tolerably handsome face, keen expression, piercing eyes sparkling with cleverness; a little cloak, a satin skull-cap over his grey hairs, a smooth collar, almost like an Abbé's, and his pocket-handkerchief always between his coat and his vest. He used to say that it was nearer his nose there. He had taken me into his friendship. He laughed very freely at the foreign princes; and always called the Dukes with whom he was familiar, "Your Ducal Highness," in ridicule of the sham Highnesses. He was extremely neat and brisk, and full of sense to the last; he was a sort of personage.

CHAPTER XXI

ON Saturday, the 19th of March, in the evening, the King was about to undress himself, when he heard cries in his chamber, which was full of courtiers; everybody calling for Fagon and Felix. Monseigneur had been taken very ill. He had passed the day at Meudon, where he had eaten only a collation; at the King's supper he had made amends by gorging himself nigh to bursting with fish. He was a great eater, like the King, and like the Queens his mother and grandmother. He had not appeared after supper, but had just gone down to his own room from the King's cabinet, and was about to undress himself, when all at once he lost consciousness. His valets, frightened out of their wits, and some courtiers who were near, ran to the King's chambers, to his chief physician and his chief surgeon with the hubbub which I have mentioned above. The King, all unbuttoned, started to his feet immediately, and descended by a little dark, narrow, and steep staircase towards the chamber of Monseigneur. Madame la Duchesse de Bourgogne arrived at the same time, and in an instant the chamber, which was vast, was filled.

They found Monseigneur half naked: his servants endeavouring to make him walk erect, and dragging rather than leading him about. He did not know the King, who spoke to him, nor anybody else; and defended himself as long as he could against Felix, who, in this pressing necessity, hazarded bleeding him, and succeeded. Consciousness returned. Monseigneur asked for a confessor; the King had already sent for the curé. Many emetics were given to him: but two hours passed before they operated. At half-past two in the morning, no further danger appearing, the King, who had shed tears, went to bed, leaving orders that he was to be awakened if any fresh accident happened. At five o'clock, however, all the effect having passed, the doctors went away, and made everybody leave the sick chamber. During the night all Paris hastened thither. Monseigneur was compelled to keep his room for eight or ten days; and took care in future not to gorge himself so much with food. Had this accident happened a quarter of an hour later, the chief *valet de chambre,* who slept in his room, would have found him dead in his bed.

Paris loved Monseigneur, perhaps because he often went to the opera. The fish-fags of the Halles thought it would be proper to exhibit their affection, and deputed four stout gossips to wait upon him: they were admitted. One of them took him round the neck and kissed him on both cheeks; the others kissed his hand. They were all very well received. Bontems showed them over the apartments, and treated them to a dinner. Monseigneur gave them some money, and the King did so also. They determined not to remain in debt, and had a fine *Te Deum* sung at Saint Eustache, and then feasted.

For some time past Monsieur had been sorely grieved that his son, M. le Duc de Chartres, had not been appointed to the command of an army. When M. de Chartres married, the King, who had converted his nephew by force into a son-in-law, promised him all kinds of favours; but except those which were written down in black and white had not given him any. M. de Chartres, annoyed at this, and at the manner in which the illegitimate children were promoted over his head, had given himself up to all kinds of youthful follies and excesses. The King was surprised to find Monsieur agree with his son's ambition; but gave a flat refusal when overtures were made to him on the subject. All hope of rising to a high command was thus forbidden to the Duc de Chartres; so that Madame had a fine excuse for sneering at the weakness which had been shown by Monsieur, who, on his part, had long before repented of it. He winked, therefore, at all the escapades performed or threatened by his son, and said nothing, not being sorry that the King should become uneasy, which was soon the case.

The King at last spoke to Monsieur; and being coldly received, reproached him for not knowing how to exercise authority over his son. Upon this Monsieur fired up; and, quite as much from foregone decision as from anger, in his turn asked the King what was to be done with a son at such an age: who was sick of treading the galleries of Versailles and the pavement of the Court; of being married as he was, and of remaining, as it were, naked, whilst his brothers-in-law were clothed in dignities, governments, establishments, and offices,—against all policy and all example. His son, he said, was worse off than any one in the King's service, for all others could earn distinction; added, that idleness was the mother of all vice, and that it gave him much pain to see his only son abandon himself to debauchery and bad company; but that it would be cruel to blame a young man, forced as it were into these follies, and to say nothing against him by whom he was thus forced.

Who was astonished to hear this straightforward language? Why, the King. Monsieur had never let out to within a thousand leagues of this tone, which was only the more annoying because supported by unanswerable reasons that did not convince. Mastering his embarrassment, however, the King answered as a brother rather than as a sovereign; endeavouring, by gentle words, to calm the excitement of Monsieur. But Monsieur was stung to the quick by the King's neglect of M. de Chartres, and would not be pacified; yet the real subject of the annoyance was never once alluded to, whilst the one kept it steadily in his mind, and the other was determined not to yield. The conversation lasted very long, and was pushed very far; Monsieur throughout taking the high tone, the King very gentle. They separated in this manner,—Monsieur frowning, but not daring to burst out; the King annoyed, but not wishing to estrange his brother, much less to let their squabble be known.

As Monsieur passed most of his summers at Saint Cloud, the separation which this occasioned put them at their ease whilst waiting for a reconciliation; and Monsieur came less often than before, but when he did filled all their private interviews with bitter talk. In public little or nothing appeared, except that familiar people remarked politeness and attention on the King's part, coldness on that of Monsieur—moods not common to either. Nevertheless, being advised not to push matters too far, he read a lecture to his son, and made him change his conduct by degrees. But Monsieur still remained irritated against the King; and this completely upset him, accustomed as he always had been to live on the best of terms with his brother, and to be treated by him in every respect as such—except that the King would not allow Monsieur to become a great personage.

Ordinarily, whenever Monsieur or Madame were unwell, even if their little finger ached, the King visited them at once; and continued his visits if the sickness lasted. But now, Madame had been laid up for six weeks with a tertian fever, for which she would do nothing, because she treated herself in her German fashion, and despised physic and doctors. The King, who, besides the affair of M. le Duc de Chartres, was secretly angered with her, as will presently be seen, had not been to see her, although Monsieur had urged him to do so during those flying visits which he made to Versailles without sleeping there. This was taken by Monsieur, who was ignorant of the private cause of indignation alluded to, for a public mark of extreme disrespect; and being proud and sensitive he was piqued thereby to the last degree.

He had other mental troubles to torment him. For some time past he had had a confessor who, although a Jesuit, kept as tight a hand over him as he could. He was a gentleman of good birth, and of Brittany, by name le Père du Trévoux. He forbade Monsieur not only certain strange pleasures, but many which he thought he could innocently indulge in as a penance for his past life. He often told him that he had no mind to be damned on his account; and that if he was thought too harsh let another confessor be appointed. He also told him to take great care of himself, as he was old, worn out with debauchery, fat, short-necked, and, according to all appearance, likely to die soon of apoplexy. These were terrible words to a prince the most voluptuous and the most attached to life that had been seen for a long time; who had always passed his days in the most luxurious idleness and who was the most incapable by nature of all serious application, of all serious reading, and of all self-examination. He was afraid of the devil; and he remembered that his former confessor had resigned for similar reasons as this new one was actuated by. He was forced now, therefore, to look a little into himself, and to live in a manner that, for him, might be considered rigid. From time to time he said many prayers; he obeyed his confessor, and rendered an account to him of the con-

duct he had prescribed in respect to play and many
other things, and patiently suffered his confessor's
long discourses. He became sad, dejected, and spoke
less than usual—that is to say, only about as much
as three or four women—so that everybody soon saw
this great change. It would have been strange if all
these troubles together had not made a great revolution in a man like Monsieur, full-bodied, and a great
eater, not only at meals, but all the day.

On Thursday, the 8th of June, he went from Saint
Cloud to dine with the King at Marly; and, as was
his custom, entered the cabinet as soon as the Council of State went out. He found the King angry with
M. de Chartres for neglecting his wife, and allowing
her to seek consolation for this neglect in the society
of others. M. de Chartres was at that time enamoured
of Mademoiselle de Sary, maid of honour to Madame,
and carried on his suit in the most open and flagrant
manner. The King took this for his theme, and very
stiffly reproached Monsieur for the conduct of his son.
Monsieur, who needed little to exasperate him, tartly
replied, that fathers who had led certain lives had little
authority over their children, and little right to blame
them. The King, who felt the point of the answer, fell
back on the patience of his daughter, and said that at
least she ought not to be allowed to see the truth so
clearly. But Monsieur was resolved to have his fling,
and recalled, in the most aggravating manner, the conduct the King had adopted towards his Queen, with
respect to his mistresses, even allowing the latter to
accompany him in his journeys—the Queen at his side,
and all in the same coach. This last remark drove the
King beyond all patience, and he redoubled his reproaches, so that presently both were shouting to each
other at the top of their voices. The door of the
room in which they wrangled was open, and only cov-

ered by a curtain, as was the custom at Marly, and the adjoining room was full of courtiers, waiting to see the King go by to dinner. On the other side was a little *salon*, devoted to very private purposes, and filled with valets, who could hear distinctly every word of what passed. The attendant without, upon hearing this noise, entered, and told the King how many people were within hearing, and immediately retired. The conversation did not stop, however; it was simply carried on in a lower tone. Monsieur continued his reproaches; said that the King, in marrying his daughter to M. de Chartres, had promised marvels, and had done nothing; that for his part he had wished his son to serve, to keep him out of the way of these intrigues, but that his demands had been vain; that it was no wonder M. de Chartres amused himself, by way of consolation, for the neglect he had been treated with. Monsieur added, that he saw only too plainly the truth of what had been predicted, namely, that he would have all the shame and dishonour of the marriage without ever deriving any profit from it. The King, more and more carried away by anger, replied, that the war would soon oblige him to make some retrenchments, and that he would commence by cutting down the pensions of Monsieur, since he showed himself so little accommodating.

At this moment the King was informed that his dinner was ready, and both he and Monsieur left the room and went to table,—Monsieur, all fury, flushed, and with eyes inflamed by anger. His face thus crimsoned induced some ladies who were at table, and some courtiers behind—but more for the purpose of saying something than anything else—to make the remark, that Monsieur, by his appearance, had great need of bleeding. The same thing had been said some time before at Saint Cloud; he was absolutely too full; and, indeed, he had himself admitted that it was true. Even the King, in spite of their squabbles, had more than once pressed him to consent. But Tancrede, his head surgeon, was old, and an unskilful bleeder: he had missed fire once. Monsieur would not be bled by him; and not to vex him was good enough to refuse being bled by another, and to die in consequence.

Upon hearing this observation about bleeding, the King spoke to him again on the subject; and said that he did not know what prevented him from having him at once taken to his room, and bled by force. The dinner passed in the ordinary manner; and Monsieur ate extremely, as he did at all his meals, to say nothing of an abundant supply of chocolate in the morning, and what he swallowed all day in the shape of fruit, pastry, preserves, and every kind of dainties, with which indeed the tables of his cabinets and his pockets were always filled.

Upon rising from the table, the King, in his carriage, alone went to Saint Germain, to visit the King and Queen of England. Other members of the family went there likewise separately; and Monsieur, after going there also, returned to Saint Cloud.

In the evening, after supper, the King was in his cabinet, with Monseigneur and the Princesses, as at Versailles, when a messenger came from Saint Cloud, and asked to see the King in the name of the Duc de Chartres. He was admitted into the cabinet, and said that Monsieur had been taken very ill while at supper; that he had been bled, that he was better, but that an emetic had been given to him. The fact was, Monsieur had supped as usual with the ladies, who were at Saint Cloud. During the meal, as he poured out a glass of liqueur for Madame de Bouillon, it was perceived that he stammered, and pointed at something with his hand. As it was customary with him sometimes to speak Spanish, some of the ladies asked what he said, others cried aloud. All this was the work of an instant, and immediately afterwards Monsieur fell in a fit of apoplexy upon M. de Chartres, who supported him. He was taken into his room, shaken, moved about, bled considerably, and had strong emetics administered to him, but scarcely any signs of life did he show.

Upon hearing this news, the King, who had been accustomed to fly to visit Monsieur for a mere nothing, went to Madame de Maintenon's, and had her waked up. He passed a quarter of an hour with her, and then, towards midnight, returning to his room, ordered his coach to be got ready, and sent the Marquis de Gesvres to Saint Cloud, to see if Monsieur was worse, in which case he was to return and wake him; and they went quickly to bed. Besides the particular relations in which they were at that time, I think that the King suspected some artifice; that he went in consequence to consult Madame de Maintenon, and preferred sinning against all laws of propriety to running the chance of being duped. Madame de Maintenon did not like Monsieur. She feared him. He paid her very little court, and despite all his timidity and his more than deference, observations escaped him at times, when he was with the King, which marked his disdain of her, and the shame that he felt of public opinion. She was not eager, therefore, to advise the King to go and visit him, still less to commence a journey by night,—the loss of rest, and the witnessing a spectacle so sad, and so likely to touch him, and make him make reflections on himself; for she hoped that if things went quietly he might be spared the trouble altogether.

A moment after the King had got into bed, a page came to say that Monsieur was better, and that he had just asked for some Schaffhausen water, which is excellent for apoplexy. An hour and a half later, another messenger came, awakened the King, and told him that the emetic had no effect, and that Monsieur was very ill. At this the King rose and set out at once. On the way he met the Marquis de Gesvres, who was coming to fetch him, and brought similar news. It may be imagined what a hubbub and disorder there was this night at Marly, and what horror at Saint Cloud, that palace of delight! Everybody who was at Marly hastened as he was best able to Saint Cloud. Whoever was first ready started together. Men and women jostled each other, and then threw themselves into the coaches without order and without regard to etiquette. Monseigneur was with Madame la Duchesse. He was so struck by what had occurred, and its resemblance to what he himself had experienced, that he could scarcely stand, and was dragged, almost carried, to the carriage, all trembling.

The King arrived at Saint Cloud before three o'clock in the morning. Monsieur had not had a moment's consciousness since his attack. A ray of intelligence came to him for an instant, while his confessor, Père du Trévoux, went to say mass, but it returned no more. The most horrible sights have often ridiculous contrasts. When the said confessor came back, he cried, "Monsieur, do you not know your confessor? Do you not know the good little Père du Trévoux, who is speaking to you?" and thus caused the less afflicted to laugh indecently.

The King appeared much moved; naturally he wept with great facility; he was, therefore, all tears. He had never had cause not to love his brother tenderly; although on bad terms with him for the last two months, these sad moments recalled all his tenderness; perhaps, too, he reproached himself for having hastened death by the scene of the morning. And finally, Monsieur was younger than he by two years, and all his life had enjoyed as good health as he, and better! The King heard mass at Saint Cloud; and, towards eight o'clock in the morning, Monsieur being past all hope, Madame de Maintenon and Madame la Duchesse de Bourgogne persuaded the King to stay no longer, and accordingly returned with him in his carriage to Marly. As he was going out and was showing some sign of affection to M. de Chartres—both weeping very much—that young Prince did not fail to take advantage of the opportunity. "Oh Sire!" he exclaimed, embracing the King's thighs, "what will become of me? I lose Monsieur, and I know that you do not like me." The King, surprised and much touched, embraced him, and said all the tender things he could.

On arriving at Marly, the King went with the Duchesse de Bourgogne to Madame de Maintenon. Three hours after came M. Fagon, who had been ordered not to leave Monsieur until he was dead or better—which could not be but by miracle. The King said, as soon as he saw him: "Well! M. Fagon, my brother is dead?" "Yes, Sire," said Fagon, "no remedy has taken effect."

The King wept a good deal. He was pressed to dine with Madame de Maintenon; but he would not do so, and had his dinner, as usual, with the ladies. The tears often ran down his cheek, during the meal, which was short. After this, he shut himself up in Madame de Maintenon's rooms until seven o'clock, and then took a turn in his garden. Afterwards he worked with Chamillart and Pontchartrain; and arranged all the funeral ceremonies of Monsieur. He supped an hour before his customary time, and went to bed soon afterwards.

At the departure from St. Cloud of the King, all the

crowd assembled there little by little withdrew, so that Monsieur dying, stretched upon a couch in his cabinet, remained exposed to the scullions and the lower officers of the household, the majority of whom, either by affection or interest, were much afflicted. The chief officers and others who lost posts and pensions filled the air with their cries; whilst all the women who were at Saint Cloud, and who lost their consideration and their amusement, ran here and there, crying, with dishevelled hair, like Bacchantes. The Duchesse de la Ferté, who had basely married her daughter to one of Monsieur's minions, named La Carte, came into the cabinet; and, whilst gazing on the Prince, who still palpitated there, exclaimed, giving vent to her profound reflections, "*Pardi!* Here is a daughter well married!"

"A very important matter!" cried Chatillon, who himself lost everything by this death. "Is this a moment to consider whether your daughter is well married or not?"

Madame, who had never had great affection or great esteem for Monsieur, but who felt her loss and her fall, meanwhile remained in her cabinet, and in the midst of her grief cried out, with all her might, "No convent! Let no one talk of a convent! I will have nothing to do with a convent!" The good Princess had not lost her judgment. She knew that, by her compact of marriage, she had to choose, on becoming a widow, between a convent and the château of Montargis. She liked neither alternative; but she had greater fear of the convent than of Montargis; and perhaps thought it would be easier to escape from the latter than the former. She knew she had much to fear from the King, although she did not yet know all, and although he had been properly polite to her, considering the occasion.

Next morning, Friday, M. de Chartres, came to the King, who was still in bed, and who spoke to him in a very friendly manner. He said that the Duke must for the future regard him as his father; that he would take care of his position and his interests; that he had forgotten all the little causes of anger he had had against him; that he hoped the Duke would also forget them; that he begged that the advances of friendship he made him might serve to attach him to him, and make their two hearts belong to one another again. It may easily be conceived how well M. de Chartres answered all this.

CHAPTER XXII

AFTER such a frightful spectacle as had been witnessed, so many tears and so much tenderness, nobody doubted that the three days which remained of the stay at Marly would be exceedingly sad. But, on the very morrow of the day on which Monsieur died, some ladies of the palace, upon entering the apartments of Madame de Maintenon, where was the King with the Duchesse de Bourgogne, about twelve o'clock, heard her from the chamber where they were, next to hers, singing opera tunes. A little while after, the King, seeing the Duchesse de Bourgogne very sad in a corner of the room, asked Madame de Maintenon, with surprise, why the said Duchess was so melancholy; set himself to work to rouse her; then played with her and some ladies of the palace he had called in to join in the sport. This was not all. Before rising from the dinner table, at a little after two o'clock, and twenty-six hours after the death of Monsieur, Monseigneur the Duc de Bourgogne asked the Duc de Montfort if he would play at *brelan*.

"At *brelan!*" cried Montfort, in extreme astonishment; "you cannot mean it! Monsieur is still warm."

"Pardon me," replied the Prince, "I do mean it though. The King does not wish that we should be dull here at Marly, and has ordered me to make everybody play; and, for fear that nobody should dare to begin, to set, myself, the example;" and with this he began to play at *brelan;* and the *salon* was soon filled with gaming tables.

Such was the affection of the King: such that of Madame de Maintenon! *She* felt the loss of Monsieur as a deliverance, and could scarcely restrain her joy; and it was with the greatest difficulty she succeeded in putting on a mournful countenance. She saw that the King was already consoled; nothing could therefore be more becoming than for her to divert him, and nothing suited her better than to bring things back into their usual course, so that there might be no more talk of Monsieur nor of affliction. For propriety of appearance she cared nothing. The thing could not fail, however, to be scandalous; and in whispers was found so. Monseigneur, though he had appeared to like Monsieur, who had given him all sorts of balls and amusements, and shown him every kind of attention and complaisance, went out wolf hunting the very day after his death; and, upon his return, finding play going on in the *salons,* went without hesitation and played himself like the rest. Monseigneur le Duc de Bourgogne and M. le Duc de Berry only saw Monsieur on public occasions, and therefore could not be much moved by his loss. But Madame la Duchesse was extremely touched by this event. He was her grandfather; and she tenderly loved her mother, who loved Monsieur; and Monsieur had always been very kind to her, and provided all kinds of diversion for her. Although not very loving to anybody, she loved Monsieur; and was much affected not to dare to show her grief, which she indulged a long time in private. What the grief of Madame was has already been seen.

As for M. de Chartres, he was much affected by his loss. The father and son loved each other extremely. Monsieur was a gentle and indulgent parent, who had never constrained his son. But if the Duke's heart was touched, his reason also was. Besides the great assistance it was to him to have a father, brother of the King, that father was, as it were, a barrier between him and the King, under whose hand he now found himself directly placed. His greatness, his consideration, the comfort of his house and his life, would, therefore, depend on him alone. Assiduity, propriety of conduct, a certain manner, and, above all, a very different deportment towards his wife, would now become the price of everything he could expect to obtain from the King. Madame la Duchesse de Chartres, although well treated by Monsieur, was glad to be delivered from him; for he was a barrier betwixt her and the King, that left her at the mercy of her husband. She was charmed to be quit of the duty of following Monsieur to Paris or Saint Cloud, where she found herself, as it were, in a foreign country, with faces which she never saw anywhere else, which did not make her welcome; and where she was exposed to the contempt and humour of Madame, who little spared her. She expected for the future never to leave the Court, and to be not only exempt from paying her court to Monsieur, but that Madame and her husband would for the future be obliged to treat her in quite another manner.

The bulk of the Court regretted Monsieur, for it was he who set all pleasure a-going; and when he left it, life and merriment seemed to have disappeared likewise. Setting aside his obstinacy with regard to the Princes, he loved the order of rank, preferences, and distinctions: he caused them to be observed as much as possible, and himself set the example. He loved great people; and was so affable and polite, that crowds came to him. The difference which he knew how to make, and which he never failed to make, between every one according to his position, contributed greatly to his popularity. In his receptions, by his greater or less, or more neglectful attention, and by his words, he always marked in a flattering manner the differences made by birth and dignity, by age and merit, and by profession; and all this with a dignity natural to him, and a constant facility which he had acquired. His familiarity obliged, and yet no rash people ever ventured to take advantage of it. He visited or sent exactly when it was proper; and under his roof he allowed a complete liberty, without injury to the respect shown him, or to a perfect court air. He had learned from the Queen his mother, and well remembered this art. The crowd, therefore, constantly flocked towards the Palais Royal.

At Saint Cloud, where all his numerous household used to assemble, there were many ladies who, to speak the truth, would scarcely have been received elsewhere, but many also of a higher set, and great store of gamblers. The pleasures of all kinds of games, and the singular beauty of the place, where a thousand calèches were always ready to whirl even the most lazy ladies through the walks, soft music and good cheer, made it a palace of delight, grace, and magnificence.

All this without any assistance from Madame, who dined and supped with the ladies and Monsieur, rode out sometimes in a calèche with one of them, often sulked with the company, made herself feared for her harsh and surly temper—frequently even for her words; and passed her days in a little cabinet she had chosen, where the windows were ten feet from the ground, gazing perpetually on the portraits of Paladins and other German princes, with which she had tapestried the walls; and writing every day with her own hand whole volumes of letters, of which she always kept autograph copies. Monsieur had never been able to bend her to a more human way of life; and lived decently with her, without caring for her person in any way.

For his part, Monsieur, who had very gallantly won the battle of Cassel, and who had always shown courage in the sieges where he had served, had only the bad qualities that distinguish women. With more knowledge of the world than wit, with no reading, though he had a vast and exact acquaintance with noble houses, their births and marriages, he was good for nothing. Nobody was so flabby in body and mind, no one so weak, so timid, so open to deception, so led by the nose, so despised by his favourites, often so roughly treated by them. He was quarrelsome in small matters, incapable of keeping any secret, suspicious, mistrustful; fond of spreading reports in his Court to make mischief, to learn what was really going on or just to amuse himself: he fetched and carried from one to the other. With so many defects, unrelated to any virtue, he had such an abominable taste, that his gifts and the fortunes that he gave to those he took into favour had rendered him publicly scandalous. He neither respected times nor places. His minions, who owed him everything, sometimes treated him most insolently; and he had often much to do to appease horrible jealousies. He lived in continual hot water with his favourites, to say nothing of the quarrels of that troop of ladies of a very decided character—many of whom were very malicious, and, most, more than malicious—with whom Monsieur used to divert himself, entering into all their wretched squabbles.

The Chevaliers de Lorraine and Chatillon had both made a large fortune by their good looks, with which he was more smitten than with those of any other of his favourites. Chatillon, who had neither head, nor sense, nor wit, got on in this way, and acquired for-

tune. The other behaved like a Guisard, who blushes
at nothing provided he succeeds; and governed Monsieur with a high hand all his life, was overwhelmed
with money and benefices, did what he liked for his
family, lived always publicly as the master with Monsieur; and as he had, with the pride of the Guises,
their art and cleverness, he contrived to get between
the King and Monsieur, to be dealt with gingerly, if
not feared by both, and was almost as important a
man with the one as with the other. He had the finest
apartments in the Palais Royal and Saint Cloud, and
a pension of ten thousand crowns. He remained in
his apartments after the death of Monsieur, but would
not from pride continue to receive the pension, which
from pride was offered him. Although it would have
been difficult to be more timid and submissive than was
Monsieur with the King—for he flattered both his
ministers and his mistresses—he, nevertheless, mingled
with his respectful demeanour the demeanour of a
brother, and the free and easy ways of one. In private, he was yet more unconstrained; always taking
an armed chair, and never waiting until the King told
him to sit. In the Cabinet, after the King appeared,
no other Prince sat besides him, not even Monseigneur. But in what regarded his service, and his
manner of approaching and leaving the King, no private person could behave with more respect; and he
naturally did everything with grace and dignity. He
never, however, was able to bend to Madame de
Maintenon completely, nor avoid making small attacks
on her to the King, nor avoid satirising her pretty
broadly in person. It was not her success that annoyed him; but simply the idea that La Scarron had
become his sister-in-law; this was insupportable to
him. Monsieur was extremely vain, but not haughty,
very sensitive, and a great stickler for what was due

to him. Upon one occasion he complained to the King that M. le Duc had for some time neglected to attend upon him, as he was bound, and had boasted that he would not do it. The King replied, that it was not a thing to be angry about, that he ought to seek an opportunity to be served by M. le Duc, and if he would not, to affront him. Accordingly, one morning at Marly, as he was dressing, seeing M. le Duc walking in the garden, Monsieur opened the window and called to him. Monsieur le Duc came up, and entered the room. Then, while one remark was leading to another, Monsieur slipped off his dressing-gown, and then his shirt. A *valet de chambre* standing by, at once slipped a clean shirt into the hands of M. le Duc, who, caught thus in a trap, was compelled to offer the garment to Monsieur, as it was his duty to do. As soon as Monsieur had received it, he burst out laughing, and said—" Good-bye, cousin, go away. I do not want to delay you longer." M. le Duc felt the point of this, and went away very angry, and continued so in consequence of the high tone Monsieur afterwards kept up on the subject.

Monsieur was a little round-bellied man, who wore such high-heeled shoes that he seemed mounted always upon stilts; was always decked out like a woman, covered everywhere with rings, bracelets, jewels; with a long black wig, powdered, and curled in front; with ribbons wherever he could put them; steeped in perfumes, and in fine a model of cleanliness. He was accused of putting on an imperceptible touch of rouge. He had a long nose, good eyes and mouth, a full but very long face. All his portraits resembled him. I was piqued to see that his features recalled those of Louis XIII., to whom, except in matters of courage, he was so completely dissimilar.

On Saturday, the 11th of June, the Court returned to

Versailles. On arriving there the King went to visit Madame and her son and daughter-in-law separately. Madame, very much troubled by reflection on her position with regard to the King, had sent the Duchesse de Ventadour to Madame de Maintenon. The latter replied to the message only in general terms; said she would visit Madame after dinner, and requested that the Duchess might be present at the interview. It was Sunday, the morning after the return from Marly. After the first compliments, every one went out except Madame de Ventadour. Then Madame requested Madame de Maintenon to sit down; and she must have felt her position keenly to bring her to this.

She began the conversation by complaining of the indifference with which the King had treated her during her illness. Madame de Maintenon allowed her to talk on; and when she had finished, said that the King had commanded her to say that their common loss effaced all the past, provided that he had reason to be better satisfied for the future, not only as regarded M. le Duc de Chartres, but other matters also. Upon this Madame exclaimed and protested that, except in as far as regarded her son, she had never given cause for displeasure; and went on alternating complaints and justifications. Precisely at the point when she was most emphatic, Madame de Maintenon drew forth a letter from her pocket and asked if the handwriting was known to her. It was a letter from Madame to the Duchess of Hanover, in which she said, after giving news of the Court, that no one knew what to say of the intercourse between the King and Madame de Maintenon, whether it was that of marriage or of concubinage; and then, touching upon other matters, launched out upon the misery of the realm: that, she said, was too great to be relieved. This letter had been opened at the post—as almost all letters were at that time, and are indeed still—and sent to the King. It may be imagined that this was a thunderstroke to Madame: it nearly killed her. She burst into tears; and Madame de Maintenon very quietly and demurely began to represent to her the contents of the letter in all its parts, especially as it was addressed to a foreign country. Madame de Ventadour interposed with some twaddle, to give Madame time to breathe and recover sufficiently to say something. The best excuse was the admission of what could not be denied, with supplications for pardon, expressions of repentance, prayers, promises. But Madame de Maintenon had not finished yet. Having got rid of the commission she had been charged with by the King, she next turned to her own business: she asked Madame how it was, that after being so friendly with her a long time ago, she had suddenly ceased to bestow any regard upon her, and had continued to treat her with coldness ever since. At this, Madame thinking herself quite safe, said that the coldness was on the part of Madame de Maintenon, who had all on a sudden discontinued the friendly intercourse which formerly existed between them. As before, Madame de Maintenon allowed Madame to talk her fill before she replied. She then said she was about to divulge a secret which had never escaped her mouth, although she had for ten years been at liberty to tell it; and she forthwith related a thousand most offensive things which had been uttered against her by Madame to the late Madame la Dauphine. This latter, falling out with Madame, had related all these things to Madame de Maintenon, who now brought them forward triumphantly.

At this new blow, Madame was thunderstruck, and stood like a statue. There was nothing for it but to behave as before—that is to say, shed tears, cry, ask pardon, humble herself, and beg for mercy. Madame de Maintenon triumphed coldly over her for a long time,—allowing her to excite herself in talking, and weeping, and taking her hands, which she did with increasing energy and humility. This was a terrible humiliation for such a haughty German. Madame de Maintenon at last gave way, as she had always meant to do after having satiated her vengeance. They embraced, promised forgetfulness on both sides, and a new friendship from that time. The King, who was not ignorant of what had occurred, took back Madame into favour. She went neither to a convent nor to Montargis, but was allowed to remain in Paris, and her pension was augmented. As for M. le Duc de Chartres, he was prodigiously well treated. The King gave him all the pensions Monsieur had enjoyed, besides allowing him to retain his own; so that he had one million eight hundred thousand livres a year; added to the Palais Royal, Saint Cloud, and other mansions. He had a Swiss guard, which none but the sons of France had ever had before; in fact he retained all the privileges his father had enjoyed, and he took the name of Duc d'Orléans. The pensions of Madame de Chartres were augmented. All these honours so great and so unheard of bestowed on M. de Chartres, and an income of a hundred thousand crowns more than his father, were due solely to the quarrel which had recently taken place between Monsieur and the King, as to the marriage M. de Chartres had made. People accustom themselves to everything, but this prodigious good fortune infinitely surprised everybody. The Princes of the blood were extremely mortified. To console them, the King immediately gave to M. le Prince all the advantages of a first Prince of the blood, and added ten thousand crowns to his pension.

Madame wore deep mourning for forty days, after which she threw it almost entirely aside, with the King's permission. He did not like to see such sad-looking things before his eyes every day. Madame went about in public, and with the Court, in her half-mourning, under pretence that being with the King, and living under his roof, she was of the family. But her conduct was not the less thought strange in spite of this excuse. During the winter, as the King could not well go to the theatre, the theatre came to him, in the apartments of Madame de Maintenon, where comedies with music were played. The King wore mourning for six months, and paid all the expenses of the superb funeral which took place on the 13th of June.

While upon the subject of Monsieur, I will relate an anecdote known to but few people, concerning the death of his first wife, Henriette d'Angleterre, whom nobody doubts was poisoned. Her gallantries made Monsieur jealous; and his tastes made her furious. His favourites, whom she hated, did all in their power to sow discord between them, in order to dispose of Monsieur at their will. The Chevalier de Lorraine, then in the prime of his first youth (having been born in 1643) completely ruled over Monsieur, and made Madame feel that he had this power. She, charming and young, could not suffer this, and complained to the King, so that M. de Lorraine was exiled. When Monsieur heard this, he swooned, then melted into tears, and throwing himself at the feet of the King, implored him to recall M. de Lorraine. But his prayers were useless, and, rushing away in fury, he retired into the country and remained there until, ashamed of a thing so publicly disgraceful, he returned to Paris and lived with Madame as before.

Although M. de Lorraine was banished, two of his intimate friends, D'Effiat and the Count de Beuvron, remained in the household of Monsieur. The absence of M. de Lorraine nipped all their hopes of success, and made them fear that some other favourite might arrive from whom they could hope for nothing. They saw no chance that M. de Lorraine's exile would speedily terminate; for Madame (Henriette d'Angleterre) was in greater favour with the King than ever, and had just been sent by him into England on a mysterious errand in which she had perfectly succeeded. She returned triumphant and very well in health. This gave the last blow to the hopes of D'Effiat and Beuvron, as to the return of M. de Lorraine, who had gone to Italy to try to get rid of his vexation. I know not which of the three thought of it first, but the Chevalier de Lorraine sent a sure and rapid poison to his two friends by a messenger who did not probably know what he carried.

At Saint Cloud, Madame was in the habit of taking a glass of endive-water, at about seven o'clock in the evening. A servant of hers used to make it, and then put it away in a cupboard where there was some ordinary water for the use of Madame if she found the other too bitter. The cupboard was in an antechamber which served as the public passage by which the apartments of Madame were reached. D'Effiat took notice of all these things, and on the 29th of June, 1670, he went to the ante-chamber; saw that he was unobserved and that nobody was near, and threw the poison into the endive-water; then hearing some one approaching, he seized the jug of common water and feigned to be putting it back in its place just as the servant, before alluded to, entered and asked him sharply what he was doing in that cupboard. D'Effiat, without losing countenance, asked his pardon, and said, that being thirsty, and knowing there was some water in the cupboard, he could not resist drinking. The servant grumbled; and D'Effiat, trying to appease him, entered the apartments of Madame, like the other courtiers, and began talking without the slightest emotion.

What followed an hour afterwards does not belong to my subject, and has made only too much stir throughout all Europe. Madame died on the morrow, June 30, at three o'clock in the morning; and the King was profoundly prostrated with grief. Apparently during the day, some indications showed him that Purnon, chief steward of Madame, was in the secret of her decease. Purnon was brought before him privately, and was threatened with instant death, unless he disclosed all; full pardon being on the contrary promised him if he did. Purnon, thus pressed, admitted that Madame had been poisoned, and under the circumstance I have just related. "And my brother," said the King, "did he know of this?" "No, Sire, not one of us was stupid enough to tell him; he has no secrecy, he would have betrayed us." On hearing this answer the King uttered a great "ah!" like a man oppressed, who suddenly breathes again.

Purnon was immediately set at liberty; and years afterwards related this narrative to M. Joly de Fleury, procureur-général of the Parliament, by which magistrate it was related to me. From this same magistrate I learned that, a few days before the second marriage of Monsieur, the King took Madame aside and told her that circumstance, assuring her that he was too honest a man to wish her to marry his brother, if that brother could be capable of such a crime. Madame profited by what she heard. Purnon remained in her service; but after a time she pretended to find faults in him, and made him resign; he sold his post accordingly, towards the end of 1674, to Maurel de Vaulonne, and quitted her service.

CHAPTER XXIII

AT the breaking out of the war in Italy this year Ségur bought the government of the Foix country from Tallard, one of the generals called away to serve in that war. Ségur had been in his youth a very handsome fellow; he was at that time in the Black Musketeers, and this company was always quartered at Nemours while the Court was at Fontainebleau. Ségur played very well upon the lute; but found life dull, nevertheless, at Nemours, made the acquaintance of the Abbesse de la Joye, a place hard by, and charmed her ears and eyes so much that she became with child by him. After some months the Abbess pleaded illness, left the convent, and set out for the waters, as she said. Putting off her journey too long, she was obliged to stop a night at Fontainebleau; and in consequence of the Court being there, could find no accommodation, except in a wretched little inn already full of company. She had delayed so long that the pangs of labour seized her in the night, and the cries she uttered brought all the house to her assistance. She was delivered of a child then and there; and the next morning this fact was the talk of the town.

The Duc de Saint Aignan, one of the first of the courtiers who learned it, went straight to the King, who was brisk and free enough in those days, and related to him what had occurred; the King laughed heartily at the poor Abbess, who, while trying to hide her shame, had come into the very midst of the Court. Nobody knew then that her abbey was only four leagues distant, but everybody learned it soon, and the Duc de Saint Aignan among the first.

When he returned to his house, he found long faces on every side. His servants made signs one to another, but nobody said a word. He perceived this, and asked what was the matter; but, for some time, no one dared to reply. At last a *valet-de-chambre* grew bold enough to say to Saint Aignan, that the Abbess, whose adventure had afforded so much mirth, was his own daughter; and that, after he had gone to the King, she had sent for assistance, in order to get out of the place where she was staying.

It was now the Duke's turn to be confused. After having made the King and all the Court laugh at this adventure, he became himself the laughing-stock of everybody. He bore the affair as well as he could; carried away the Abbess and her baggage; and, as the scandal was public, made her send in her resignation and hide herself in another convent, where she lived more than forty years.

That worthy man, Saint-Herem, died this year at his house in Auvergne, to which he had retired. Everybody liked him; and M. de Rochefoucauld had reproached the King for not making him Chevalier of the Order. The King had confounded him with Courtine, his brother-in-law, for they had married two sisters; but when put right had not given the favour.

Madame de Saint-Herem was the most singular creature in the world, not only in face but in manners. She half boiled her thigh one day in the Seine, near Fontainebleau, where she was bathing. The river was too cold; she wished to warm it, and had a quantity of water heated and thrown into the stream just above her. The water reaching her before it could grow cold, scalded her so much that she was forced to keep her bed.

When it thundered, she used to squat herself under a couch and make all her servants lie above, one upon the other, so that if the thunderbolt fell, it might have its effect upon them before penetrating to her. She had ruined herself and her husband, though they were rich, through sheer imbecility; and it is incredible the amount of money she spent in her absurdities.

The best adventure which happened to her, among a thousand others, was at her house in the Place Royale, where she was one day attacked by a madman, who, finding her alone in her chamber, was very enterprising. The good lady, hideous at eighteen, but who was at this time eighty and a widow, cried aloud as well as she could. Her servants heard her at last, ran to her assistance, and found her all disordered, struggling in the hands of this raging madman. The man was found to be really out of his senses when brought before the tribunal, and the story amused everybody.

The health of the King of England (James II.), which had for some time been very languishing, grew weaker towards the middle of August of this year, and by the 8th of September completely gave way. There was no longer any hope. The King, Madame de Maintenon, and all the royal persons, visited him often. He received the last sacrament with a piety in keeping with his past life, and his death was expected every instant. In this conjuncture the King made a resolve more worthy of Louis XII., or Francis I., than of his own wisdom. On Tuesday, the 13th of September, he went from Marly to Saint Germain. The King of England was so ill that when the King was announced to him he scarcely opened his eyes for an instant. The King told him that he might die in peace respecting the Prince of Wales, whom he would recognise as King of England, Scotland, and Ireland.

The few English who were there threw themselves upon their knees, but the King of England gave no signs of life. The gratitude of the Prince of Wales and of his mother, when they heard what the King had said, may be imagined. Returned to Marly, the King repeated to all the Court what he had said. Nothing was heard but praises and applause.

Yet reflections did not fail to be made promptly, if not publicly. It was seen, that to recognise the Prince of Wales was to act in direct opposition to the recognition of the Prince of Orange as King of England, that the King had declared at the Peace of Ryswick. It was to wound the Prince of Orange in the tenderest point, and to invite England and Holland to become allies of the Emperor against France. As for the Prince of Wales, this recognition was no solid advantage to him, but was calculated to make the party opposed to him in England only more bitter and vigilant in their opposition.

The King of England, in the few intervals of intelligence he had, appeared much impressed by what the King had done. He died about three o'clock in the afternoon of the 16th September of this year, 1701. He had requested that there might be no display at his funeral, and his wish was faithfully observed. He was buried on the Saturday, at seven o'clock in the evening, in the church of the English Benedictines at Paris, Rue St. Jacques, without pomp, and attended by but few mourners. His body rests in the chapel, like that of the simplest private person, until the time, apparently very distant, when it shall be transported to England. His heart is at the Filles de Sainte Marie, of Chaillot.

Immediately afterwards, the Prince of Wales was received by the King as King of England, with all the formalities and state with which his father before him had been received. Soon afterwards he was recognised by the new King of Spain.

The Count of Manchester, English ambassador in France, ceased to appear at Versailles after this recognition of the Prince of Wales by the King, and immediately quitted his post and left the country without any leave-taking. King William heard, while in Holland, of the death of James II. and of this recognition. He was at table with some German princes and other lords when the news arrived; did not utter a word, except to announce the death; but blushed, pulled down his hat, and could not keep his countenance. He sent orders to London, to drive out Poussin, acting as French ambassador, immediately; and Poussin directly crossed the sea and arrived at Calais.

This event was itself followed by the signing of the great treaty of alliance, offensive and defensive, against France and Spain, by Austria, England, and Holland; in which they afterwards succeeded in engaging other powers, which compelled the King to increase the number of his troops.

Just after the return of the Court from Fontainebleau, a strange scene happened at St. Maur, in a pretty house there which M. le Duc possessed. He was at this house one night with five or six intimate friends, whom he had invited to pass the night there. One of these friends was the Comte de Fiesque. At table, and before the wine had begun to circulate, a dispute upon some historical point arose between him and M. le Duc. The Comte de Fiesque, who had some intellect and learning, strongly sustained his opinion. M. le Duc sustained his; and for want of better reasons, threw a plate at the head of Fiesque, drove him from the table and out of the house. So sudden and strange a scene frightened the guests. The Comte de Fiesque, who had gone to M. le Duc's house with the intention of passing the night there, had not retained a carriage, went to ask shelter of the curé, and got back to Paris the next day as early in the morning as he could. It may be imagined that the rest of the supper and of the evening was terribly dull. M. le Duc remained fuming (perhaps against himself, but without saying so), and could not be induced to apologise for the affront. It made a great stir in society, and things remained thus several months. After a while, friends mixed themselves in the matter; M. le Duc, completely himself again, made all the advances towards a reconciliation. The Comte de Fiesque received them, and the reconciliation took place. The most surprising thing is, that after this they continued on as good terms as though nothing had passed between them.

The year 1702 commenced with balls at Versailles, many of which were masquerades. Madame du Maine gave several in her chamber, always keeping her bed because she was in the family-way; which made rather a singular spectacle. There were several balls at Marly, but the majority were not masquerades. The King often witnessed, but in strict privacy, and always in the apartments of Madame de Maintenon, sacred dramas such as "Absalon," "Athalie," &c. Madame la Duchesse de Bourgogne, M. le Duc d'Orléans, the Comte and Comtesse d'Anjou, the young Comte de Noailles, Mademoiselle de Melun, urged by the Noailles, played the principal characters in very magnificent stage dresses. Baron, the excellent old actor, instructed them and played with them. M. de Noailles and his clever wife were the inventors and promoters of these interior pleasures, for the purpose of intruding themselves more and more into the society of the King, in support of the alliance of Madame de Maintenon.

Only forty spectators were admitted to the representations. Madame was sometimes invited by the King, because she liked plays. This favour was much sought after. Madame de Maintenon wished to show that she had forgotten the past.

Longepierre had written a very singular piece called "Electra," which was played on a magnificent stage erected in Madame de Conti's house, and all the Court flocked several times to see it. This piece was without love, but full of other passions and of most interesting situations. I think it had been written in the hopes that the King would go and see it. But he contented himself with hearing it talked about, and the representation was confined to the Hôtel de Conti. Longepierre would not allow it to be given elsewhere. He was an intriguing fellow of much wit, gentle, insinuating, and who, under a tranquillity and indifference and a very deceitful philosophy, thrust himself everywhere, and meddled with everything in order to make his fortune. He succeeded in intruding himself into favour with the Duc d'Orléans, but behaved so badly that he was driven away.

The death of the Abbé de Vatteville occurred at the commencement of this year, and made some noise, on account of the prodigies of the Abbé's life. This Vatteville was the younger son of a Franche-Comté family; early in life he joined the Order of the Chartreux monks, and was ordained priest. He had much intellect, but was of an impetuous spirit, and soon began to chafe under the yoke of a religious life. He determined, therefore, to set himself free from it, and procured some secular habits, pistols, and a horse. Just as he was about to escape over the walls of the monastery by means of a ladder, the prior entered his cell. Vatteville made no to-do, but at once drew a pistol, shot the prior dead, and effected his escape.

Two or three days afterwards, travelling over the

country and avoiding as much as possible the frequented places, he arrived at a wretched road-side inn, and asked what there was in the house. The landlord replied—"A leg of mutton and a capon." "Good!" replied our unfrocked monk; "put them down to roast."

The landlord replied that they were too much for a single person, and that he had nothing else for the whole house. The monk upon this flew into a passion, and declared that the least the landlord could do was to give him what he would pay for; and that he had sufficient appetite to eat both leg of mutton and capon. They were accordingly put down to the fire, the landlord not daring to say another word. While they were cooking, a traveller on horseback arrived at the inn, and learning that they were for one person, was much astonished. He offered to pay his share to be allowed to dine off them with the stranger who had ordered this dinner; but the landlord told him he was afraid the gentleman would not consent to the arrangement. Thereupon the traveller went upstairs, and civilly asked Vatteville if he might dine with him on paying half of the expense. Vatteville would not consent, and a dispute soon arose between the two; to be brief, the monk served this traveller as he had served the prior, killed him with a pistol shot. After this he went downstairs tranquilly, and in the midst of the fright of the landlord and of the whole house, had the leg of mutton and capon served up to him, picked both to the very bone, paid his score, remounted his horse, and went his way.

Not knowing what course to take, he went to Turkey, and in order to succeed there, had himself circumcised, put on the turban, and entered into the militia. His blasphemy advanced him, his talents and his colour distinguished him; he became *Bacha,* and the confidential man in the Morea, where the Turks were making war against the Venetians. He determined to make use of this position in order to advance his own interests, and entering into communication with the generalissimo of the Republic, promised to betray into his hands several secret places belonging to the Turks, but on certain conditions. These were, absolution from the Pope for all crimes of his life, his murders and his apostasy included; security against the Chartreux and against being placed in any other Order; full restitution of his civil rights, and liberty to exercise his profession of priest with the right of possessing all benefices of every kind. The Venetians thought the bargain too good to be refused, and the Pope, in the interest of the Church, accorded all the demands of the *Bacha*. When Vatteville was quite assured that his conditions would be complied with, he took his measures so well that he executed perfectly all he had undertaken. Immediately after he threw himself into the Venetian army, and passed into Ialy. He was well received at Rome by the Pope, and returned to his family in Franche-Comté, and amused himself by braving the Chartreux.

At the first conquest of the Franche-Comté, he intrigued so well with the Queen-mother and the ministry, that he was promised the Archbishopric of Besançon; but the Pope cried out against this on account of his murders, circumcision, and apostasy. The King sided with the Pope, and Vatteville was obliged to be contented with the abbey of Baume, another good abbey in Picardy, and divers other advantages.

Except when he came to the Court, where he was always received with great distinction, he remained at his abbey of Baume, living there like a grand seigneur, keeping a fine pack of hounds, a good table, entertaining jovial company, keeping mistresses very freely;

tyrannising over his tenants and his neighbours in the most absolute manner. The intendants gave way to him, and by express orders of the Court allowed him to act much as he pleased, even with the taxes, which he regulated at his will, and in his conduct was oftentimes very violent. With these manners and this bearing, which caused him to be both feared and respected, he would often amuse himself by going to see the Chartreux, in order to plume himself on having quitted their frock. He played much at *hombre,* and frequently gained *codille* (a term of the game), so that the name of the Abbé Codille was given to him. He lived in this manner always with the same licence and in the same consideration, until nearly ninety years of age.

CHAPTER XXIV

THE changes which took place in the army after the Peace of Ryswick, were very great and very strange. The excellence of the regiments, the merits of the officers, those who commanded, all were forgotten by Barbezieux, young and impetuous, whom the King allowed to act as he liked. My regiment was disbanded, and my company was incorporated with that of Count d'Uzès, brother-in-law of Duras, who looked well after the interests of his relative. I was thus deprived of command, without regiment, without company, and the only opportunity offered me was to serve in a regiment commanded by Saint Morris, where I should have been, as it were, at the lowest step of the ladder, with my whole military career to begin over again.

I had served at the head of my regiment during four campaigns, with applause and reputation, I am bold enough to say it. I thought therefore I was entitled to better treatment than this. Promotions were made; five officers, all my juniors, were placed over my head. I resolved then to leave the service, but not to take a rash step. I consulted first with several friends before sending in my resignation. All whom I consulted advised me to quit the service, but for a long time I could not resolve to do so. Nearly three months passed, during which I suffered cruel anguish of mind from my irresolution. I knew that if I left the army I should be certain to incur the anger of the King, and I do not hesitate to say that this was not a matter of indifference to me. The King was always annoyed when anybody ceased to serve; he called it "quitting him;" and made his anger felt for a long time. At last, however, I determined on my course of action.

I wrote a short letter to the King, in which, without making any complaints, I said that as my health was not good (it had given me some trouble on different occasions) I begged to be allowed to quit his service, and said that I hoped I should be permitted to console myself for leaving the army by assiduously attending upon him at the Court. After despatching this letter I went away immediately to Paris.

I learnt afterwards from my friends, that upon receiving my letter the King called Chamillart to him, and said with emotion: "Well! Monsieur, here is another man who quits us!" and he read my letter word for word. I did not learn that anything else escaped him.

As for me, I did not return to Versailles for a whole week, or see the King again until Easter Monday. After his supper that evening, and when about to undress himself, he paid me a distinction,—a mere trifle I admit, and which I should be ashamed to mention if it did not under the circumstances serve as a characteristic of him.

Although the place he undressed in was very well illuminated, the chaplain at the evening prayers there held in his hand a lighted candle, which he gave afterwards to the chief *valet-de-chambre,* who carried it before the King until he reached his arm-chair, and then handed it to whomever the King ordered him to give it to. On this evening the King, glancing all around him, cast his eye upon me, and told the valet to give the candle to me. It was an honour which he bestowed sometimes upon one, sometimes upon another, according to his whim, but which, by his manner of bestowing it, was always coveted, as a great distinction. My surprise may be imagined when I heard myself named aloud for this office, not only on this but on many other occasions. It was not that there was any lack of people of consideration to hold the candle; but the King was sufficiently piqued by my retirement not to wish everybody to see that he was so.

For three years he failed not to make me feel to what extent he was angry with me. He spoke to me no longer; he scarcely bestowed a glance upon me, and never once alluded to my letter. To show that his annoyance did not extend to my wife, but that it was solely and wholly directed against me, he bestowed, about eight months after, several marks of favour upon Madame de Saint-Simon. She was continually invited to the suppers at Trianon—an honour which had never before been granted her. I only laughed at this. Madame de Saint-Simon was not invited to Marly, because the husbands always, by right, accompanied their wives there, apartments being given for both. At Trianon it was different. Nobody was allowed to sleep there except those absolutely in attendance. The King wished, therefore, the better to mark by this distinction that the exclusion was intended for me alone, and that my wife had no part in it.

Notwithstanding this, I persevered in my ordinary assiduity, without ever asking to be invited to Marly, and lived agreeably with my wife and my friends. I have thought it best to finish with this subject at once—now I must go back to my starting point.

At the commencement of this year (1702) it seemed as though the flatterers of the King foresaw that the prosperity of his reign was at an end, and that henceforth they would only have to praise him for his constancy. The great number of medals that had been struck on all occasions—the most ordinary not having been forgotten—were collected, engraved, and destined for a medallic history. The Abbés Tallemant, Toureil, and Dacier, three learned members of the Academy, were charged with the explanation to be placed opposite each of these medals, in a large volume of the most magnificent impression of the Louvre. As the history commenced at the death of Louis XIII., his medal was placed at the head of the book, and thus it became necessary to say something of him in the preface.

As it was known that I had a correct knowledge of Louis XIII., I was asked to write that portion of the preface which related to him. I consented to this, but on condition that I should be spared the ridicule of it in society, and that the matter should be faithfully kept secret. I wrote my theme then, which cost me little more than a morning, being of small extent. I had the fate of authors: my writing was praised, and appeared to answer all expectations. I congratulated myself, delighted at having devoted two or three hours to a grateful duty—for so I considered it.

But when my essay was examined, the three gentlemen above-named were affrighted. There are truths the unstudied simplicity of which emits a lustre which obscures all the results of an eloquence which exaggerates or extenuates; Louis XIII. furnished such proofs in abundance. I had contented myself by showing them forth; but this picture tarnished those which followed—so at least it appeared to those who had gilded the latter. They applied themselves, therefore, to cut out, or weaken, everything that might, by comparison, obscure their hero. But as they found at last that it was not me they had to correct, but the thing itself, they gave up the task altogether, threw aside my writing, and printed the history without any notice whatever of Louis XIII. under his portrait—except to note that his death caused his son to ascend the throne.

Reflections upon this kind of iniquity would carry me too far.

In the early part of this year (1702), King William (of England), worn out before his time with labours and business, in which he had been engaged all his life, and which he had carried on with a capacity, an address, a superiority of genius that acquired for him supreme authority in Holland, the crown of England, the confidence, and, to speak the truth, the complete dictatorship of all Europe—except France;—King William, I say, had fallen into a wasting of strength and of health which, without attacking or diminishing his intellect, or causing him to relax the infinite labours of his cabinet, was accompanied by a deficiency of breath, which aggravated the asthma he had had for several years. He felt his condition, and his powerful genius did not disavow it. Under forged names he consulted the most eminent physicians of Europe, among others, Fagon; who, having to do, as he thought, with a *curé*, replied in all sincerity, and without dissimulation, that he must prepare for a speedy death. His illness increasing, William consulted Fagon, anew, but this time openly. The physician recognised the malady of the *curé*—he did not change his opinion, but expressed it in a less decided manner, and prescribed with much feeling the remedies most likely if not to cure, at least to prolong. These remedies were followed and gave relief; but at last the time had arrived when William was to feel that the greatest men finish like the humblest—and to see the nothingness of what the world calls great destinies.

He rode out as often as he could; but no longer having the strength to hold himself on horseback, received a fall, which hastened his end by the shock it gave him. He occupied himself with religion as little as he had all his life. He ordered everything, and spoke to his ministers and his familiars with a surprising tranquillity, which did not abandon him until the last moment. Although crushed with pain, he had the satisfaction of thinking that he had consummated a great alliance, which would last after his death, and that it would strike the great blow against France, which he had projected. This thought, which flattered him even in the hour of death, stood in place of all other consolation,—a consolation frivolous and cruelly deceitful, which left him soon the prey to eternal truths! For two days he was sustained by strong waters and spirituous liquors. His last nourishment was a cup of chocolate. He died the 19th March, 1702, at ten o'clock in the morning.

The Princess Anne, his sister-in-law, wife of Prince George of Denmark, was at the same time proclaimed queen. A few days after, she declared her husband Grand Admiral and Commander-in-Chief (*generalissimo*), recalled the Earl of Rochester, her maternal uncle, and the Earl of Sunderland, and sent the Count of Marlborough, afterwards so well known, to Holland to follow out there all the plans of his predecessor.

The King did not learn this death until the Saturday morning following, by a courier from Calais. A boat had escaped, in spite of the vigilance which had closed the ports. The King was silent upon the news, except to Monseigneur and to Madame de Maintenon. On the next day confirmation of the intelligence arrived from all parts. The King no longer made a secret of it, but spoke little on the subject, and affected much indifference respecting it. With the recollection of all the indecent follies committed in Paris during the last war, when it was believed that William had been killed at the battle of the Boyne in Ireland, the necessary precautions against falling into the same error were taken by the King's orders.

The King simply declared that he would not wear mourning, and prohibited the Duc de Bouillon, the Maréchal de Duras and the Maréchal de Lorges, who were all related to William, from doing so—an act probably without example. Nearly all England and the United Provinces mourned the loss of William. Some good republicans alone breathed again with joy in secret, at having recovered their liberty. The grand alliance was very sensibly touched by this loss, but found itself so well cemented, that the spirit of William continued to animate it; and Heinsius, his confidant, perpetuated it, and inspired all the chiefs of the republic, their allies and their generals, with it, so that it scarcely appeared that William was no more.

I have related, in its proper place, all that happened to Catinat in Italy, when the schemes of Tessé and M. de Vaudemont caused him to be dismissed from the command of the army. After the signing of the alliance against France by the Emperor, England, and Holland, the war took a more extended field. It became necessary to send an army to the Rhine. There was nothing for it but to have recourse to Catinat.

Since his return from Italy, he had almost always lived at his little house of Saint Gratien, beyond Saint Denis, where he bore with wisdom the injury that had been done him and the neglect he had experienced upon his return, surrounded by his family and a small number of friends. Chamillart one day sent for him, saying that he had the King's order to talk with him. Catinat went accordingly to Chamillart, from whom he learned that he was destined for the Rhine; he refused the command, and only accepted it after a long dispute, by the necessity of obedience.

On the morrow, the 11th of March, the King called

Catinat into his cabinet. The conversation was amiable on the part of the King, serious and respectful on the part of Catinat. The King, who perceived this, wished to make him speak about Italy, and pressed him to explain what had really passed there. Catinat excused himself, saying that everything belonged to the past, and that it was useless now to rake up matters which would give him a bad opinion of the people who served him, and nourish eternal enmity. The King admired the sagacity and virtue of Catinat, but, wishing to sound the depths of certain things, and discover who was really to blame, pressed him more and more to speak out; mentioning certain things which Catinat had not rendered an account of, and others he had been silent upon, all of which had come to him from other sources.

Catinat, who, by his conversation of the previous evening with Chamillart, suspected that the King would say something to him, had brought his papers to Versailles. Sure of his position, he declared that he had not in any way failed to render account to Chamillart or to the King, and detailed the very things that had just been mentioned to him. He begged that a messenger might be despatched in order to search his *cassette,* in which the proofs of what he had advanced could be seen,—truths that Chamillart, if present, he said, would not dare to disavow. The King took him at his word, and sent in search of Chamillart.

When he arrived, the King related to him the conversation that had just taken place. Chamillart replied with an embarrassed voice, that there was no necessity to wait for the *cassette* of Catinat, for he admitted that the accusation against him was true in every respect. The King, much astonished, reproved him for his infidelity in keeping silence upon these comments, whereby Catinat had lost his favour.

Chamillart, his eyes lowered, allowed the King to say on; but as he felt that his anger was rising, said. "Sire, you are right; but it is not my fault."

"And whose is it, then?" replied the King warmly. "Is it mine?"

"Certainly not, Sire," said Chamillart, trembling; "but I am bold enough to tell you, with the most exact truth, that it is not mine."

The King insisting, Chamillart was obliged to explain, that having shown the letters of Catinat to Madame de Maintenon, she had commanded him to keep them from his Majesty, and to say not a syllable about them. Chamillart added, that Madame de Maintenon was not far off, and supplicated the King to ask her the truth of this matter.

In his turn, the King was now more embarrassed than Chamillart; lowering his voice, he said that it was inconceivable how Madame de Maintenon felt interested in his comfort, and endeavoured to keep from him everything that might vex him, and without showing any more displeasure, turned to Marshal Catinat, said he was delighted with an explanation which showed that nobody was wrong; addressed several gracious remarks to the Marshal; begged him to remain on good terms with Chamillart, and hastened to quit them and enter into his private cabinet.

Catinat, more ashamed of what he had just heard and seen than pleased with a justification so complete, paid some compliments to Chamillart, who, out of his wits at the perilous explanation he had given, received them, and returned them as well as he could. They left the cabinet soon after, and the selection of Catinat by the King for the command of the army of the Rhine was declared.

Reflections upon this affair present themselves of their own accord. The King verified what had been said that very evening with Madame de Maintenon. They were only on better terms than ever in consequence. She approved of Chamillart for avowing all; and this minister was only the better treated afterwards by the King and by Madame de Maintenon.

As for Catinat, he took the command he had been called to, but did not remain long in it. The explanations that had passed, all the more dangerous because in his favour, were not of a kind to prove otherwise than hurtful to him. He soon resigned his command, finding himself too much obstructed to do anything, and retired to his house of Saint Gratien, near Saint Denis, which he scarcely ever left, and where he saw only a few private friends, sorry that he had ever left it, and that he had listened to the cajoleries of the King.

CHAPTER XXV

CANAPLES, brother of the Maréchal de Crequi, wished to marry Mademoiselle de Vivonne, who was no longer young, but was distinguished by talent, virtue, and high birth; she had not a penny. The Cardinal de Coislin, thinking Canaples too old to marry, told him so. Canaples said he wanted to have children. "Children!" exclaimed the Cardinal. "But she is so virtuous!" Everybody burst out laughing; and the more willingly, as the Cardinal, very pure in his manners, was still more so in his language. His saying was verified by the event: the marriage proved sterile.

The Duc de Coislin died about this time. I have related in its proper place an adventure that happened to him and his brother, the Chevalier de Coislin: now I will say something more of the Duke. He was a very little man, of much humour and virtue, but of a politeness that was unendurable, and that passed all bounds, though not incompatible with dignity. He had been lieutenant-general in the army. Upon one occasion, after a battle in which he had taken part, one of the Rhingraves who had been made prisoner, fell to his lot. The Duc de Coislin wished to give up to the other his bed, which consisted indeed of but a mattress. They complimented each other so much, the one pressing, the other refusing, that in the end they both slept upon the ground, leaving the mattress between them. The Rhingrave in due time came to Paris and called on the Duc de Coislin. When he was going, there was such a profusion of compliments, and the Duke insisted so much on seeing him out, that the Rhingrave, as a last resource, ran out of the room, and double locked the door outside. M. de Coislin was not thus to be outdone. His apartments were only a few feet above the ground. He opened the window accordingly, leaped out into the court, and arrived thus at the entrance-door before the Rhingrave, who thought the devil must have carried him there. The Duc de Coislin, however, had managed to put his thumb out of joint by this leap. He called in Felix, chief surgeon of the King, who soon put the thumb to rights. Soon afterwards Felix made a call upon M. de Coislin to see how he was, and found that the cure was perfect. As he was about to leave, M. de Coislin must needs open the door for him. Felix, with a shower of bows, tried hard to prevent this, and while they were thus vying in politeness, each with a hand upon the door, the Duke suddenly drew back; he had put his thumb out of joint again, and Felix was obliged to attend to it on the spot! It may be imagined what laughter this story caused the King, and everybody else, when it became known.

There was no end to the outrageous civilities of M. de Coislin. On returning from Fontainebleau one day, we, that is Madame de Saint-Simon and myself, encountered M. de Coislin and his son, M. de Metz, on foot upon the pavement of Ponthierry, where their coach had broken down. We sent word, accordingly, that we should be glad to accommodate them in ours. But message followed message on both sides; and at last I was compelled to alight and to walk through the mud, begging them to mount into my coach. M. de Coislin, yielding to my prayers, consented to this. M. de Metz was furious with him for his compliments, and at last prevailed on him. When M. de Coislin had accepted my offer and we had nothing more to do than to gain the coach, he began to capitulate, and to protest that he would not displace the two young ladies he saw seated in the vehicle. I told him that the two young ladies were chambermaids, who could well afford to wait until the other carriage was mended, and then continue their journey in that. But he would not hear of this; and at last all that M. de Metz and I could do was to compromise the matter by agreeing to take one of the chambermaids with us. When we arrived at the coach, they both descended, in order to allow us to mount. During the compliments that passed—and they were not short—I told the servant who held the coach-door open, to close it as soon as I was inside, and to order the coachman to drive on at once. This was done; but M. de Coislin immediately began to cry aloud that he would jump out if we did not stop for the young ladies; and he set himself to do so in such an odd manner, that I had only time to catch hold of the belt of his breeches and hold him back; but he still, with his head hanging out of the window, exclaimed that he *would* leap out, and pulled against me. At this absurdity I called to the coachman to stop; the Duke with difficulty recovered himself, and persisted that he would have thrown himself out. The chambermaid was ordered to mount, and mount she did, all covered with mud, which daubed us; and she nearly crushed M. de Metz and me in this carriage fit only for four.

M. de Coislin could not bear that at parting anybody should give him the "last touch;" a piece of sport, rarely cared for except in early youth, and out of which arises a chase by the person touched, in order to catch him by whom he has been touched. One evening, when the Court was at Nancy, and just as everybody was going to bed, M. de Longueville spoke a few words in private to two of his torch-bearers, and then touching the Duc de Coislin, said he had given him the last touch, and scampered away, the Duke hotly pursuing him. Once a little in advance, M. de Longueville hid himself in a doorway, allowed M. de Coislin to pass on, and then went quietly home to bed. Meanwhile the Duke, lighted by the torch-bearers, searched for M. de Longueville all over the town, but meeting with no success, was obliged to give up the chase, and went home all in a sweat. He was obliged of course to laugh a good deal at this joke, but he evidently did not like it over much.

With all his politeness, which was in no way put on, M. de Coislin could, when he pleased, show a great deal of firmness, and a resolution to maintain his proper dignity worthy of much praise. At Nancy, on this same occasion, the Duc de Crequi, not finding apartments provided for him to his taste on arriving in town, went, in his brutal manner, and seized upon those allotted to the Duc de Coislin. The Duke, arriving a moment after, found his servants turned into the street, and soon learned who had sent them there. M. de Crequi had precedence of him in rank; he said not a word, therefore, but went to the apartments provided for the Maréchal de Crequi (brother of the other), served him exactly as he himself had just been served, and took up his quarters there. The Maréchal de Crequi arrived in his turn, learned what had occurred, and immediately seized upon the apartments of Cavoye, in order to teach him how to provide quarters in future so as to avoid all disputes.

On another occasion, M. de Coislin went to the Sorbonne to listen to a thesis sustained by the second son of M. de Bouillon. When persons of distinction gave these discourses, it was customary for the Princes of the blood, and for many of the Court, to go and hear them. M. de Coislin was at that time almost last in order of precedence among the Dukes. When he took his seat, therefore, knowing that a number of them would probably arrive, he left several rows of vacant places in front of him, and sat himself down. Immediately afterwards, Novion, Chief President of the Parliament, arrived, and seated himself in front of M. de Coislin. Astonished at this act of madness, M. de Coislin said not a word, but took an arm-chair, and, while Novion turned his head to speak to Cardinal de Bouillon, placed that arm-chair in front of the Chief President in such a manner that he was as it were imprisoned, and unable to stir. M. de Coislin then sat down. This was done so rapidly, that nobody saw it until it was finished. When once it was observed, a great stir arose. Cardinal de Bouillon tried to intervene. M. de Coislin replied, that since the Chief President had forgotten his position he must be taught it, and would not budge. The other presidents were in a fright, and Novion, enraged by the offence put on him, knew not what to do. It was in vain that Cardinal de Bouillon on one side, and his brother on the other, tried to persuade M. de Coislin to give way. He would not listen to them. They sent a message to him to say that somebody wanted to see him at the door on most important business. But this had no effect. "There is no business so important," replied M. de Coislin, "as that of teaching M. le Premier Président what he owes me, and nothing will make me go from this place unless M. le Président, whom you see behind me, goes away first."

At last M. le Prince was sent for, and he with much persuasion endeavoured to induce M. de Coislin to release the Chief President from his prison. But for some time M. de Coislin would listen as little to M. le Prince as he had listened to the others, and threatened to keep Novion thus shut up during all the thesis. At length, he consented to set the Chief President free, but only on condition that he left the building immediately; that M. le Prince should guarantee this; and that no "juggling tricks" (that was the term he made use of), should be played off to defeat the agreement. M. le Prince at once gave his word that everything should be as he required, and M. de Coislin then rose, moved away his arm-chair, and said to the Chief President, "Go away, sir! go away, sir!" Novion did on the instant go away, in the utmost confusion, and jumped into his coach. M. de Coislin thereupon took back his chair to its former position and composed himself to listen again.

On every side M. de Coislin was praised for the firmness he had shown. The Princes of the blood called upon him the same evening, and complimented him for the course he had adopted; and so many other visitors came during the evening that his house was quite full until a late hour. On the morrow the King also praised him for his conduct, and severely blamed the Chief President. Nay more, he commanded the latter to go to M. de Coislin, at his house, and beg pardon of him. It is easy to comprehend the shame and despair of Novion at being ordered to take so humiliating a step, especially after what had already happened to him. He prevailed upon M. le Coislin, through the mediation of friends, to spare him this pain, and M. de Coislin had the generosity to do so. He agreed therefore that when Novion called upon him he would pretend to be out, and this was done. The King, when he heard of it, praised very highly the forbearance of the Duke.

He was not an old man when he died, but was eaten up with the gout, which he sometimes had in his eyes, in his nose, and in his tongue. When in this state, his room was filled with the best company. He was very generally liked, was truth itself in his dealings and his words, and was one of my friends, as he had been the friend of my father before me.

The Président de Novion, above alluded to, was a man given up to iniquity, whom money and obscure mistresses alone influenced. Lawyers complained of his caprices, and pleaders of his injustice. At last, he went so far as to change decisions of the court when they were given him to sign, which was not found out for some time, but which led to his disgrace. He was replaced by Harlay in 1689; and lived in ignominy for four years more.

About this time died Petit, a great physician, who had wit, knowledge, experience, and probity; and yet lived to the last without being ever brought to admit the circulation of the blood.

A rather strange novelty was observed at Fontainebleau: Madame publicly at the play, in the second year of her mourning for Monsieur! She made some objections at first, but the King persuaded her, saying that what took place in his palace ought not to be considered as public.

On Saturday, the 22nd of October of this year (1702), at about ten in the morning, I had the misfortune to lose my father-in-law, the Maréchal de Lorges, who died from the effects of an unskilful operation performed upon him for the stone. He had been brought up as a Protestant, and had practised that religion. But he had consulted on the one hand with Bossuet, and on the other hand with M. Claude, (Protestant) minister of Charenton, without acquainting them that he was thus in communication with both. In the end the arguments of Bossuet so convinced him that he lost from that time all his doubts, became steadfastly attached to the Catholic religion, and strove hard to convert to it all the Protestants with whom he spoke. M. de Turenne, with whom he was intimately allied, was in a similar state of mind, and, singularly enough, his doubts were resolved at the same time, and in exactly the same manner, as those of M. de Lorges. The joy of the two friends, who had both feared they should be estranged from each other when they announced their conversion, was very great. The Comtesse de Roye, sister to M. de Lorges, was sorely affected at this change, and she would not consent to see him except on condition that he never spoke of it.

M. de Lorges commanded with great distinction in Holland and elsewhere, and at the death of M. de Turenne, took for the time, and with great honour, his place. He was made Marshal of France on the 21st of February, 1676, not before he had fairly won that distinction. The remainder of his career showed his capacity in many ways, and acquired for him the esteem of all. His family were affected beyond measure at his loss. That house was in truth terrible to see. Never was man so tenderly or so universally regretted, or so worthy of being so. Besides my own grief, I had to sustain that of Madame de Saint-Simon, whom many times I thought I should lose. Nothing was comparable to the attachment she had for her father, or the tenderness he had for her; nothing more perfectly alike than their hearts and their dispositions. As for me, I loved him as a father, and he loved me as a son, with the most entire and sweetest confidence.

About the same time died the Duchesse de Gesvres, separated from a husband who had been the scourge of his family, and had dissipated millions of her fortune. She was a sort of witch, tall and lean, who walked like an ostrich. She sometimes came to Court, with the odd look and famished expression to which her husband had brought her. Virtue, wit, and dignity distinguished her. I remember that one summer the King took to going very often in the evening to Trianon, and that once for all he gave permission to all the Court, men and women, to follow him. There was a grand collation for the Princesses, his daughters, who took their friends there, and indeed all the women went to it if they pleased. One day the Duchesse de Gesvres took it into her head to go to Trianon and partake of this meal; her age, her rarity at Court, her accoutrements, and her face, provoked the Princesses to make fun of her in whispers with their fair visitors. She perceived this, and without being embarrassed, took them up so sharply, that they were silenced, and looked down. But this was not all: after the collation she began to talk so freely and yet so humorously about them that they were frightened, and went and made their excuses, and very frankly asked for quarter. Madame de Gesvres was good enough to grant them this, but said it was only on condition that they learned how to behave. Never afterwards did they venture to look at her impertinently. Nothing was ever so magnificent as these *soirées* of Trianon. All the flowers of the parterres were renewed every day; and I have seen the King and all the Court obliged to go away because of the tuberoses, the odour of which perfumed the air, but so powerfully, on account of their quantity, that nobody could remain in the garden, although very vast, and stretching like a terrace all along the canal.

CHAPTER XXVI

THE Prince d'Harcourt at last obtained permission to wait on the King, after having never appeared at Court for seventeen years. He had followed the King in all his conquests in the Low Countries and Franche-Comté; but he had remained little at the Court since his voyage to Spain, whither he had accompanied the daughter of Monsieur to the King, Charles II., her husband. The Prince d'Harcourt took service with Venice, and fought in the Morea until the Republic made peace with the Turks. He was tall, well made; and, although he looked like a nobleman and had wit, reminded one at the same time of a country actor. He was a great liar, and a libertine in body and mind; a great spendthrift, a great and impudent swindler, with a tendency to low debauchery, that cursed him all his life. Having fluttered about a long time after his return, and found it impossible either to live with his wife—which is not surprising—or accommodate himself to the Court or to Paris, he set up his rest at Lyons with wine, street-walkers, a society to match, a pack of hounds, and a gaming-table to support his extravagance and enable him to live at the expense of the dupes, the imbeciles, and the sons of fat tradesmen, whom he could lure into his nets. Thus he spent many years, and seemed to forget that there existed in the world another country besides Lyons. At last he got tired, and returned to Paris. The King, who despised him, let him alone, but would not see him; and it was only after two months of begging for him by the Lorraines, that he received permission to present himself. His wife, the Princesse d'Harcourt, was a favourite of Madame de Maintenon. The origin of their friendship is traced to the fact that Brancas, the father of the Princess, had been one of the lovers of Madame de Maintenon. No claim less powerful could have induced the latter to take into her favour a person who was so little worthy. Like all women who know nothing but what chance has taught them, and who have long languished in obscurity before arriving at splendour, Madame de Maintenon was dazzled by the very name of Princess, even if assumed: as to a real Princess, nothing equalled her in her opinion. The Princess then tried hard to get the Prince invited to Marly, but without success. Upon this she pretended to sulk, in hopes that Madame de Maintenon would exert all her influence; but in this she was mistaken. The Prince accordingly by degrees got disgusted with the Court, and retired into the provinces for a time.

The Princesse d'Harcourt was a sort of personage whom it is good to make known, in order better to lay bare a Court which did not scruple to receive such as she. She had once been beautiful and gay; but though not old, all her grace and beauty had vanished. The rose had become an ugly thorn. At the time I speak of she was a tall, fat creature, mightily brisk in her movements, with a complexion like milk-porridge; great, ugly, thick lips, and hair like tow, always sticking out and hanging down in disorder, like all the rest of her fittings out. Dirty, slatternly, always intriguing, pretending, enterprising, quarrelling—always low as the grass or high as the rainbow, according to the person with whom she had to deal: she was a blonde Fury, nay more, a harpy: she had all the effrontery of one, and the deceit and violence; all the avarice and the audacity; moreover, all the gluttony, and all the promptitude to relieve herself from the effects thereof; so that she drove out of their wits those at whose house she dined; was often a victim of her confidence; and was many a time sent to the devil by the servants of M. du Maine and M. le Grand. She, however, was never in the least embarrassed, tucked up her petticoats and went her way; then returned, saying she had been unwell. People were accustomed to it.

Whenever money was to be made by scheming and bribery, she was there to make it. At play she always cheated, and if found out stormed and raged; but pocketed what she had won. People looked upon her as they would have looked upon a fish-fag, and did not like to commit themselves by quarrelling with her. At the end of every game she used to say that she gave whatever might have been unfairly gained to those who had gained it, and hoped that others would do likewise. For she was very devout by profession, and thought by so doing to put her conscience in safety; because, she used to add, in play there is always some mistake. She went to church always, and constantly took the sacrament, very often after having played until four o'clock in the morning.

One day, when there was a grand *fête* at Fontainebleau, Madame la Maréchale de Villeroy persuaded her, out of malice, to sit down and play, instead of going to evening prayers. She resisted some time, saying that Madame de Maintenon was going; but the Maréchale laughed at her for believing that her patron could see who was and who was not at the chapel: so down they sat to play. When the prayers were over, Madame de Maintenon, by the merest accident—for she scarcely ever visited any one—went to the apartments of the Maréchale de Villeroy. The door was flung back, and she was announced. This was a thunderbolt for the Princesse d'Harcourt. " I am ruined," cried she, unable to restrain herself; "she will see me playing, and I ought to have been at chapel!" Down fell the cards from her hands, and down fell she all abroad in her chair. The Maréchale laughed most heartily at so complete an adventure. Madame de Maintenon entered slowly, and found the Princess in this state, with five or six persons. The Maréchale de Villeroy, who was full of wit, began to say that, whilst doing her a great honour, Madame was the cause of great disorder; and showed her the Princesse d'Harcourt in her state of discomfiture. Madame de Maintenon smiled with majestic kindness, and addressing the Princesse d'Harcourt, "Is this the way," said she, "that you go to prayers?" Thereupon the Princess flew out of her half-faint into a sort of fury; said that this was the kind of trick that was played off upon her; that no doubt the Maréchale knew that Madame de Maintenon was coming, and for that reason had persecuted her to play. "Persecuted!" exclaimed the Maréchale, "I thought I could not receive you better than by proposing a game; it is true you were for a moment troubled at missing the chapel, but your tastes carried the day.—This, Madame, is my whole crime," continued she, addressing Madame de Maintenon. Upon this, everybody laughed louder than before. Madame de Maintenon, in order to stop the quarrel, commanded them both to continue their game; and they continued accordingly, the Princesse d'Harcourt, still grumbling, quite beside herself, blinded with fury, so as to commit fresh mistakes every minute. So ridiculous an adventure diverted the Court for several days; for this beautiful Princess was equally feared, hated, and despised.

Monseigneur le Duc and Madame la Duchesse de Bourgogne continually played off pranks upon her. They put, one day, crackers all along the avenue of the château at Marly, that led to the Perspective where she lodged. She was horribly afraid of everything. The Duke and Duchess bribed two porters to be ready to take her into the mischief. When she was right in the middle of the avenue the crackers began to go off, and she to cry aloud for mercy; the chairman set her down and ran for it. There she was, then, struggling in her chair, furiously enough to upset it, and yelling like a demon. At this the company, which had gathered at the door of the château to see the fun, ran to her assistance, in order to have the pleasure of enjoying the scene more fully. Thereupon she set to abusing everybody right and left, commencing with Monseigneur and Madame la Duchesse de Bourgogne. At another time M. de Bourgogne put a cracker under her chair in the *salon,* where she was playing at *piquet.* As he was about to set fire to this cracker, some charitable soul warned him that it would maim her, and he desisted.

Sometimes they used to send about twenty Swiss guards, with drums, into her chamber, who roused her from her first sleep by their horrid din. Another time—and these scenes were always at Marly—they waited until very late for her to go to bed and sleep. She lodged not far from the post of the captain of the guards, who was at that time the Maréchal de Lorges. It had snowed very hard, and had frozen. Madame la Duchesse de Bourgogne and her suite gathered snow from the terrace which is on a level with their lodgings; and, in order to be better supplied, waked up, to assist them, the Maréchal's people, who did not let them want for ammunition. Then, with a false key, and lights, they gently slipped into the chamber of the Princesse d'Harcourt; and, suddenly drawing the curtains of her bed, pelted her amain with snowballs. The filthy creature, waking up with a start, bruised and stifled in snow, with which even her ears were filled, with dishevelled hair, yelling at the top of her voice, and wriggling like an eel, without knowing where to hide, formed a spectacle that diverted people more than half an hour: so that at last the nymph swam in her bed, from which the water flowed everywhere, slushing all the chamber. It was enough to make one die of laughter. On the morrow she sulked, and was more than ever laughed at for her pains.

Her fits of sulkiness came over her either when the tricks played were too violent, or when M. le Grand abused her. He thought, very properly, that a person who bore the name of Lorraine should not put herself so much on the footing of a buffoon; and, as he was a rough speaker, he sometimes said the most abominable things to her at table; upon which the Princess would burst out crying, and then, being enraged, would sulk. The Duchesse de Bourgogne used then to pretend to sulk, too; but the other did not hold out long, and came crawling back to her, crying, begging pardon for having sulked, and praying that she might not cease to be a source of amusement! After some time the Duchess would allow herself to be melted, and the Princess was more villainously treated than ever, for the Duchesse de Bourgogne had her own way in everything. Neither the King nor Madame de Maintenon found fault with what she did, so that the Princesse d'Harcourt had no resource; she did not even dare to complain of those who aided in tormenting her; yet it would not have been prudent in any one to make her an enemy.

The Princesse d'Harcourt paid her servants so badly that they concocted a plan, and one fine day drew up on the Pont Neuf. The coachman and footmen got down, and came and spoke to her at the door, in language she was not used to hear. Her ladies and chambermaid got down, and went away, leaving her to shift as she might. Upon this she set herself to harangue the blackguards who collected, and was only too happy to find a man, who mounted upon the seat and drove her home. Another time, Madame de Saint-Simon, returning from Versailles, overtook her, walking in full dress in the street, and with her train under her arms. Madame de Saint-Simon stopped, offered her assistance, and found that she had been left by her servants, as on the Pont Neuf. It was volume the second of that story; and even when she came back she found her house deserted, every one having gone away at once by agreement. She was very violent with her servants, beat them, and changed them every day.

Upon one occasion, she took into her service a strong and robust chambermaid, to whom, from the first day of her arrival, she gave many slaps and boxes on the ear. The chambermaid said nothing, but after submitting to this treatment for five or six days, conferred with the other servants; and one morning, while in her mistress's room, locked the door without being perceived, said something to bring down punishment upon her, and at the first box on the ear she received, flew upon the Princesse d'Harcourt, gave her no end of thumps and slaps, knocked her down, kicked her, mauled her from her head to her feet, and when she was tired of this exercise, left her on the ground, all torn and dishevelled, howling like a devil. The chambermaid then quitted the room, double-locked the door on the outside, gained the staircase, and fled the house.

Every day the Princess was fighting, or mixed up in some adventures. Her neighbours at Marly said they could not sleep for the riot she made at night; and I remember that, after one of these scenes, everybody went to see the room of the Duchesse de Villeroy and that of Madame d'Espinoy, who had put their bed in the middle of their room, and who related their night vigils to every one.

Such was this favourite of Madame de Maintenon; so insolent and so insupportable to every one, but who had favours and preferences for those who brought her over, and who had raised so many young men, amassed their wealth, and made herself feared even by the Prince and minister.

CHAPTER XXVII

IN a previous page I have alluded to the Princesse des Ursins, when she was appointed *Camerera Mayor* to the Queen of Spain on her marriage. As I have now to occupy myself more particularly with her, it may be as well to give a description of this extraordinary woman, which I omitted when I first spoke of her.

Anne Marie de la Trémoille, was daughter of M. de Noirmoutiers, who figured sufficiently in the troubles of the minority to be made a *Duc à brevet*. She first married M. Talleyrand, who called himself Prince de Chalais, and who was obliged to quit the kingdom for engaging in the famous duel against Messieurs de la Frette. She followed her husband to Spain, where he died. Having gone to Rome, she got into favour with the Cardinals de Bouillon and d'Estrées, first on account of her name and nation, and afterwards for more tender reasons. In order to detain her at Rome, these dignitaries thought of obtaining her an establishment. She had no children, and almost no fortune, they wrote to Court that so important a man as the Duc de Bracciano, Prince des Ursins, was worth gaining; and that the way to arrive at this result was to have him married to Madame de Chalais. The Duke was persuaded by the two Cardinals that he was in love with Madame de Chalais: and so the affair was arranged. Madame des Ursins displayed all her wit and charms at Rome; and soon her palace became a sort of court, where all the best company assembled. It grew to be the fashion to go there.

The husband amidst all this counts for not much. There was sometimes a little disagreement between the two, without open rupture; yet they were now and then glad to separate. This is why the Duchesse de Bracciano made two journeys to France: the second time she spent four or five years there. It was then I knew her, or rather formed a particular friendship with her. My mother had made her acquaintance during her previous visit. She lodged near us. Her wit, her grace, her manners enchanted me: she received me with tenderness and I was always at her house. It was she who proposed to me a marriage with Mlle. de Royan, which I rejected for the reason already given.

When Madame des Ursins was appointed *Camerera Mayor,* she was a widow, without children. No one could have been better suited for the post. A lady of our court would not have done: a Spanish lady was not to be depended on, and might have easily disgusted the Queen. The Princesse des Ursins appeared to be a middle term. She was French, had been in Spain, and she passed a great part of her life at Rome, and in Italy. She was of the house of La Trémoille: her husband was chief of the house of Ursins, a grandee of Spain, and Prince of the Soglio. She was also on very good terms with the Duchess of Savoy, and with the Queen of Portugal. The Cardinal d'Estrées, also, was known to have remained her friend, after having been something more in their youth; and he gave information that the Cardinal Portocarrero had been much in love with her at Rome, and that they were then on very good terms. As it was through the latter Cardinal that it was necessary to govern everything, this circumstance was considered very important.

Age and health were also appropriate; and likewise her appearance. She was rather tall than otherwise, a brunette, with blue eyes of the most varied expression, in figure perfect, with a most exquisite bosom; her face, without being beautiful, was charming; she was extremely noble in air, very majestic in demeanour, full of graces so natural and so continual in everything, that I have never seen any one approach her, either in form or mind. Her wit was copious and of all kinds: she was flattering, caressing, insinuating, moderate, wishing to please for pleasing's sake, with charms irresistible when she strove to persuade and win over; accompanying all this, she had a grandeur that encouraged instead of frightening; a delicious conversation, inexhaustible and very amusing, for she had seen many countries and persons; a voice and way of speaking extremely agreeable, and full of sweetness. She had read much, and reflected much. She knew how to choose the best society, how to receive them, and could even have held a court; was polite, distinguished; and above all was careful never to take a step in advance without dignity and discretion. She was eminently fitted for intrigue, in which, from taste, she had passed her time at Rome; with much ambition, but of that vast kind, far above her sex, and the common run of men—a desire to occupy a great position and to govern. A love for gallantry and personal vanity were her foibles, and these clung to her until her latest day; consequently, she dressed in a way that no longer became her, and as she advanced in life, removed further from propriety in this particular. She was an ardent and excellent friend—of a friendship that time and absence never enfeebled; and, consequently, an implacable enemy, pursuing her hatred to the infernal regions. While caring little for the means by which she gained her ends, she tried as much as possible to reach them by honest means. Secret, not only for herself, but for her friends, she was yet of a decorous gaiety, and so governed her humours, that at all times and in everything she was mistress of herself. Such was the Princesse des Ursins.

From the first moment on which she entered the service of the Queen of Spain, it became her desire to govern not only the Queen, but the King; and by this means the realm itself. Such a grand project had need of support from our King, who, at the commencement, ruled the Court of Spain as much as his own Court, with entire influence over all matters.

The young Queen of Spain had been not less carefully educated than her sister, the Duchesse de Bourgogne. She had even when so young much intelligence and firmness, without being incapable of restraint; and as time went on, improved still further, and displayed a constancy and courage which were admirably set off by her meekness and natural graces. According to everything I have heard said in France and in Spain, she possessed all qualities that were necessary to make her adored. Indeed she became a divinity among the Spaniards, and to their affection for her, Philip V. was more than once indebted for his crown. Lords, ladies, soldiers, and the people still remember her with tears in their eyes; and even after the lapse of so many years, are not yet consoled for her loss.

Madame des Ursins soon managed to obtain the entire confidence of this Queen; and during the absence of Philip V. in Italy, assisted her in the administration of all public offices. She even accompanied her to the Junta, it not being thought proper that the Queen should be alone amid such an assemblage of men. In this way she became acquainted with everything that was passing, and knew all the affairs of the Government.

This step gained, it will be imagined that the Prin-

cesse des Ursins did not forget to pay her court most
assiduously to our King and to Madame de Maintenon. She continually sent them an exact account of
everything relating to the Queen—making her appear
in the most favourable light possible. Little by little
she introduced into her letters details respecting public
events; without, however, conveying a suspicion of
her own ambition, or that she wished to meddle in
these matters. Anchored in this way, she next began
to flatter Madame de Maintenon, and by degrees to
hint that she might rule over Spain, even more firmly
than she ruled over France, if she would entrust her
commands to Madame des Ursins. Madame des
Ursins offered, in fact, to be the instrument of Madame de Maintenon; representing how much better it
would be to rule affairs in this manner, than through
the instrumentality of the ministers of either country.

Madame de Maintenon, whose passion it was to
know everything, to mix herself in everything, and
to govern everything, was enchanted by the siren.
This method of governing Spain without ministers
appeared to her an admirable idea. She embraced it
with avidity, without reflecting that she would govern
only in appearance, since she would know nothing
except through the Princesse des Ursins, see nothing
except in the light in which she presented it. From
that time dates the intimate union which existed between these two important women, the unbounded
authority of Madame des Ursins, the fall of all those
who had placed Philip V. upon the throne, and of all
our ministers in Spain who stood in the way of the
new power.

Such an alliance being made between the two
women, it was necessary to draw the King of Spain
into the same net. This was not a very arduous task.
Nature and art indeed had combined to make it easy.

Younger brother of an excitable, violent, and robust Prince, Philip V. had been bred up in a submission and dependence that were necessary for the repose of the Royal family. Until the testament of Charles II., the Duc d'Anjou was necessarily regarded as destined to be a subject all his life; and therefore could not be too much abased by education, and trained to patience and obedience. That supreme law, the reason of state, demanded this preference, for the safety and happiness of the kingdom, of the elder over the younger brother. His mind for this reason was purposely narrowed and beaten down, and his natural docility and gentleness greatly assisted in the process. He was quite formed to be led, although he had enough judgment left to choose the better of two courses proposed to him, and even to express himself in good phrase, when the slowness, not to say the laziness, of his mind did not prevent him from speaking at all. His great piety contributed to weaken his mind; and, being joined to very lively passions, made it disagreeable and even dangerous for him to be separated from his Queen. It may easily be conceived, therefore, how he loved her, and that he allowed himself to be guided by her in all things. As the Queen herself was guided in all things by Madame des Ursins, the influence of this latter was all-powerful.

Soon, indeed, the Junta became a mere show. Everything was brought before the King in private, and he gave no decision until the Queen and Madame des Ursins had passed theirs. This conduct met with no opposition from our Court, but our ministers at the Court of Spain and the Spanish ministers here soon began to complain of it. The first to do so were Cardinals d'Estrées and Portocarrero. Madame de Maintenon laughed at them, and Madame des Ursins, of whom they were old friends, soon showed them that she did not mean to abate one jot of her power. She first endeavoured to bring about a coldness between the two, and this succeeded so well, that in consequence of the quarrels that resulted, the Spanish Cardinal, Portocarrero (who, it will be remembered, had played an important part in bringing Philip to the Spanish throne) wished to quit the Junta. But Madame des Ursins, who thought that the time had not yet arrived for this step, persuaded him to remain, and endeavoured to flatter his vanity by an expedient altogether ridiculous. She gave him the command of a regiment of guards, and he, priest, archbishop, primate and cardinal, accepted it, and was, of course, well laughed at by everybody for his pains. The two cardinals soon after became reconciled to each other, feeling, perhaps, the necessity of uniting against the common enemy. But they could come to no better understanding with her. Disagreements continued, so that at last, feeling her position perfectly secure, the Princesse des Ursins begged permission to retire into Italy, knowing full well that she would not be taken at her word, and hoping by this means to deliver herself of these stumbling-blocks in her path.

Our ministers, who felt they would lose all control over Spanish affairs if Madame des Ursins was allowed to remain mistress, did all in their power to support the D'Estrées. But Madame de Maintenon pleaded so well with the King, representing the good policy of allowing a woman so much attached to him, and to the Spanish Queen, as was Madame des Ursins, to remain where she was, that he entirely swallowed the bait; the D'Estrées were left without support; the French ambassador at Madrid was virtually deprived of all power: the Spanish ministers were fettered in their every movement, and the authority of Madame des Ursins became stronger than ever. All public affairs passed through her hands. The King decided nothing without conferring with the Queen and her.

While excluding almost all the ministers from public offices, Madame des Ursins admitted a few favourites into her confidence. Amongst them was D'Harcourt, who stood well with Madame de Maintenon, and who cared little for the means by which he obtained consideration; Orry, who had the management of the finances; and D'Aubigny, son of a Procureur in Paris. The last was a tall, handsome fellow, well made, and active in mind and body; who for many years had been with the Princess, as a sort of squire, and on very intimate terms with her. One day, when, followed by some of the ministers, she entered a room in which he was writing, he burst out into exclamations against her, without being aware that she was not alone, swore at her, asked her why she could not leave him an hour in peace, called her by the strangest names, and all this with so much impetuosity that she had no time to show him who were behind her. When he found it out, he ran from the room, leaving Madame des Ursins so confused that the ministers looked for two or three minutes upon the walls of the room in order to give her time to recover herself. Soon after this, D'Aubigny had a splendid suite of apartments, that had formerly been occupied by Maria Theresa (afterwards wife of Louis XIV.), placed at his disposal, with some rooms added, in despite of the murmurs that arose at a distinction so strange accorded to this favourite.

At length, Cardinal d'Estrées, continually in arms against Madame des Ursins, and continually defeated, could not bear his position any longer, but asked to be immediately recalled. All that the ministry could do was to obtain permission for the Abbé d'Estrées (nephew of the Cardinal) to remain as Ambassador of

France at Madrid. As for Portocarrero, seeing the step his associate had taken, he resolved to quit public business also, and resigned his place accordingly. Several others who stood in the way of the Princesse des Ursins were got rid of at the same time, so that she was now left mistress of the field. She governed absolutely in all things; the ministers became instruments in her hands; the King and Queen agents to work out her will. She was at the highest pinnacle of power. Together with Orry she enjoyed a power such as no one had ever attained since the time of the Duke of Lerma and of Olivares.

In the mean time the Archduke was declared King of Spain by the Emperor, who made no mystery of his intention of attacking Spain by way of Portugal. The Archduke soon afterwards was recognised by Holland, England, Portugal, Brandenburg, Savoy, and Hanover, as King of Spain, under the title of Charles III., and soon after by the other powers of Europe. The Duke of Savoy had been treacherous to us, had shown that he was in league with the Emperor. The King accordingly had broken off all relations with him, and sent an army to invade his territory. It need be no cause of surprise, therefore, that the Archduke was recognised by Savoy. While our armies were fighting with varied fortune those of the Emperor and his allies, in different parts of Europe, notably upon the Rhine, Madame des Ursins was pressing matters to extremities in Spain. Dazzled by her success in expelling the two cardinals from public affairs, and all the ministers who had assisted in placing Philip V. upon the throne, she committed a blunder of which she soon had cause to repent.

I have said, that when Cardinal d'Estrées quitted Spain, the Abbé d'Estrées was left behind, so that France should not be altogether unrepresented in an official manner at the Court of Madrid. Madame des Ursins did not like this arrangement, but as Madame de Maintenon insisted upon it, she was obliged to accept it with as good grace as possible. The Abbé, vain of his family and of his position, was not a man much to be feared as it seemed. Madame des Ursins accordingly laughed at and despised him. He was admitted to the council, but was quite without influence there, and when he attempted to make any representations to Madame des Ursins or to Orry, they listened to him without attending in the least to what he said. The Princess reigned supreme, and thought of nothing but getting rid of all who attempted to divide her authority. At last she obtained such a command over the poor Abbé d'Estrées, so teased and hampered him, that he consented to the hitherto unheard-of arrangement, that the Ambassador of France should not write to the King without first concerting his letter with her, and then show her its contents before he despatched it. But such restraint as this became, in a short time, so fettering, that the Abbé determined to break away from it. He wrote a letter to the King, without showing it to Madame des Ursins. She soon had scent of what he had done; seized the letter as it passed through the post, opened it, and, as she expected, found its contents were not of a kind to give her much satisfaction. But what piqued her most was, to find details exaggerating the authority of D'Aubigny, and a statement to the effect that it was generally believed she had married him. Beside herself with rage and vexation, she wrote with her own hand upon the margin of the letter, *Pour mariée non* ("At any rate, not married"), showed it in this state to the King and Queen of Spain, to a number of other people, always with strange clamouring, and finally crowned her folly by sending it to the King (Louis XIV.), with furious complaints against the Abbé for writing it without her knowledge, and for inflicting upon her such an atrocious injury as to mention this pretended marriage. Her letter and its enclosure reached the King at a very inopportune moment. Just before, he had received a letter, which, taken in connection with this of the Princesse des Ursins, struck a blow at her power of the most decisive kind.

CHAPTER XXVIII

SOME little time previously it had been thought necessary to send an army to the frontiers of Portugal to oppose the Archduke. A French general was wanted to command this army. Madame des Ursins, who had been very intimate with the King of England (James II.) and his Queen, thought she would please them if she gave this post to the Duke of Berwick, illegitimate son of King James. She proposed this therefore; and our King, out of regard for his brother monarch, and from a natural affection for bastards, consented to the appointment; but as the Duke of Berwick had never before commanded an army, he stipulated that Puységur, known to be a skilful officer, should go with him and assist him with his counsels and advice.

Puységur set out before the Duke of Berwick. From the Pyrenees as far as Madrid, he found every provision made for the subsistence of the French troops, and sent a very advantageous account to the King of this circumstance. Arrived at Madrid, he had interviews with Orry (who, as I have already mentioned, had the finances under his control, and who was a mere instrument in the hands of Madame des Ursins), and was assured by the minister that all the magazines along the line of route to the frontiers of Portugal were abundantly filled with supplies for the French troops, that all the money necessary was ready, and that nothing, in fact, should fail in the course of the campaign. Puységur, who had found nothing wanting up to that time, never doubted but that these statements were perfectly correct; and had no suspicion that a minister would have the effrontery to show him in detail all these precautions if he had taken none. Pleased, then, to the utmost degree, he wrote to the King in praise of Orry, and consequently of Madame des Ursins and her wise government. Full of these ideas, he set out for the frontier of Portugal to reconnoitre the ground himself, and arrange everything for the arrival of the army and its general. What was his surprise, when he found that from Madrid to the frontier not a single preparation had been made for the troops, and that in consequence all that Orry had shown him, drawn out upon paper, was utterly fictitious. His vexation upon finding that nothing upon which he had reckoned was provided, may be imagined. He at once wrote to the King, in order to contradict all that he had recently written.

This conduct of Orry—his impudence, I may say—in deceiving a man who immediately after would have under his eyes the proof of his deceit, is a thing past all comprehension. It is easy to understand that rogues should steal, but not that they should have the audacity to do so in the face of facts which so quickly and so easily could prove their villainy.

It was Puységur's letter then, detailing this rascality on the part of Orry, that had reached the King just before that respecting the Abbé d'Estrées. The two disclosed a state of things that could not be allowed any longer to exist. Our ministers, who, step by step, had been deprived of all control over the affairs of Spain, profited by the discontentment of the King to reclaim their functions. Harcourt and Madame de Maintenon did all they could to ward off the blow from Madame des Ursins, but without effect. The King determined to banish her to Rome and to dismiss Orry from his post.

It was felt, however, that these steps must be taken cautiously, to avoid offending too deeply the King and Queen of Spain, who supported their favourite through every emergency.

In the first place, then, a simple reprimand was sent to the Princesse des Ursins for the violation of the respect due to the King, by opening a letter addressed to him by one of his ambassadors. The Abbé d'Estrées, who expected that Madame des Ursins would be at once disgraced, and who had made a great outcry when his letter was opened, fell into such despair when he saw how lightly she was let off, that he asked for his dismissal. He was taken at his word; and this was a new triumph for Madame des Ursins, who thought herself more secure than ever. Her triumph was of but short duration. The King wrote to Philip, recommending him to head in person the army for the frontiers of Portugal, which, in spite of Orry's deception, it was still determined to send. No sooner was Philip fairly away, separated from the Queen and Madame des Ursins, and no longer under their influence, than the King wrote to the Queen of Spain, requesting her, in terms that could not be disputed, to dismiss at once and for ever her favourite *Camerera Mayor*. The Queen, in despair at the idea of losing a friend and adviser to whom she had been so much attached, believed herself lost. At the same time that the King wrote to the Queen of Spain, he also wrote to the Princesse des Ursins, ordering her to quit Madrid immediately, to leave Spain, and to retire into Italy.

At this conjuncture of affairs, when the Queen was in despair, Madame des Ursins did not lose her composure. She opened her eyes to all that had passed since she had violated D'Estrées' letter, and saw the vanity of the triumph she had recently enjoyed. She felt at once that for the present all was lost, that her only hope was to be allowed to remain in France. She made all her arrangements, therefore, so that affairs might proceed in her absence as much as possible as though she were present, and then prepared to set out. Dawdling day by day, she put off her departure as long as could be, and when at length she left Madrid only went to Alcala, a few leagues distant. She stopped there under various pretexts, and at length, after five weeks of delay, set out for Bayonne, journeying as slowly as she could and stopping as often as she dared.

She lost no opportunity of demanding an audience at Versailles, in order to clear herself of the charge which weighed upon her, and her importunities at length were not without effect. The most terrible storms at Court soon blow over. The King (Louis XIV.) was satisfied with the success of his plans. He had been revenged in every way, and had humbled the pride of the Princesse des Ursins. It was not necessary to excite the anger of the Queen and King of Spain by too great harshness against their fallen friend. Madame de Maintenon took advantage of this change in the temper of the King, and by dint of persuasion and scheming succeeded in obtaining from him the permission for Madame des Ursins to remain in France. Toulouse was fixed upon for her residence. It was a place that just suited her, and from which communication with Spain was easy. Here accordingly she took up her residence, determined to watch well the course of events, and to avail herself of every opportunity that could bring about her complete reconciliation with the King (Louis XIV.), and obtain for her in consequence the permission to return to Madrid.

In the mean time, the King and Queen of Spain,

distressed beyond measure at the loss of their favourite, thought only of the best means of obtaining her recall. They plotted with such ministers as were favourable to her; they openly quarrelled with and thwarted those who were her opponents, so that the most important matters perished in their hands. Nay more, upon the King of Spain's return, the Queen persuaded him to oppose in all things the wishes of the King (Louis XIV.), his grandfather, and to neglect his counsels with studied care. Our King complained of this with bitterness. The aim of it was to tire him out, and to make him understand that it was only Madame des Ursins, well treated and sent back, who could restore Spanish affairs to their original state, and cause his authority to be respected. Madame de Maintenon, on her side, neglected no opportunity of pressing the King to allow Madame des Ursins, not to return into Spain—that would have been to spoil all by asking too much—but simply to come to Versailles in order to have the opportunity of justifying herself for her past conduct. From other quarters the King was similarly importuned. Tired at last of the obstinate opposition he met with in Spain from the Queen, who governed completely her husband, he gave permission to Madame des Ursins to come to Versailles to plead her own cause. Self-imprisoned as he was in seclusion, the truth never approached him, and he was the only man in the two kingdoms who had no suspicion that the arrival of Madame des Ursins at the Court was the certain sign of her speedy return to Spain more powerful than ever. But he was fatigued with the constant resistance he met with; with the disorder which this occasioned in public affairs at a time too when, as I will afterwards explain, the closest union was necessary between the two crowns in order to repel the common enemy; and these motives induced him, to the astonishment of his ministers, to grant the favour requested of him.

However well informed Madame des Ursins might be of all that was being done on her account, this permission surpassed her hopes. Her joy accordingly was very great; but it did not at all carry her away. She saw that her return to Spain would now depend upon herself. She determined to put on the air of one who is disgraced, but who hopes, and yet is humiliated. She instructed all her friends to assume the same manner; took all measures with infinite presence of mind; did not hurry her departure, and yet set out with sufficient promptness to prevent any coldness springing up, and to show with what eagerness she profited by the favour accorded to her, and which she had so much wished.

No sooner was the courier gone who carried this news to her, than the rumour of her return was whispered all over the Court, and became publicly confirmed a few days afterwards. The movement that it produced at Court was inconceivable. Only the friends of Madame des Ursins were able to remain in a tolerably tranquil state. Everybody opened his eyes and comprehended that the return of such an important personage was a fact that could not be insignificant. People prepared themselves for a sort of rising sun that was going to change and renew many things in nature. On every side were seen people who had scarcely ever uttered her name, and who now boasted of their intimacy with her and of her friendship for them. Other people were seen, who, although openly allied with her enemies, had the baseness to affect transports of joy at her forthcoming return, and to flatter those whom they thought likely to favour them with her.

She reached Paris on Sunday, the 4th of January,

1705. The Duc d'Albe met her several miles out of the city, escorted her to his house, and gave a *fête* in her honour there. Several persons of distinction went out to meet her. Madame des Ursins had reason to be surprised at an entry so triumphant: she would not, however, stay with the Duc and Duchesse d'Albe, but took up her quarters with the Comtesse d'Egmont, niece of the Archbishop of Aix; the said Archbishop having been instrumental in obtaining her recall. The King was at Marly. I was there with Madame de Saint-Simon. During the remainder of the stay at Marly everybody flocked to the house of Madame des Ursins, anxious to pay her their court. However flattered she may have been by this concourse, she had matters to occupy her, pleaded want of repose, and shut her door to three people out of four who called upon her. Curiosity, perhaps fashion, drew this great crowd to her. The ministers were startled by it. Torcy had orders from the King to go and see her: he did so; and from that moment Madame des Ursins changed her tone. Until then her manner had been modest, supplicating, nearly timid. She now saw and heard so much that from defendant, which she had intended to be, she thought herself in a condition to become accuser; and to demand justice of those who, abusing the confidence of the King, had drawn upon her such a long and cruel punishment, and made her a show for the two kingdoms. All that happened to her surpassed her hopes. Several times when with me she has expressed her astonishment; and with me has laughed at many people, often of much consideration, whom she scarcely knew, or who had been strongly opposed to her, and who basely crouched at her feet.

The King returned to Versailles on Saturday, the 10th of January. Madame des Ursins arrived there the same day. I went immediately to see her, not having been able to do so before, because I could not quit Marly. My mother had seen a great deal of Madame des Ursins at Paris. I had always been on good terms with her, and had received on all occasions proofs of her friendship. She received me very well, spoke with much freedom, and said she promised herself the pleasure of seeing me again, and of talking with me more at her ease. On the morrow, Sunday, she dined at home alone, dressed herself in grand style, and went to the King, with whom she remained alone two hours and a half conversing in his cabinet. From there she went to the Duchesse de Bourgogne, with whom she also conversed a long time alone. In the evening, the King said, while in Madame de Maintenon's apartments, that there were still many things upon which he had not yet spoken to Madame des Ursins. The next day she saw Madame de Maintenon in private for a long time, and much at her ease. She had an interview soon after with the King and Madame de Maintenon, which was also very long.

A month after this a special courier arrived from the King and Queen of Spain, to thank the King (Louis XIV.) for his conduct towards the Princesse des Ursins. From that moment it was announced that she would remain at Court until the month of April, in order to attend to her affairs and her health. It was already to have made a grand step to be mistress enough to announce thus her stay. Nobody in truth doubted of her return to Spain, but the word was not yet said. She avoided all explanations, and it may be believed did not have many indiscreet questions put to her upon the subject.

So many and such long audiences with the King, followed by so much serenity, had a great effect upon the world, and the crowd that flocked to see Madame des Ursins was greater than ever; but under various pretences she shut herself up and would see only a few intimate friends, foremost among which were Madame de Saint-Simon and myself. Whilst triumphant beyond all her hopes in Paris, she was at work in Spain, and with equal success. Rivas, who had drawn up the will of the late King Charles II., was disgraced, and never afterwards rose to favour. The Duc de Grammont, our ambassador at Madrid, was so overwhelmed with annoyance, that he asked for his recall. Amelot, whom Madame des Ursins favoured, was appointed in his place, and many who had been disgraced were reinstated in office; everything was ordered according to her wishes.

We returned to Marly, where many balls took place. It need not be doubted that Madame des Ursins was among the invited. Apartments were given her, and nothing could equal the triumphant air with which she took possession of them, the continual attentions of the King to her, as though she were some little foreign queen just arrived at his Court, or the majestic fashion in which she received them, mingled with grace and respectful politeness, then almost out of date, and which recalled the stately old dames of the Queen-mother. She never came without the King, who appeared to be completely occupied with her, talking with her, pointing out objects for her inspection, seeking her opinion and her approbation with an air of gallantry, even of flattery, which never ceased. The frequent private conversations that she had with him in the apartment of Madame de Maintenon, and which lasted an hour, and sometimes double that time; those that she very often had in the morning alone with Madame de Maintenon, rendered her the divinity of the Court. The Princesses encircled her the moment she appeared anywhere, and went to see her in her chamber. Nothing was more surprising than the servile eagerness with which the greatest people, the highest in power and the most in favour, clustered around her. Her very glances were counted, and her words, addressed even to ladies of the highest rank, imprinted upon them a look of ravishment.

I went nearly every morning to her house: she always rose very early, dressed herself at once, so that she was never seen at her toilette. I was in advance of the hour fixed for the most important visitors, and we talked with the same liberty as of yore. I learnt from her many details, and the opinion of the King and of Madame de Maintenon upon many people. We often used to laugh in concert at the truckling to her of persons the most considerable, and of the disdain they drew upon themselves, although she did not testify it to them. We laughed too at the falsehood of others, who after having done her all the injury in their power ever since her arrival, lavished upon her all kinds of flatteries, and boasted of their affection for her and of zeal in her cause. I was flattered with this confidence of the dictatress of the Court. It drew upon me a sudden consideration; for people of the greatest distinction often found me alone with her in the morning, and the messengers who rained down at that time reported that they had found me with her, and that they had not been able to speak to her. Oftentimes in the *salon* she called me to her, or at other times I went to her and whispered a word in her ear, with an air of ease and liberty much envied but little imitated. She never met Madame de Saint-Simon without going to her, praising her, making her join in the conversation that was passing around; oftentimes leading her to the glass and adjusting her head-dress or her robe as she might have done in private to a daughter. People asked with surprise and much annoyance whence came such a great friendship which had never been suspected by anybody? What completed the torment of the majority, was to see Madame des Ursins, as soon as she quitted the chamber of Madame de Maintenon, go immediately to Madame de Saint-Simon, lead her aside, and speak to her in a low tone. This opened the eyes of everybody and drew upon us many civilities.

A more solid gratification to us were the kind things Madame des Ursins said in our behalf to the King and Madame de Maintenon. She spoke in the highest praise of Madame de Saint-Simon, and declared that there was no woman at Court so fitting as she, so expressly made by her virtue, good conduct, and ability, to be lady of the Palace, or even lady-of-honour to Madame la Duchesse de Bourgogne, should the post become vacant. Madame des Ursins did not forget me; but a woman was more susceptible of her praise. It made, therefore, all the more impression. This kind manner towards us did not change during all her stay at Court.

At all the balls which Madame des Ursins attended, she was treated with much distinction, and at one she obtained permission for the Duc and Duchesse d'Albe to be present, but with some little trouble. I say with some little trouble, because no ambassador, no foreigner, had ever, with one exception, been admitted to Marly. It was a great favour, therefore, for Madame des Ursins to obtain. The King, too, treated the Duc and Duchesse d'Albe, throughout the evening with marked respect, and placed the latter in the most distinguished position, not only in the ball-room but at supper. When he went to bed, too, he gave the Duc d'Albe his candlestick; an honour the importance of which I have already described.

At the other balls Madame des Ursins seated herself near the Grand Chamberlain, and looked at everybody with her *lorgnette*. At every moment the King turned round to speak to her and Madame de Maintenon, who came for half an hour or so to these balls, and on her account displaced the Grand Chamberlain, who put himself behind her. In this manner she joined Madame des Ursins, and was close to the King—the conversation between the three being continual. What appeared extremely singular was to see Madame des Ursins in the *salon* with a little spaniel in her arms, as though she had been in her own house. People could not sufficiently express their astonishment at a familiarity which even Madame la Duchesse de Bourgogne would not have dared to venture; still less could they do so when they saw the King caress this little dog over and over again. In fine, such a high flight has never been seen. People could not accustom themselves to it, and those who knew the King and his Court are surprised still, when they think of it, after so many years. There was no longer any doubt that Madame des Ursins would return into Spain. All her frequent private conversations with the King and Madame de Maintenon were upon that country. I will only add here that her return took place in due time; and that her influence became more paramount than ever.

The Surrender of Marshal Tallard after the battle of Blenheim. —p. 363

From the painting by R. Caton Woodville.

CHAPTER XXIX

IN relating what happened to Madame des Ursins upon her return to Spain, I have carried the narrative into the year 1705. It is not necessary to retrace our steps. Towards the end of 1703 Courtin died. He had early shone at the Council, and had been made Intendant of Picardy. M. de Chaulnes, whose estates were there, begged him to tax them as lightly as possible. Courtin, who was a very intimate friend of M. de Chaulnes, complied with his request; but the next year, in going over his accounts, he found that to do a good turn to M. de Chaulnes he had done an ill turn to many others—that is to say, he had relieved M. de Chaulnes at the expense of other parishes, which he had overcharged. The trouble this caused him made him search deeply into the matter, and he found that the wrong he had done amounted to forty thousand francs. Without a second thought he paid back this money, and asked to be recalled. As he was much esteemed, his request was not at once complied with, but he represented so well that he could not pass his life doing wrong, and unable to serve his friends, that at last what he asked was granted. He afterwards had several embassies, went to England as ambassador, and was very successful in that capacity. I cannot quit Courtin without relating an adventure he had one day with Fieubet, a Councillor of State like himself. As they were going to Saint Germain they were stopped by several men and robbed; robbery was common in those days, and Fieubet lost all he had in his pockets. When the thieves had left them, and while Fieubet was complaining of his misfortune, Courtin began to applaud himself for having saved his watch and fifty pistoles that he had time to slip into his trowsers. Immediately on hearing this, Fieubet put his head out of the coach window, and called back the thieves, who came sure enough to see what he wanted.

"Gentlemen," said he, "you appear to be honest folks in distress; it is not reasonable that you should be the dupes of this gentleman, who has swindled you out of fifty pistoles and his watch." And then turning to Courtin, he smilingly said: "You told me so yourself, monsieur; so give the things up like a man, without being searched."

The astonishment and indignation of Courtin were such that he allowed money and watch to be taken from him without uttering a single word; but when the thieves were gone away, he would have strangled Fieubet had not this latter been the stronger of the two. Fieubet only laughed at him; and upon arriving at Saint Germain told the adventure to everybody he met. Their friends had all the trouble in the world to reconcile them.

The year finished with an affair in which I was not a little interested. During the year there were several grand *fêtes,* at which the King went to High Mass and vespers. On these occasions a lady of the Court, named by the Queen, or when there was none, by the Dauphiness, made a collection for the poor. The house of Lorraine, always anxious to increase its importance, shirked impudently this duty, in order thereby to give itself a new distinction, and assimilate its rank to that of the Princes of the blood. It was a long time before this was perceived. At last the Duchesse de Noailles, the Duchesse de Guiche, her daughter, the Maréchal de Boufflers, and others, took notice of it; and I was soon after informed of it. I determined that the matter should be arranged, and that justice should be done.

The Duchesse de Lude was first spoken to on the subject; she, weak and timid, did not dare to do anything; but at last was induced to speak to Madame la Duchesse de Bourgogne, who, wishing to judge for herself as to the truth of the matter, ordered Madame de Montbazon to make the collection for the poor at the next *fête* that took place. Although very well, Madame de Montbazon pretended to be ill, stopped in bed half a day, and excused herself on this ground from performing the duty. Madame de Bourgogne was annoyed, but she did not dare to push matters farther; and, in consequence of this refusal, none of the Duchesses would make the collection. Other ladies of quality soon perceived this, and they also refused to serve; so that the collection fell into all sorts of hands, and sometimes was not made at all. Matters went on so far, indeed, that the King at last grew angry, and threatened to make Madame de Bourgogne herself take this office. But refusals still followed upon refusals, and the bomb thus at length was ready to burst!

The King, who at last ordered the daughter of M. le Grand to take the plate on New Year's Day, 1704, had, it seems, got scent of the part I was taking in this matter, and expressed himself to Madame de Maintenon, as I learnt, as very discontented with me and one or two other Dukes. He said that the Dukes were much less obedient to him than the Princes; and that although many Duchesses had refused to make the collection, the moment he had proposed that the daughter of M. le Grand should take it, M. le Grand consented. On the next day, early in the morning, I saw Chamillart, who related to me that on the previous evening, before he had had time to open his business, the King had burst out in anger against me, saying it was very strange, but that since I had quitted the army I did nothing but meddle in matters of rank and bring actions against everybody; finishing, by declaring that if he acted well he should send me so far away that I should be unable to importune him any more. Chamillart added, that he had done all in his power to appease the King, but with little effect.

After consulting with my friends, I determined to go up to the King and boldly ask to speak to him in his cabinet, believing that to be the wisest course I could pursue. He was not yet so reconciled to me as he afterwards became, and, in fact, was sorely out of humour with me. This step did not seem, therefore, altogether unattended with danger; but, as I have said, I resolved to take it. As he passed, therefore, from his dinner that same day, I asked permission to follow him into his cabinet. Without replying to me, he made a sign that I might enter, and went into the embrasure of the window.

When we were quite alone I explained, at considerable length, my reasons for acting in this matter, declaring that it was from no disrespect to his Majesty that I had requested Madame de Saint-Simon and the other Duchesses to refuse to collect for the poor, but simply to bring those to account who had claimed without reason to be exempt from this duty. I added, keeping my eyes fixed upon the King all the time, that I begged him to believe that none of his subjects were more submissive to his will or more willing to acknowledge the supremacy of his authority in all things than the Dukes. Until this his tone and manner had been very severe; but now they both softened, and he said, with much goodness and familiarity, that "that was how it was proper to speak and think," and other remarks equally gracious. I took then the opportunity of expressing the sorrow I felt at seeing, that while my sole endeavour was to please him, my enemies did all they could to blacken me in his eyes, indicating that I suspected M. le Grand, who had never pardoned me for the part I took in the affair of the Princesse d'Harcourt, was one of the number. After I had finished the King remained still a moment, as if ready to hear if I had anything more to say, and then quitted me with a bow, slight but very gracious, saying it was well, and that he was pleased with me.

I learnt afterwards that he said the same thing of me in the evening to Chamillart, but, nevertheless, that he did not seem at all shaken in his prejudice in favour of M. le Grand. The King was in fact very easy to prejudice, difficult to lead back, and most unwilling to seek enlightenment, or to listen to any explanations, if authority was in the slightest degree at stake. Whoever had the address to make a question take this shape, might be assured that the King would throw aside all consideration of justice, right, and reason, and dismiss all evidence. It was by playing on this chord that his ministers knew how to manage him with so much art, and to make themselves despotic masters, causing him to believe all they wished, while at the same time they rendered him inaccessible to explanation, and to those who might have explained.

I have, perhaps, too much expanded an affair which might have been more compressed. But in addition to the fact that I was mixed up in it, it is by these little private details, as it seems to me, that the characters of the Court and King are best made known.

In the early part of the next year, 1704, the King made La Queue, who was a captain of cavalry, campmaster. This La Queue was seigneur of the place of which he bore the name, distant six leagues from Versailles, and as much from Dreux. He had married a girl that the King had had by a gardener's wife. Bontems, the confidential valet of the King, had brought about the marriage without declaring the names of the father or the mother of the girl; but La Queue knew it, and promised himself a fortune. The girl herself was tall and strongly resembled the King. Unfortunately for her, she knew the secret of her birth, and much envied her three sisters—recognised, and so grandly married. She lived on very good terms with her husband—always, however, in the greatest privacy—and had several children by him. La Queue himself, although by this marriage son-in-law of the King, seldom appeared at the Court, and, when there, was on the same footing as the simplest soldier. Bontems did not fail from time to time to give him money. The wife of La Queue lived very melancholily for twenty years in her village, never left it, and scarcely ever went abroad for fear of betraying herself.

On Wednesday, the 25th of June, Monseigneur le Duc de Bourgogne had a son born to him. This event caused great joy to the King and the Court. The town shared their delight, and carried their enthusiasm almost to madness, by the excess of their demonstration and their *fêtes*. The King gave a *fête* at Marly, and made the most magnificent presents to Madame la Duchesse de Bourgogne when she left her bed. But we soon had reason to repent of so much joy, for the child died in less than a year—and of so much money unwisely spent in *fêtes* when it was wanted for more pressing purposes. Even while these rejoicings were being celebrated, news reached us which spread consternation in every family, and cast a gloom over the whole city.

I have already said that a grand alliance, with the Emperor at its head, had been formed against France, and that our troops were opposing the Allies in various parts of Europe. The Elector of Bavaria had joined his forces to ours, and had already done us some service. On the 12th of August he led his men into the plain of Hochstedt, where, during the previous year, he had gained a victory over the Imperialists. In this plain he was joined by our troops, who took up positions right and left of him, under the command of Tallard and Marsin. The Elector himself had command of all. Soon after their arrival at Hochstedt, they received intelligence that Prince Eugène, with the Imperialist forces, and the Duke of Marlborough with the English were coming to meet them. Our generals had, however, all the day before them to choose their ground, and to make their dispositions. It would have been difficult to succeed worse, both with the one and the other. A brook, by no means of a miry kind, ran parallel to our army; and in front of it a spring, which formed a long and large quagmire, nearly separated the two lines of Marshal Tallard. It was a strange situation for a general to take up, who is master of a vast plain; and it became, as will be seen, a very sad one. At his extreme right was the large village of Blenheim, in which, by a blindness without example, he had placed twenty-six battalions of infantry, six regiments of dragoons, and a brigade of cavalry. It was an entire army merely for the purpose of holding this village, and supporting his right, and of course he had all these troops the less to aid him in the battle which took place. The first battle of Hochstedt afforded a lesson which ought to have been studied on this occasion. There were many officers present, too, who had been at that battle; but they were not consulted. One of two courses was open, either to take up a position behind the brook, and parallel to it, so as to dispute its passage with the enemies, or to take advantage of the disorder they would be thrown into in crossing it by attacking them then. Both these plans were good; the second was the better; but neither was adopted. What was done was, to leave a large space between our troops and the brook, that the enemy might pass at their ease, and be overthrown afterwards, as was said. With such dispositions it is impossible to doubt but that our chiefs were struck with blindness. The Danube flowed near enough to Blenheim to be of sufficient support to our right, better indeed than that village, which consequently there was no necessity to hold.

The enemies arrived on the 13th of August at the dawn, and at once took up their position on the banks of the brook. Their surprise must have been great to see our army so far off, drawn up in battle array. They profited by the extent of ground left to them, crossed the brook at nearly every point, formed themselves in several lines on the side to which they crossed, and then extended themselves at their ease, without receiving the slightest opposition. This is exact truth, but without any appearance of being so; and posterity will with difficulty believe it. It was nearly eight o'clock before all these dispositions, which our troops saw made without moving, were completed. Prince Eugène with his army had the right; the Duke of Marlborough the left. The latter thus opposed to the forces of Tallard, and Prince Eugène to those of Marsin.

The battle commenced; and in one part was so far favourable to us that the attack of Prince Eugène was repulsed by Marsin, who might have profited by this circumstance but for the unfortunate position of our right. Two things contributed to place us at a disadvantage. The second line, separated by the quagmire I have alluded to from the first line, could not sustain it properly; and in consequence of the long bend it was necessary to make round this quagmire, neither line, after receiving or making a charge, could retire quickly to rally and return again to the attack. As for the infantry, the twenty-six battalions shut up in Blenheim left a great gap in it that could not fail to be felt. The English, who soon perceived the advantage they might obtain from this want of infantry, and from the difficulty with which our cavalry of the right was rallied, profited by these circumstances with the readiness of people who have plenty of ground at their disposal. They redoubled their charges, and to say all in one word, they defeated at their first attack all this army, notwithstanding the efforts of our general officers and of several regiments to repel them. The army of the Elector, entirely unsupported, and taken in flank by the English, wavered in its turn. All the valour of the Bavarians, all the prodigies of the Elector, were unable to remedy the effects of this wavering. Thus was seen, at one and the same time, the army of Tallard beaten and thrown into the utmost disorder; that of the Elector sustaining itself with great intrepidity, but already in retreat; and that of Marsin charging and gaining ground upon Prince Eugène. It was not until Marsin learnt of the defeat of Tallard and of the Elector, that he ceased to pursue his advantages, and commenced his retreat. This retreat he was able to make without being pursued.

In the mean time the troops in Blenheim had been twice attacked, and had twice repulsed the enemy. Tallard had given orders to these troops on no account to leave their positions, nor to allow a single man even to quit them. Now, seeing his army defeated and in flight, he wished to countermand these orders. He was riding in hot haste to Blenheim to do so, with only two attendants, when all three were surrounded, recognised, and taken prisoners.

These troops shut up in Blenheim had been left under the command of Blansac, camp-marshal, and Clérembault, lieutenant-general. During the battle this latter was missed, and could nowhere be found. It was known afterwards that, for fear of being killed, he had endeavoured to escape across the Danube on horseback attended by a single valet. The valet passed over the river in safety, but his master went to the bottom. Blansac, thus left alone in command, was much troubled by the disorders he saw and heard, and by the want which he felt of fresh orders. He sent a messenger to Tallard for instructions how to act, but his messenger was stopped on the road, and taken prisoner. I only repeat what Blansac himself reported in his defence, which was equally ill-received by the King and the public, but which had no contradictors, for nobody was witness of what took place at Blenheim except those actually there, and they all, the principals at least, agreed in their story. What some of the soldiers said was not of a kind that could altogether be relied upon.

While Blansac was in this trouble, he saw Denonville, one of our officers who had been taken prisoner, coming towards the village, accompanied by an officer who waved a handkerchief in the air and demanded a parley. Denonville was a young man, very handsome and well made, who being a great favourite with Monseigneur le Duc de Bourgogne had become presumptuous and somewhat audacious. Instead of speaking in private to Blansac and the other principal officers—since he had undertaken so strange a mission—Denonville, who had some intellect, plenty of fine talk, and a mighty opinion of himself, set to work haranguing the troops, trying to persuade them to surrender themselves prisoners of war, so that they might preserve themselves for the service of the King. Blansac, who saw the wavering this caused among the troops, sharply told Denonville to hold his tongue, and began himself to harangue the troops in a contrary spirit. But it was too late. The mischief was done. Only one regiment, that of Navarre, applauded him, all the rest maintained a dull silence. I remind my readers that it is Blansac's version of the story I am giving.

Soon after Denonville and his companion had returned to the enemy, an English lord came, demanding a parley with the commandant. He was admitted to Blansac, to whom he said that the Duke of Marlborough had sent him to say that he had forty battalions and sixty pieces of cannon at his disposal, with reinforcements to any extent at command; that he should surround the village on all sides; that the army of Tallard was in flight, and the remains of that of the Elector in retreat; that Tallard and many general officers were prisoners; that Blansac could hope for no reinforcements; and that, therefore, he had better at once make an honourable capitulation, and surrender himself with all his men prisoners of war, than attempt a struggle in which he was sure to be worsted with great loss. Blansac wanted to dismiss this messenger at once, but the Englishman pressed him to advance a few steps out of the village, and see with his own eyes the defeat of the Electoral army, and the preparations that were made on the other side to continue the battle. Blansac accordingly, attended by one of his officers, followed this lord, and was astounded to see with his own eyes that all he had just heard was true. Returned into Bleinheim, Blansac assembled all his principal officers, made them acquainted with the proposition that had been made, and told them what he had himself seen. Every one comprehended what a frightful shock it would be for the country when it learnt that they had surrendered themselves prisoners of war; but all things well considered, it was thought best to accept these terms, and so preserve to the King the twenty-six battalions and the twelve squadrons of dragoons who were there. This terrible capitulation was at once, therefore, drawn up and signed by Blansac, the general officers, and the heads of every corps except that of Navarre, which was thus the sole one which refused.

The number of prisoners that fell to the enemy in this battle was infinite. The Duke of Marlborough took charge of the most distinguished, until he could carry them away to England, to grace his triumph there. He treated them all, even the humblest, with the utmost attention, consideration, and politeness, and with a modesty that did him even more honour than his victory. Those that came under the charge of Prince Louis of Baden were much less kindly treated.

The King received the cruel news of this battle on the 21st of August, by a courier from the Maréchal de Villeroy. By this courier the King learnt that a battle had taken place on the 13th; had lasted from eight o'clock in the morning until evening; that the entire army of Tallard was killed or taken prisoners; that it was not known what had become of Tallard himself, or whether the Elector and Marsin had been at the action. The private letters that arrived were all opened to see what news they contained, but no fresh information could be got from them. For six days the King remained in this uncertainty as to the real losses that had been sustained. Everybody was afraid to write bad news; all the letters which from time to time arrived, gave, therefore, but an unsatisfactory account of what had taken place. The King used every means in his power to obtain some news. Every post that came in was examined by him, but there was little found to satisfy him. Neither the King nor anybody else could understand, from what had reached them, how it was that an entire army had been placed inside a village, and had surrendered itself by a signed capitulation. It puzzled every brain. At last the details, that had oozed out little by little, augmented to a perfect stream, by the arrival of one of our officers, who, taken prisoner, had been allowed by the Duke of Marlborough to go to Paris to relate to the King the misfortune that had happened to him.

We were not accustomed to misfortunes. This one, very reasonably, was utterly unexpected. It seemed in every way the result of bad generalship, of an unjustifiable disposition of troops, and of a series of gross and incredible errors. The commotion was general. There was scarcely an illustrious family that had not had one of its members killed, wounded, or taken prisoner. Other families were in the same case. The public sorrow and indignation burst out without restraint. Nobody who had taken part in this humiliation was spared; the generals and the private soldiers alike came in for blame. Denonville was ignominiously broken for the speech he had made at Blenheim. The generals, however, were entirely let off. All the punishment fell upon certain regiments, which were broken, and upon certain unimportant officers—the guilty and innocent mixed together. The outcry was universal. The grief of the King at this ignominy and this loss, at the moment when he imagined that the fate of the Emperor was in his hands, may be imagined. At a time when he might have counted upon striking a decisive blow, he saw himself reduced to act simply on the defensive, in order to preserve his troops; and had to repair the loss of an entire army, killed or taken prisoners. The sequel showed not less that the hand of God was weighty upon us. All judgment was lost. We trembled even in the midst of Alsace.

In the midst of all this public sorrow, the rejoicings and the *fêtes* for the birth of the Duc de Bretagne, son of Monseigneur le Duc de Bourgogne, were not discontinued. The city gave a firework *fête* upon the river, that Monseigneur, the Princes, his sons, and Madame la Duchesse de Bourgogne, with many ladies and courtiers, came to see from the windows of the Louvre, magnificent cheer and refreshments being provided for them. This was a contrast which irritated the people, who would not understand that it was meant for magnanimity. A few days afterwards the King gave an illumination and a *fête* at Marly, to which the Court of Saint Germain was invited, and which was all in honour of Madame la Duchesse de Bourgogne. He thanked the *Prévôt des Marchands* for the fireworks upon the river, and said that Monseigneur and Madame had found them very beautiful.

Shortly after this, I received a letter from one of my friends, the Duc de Montfort, who had always been in the army of the Maréchal de Villeroy. He sent word to me, that upon his return he intended to break his sword, and retire from the army. His letter was written in such a despairing tone that, fearing lest with his burning courage he might commit some martial folly, I conjured him not to throw himself into danger for the sake of being killed. It seemed that I had anticipated his intentions. A convoy of money was to be sent to Landau. Twice he asked to be allowed to take charge of this convoy, and twice he was told it was too insignificant a charge for a camp-marshal to undertake. The third time that he asked this favour, he obtained it by pure importunity. He carried the money safely into Landau, without meeting with any obstacle. On his return he saw some hussars roving about. Without a moment's hesitation he resolved to give chase to them.

He was with difficulty restrained for some time, and at last, breaking away, he set off to attack them, followed by only two officers. The hussars dispersed themselves, and retreated; the Duc de Montfort followed them, rode into the midst of them, was surrounded on all sides, and soon received a blow which overturned him. In a few moments after, being carried off by his men, he died, having only had time to confess himself, and to arrive at his quarters. He was infinitely regretted by everybody who had known him. The grief of his family may be imagined.

CHAPTER XXX

THE King did not long remain without some consolation for the loss of the battle of Hochstedt (Blenheim). The Comte de Toulouse—very different in every respect from his brother, the Duc du Maine—was wearied with cruising in the Mediterranean, without daring to attack enemies that were too strong for him. He had, therefore, obtained reinforcements this year, so that he was in a state to measure his forces with any opponent. The English fleet was under the command of Admiral Rooke. The Comte de Toulouse wished above all things to attack. He asked permission to do so, and, the permission being granted, he set about his enterprise. He met the fleet of Admiral Rooke near Malaga, on the 24th of September of this year, and fought with it from ten o'clock in the morning until eight o'clock in the evening. The fleets, as far as the number of vessels was concerned, were nearly equal. So furious or so obstinate a sea-fight had not been seen for a long time. They had always the wind upon our fleet, yet all the advantage was on the side of the Comte de Toulouse, who could boast that he had obtained the victory, and whose vessel fought that of Rooke, dismasted it, and pursued it all next day towards the coast of Barbary, where the Admiral retired. The enemy lost six thousand men; the ship of the Dutch Vice-Admiral was blown up; several others were sunk, and some dismasted. Our fleet lost neither ship nor mast, but the victory cost the lives of many distinguished people, in addition to those of fifteen hundred soldiers or sailors killed or wounded.

Towards evening on the 25th, by dint of manœuvres, aided by the wind, our fleet came up again with that of Rooke. The Comte de Toulouse was for attacking it again on the morrow, and showed that if the attack were successful, Gibraltar would be the first result of the victory. That famous place, which commands the important strait of the same name, had been allowed to fall into neglect, and was defended by a miserable garrison of forty men. In this state it had of course easily fallen into the hands of the enemies. But they had not yet had time to man it with a much superior force, and Admiral Rooke once defeated, it must have surrendered to us.

The Comte de Toulouse urged his advice with all the energy of which he was capable, and he was supported in opinion by others of more experience than himself. But D'O, the mentor of the fleet, against whose counsel he had been expressly ordered by the King never to act, opposed the project of another attack with such disdainful determination, that the Comte had no course open but to give way. The annoyance which this caused throughout the fleet was very great. It soon was known what would have become of the enemy's fleet had it been attacked, and that Gibraltar would have been found in exactly the same state as when abandoned. The Comte de Toulouse acquired great honour in this campaign, and his stupid teacher lost little, because he had little to lose.

M. de Mantua having surrendered his state to the King, thereby rendering us a most important service in Italy, found himself ill at ease in his territory, which had become the theatre of war, and had come *incognito* to Paris. He had apartments provided for him in the Luxembourg, furnished magnificently with the Crown furniture, and was very graciously received by the King. The principal object of his journey was to marry some French lady; and as he made no secret of this intention, more than one plot was laid in order to provide him with a wife. M. de Vaudemont, intent upon aggrandising the house of Lorraine, wished M. de Mantua to marry a member of that family, and fixed upon Mademoiselle d'Elbœuf for his bride. The Lorraines did all in their power to induce M. de Mantua to accept her. But M. le Prince had also his designs in this matter. He had a daughter, whom he knew not how to get off his hands, and he thought that in more ways than one it would be to his advantage to marry her to the Duke of Mantua. He explained his views to the King, who gave him permission to follow them out, and promised to serve him with all his protection. But when the subject was broached to M. de Mantua, he declined this match in such a respectful, yet firm, manner that M. le Prince felt he must abandon all hope of carrying it out. The Lorraines were not more successful in their designs. When M. de Vaudemont had first spoken of Mademoiselle d'Elbœuf, M. de Mantua had appeared to listen favourably. This was in Italy. Now that he was in Paris he acted very differently. It was in vain that Mademoiselle d'Elbœuf was thrust in his way, as though by chance, at the promenades, in the churches; her beauty, which might have touched many others, made no impression upon him. The fact was that M. de Mantua, even long before leaving his state, had fixed upon a wife.

Supping one evening with the Duc de Lesdiguières, a little before the death of the latter, he saw a ring with a portrait in it, upon the Duke's finger. He begged to be allowed to look at the portrait, was charmed with it, and said he should be very happy to have such a beautiful mistress. The Duke at this burst out laughing, and said it was the portrait of his wife. As soon as the Duc de Lesdiguières was dead, M. de Mantua thought only of marrying the young widowed Duchess. He sought her everywhere when he arrived in Paris, but without being able to find her, because she was in the first year of her widowhood. He therefore unbosomed himself to Torcy, who reported the matter to the King. The King approved of the design of M. de Mantua, and charged the Maréchal de Duras to speak to the Duchesse de Lesdiguières, who was his daughter. The Duchess was equally surprised and afflicted when she learned what was in progress. She testified to her father her repugnance to abandon herself to the caprices and the jealousy of an old Italian *débauché;* the horror she felt at the idea of being left alone with him in Italy; and the reasonable fear she had of her health, with a man whose own could not be good.

I was promptly made acquainted with this affair; for Madame de Lesdiguières and Madame de Saint-Simon were on the most intimate terms. I did everything in my power to persuade Madame de Lesdiguières to consent to the match, insisting at once on her family position, on the reason of state, and on the pleasure of ousting Madame d'Elbœuf,—but it was all in vain. I never saw such firmness. Pontchartrain, who came and reasoned with her, was even less successful than I, for he excited her by threats and menaces. M. le Prince himself supported us—having no longer any hope for himself, and fearing, above all things, M. de Mantua's marriage with a Lorraine—and did all he could to persuade Madame de Lesdiguières to give in. I renewed my efforts in the same direction, but with no better success than before. Nevertheless, M. de Mantua, irritated by not being able to see Madame de Lesdiguières, resolved to go and wait for her on a Sunday at the Minimes. He found her shut up in a chapel, and drew near the door in order to see her as she went out. He was not much gratified; her thick crape veil was lowered; it was with difficulty he could get a glance at her. Resolved to succeed, he spoke to Torcy, intimating that Madame de Lesdiguières ought not to refuse such a slight favour as to allow herself to be seen in a church. Torcy communicated this to the King, who sent word to Madame de Lesdiguières that she must consent to the favour M. de Mantua demanded. She could not refuse after this. M. de Mantua went accordingly, and waited for her in the same place, where he had once already so badly seen her. He found her in the chapel, and drew near the door, as before. She came out, her veil raised, passed lightly before him, made him a sliding courtesy as she glided by, in reply to his bow, and reached her coach.

M. de Mantua was charmed; he redoubled his efforts with the King and M. de Duras; the matter was discussed in full council, like an affair of state—indeed it *was* one; and it was resolved to amuse M. de Mantua, and yet at the same time to do everything to vanquish this resistance of Madame de Lesdiguières, except employing the full authority of the King, which the King himself did not wish to exert. Everything was promised to her on the part of the King: that it should be his Majesty who would make the stipulations of the marriage contract; that it should be his Majesty who would give her a dowry, and would guarantee her return to France if she became a widow, and assure her his protection while she remained a wife; in one word, everything was tried, and in the gentlest and most honourable manner, to persuade her. Her mother lent us her house one afternoon, in order that we might speak more at length and more at our ease there to Madame de Lesdiguières than we could at the Hôtel de Duras. We only gained a torrent of tears for our pains.

A few days after this, I was very much astonished to hear Chamillart relate to me all that had passed at this interview. I learnt afterwards that Madame de Lesdiguières, fearing that if, entirely unsupported, she persisted in her refusal, it might draw upon her the anger of the King, had begged Chamillart to implore his Majesty not to insist upon this marriage. M. de Mantua hearing this, turned his thoughts elsewhere; and she was at last delivered of a pursuit which had become a painful persecution to her. Chamillart served her so well that the affair came to an end; and the King, flattered perhaps by the desire this young Duchess showed to remain his subject instead of becoming a sovereign, passed a eulogium upon her the same evening in his cabinet to his family and to the Princesses, by whom it was spread abroad through society.

I may as well finish this matter at once. The Lorraines, who had watched very closely the affair up to this point, took hope again directly they heard of the resolution M. de Mantua had formed to abandon his pursuit of Madame de Lesdiguières. They, in their turn, were closely watched by M. le Prince, who so excited the King against them, that Madame d'Elbœuf received orders from him not to continue pressing her suit upon M. de Mantua. That did not stop them. They felt that the King would not interfere with them by an express prohibition, and sure, by past experience, of being on better terms with him afterwards than before, they pursued their object with obstinacy. By dint of much plotting and scheming, and by the aid of their creatures, they contrived to overcome the repugnance of M. de Mantua to Mademoiselle d'Elbœuf, which at bottom could be only caprice—her beauty, her figure, and her birth taken into account. But Mademoiselle d'Elbœuf, in her turn, was as opposed to marriage with M. de Mantua as Madame de Lesdiguières had been. She was, however, brought round ere long, and then the consent of the King was the only thing left to be obtained. The Lorraines made use of their usual suppleness in order to gain that. They represented the impolicy of interfering with the selection of a sovereign who was the ally of France, and who wished to select a wife from among her subjects, and succeeded so well, that the King determined to become neutral; that is to say, neither to prohibit nor to sanction this match. M. le Prince was instrumental in inducing the King to take this neutral position; and he furthermore caused the stipulation to be made, that it should not be celebrated in France, but at Mantua.

After parting with the King, M. de Mantua, on the 21st of September, went to Nemours, slept there, and then set out for Italy. At the same time Madame and Mademoiselle d'Elbœuf, with Madame de Pompadour, sister of the former, passed through Fontainebleau without going to see a soul, and followed their prey lest he should change his mind and escape them— until the road he was to take branched off from that they were to go by; he in fact intending to travel by sea and they by land. On the way their fears redoubled. Arrived at Nevers, and lodged in a hostelrie, they thought it would not be well to commit themselves further without more certain security. Madame de Pompadour therefore proposed to M. de Mantua not to delay his happiness any longer, but to celebrate his marriage at once. He defended himself as well as he could, but was at last obliged to give in. During this indecent dispute, the Bishop was sent to. He had just died, and the Grand Vicar, not knowing what might be the wishes of the King upon this marriage, refused to celebrate it. The chaplain was therefore appealed to, and he at once married Mademoiselle d'Elbœuf to M. de Mantua in the hotel. As soon as the ceremony was over, Madame d'Elbœuf wished to leave her daughter alone with M. de Mantua, and although he strongly objected to this, everybody quitted the room, leaving only the newly married couple there, and Madame de Pompadour outside upon the step listening to what passed between them. But finding after a while that both were very much embarrassed, and that M. de Mantua did little but cry out for the company to return, she conferred with her sister, and they agreed to give him his liberty. Immediately he had obtained it, he mounted his horse, though it was not early, and did not see them again until they reached Italy—though all went the same road as far as Lyons. The news of this strange celebration of marriage was soon spread abroad with all the ridicule which attached to it.

The King was very much annoyed when he learnt that his orders had been thus disobeyed. The Lorraines plastered over the affair by representing that they feared an affront from M. de Mantua, and indeed it did not seem at all unlikely that M. de Mantua, forced as it were into compliance with their wishes, might have liked nothing better than to reach Italy and then laugh at them. Meanwhile, Madame d'Elbœuf and her daughter embarked on board the royal galleys and started for Italy. On the way they were fiercely chased by some African corsairs, and it is a great pity they were not taken to finish the romance.

However, upon arriving in Italy, the marriage was again celebrated, this time with all the forms necessary for the occasion. But Madame d'Elbœuf had no cause to rejoice that she had succeeded in thus disposing of her daughter. The new Duchesse de Mantua was guarded by her husband with the utmost jealousy. She was not allowed to see anybody except her mother, and that only for an hour each day. Her women entered her apartment only to dress and undress her. The Duke walled up very high all the windows of his house, and caused his wife to be guarded by old women. She passed her days thus in a cruel prison. This treatment, which I did not expect, and the little consideration, not to say contempt, shown here for M. de Mantua since his departure, consoled me much for the invincible obstinacy of Madame de Lesdiguières. Six months after, Madame d'Elbœuf returned, beside herself with vexation, but too vain to show it. She disguised the misfortune of her daughter, and appeared to be offended if it was spoken of; but all our letters from the army showed that the news was true. The strangest thing of all is, that the Lorraines after this journey were as well treated by the King as if they had never undertaken it; a fact which shows their art and ascendency.

I have dwelt too long perhaps upon this matter. It appeared to me to merit attention by its singularity, and still more so because it is by facts of this sort that is shown what was the composition of the Court of the King.

About this time the Comtesse d'Auvergne finished a short life by an illness very strange and uncommon. When she married the Comte d'Auvergne she was a Huguenot, and he much wanted to make her turn Catholic. A famous advocate of that time, who was named Chardon, had been a Huguenot, and his wife also; they had made a semblance, however, of abjuring, but made no open profession of Catholicism. Chardon was sustained by his great reputation, and by the number of protectors he had made for himself.

One morning he and his wife were in their coach before the Hôtel-Dieu, waiting for a reply that their lackey was a very long time in bringing them. Madame Chardon glanced by chance upon the grand portal of Notre Dame, and little by little fell into a profound reverie, which might be better called reflection. Her husband, who at last perceived this, asked her what had sent her into such deep thought, and pushed her elbow even to draw a reply from her. She told him then what she was thinking about. Pointing to Notre Dame, she said that it was many centuries before Luther and Calvin that those images of saints had been sculptured over that portal; that this proved that saints had long since been invoked; the opposition of the reformers to this ancient opinion was a novelty; that this novelty rendered suspicious other dogmas against the antiquity of Catholicism that they taught; that these reflections, which she had never before made, gave her much disquietude, and made her form the resolution to seek to enlighten herself.

Chardon thought his wife right, and from that day they laid themselves out to seek the truth, then to consult, then to be instructed. This lasted a year, and then they made a new abjuration, and both ever afterwards passed their lives in zeal and good works. Madame Chardon converted many Huguenots. The Comte d'Auvergne took his wife to her. The Countess was converted by her, and became a very good Catholic. When she died she was extremely regretted by all the relatives of her husband, although at first they had looked upon her coldly.

In the month of this September, a strange attempt at assassination occurred. Vervins had been forced into many suits against his relatives, and was upon the point of gaining them all, when one of his cousins-german, who called himself the Abbé de Pré, caused him to be attacked as he passed in his coach along the Quai de la Tournelle, before the community of Madame de Miramion. Vervins was wounded with several sword cuts, and also his coachman, who wished to defend him. In consequence of the complaint Vervins made, the Abbé escaped abroad, whence he never returned, and soon after, his crime being proved, was condemned to be broken alive on the wheel. Vervins had long been menaced with an attack by the Abbé. Vervins was an agreeable, well-made man, but very idle. He had entered the army; but quitted it soon, and retired to his estates in Picardy. There he shut himself up without any cause of disgust or of displeasure, without being in any embarrassment, for on the contrary he was well to do, and all his affairs were in good order, and he never married; without motives of piety, for piety was not at all in his vein; without being in bad health, for his health was always perfect; without a taste for improvement, for no workmen were ever seen in his house; still less on account of the chase, for he never went to it. Yet he stayed in his house for several years, without intercourse with a soul, and, what is most incomprehensible, without budging from his bed, except to allow it to be made. He dined there, and often all alone; he transacted what little business he had to do there, and received while there the few people he could not refuse admission to; and each day, from the moment he opened his eyes until he closed them again, worked at tapestry, or read a little; he persevered until his death in this strange fashion of existence; so uniquely singular, that I have wished to describe it.

CHAPTER XXXI

THERE presents itself to my memory an anecdote which it would be very prudent perhaps to be silent upon, and which is very curious for anybody who has seen things so closely as I have, to describe. What determines me to relate it is that the fact is not altogether unknown, and that every Court swarms with similar adventures. Must it be said then? We had amongst us a charming young Princess who, by her graces, her attentions, and her original manners, had taken possession of the hearts of the King, of Madame de Maintenon, and of her husband, Monseigneur le Duc de Bourgogne. The extreme discontent so justly felt against her father, M. de Savoie, had not made the slightest alteration in their tenderness for her. The King, who hid nothing from her, who worked with his ministers in her presence whenever she liked to enter, took care not to say a word in her hearing against her father. In private, she clasped the King round the neck at all hours, jumped upon his knees, tormented him with all sorts of sportiveness, rummaged among his papers, opened his letters and read them in his presence, sometimes in spite of him; and acted in the same manner with Madame de Maintenon. Despite this extreme liberty, she never spoke against any one: gracious to all, she endeavoured to ward off blows from all whenever she could; was attentive to the private comforts of the King, even the humblest: kind to all who served her, and living with her ladies, as with friends, in complete liberty, old and young; she was the darling of the Court, adored by all; everybody, great and small, was anxious to please her; everybody missed her when she was away; when she reappeared the void was filled up; in a word, she had attached all hearts to her; but while in this brilliant situation she lost her own.

Nangis, now a very commonplace Marshal of France, was at that time in full bloom. He had an agreeable but not an uncommon face; was well made, without anything marvellous; and had been educated in intrigue by the Maréchale de Rochefort, his grandmother, and Madame de Blansac, his mother, who were skilled mistresses of that art. Early introduced by them into the great world of which they were, so to speak, the centre, he had no talent but that of pleasing women, of speaking their language, and of monopolising the most desirable by a discretion beyond his years, and which did not belong to his time. Nobody was more in vogue than he. He had had the command of a regiment when he was quite a child. He had shown firmness, application, and brilliant valour in war, that the ladies had made the most of, and they sufficed at his age; he was of the Court of Monseigneur le Duc de Bourgogne, about the same age, and well treated by him.

The Duc de Bourgogne, passionately in love with his wife, was not so well made as Nangis; but the Princess reciprocated his ardour so perfectly that up to his death he never suspected that her glances had wandered to any one else. They fell, however, upon Nangis, and soon redoubled. Nangis was not ungrateful, but he feared the thunderbolt; and his heart, too, was already engaged. Madame de la Vrillière, who, without beauty, was pretty and grateful as Love, had made this conquest. She was, as I have said, daughter of Madame de Mailly, Dame d'Atours of Madame la Duchesse de Bourgogne; and was always near her. Jealousy soon enlightened her as to what was taking place. Far from yielding her conquest to the Duchess, she made a point of preserving it, of disputing its possession, and carrying it off. This struggle threw Nangis into a terrible embarrassment. He feared the fury of Madame de la Vrillière, who affected to be more ready to break out than in reality she was. Besides his love for her, he feared the result of an outburst, and already saw his fortune lost. On the other hand, any reserve of his towards the Duchess, who had so much power in her hands—and seemed destined to have more—and who he knew was not likely to suffer a rival—might, he felt, be his ruin. This perplexity, for those who were aware of it, gave rise to continual scenes. I was then a constant visitor of Madame de Blansac, at Paris, and of the Maréchale de Rochefort, at Versailles; and, through them and several other ladies of the Court, with whom I was intimate, I learnt, day by day, everything that passed. In addition to the fact that nothing diverted me more, the results of this affair might be great; and it was my especial ambition to be well informed of everything. At length, all members of the Court who were assiduous and enlightened understood the state of affairs; but either through fear or from love to the Duchess, the whole Court was silent, saw everything, whispered discreetly, and actually kept the secret that was not entrusted to it. The struggle between the two ladies, not without bitterness, and sometimes insolence on the part of Madame de la Vrillière, nor without suffering and displeasure gently manifested on the part of Madame de Bourgogne, was for a long time a singular sight.

Whether Nangis, too faithful to his first love, needed some grains of jealousy to excite him, or whether things fell out naturally, it happened that he found a rival. Maulevrier, son of a brother of Colbert who had died of grief at not being named Marshal of France, was this rival. He had married a daughter of the Maréchal de Tessé, and was not very agreeable in appearance—his face, indeed, was very commonplace. He was by no means framed for gallantry; but he had wit, and a mind fertile in intrigues, with a measureless ambition that was sometimes pushed to madness. His wife was pretty, not clever, quarrelsome, and under a virginal appearance, mischievous to the last degree. As daughter of a man for whom Madame de Bourgogne had much gratitude for the part he had taken in negotiating her marriage, and the Peace of Savoy, she was easily enabled to make her way at Court, and her husband with her. He soon sniffed what was passing in respect to Nangis, and obtained means of access to Madame de Bourgogne, through the influence of his father-in-law; was assiduous in his attentions; and at length, excited by example, dared to sigh. Tired of not being understood, he ventured to write. It is pretended that he sent his letters through one of the Court ladies, who thought they came from Tessé, delivered them, and handed him back the answers, as though for delivery by him. I will not add what more was believed. I will simply say that this affair was as soon perceived as had been the other, and was treated with the same silence.

Under pretext of friendship, Madame de Bourgogne went more than once—on account of the speedy departure of her husband (for the army), attended sometimes by La Maintenon,—to the house of Madame de Maulevrier, to weep with her. The Court smiled. Whether the tears were for Madame de Maulevrier or for Nangis, was doubtful. But Nangis, nevertheless, aroused by this rivalry, threw Madame de la Vrillière into terrible grief, and into a humour over which she was not mistress.

This tocsin made itself heard by Maulevrier. What will not a man think of doing when possessed to excess by love or ambition? He pretended to have something the matter with his chest, put himself on a milk diet, made believe that he had lost his voice, and was sufficiently master of himself to refrain from uttering an intelligible word during a whole year; by these means evading the campaign and remaining at the Court. He was mad enough to relate this project, and many others, to his friend the Duc de Lorges, from whom, in turn, I learnt it. The fact was, that bringing himself thus to the necessity of never speaking to anybody except in their ear, he had the liberty of speaking low to Madame la Duchesse de Bourgogne before all the Court without impropriety and without suspicion. In this manner he said to her whatever he wished day by day, and was never overheard. He also contrived to say things the short answers to which were equally unheard. He so accustomed people to this manner of speaking that they took no more notice of it than was expressed in pity for such a sad state; but it happened that those who approached the nearest to Madame la Duchesse de Bourgogne when Maulevrier was at her side, soon knew enough not to be eager to draw near her again when she was thus situated. This trick lasted more than a year: his conversation was principally composed of reproaches—but reproaches rarely succeed in love. Maulevrier, judging by the ill-humour of Madame de la Vrillière, believed Nangis to be happy. Jealousy and rage transported him at last to the extremity of folly.

One day, as Madame de Bourgogne was coming from mass and he knew that Dangeau, her chevalier d'honneur, was absent, he gave her his hand. The attendants had accustomed themselves to let him have this honour, on account of his distinguished voice, so as to allow him to speak by the way, and retired respectfully so as not to hear what he said. The ladies always followed far behind, so that, in the midst of all the Court, he had, from the chapel to the apartments of Madame de Bourgogne, the full advantages of a private interview—advantages that he had availed himself of several times. On this day he railed against Nangis to Madame de Bourgogne, called him by all sorts of names, threatened to tell everything to the King and to Madame de Maintenon, and to the Duc de Bourgogne, squeezed her fingers as if he would break them, and led her in this manner, like a madman as he was, to her apartments. Upon entering them she was ready to swoon. Trembling all over she entered her wardrobe, called one of her favourite ladies, Madame de Nogaret, to her, related what had occurred, saying she knew not how she had reached her rooms, or how it was she had not sunk beneath the floor, or died. She had never been so dismayed. The same day Madame de Nogaret related this to Madame de Saint-Simon and to me, in the strictest confidence. She counselled the Duchess to behave gently with such a dangerous madman, and to avoid committing herself in any way with him. The worst was, that after this he threatened and said many things against Nangis, as a man with whom he was deeply offended, and whom he meant to call to account. Although he gave no reason for this, the reason was only too evident. The fear of Madame de Bourgogne at this may be imagined, and also that of Nangis. He was brave and cared for nobody; but to be mixed up in such an affair as this made him quake with fright. He beheld his fortune and his happiness in the hands of a furious madman. He shunned Maulevrier from that time as much as possible, showed himself but little, and held his peace.

For six weeks Madame de Bourgogne lived in the most measured manner, and in mortal tremors of fear, without, however, anything happening. I know not who warned Tessé of what was going on. But when he learnt it he acted like a man of ability. He persuaded his son-in-law, Maulevrier, to follow him to Spain, as to a place where his fortune was assured to him. He spoke to Fagon, who saw all and knew all. He understood matters in a moment, and at once said, that as so many remedies had been tried ineffectually for Maulevrier, he must go to a warmer climate, as a winter in France would inevitably kill him. It was then as a remedy, and as people go to the waters, that he went to Spain. The King and all the Court believed this, and neither the King nor Madame de Maintenon offered any objections. As soon as Tessé knew this he hurried his son-in-law out of the realm, and so put a stop to his follies and the mortal fear they had caused. To finish this adventure at once, although it will lead me far beyond the date of other matters to be spoken of after, let me say what became of Maulevrier after this point of the narrative.

He went first to Spain with Tessé. On the way they had an interview with Madame des Ursins, and succeeded in gaining her favour so completely, that, upon arriving at Madrid, the King and Queen of Spain, informed of this, welcomed them with much cordiality. Maulevrier soon became a great favourite with the Queen of Spain. It has been said that he wished to please her, and that he succeeded. At all events he often had long interviews with her in private, and these made people think and talk.

Maulevrier began to believe it time to reap after

having so well sown. He counted upon nothing less than being made grandee of Spain, and would have obtained this favour but for his indiscretion. News of what was in store for him was noised abroad. The Duc de Grammont, then our ambassador at Madrid, wrote word to the King of the rumours that were in circulation of Maulevrier's audacious conduct towards the Queen of Spain, and of the reward it was to meet with. The King at once sent a very strong letter to the King of Spain about Maulevrier, who, by the same courier, was prohibited from accepting any favour that might be offered him. He was ordered at the same time to join Tessé at Gibraltar. He had already done so at the instance of Tessé himself; so the courier went from Madrid to Gibraltar to find him. His rage and vexation upon seeing himself deprived of the recompense he had considered certain were very great. But they yielded in time to the hopes he formed of success, and he determined to set off for Madrid and thence to Versailles. His father-in-law tried to retain him at the siege, but in vain. His representations and his authority were alike useless. Maulevrier hoped to gain over the King and Queen of Spain so completely, that our King would be forced, as it were, to range himself on their side; but the Duc de Grammont at once wrote word that Maulevrier had left the siege of Gibraltar and returned to Madrid. This disobedience was at once chastised. A courier was immediately despatched to Maulevrier, commanding him to set out for France. He took leave of the King and Queen of Spain like a man without hope, and left Spain. The most remarkable thing is, that upon arriving at Paris, and finding the Court at Marly, and his wife there also, he asked permission to go too, the husbands being allowed by right to accompany their wives there, and the King, to avoid a disturbance, did not refuse him.

At first everything seemed to smile upon Maulevrier. He had, as I have said, made friends with Madame des Ursins when he was on the road to Spain. He had done so chiefly by vaunting his intimacy with Madame de Bourgogne, and by showing to Madame des Ursins that he was in many of the secrets of the Court. Accordingly, upon his return, she took him by the hand and showed a disposition towards him which could not fail to reinstate him in favour. She spoke well of him to Madame de Maintenon, who, always much smitten with new friends, received him well, and often had conversations with him which lasted more than three hours. Madame de Maintenon mentioned him to the King, and Maulevrier, who had returned out of all hope, now saw himself in a more favourable position than ever.

But the old cause of trouble still existed, and with fresh complications. Nangis was still in favour, and his appearance made Maulevrier miserable. There was a new rival too in the field, the Abbé de Polignac.

Pleasing, nay most fascinating in manner, the Abbé was a man to gain all hearts. He stopped at no flattery to succeed in this. One day when following the King through the gardens of Marly, it came on to rain. The King considerately noticed the Abbé's dress, little calculated to keep off rain. "It is no matter, Sire," said De Polignac, "the rain of Marly does not wet." People laughed much at this, and these words were a standing reproach to the soft-spoken Abbé.

One of the means by which the Abbé gained the favour of the King was by being the lover of Madame du Maine. His success at length was great in every direction. He even envied the situations of Nangis and Maulevrier; and sought to participate in the same happiness. He took the same road. Madame d'O and the Maréchale de Cœuvres became his friends.

He sought to be heard, and *was* heard. At last he faced the danger of the Swiss, and on fine nights was seen with the Duchess in the gardens. Nangis diminished in favour. Maulevrier on his return increased in fury. The Abbé met with the same fate as they: everything was perceived: people talked about the matter in whispers, but silence was kept. This triumph, in spite of his age, did not satisfy the Abbé: he aimed at something more solid. He wished to arrive at the cardinalship, and to further his views he thought it advisable to ingratiate himself into the favour of Monsieur de Bourgogne. He sought introduction to them through friends of mine, whom I warned against him as a man without scruple, and intent only upon advancing himself. My warnings were in vain. My friends would not heed me, and the Abbé de Polignac succeeded in gaining the confidence of Monsieur de Bourgogne, as well as the favour of Madame de Bourgogne.

Maulevrier had thus two sources of annoyance—the Abbé de Polignac and Nangis. Of the latter he showed himself so jealous, that Madame de Maulevrier, out of pique, made advances to him. Nangis, to screen himself the better, replied to her. Maulevrier perceived this. He knew his wife to be sufficiently wicked to make him fear her. So many troubles of heart and brain transported him. He lost his head.

One day the Maréchale de Cœuvres came to see him, apparently on some message of reconciliation. He shut the door upon her; barricaded her within, and through the door quarrelled with her, even to abuse, for an hour, during which she had the patience to remain there without being able to see him. After this he went rarely to Court, but generally kept himself shut up at home.

Sometimes he would go out all alone at the strangest hours, take a fiacre and drive away to the back of the Chartreux or to other remote spots. Alighting there, he would whistle, and a grey-headed old man would advance and give him a packet, or one would be thrown to him from a window, or he would pick up a box filled with despatches, hidden behind a post. I heard of these mysterious doings from people to whom he was vain and indiscreet enough to boast of them. He continually wrote letters to Madame de Bourgogne, and to Madame de Maintenon, but more frequently to the former. Madame Cantin was their agent; and I know people who have seen letters of hers in which she assured Maulevrier, in the strongest terms, that he might ever reckon on the Duchess.

He made a last journey to Versailles, where he saw his mistress in private, and quarrelled with her cruelly After dining with Torcy he returned to Paris. There, torn by a thousand storms of love, of jealousy, of ambition, his head was so troubled that doctors were obliged to be called in, and he was forbidden to see any but the most indispensable persons, and those at the hours when he was least ill. A hundred visions passed through his brain. Now like a madman he would speak only of Spain, of Madame de Bourgogne, of Nangis, whom he wished to kill or to have assassinated; now full of remorse towards M. de Bourgogne, he made reflections so curious to hear, that no one dared to remain with him, and he was left alone. At other times, recalling his early days, he had nothing but ideas of retreat and penitence. Then a confession was necessary in order to banish his despair as to the mercy of God. Often he thought himself very ill and upon the point of death.

The world, however, and even his nearest friends persuaded themselves that he was only playing a part;

and hoping to put an end to it, they declared to him that he passed for mad in society, and that it behoved him to rise out of such a strange state and show himself. This was the last blow and it overwhelmed him. Furious at finding that this opinion was ruining all the designs of his ambition, he delivered himself up to despair. Although watched with extreme care by his wife, by particular friends, and by his servants, he took his measures so well, that on the Good Friday of the year 1706, at about eight o'clock in the morning, he slipped away from them all, entered a passage behind his room, opened the window, threw himself into the court below, and dashed out his brains upon the pavement. Such was the end of an ambitious man, who, by his wild and dangerous passions, lost his wits, and then his life, a tragic victim of himself.

Madame de Bourgogne learnt the news at night. In public she showed no emotion, but in private some tears escaped her. They might have been of pity, but were not so charitably interpreted. Soon after, it was noticed that Madame de Maintenon seemed embarrassed and harsh towards Madame de Bourgogne. It was no longer doubted that Madame de Maintenon had heard the whole story. She often had long interviews with Madame de Bourgogne, who always left them in tears. Her sadness grew so much, and her eyes were so often red, that Monsieur de Bourgogne at last became alarmed. But he had no suspicion of the truth, and was easily satisfied with the explanation he received. Madame de Bourgogne felt the necessity, however, of appearing gayer, and showed herself so. As for the Abbé de Polignac, it was felt that that dangerous person was best away. He received therefore a post which called him away, as it were, into exile; and though he delayed his departure as long as possible, was at length obliged to go. Madame de Bourgogne took leave of him in a manner that showed how much she was affected. Some rather insolent verses were written upon this event; and were found written on a balustrade by Madame, who was not discreet enough or good enough to forget them. But they made little noise; everybody loved Madame de Bourgogne, and hid these verses as much as possible.

CHAPTER XXXII

AT the beginning of October, news reached the Court, which was at Fontainebleau, that M. de Duras was at the point of death. Upon hearing this, Madame de Saint-Simon and Madame de Lauzun, who were both related to M. Duras, wished to absent themselves from the Court performances that were to take place in the palace that evening. They expressed this wish to Madame de Bourgogne, who approved of it, but said she was afraid the King would not do the same. He had been very angry lately because the ladies had neglected to go full dressed to the Court performances. A few words he had spoken made everybody take good care not to rouse his anger on this point again. He expected so much accordingly from everybody who attended the Court, that Madame de Bourgogne was afraid he would not consent to dispense with the attendance of Madame de Saint-Simon and Madame de Lauzun on this occasion. They compromised the matter, therefore, by dressing themselves, going to the room where the performance was held, and, under pretext of not finding places, going away; Madame de Bourgogne agreeing to explain their absence in this way to the King. I notice this very insignificant bagatelle to show how the King thought only of himself, and how much he wished to be obeyed; and that that which would not have been pardoned to the nieces of a dying man, except at the Court, was a duty there, and one which it needed great address to escape from, without seriously infringing the etiquette established.

After the return of the Court from Fontainebleau this year, Puysieux came back from Switzerland, having been sent there as ambassador. Puysieux was a little fat man, very agreeable, pleasant, and witty, one of the best fellows in the world, in fact. As he had much wit, and thoroughly knew the King, he bethought himself of making the best of his position; and as his Majesty testified much friendship for him on his return, and declared himself satisfied with his mission in Switzerland, Puysieux asked if what he heard was not mere compliment, and whether he could count upon it. As the King assured him that he might do so, Puysieux assumed a brisk air, and said that he was not so sure of that, and that he was not pleased with his Majesty.

"And why not?" said the King.

"Why not?" replied Puysieux; "why, because although the most honest man in your realm, you have not kept to a promise you made me more than fifty years ago."

"What promise?" asked the King.

"What promise, Sire?" said Puysieux; "you have a good memory, you cannot have forgotten it. Does not your Majesty remember that one day, having the honour to play at blindman's buff with you at my grandmother's, you put your *cordon bleu* on my back, the better to hide yourself; and that when, after the game, I restored it to you, you promised to give it me when you became master; you have long been so, thoroughly master, and nevertheless that *cordon bleu* is still to come."

The King, who recollected the circumstance, here burst out laughing, and told Puysieux he was in the right, and that a chapter should be held on the first day of the new year expressly for the purpose of receiving him into the order. And so in fact it was, and

Puysieux received the *cordon bleu* on the day the King had named. This fact is not important, but it is amusing. It is altogether singular in connection with a prince as serious and as imposing as Louis XIV.; and it is one of those little Court anecdotes which are curious.

Here is another more important fact, the consequences of which are still felt by the State. Pontchartrain, Secretary of State for the Navy, was the plague of it, as of all those who were under his cruel dependence. He was a man who, with some amount of ability, was disagreeable and pedantic to an excess; who loved evil for its own sake; who was jealous even of his father; who was a cruel tyrant towards his wife, a woman all docility and goodness; who was in one word a monster, whom the King kept in office only because he feared him. An admiral was the abhorrence of Pontchartrain, and an admiral who was an illegitimate son of the King, he loathed. There was nothing, therefore, that he had not done during the war to thwart the Comte de Toulouse; he laid some obstacles everywhere in his path; he had tried to keep him out of the command of the fleet, and failing this, had done everything to render the fleet useless.

These were bold strokes against a person the King so much loved, but Pontchartrain knew the weak side of the King; he knew how to balance the father against the master, to bring forward the admiral and set aside the son. In this manner the Secretary of State was able to put obstacles in the way of the Comte de Toulouse that threw him almost into despair, and the Count could do little to defend himself. It was a well-known fact at sea and in the ports where the ships touched, and it angered all the fleet. Pontchartrain accordingly was abhorred there, while the Comte de Toulouse, by his amiability and other good qualities, was adored.

At last, the annoyance he caused became so unendurable, that the Comte de Toulouse, at the end of his cruise in the Mediterranean, returned to Court and determined to expose the doings of Pontchartrain to the King.

The very day he had made up his mind to do this, and just before he intended to have his interview with the King, Madame Pontchartrain, casting aside her natural timidity and modesty, came to him, and with tears in her eyes begged him not to bring about the ruin of her husband. The Comte de Toulouse was softened. He admitted afterwards that he could not resist the sweetness and sorrow of Madame de Pontchartrain, and that all his resolutions, his weapons, fell from his hands at the thought of the sorrow which the poor woman would undergo, after the fall of her brutal husband, left entirely in the hands of such a furious Cyclops. In this manner Pontchartrain was saved, but it cost dear to the State. The fear he was in of succumbing under the glory or under the vengeance of an admiral who was son of the King determined him to ruin the fleet itself, so as to render it incapable of receiving the admiral again. He determined to do this, and kept to his word, as was afterwards only too clearly verified by the facts. The Comte de Toulouse saw no more either ports or vessels, and from that time only very feeble squadrons went out, and even those very seldom. Pontchartrain had the impudence to boast of this before my face.

When I last spoke of Madame des Ursins, I described her as living in the midst of the Court, flattered and caressed by all, and on the highest terms of favour with the King and Madame de Maintenon. She found her position, indeed, so far above her hopes, that she began to waver in her intention of returning to Spain. The age and the health of Madame de Maintenon tempted her. She would have preferred to govern here rather than in Spain. Flattered by the attentions paid her, she thought those attentions, or, I may say, rather those servile adorations, would continue for ever, and that in time she might arrive at the highest point of power. The Archbishop of Aix and her brother divined her thoughts, for she did not dare to avow them, and showed her in the clearest way that those thoughts were calculated to lead her astray. They explained to her that the only interest Madame de Maintenon had in favouring her was on account of Spain. Madame des Ursins once back in that country, Madame de Maintenon looked forward to a recommencement of those relations which had formerly existed between them, by which the government of Spain in appearance, if not in reality, passed through her hands. They therefore advised Madame des Ursins on no account to think of remaining in France, at the same time suggesting that it would not be amiss to stop there long enough to cause some inquietude to Madame de Maintenon, so as to gain as much advantage as possible from it.

The solidity of these reasons persuaded Madame des Ursins to follow the advice given her. She resolved to depart, but not until after a delay by which she meant to profit to the utmost. We shall soon see what success attended her schemes. The terms upon which I stood with her enabled me to have knowledge of all the sentiments that had passed through her mind:— her extreme desire, upon arriving in Paris, to return to Spain; the intoxication which seized her in consequence of the treatment she received, and which made her balance this desire; and her final resolution. It was not until afterwards, however, that I learnt all the details I have just related.

It was not long before Madame de Maintenon began

to feel impatient at the long-delayed departure of Madame des Ursins. She spoke at last upon the subject, and pressed Madame des Ursins to set out for Spain. This was just what the other wanted. She said that as she had been driven out of Spain like a criminal, she must go back with honour, if Madame de Maintenon wished her to gain the confidence and esteem of the Spaniards. That although she had been treated by the King with every consideration and goodness, many people in Spain were, and would be, ignorant of it, and that, therefore, her return to favour ought to be made known in as public and convincing a manner as was her disgrace. This was said with all that eloquence and persuasiveness for which Madame des Ursins was remarkable. The effect of it exceeded her hopes.

The favours she obtained were prodigious. Twenty thousand livres by way of annual pension, and thirty thousand for her journey. One of her brothers, M. de Noirmoutiers, blind since the age of eighteen or twenty, was made hereditary duke; another, the Abbé de la Trémoille, of exceeding bad life, and much despised in Rome, where he lived, was made cardinal. What a success was this! How many obstacles had to be overcome in order to attain it! Yet this was what Madame des Ursins obtained, so anxious was Madame de Maintenon to get rid of her and to send her to reign in Spain, that she might reign there herself. Pleased and loaded with favour as never subject was before, Madame des Ursins set out towards the middle of July, and was nearly a month on the road. It may be imagined what sort of a reception awaited her in Spain. The King and the Queen went a day's journey out of Madrid to meet her. Here, then, we see again at the height of power this woman, whose fall the King but a short time since had so ardently desired, and whose separation from the King and Queen of Spain he had applauded himself for bringing about with so much tact. What a change in a few months!

The war continued this year, but without bringing any great success to our arms. Villars, at Circk, outmanœuvred Marlborough in a manner that would have done credit to the greatest general. Marlborough, compelled to change the plan of campaign he had determined on, returned into Flanders, where the Maréchal de Villeroy was stationed with his forces. Nothing of importance occurred during the campaign, and the two armies went into winter quarters at the end of October.

I cannot quit Flanders without relating another instance of the pleasant malignity of M. de Lauzun. In marrying a daughter of the Maréchal de Lorges, he had hoped, as I have already said, to return into the confidence of the King by means of the Maréchal, and so be again entrusted with military command. Finding these hopes frustrated, he thought of another means of reinstating himself in favour. He determined to go to the waters of Aix-la-Chapelle, not, as may be believed, for his health, but in order to ingratiate himself with the important foreigners whom he thought to find there, learn some of the enemy's plans, and come back with an account of them to the King, who would, no doubt, reward him for his zeal. But he was deceived in his calculation. Aix-la-Chapelle, generally so full of foreigners of rank, was this year, owing to the war, almost empty. M. de Lauzun found, therefore, nobody of consequence from whom he could obtain any useful information. Before his return, he visited the Maréchal de Villeroy, who received him with all military honours, and conducted him all over the army, pointing out to him the enemy's posts; for the two armies were then quite close to each other. His extreme anxiety, however, to get information, and the multitude of his questions, irritated the officers who were ordered to do the honours to him; and, in going about, they actually, at their own risk, exposed him often to be shot or taken. They did not know that his courage was extreme; and were quite taken aback by his calmness, and his evident readiness to push on even farther than they chose to venture.

On returning to Court, M. de Lauzun was of course pressed by everybody to relate all he knew of the position of the two armies. But he held himself aloof from all questioners, and would not answer. On the day after his arrival he went to pay his court to Monseigneur, who did not like him, but who also was no friend to the Maréchal de Villeroy. Monseigneur put many questions to him upon the situation of the two armies, and upon the reasons which had prevented them from engaging each other. M. de Lauzun shirked reply, like a man who wished to be pressed; did not deny that he had well inspected the position of the two armies, but instead of answering Monseigneur, dwelt upon the beauty of our troops, their gaiety at finding themselves so near an enemy, and their eagerness to fight. Pushed at last to the point at which he wished to arrive, "I will tell you, Monseigneur," said he, "since you absolutely command me; I scanned most minutely the front of the two armies to the right and to the left, and all the ground between them. It is true there is no brook, and that I saw; neither are there any ravines, nor hollow roads ascending or descending; but it is true that there were other hindrances which I particularly remarked."

"But what hindrance could there be," said Monseigneur, " since there was nothing between the two armies?"

M. de Lauzun allowed himself to be pressed upon this point, constantly repeating the list of hindrances that did not exist, but keeping silent upon the others. At last, driven into a corner, he took his snuff-box from his pocket.

"You see," said he, to Monseigneur, "there is one thing which much embarrasses the feet, the furze that grows upon the ground, where M. le Maréchal de Villeroy is encamped. The furze, it is true, is not mixed with any other plant, either hard or thorny; but it is a high furze, as high, as high, let me see, what shall I say?"—and he looked all around to find some object of comparison—" as high, I assure you, as this snuff-box!"

Monseigneur burst out laughing at this sally, and all the company followed his example, in the midst of which M. de Lauzun turned on his heel and left the room. His joke soon spread all over the Court and the town, and in the evening was told to the King. This was all the thanks M. de Villeroy obtained from M. de Lauzun for the honours he had paid him; and this was M. de Lauzun's consolation for his ill-success at Aix-la-Chapelle.

In Italy our armies were not more successful than elsewhere. From time to time, M. de Vendôme attacked some unimportant post, and, having carried it, despatched couriers to the King, magnifying the importance of the exploit. But the fact was, all these successes led to nothing. On one occasion, at Cassano, M. de Vendôme was so vigorously attacked by Prince Louis of Baden that, in spite of his contempt and his audacity, he gave himself up for lost. When danger was most imminent, instead of remaining at his post, he retired from the field of battle to a distant country-house, and began to consider how a retreat might be managed. The Grand Prieur, his brother, was in command under him, and was ordered to remain upon the field; but he was more intent upon saving his skin than on obeying orders, and so, at the very outset of the fight, ran away to a country-house hard by. M. de Vendôme strangely enough had sat down to eat at the country-house whither he had retired, and was in the midst of his meal when news was brought him that, owing to the prodigies performed by one of his officers, Le Guerchois, the fortunes of the day had changed, and Prince Louis of Baden was retiring. M. Vendôme had great difficulty to believe this, but ordered his horse, mounted, and, pushing on, concluded the combat gloriously. He did not fail, of course, to claim all the honours of this victory, which in reality was a barren one; and sent word of his triumph to the King. He dared to say that the loss of the enemy was more than thirteen thousand; and our loss less than three thousand—whereas, the loss was at least equal. This exploit, nevertheless, resounded at the Court and through the town as an advantage the most complete and the most decisive, and due entirely to the vigilance, valour, and capacity of Vendôme. Not a word was said of his country-house, or the interrupted meal. These facts were only known after the return of the general officers. As for the Grand Prieur, his poltroonery had been so public, his flight so disgraceful—for he had taken troops with him to protect the country-house in which he sought shelter—that he could not be pardoned. The two brothers quarrelled upon these points, and in the end the Grand Prieur was obliged to give up his command. He retired to his house at Clichy, near Paris; but, tiring of that place, he went to Rome, made the acquaintance there of the Marquise de Richelieu, a wanderer like himself, and passed some time with her at Genoa. Leaving that city, he went to Chalons-sur-Saône, which had been fixed upon as the place of his exile, and there gave himself up to the debaucheries in which he usually lived. From this time until the Regency we shall see nothing more of him. I shall only add, therefore, that he never went sober to bed during thirty years, but was always carried thither dead drunk: was a liar, swindler, and thief; a rogue to the marrow of his bones, rotted with vile diseases; the most contemptible and yet most dangerous fellow in the world.

CHAPTER XXXIII

TWO very different persons died towards the latter part of this year. The first was Lamoignon, Chief President; the second, Ninon, known by the name of Mademoiselle de l'Enclos. Of Lamoignon I will relate a single anecdote, curious and instructive, which will show the corruption of which he was capable.

One day—I am speaking of a time many years previous to the date of the occurrences just related—one day there was a great hunting party at Saint Germain. The chase was pursued so long, that the King gave up, and returned to Saint Germain. A number of courtiers, among whom was M. de Lauzun, who related this story to me, continued their sport; and just as darkness was coming on, discovered that they had lost their way. After a time, they espied a light, by which they guided their steps, and at length reached the door of a kind of castle. They knocked, they called aloud, they named themselves, and asked for hospitality. It was then between ten and eleven at night, and towards the end of autumn. The door was opened to them. The master of the house came forth. He made them take their boots off, and warm themselves; he put their horses into his stables; and at the same time had a supper prepared for his guests, who stood much in need of it. They did not wait long for the meal; yet when served it proved excellent; the wines served with it, too, were of several kinds, and excellent likewise: as for the master of the house, he was so polite and respectful, yet without being ceremonious or eager, that it was evident he had frequented the best company. The courtiers soon learnt that his name was Fargues, that the place was called Courson, and that he had lived there in retirement several years. After having supped, Fargues showed each of them into a separate bedroom, where they were waited upon by his valets with every proper attention. In the morning, as soon as the courtiers had dressed themselves, they found an excellent breakfast awaiting them; and upon leaving the table they saw their horses ready for them, and as thoroughly attended to as they had been themselves. Charmed with the politeness and with the manners of Fargues, and touched by his hospitable reception of them, they made him many offers of service, and made their way back to Saint Germain. Their non-appearance on the previous night had been the common talk, their return and the adventure they had met with was no less so.

These gentlemen were then the very flower of the Court, and all of them very intimate with the King. They related to him, therefore, their story, the manner of their reception, and highly praised the master of the house and his good cheer. The King asked his name, and, as soon as he heard it, exclaimed, "What, Fargues! is he so near here, then?" The courtiers redoubled their praises, and the King said no more; but soon after went to the Queen-mother, and told her what had happened.

Fargues, indeed, was no stranger, either to her or to the King. He had taken a prominent part in the movements of Paris against the Court and Cardinal Mazarin. If he had not been hanged, it was because he was well supported by his party, who had him included in the amnesty granted to those who had been engaged in these troubles. Fearing, however, that the hatred of his enemies might place his life in danger if he remained in Paris, he retired from the capital to this country-house which has just been mentioned, where he continued to live in strict privacy, even when the death of Cardinal Mazarin seemed to render such seclusion no longer necessary.

The King and the Queen-mother, who had pardoned Fargues in spite of themselves, were much annoyed at finding that he was living in opulence and tranquillity so near the Court; thought him extremely bold to do so; and determined to punish him for this and for his former insolence. They directed Lamoignon, therefore, to find out something in the past life of Fargues for which punishment might be awarded; and Lamoignon, eager to please, and make a profit out of his eagerness, was not long in satisfying them. He made researches, and found means to implicate Fargues in a murder that had been committed in Paris at the height of the troubles. Officers were accordingly sent to Courson, and its owner was arrested.

Fargues was much astonished when he learnt of what he was accused. He exculpated himself, nevertheless, completely; alleging, moreover, that as the murder of which he was accused had been committed during the troubles, the amnesty in which he was included effaced all memory of the deed, according to law and usage, which had never been contested until this occasion. The courtiers who had been so well treated by the unhappy man, did everything they could with the judges and the King to obtain the release of the accused. It was all in vain. Fargues was decapitated at once, and all his wealth was given by way of recompense to the Chief-President Lamoignon, who had no scruple thus to enrich himself with the blood of the innocent.

The other person who died at the same time was, as I have said, Ninon, the famous courtesan, known, since age had compelled her to quit that trade, as Mademoiselle de l'Enclos. She was a new example of the triumph of vice carried on cleverly and repaired by some virtue. The stir that she made, and still more the disorder that she caused among the highest and most brilliant youth, overcame the extreme indulgence that, not without cause, the Queen-mother entertained for persons whose conduct was gallant, and more than gallant, and made her send her an order to retire into a convent. But Ninon, observing that no especial convent was named, said, with a great courtesy, to the officer who brought the order, that, as the option was left to her, she would choose "the convent of the Cordeliers at Paris;" which impudent joke so diverted the Queen that she left her alone for the future. Ninon never had but one lover at a time—but her admirers were numberless—so that when wearied of one incumbent she told him so frankly, and took another. The abandoned one might groan and complain; her decree was without appeal; and this creature had acquired such an influence, that the deserted lovers never dared to take revenge on the favoured one, and were too happy to remain on the footing of friend of the house. She sometimes kept faithful to one, when he pleased her very much, during an entire campaign.

Ninon had illustrious friends of all sorts, and had so much wit that she preserved them all and kept them on good terms with each other; or, at least, no quarrels ever came to light. There was an external respect and decency about everything that passed in her house, such as princesses of the highest rank have rarely been able to preserve in their intrigues.

In this way she had among her friends a selection of the best members of the Court; so that it became the fashion to be received by her, and it was useful to be so, on account of the connections that were thus formed.

There was never any gambling there, nor loud laughing, nor disputes, nor talk about religion or politics; but much and elegant wit, ancient and modern stories, news of gallantries, yet without scandal. All was delicate, light, measured; and she herself maintained the conversation by her wit and her great knowledge of facts. The respect which, strange to say, she had acquired, and the number and distinction of her friends and acquaintances, continued when her charms ceased to attract; and when propriety and fashion compelled her to use only intellectual baits. She knew all the intrigues of the old and the new Court, serious and otherwise; her conversation was charming; she was disinterested, faithful, secret, safe to the last degree; and, setting aside her frailty, virtuous and full of probity. She frequently succoured her friends with money and influence; constantly did them the most important services, and very faithfully kept the secrets or the money deposits that were confided to her.

She had been intimate with Madame de Maintenon during the whole of her residence at Paris; but Madame de Maintenon, although not daring to disavow this friendship, did not like to hear her spoken about. She wrote to Ninon with amity from time to time, even until her death; and Ninon in like manner, when she wanted to serve any friend in whom she took great interest, wrote to Madame de Maintenon, who did her what service she required efficaciously and with promptness. But since Madame de Maintenon came to power, they had only seen each other two or three times, and then in secret.

Ninon was remarkable for her repartees. One that she made to the last Maréchal de Choiseul is worth repeating. The Maréchal was virtue itself, but not fond of company or blessed with much wit. One day, after a long visit he had paid her, Ninon gaped, looked at the Maréchal, and cried:—

"Oh, my lord! how many virtues you make me detest!"

A line from I know not what play. The laughter at this may be imagined. L'Enclos lived long beyond her eightieth year, always healthy, visited, respected. She gave her last years to God, and her death was the news of the day. The singularity of this personage has made me extend my observations upon her.

A short time after the death of Mademoiselle de l'Enclos, a terrible adventure happened to Courtenvaux, eldest son of M. de Louvois. Courtenvaux was commander of the Cent-Suisses, fond of obscure debauches; with a ridiculous voice, miserly, quarrelsome, though modest and respectful; and in fine a very stupid fellow. The King, more eager to know all that was passing than most people believed, although they gave him credit for not a little curiosity in this respect, had authorised Bontems to engage a number of Swiss in addition to those posted at the doors, and in the parks and gardens. These attendants had orders to stroll morning, noon, and night, along the corridors, the passages, the staircases, even into the private places, and, when it was fine, in the court-yards and gardens; and in secret to watch people, to follow them, to notice where they went, to notice who was there, to listen to all the conversation they could hear, and to make reports of their discoveries. This was assiduously done at Versailles, at Marly, at Trianon, at Fontainebleau, and in all the places where the King was. These new attendants vexed Courtenvaux considerably, for over such new-comers he had no sort of authority. This season, at Fontainebleau, a room, which had formerly been occupied by a party of the Cent-Suisses and of the body-guard, was given up entirely to the new corps. The room was in a public passage of communication indispensable to all in the château, and in consequence, excellently well adapted for watching those who passed through it. Courtenvaux, more than ever vexed by this new arrangement, regarded it as a fresh encroachment upon his authority, and flew into a violent rage with the new-comers, and railed at them in good set terms. They allowed him to fume as he would; they had their orders, and were too wise to be disturbed by his rage. The King, who heard of all this, sent at once for Courtenvaux. As soon as he appeared in the cabinet, the King called to him from the other end of the room, without giving him time to approach, and in a rage so terrible, and for him so novel, that not only Courtenvaux, but Princes, Princesses, and everybody in the chamber, trembled. Menaces that his post should be taken away from him, terms the most severe and the most unusual, rained upon Courtenvaux, who, fainting with fright, and ready to sink under the ground, had neither the time nor the means to prefer a word. The reprimand finished by the King saying, "Get out." He had scarcely the strength to obey.

The cause of this strange scene was that Courtenvaux, by the fuss he had made, had drawn the attention of the whole Court to the change effected by the King, and that, when once seen, its object was clear to all eyes. The King, who hid his spy system with the greatest care, had counted upon this change passing unperceived, and was beside himself with anger when he found it made apparent to everybody by Courtenvaux's noise. He never regained the King's favour during the rest of his life; and but for his family he would certainly have been driven away, and his office taken from him.

Let me speak now of something of more moment.

The war, as I have said, still continued, but without bringing us any advantages. On the contrary, our losses in Germany and Italy by sickness, rather than by the sword, were so great that it was resolved to augment each company by five men; and, at the same time, twenty-five thousand militia were raised, thus causing great ruin and great desolation in the provinces. The King was rocked into the belief that the people were all anxious to enter this militia, and, from time to time, at Marly, specimens of those enlisted were shown to him, and their joy and eagerness to serve made much of. I have heard this often; while, at the same time, I knew from my own tenantry, and from everything that was said, that the raising of this militia carried despair everywhere, and that many people mutilated themselves in order to exempt themselves from serving. Nobody at the Court was ignorant of this. People lowered their eyes when they saw the deceit practised upon the King, and the credulity he displayed, and afterwards whispered one to another what they thought of flattery so ruinous. Fresh regiments, too, were raised at this time, and a crowd of new colonels and staffs created, instead of giving a new battalion or a squadron additional to regiments already in existence. I saw quite plainly towards what rock we were drifting. We had met losses at Hochstedt, Gibraltar, and Barcelona; Catalonia and the neighbouring countries were in revolt; Italy yielding us nothing but miserable successes; Spain exhausted; France, failing in men and money, and with incapable generals, protected by the Court against their faults. I saw all these things so plainly that I could not avoid making reflections, or reporting them to my friends in office. I thought that it was time to finish the war before we sank still lower, and that it might be finished by giving to the Archduke what we could not defend, and making a division of the rest. My plan was to leave Philip V. possession of all Italy, except those parts which belonged to the Grand Duke, the republics of Venice and Genoa, and the ecclesiastical states of Naples and Sicily; our King to have Lorraine and some other slight additions of territory; and to place elsewhere the Dukes of Savoy, of Lorraine, of Parma, and of Modena. I related this plan to the Chancellor and to Chamillart, amongst others. The contrast between their replies was striking. The Chancellor, after having listened to me very attentively, said, if my plan were adopted, he would most willingly kiss my toe for joy. Chamillart, with gravity replied, that the King would not give up a single mill of all the Spanish succession. Then I felt the blindness which had fallen upon us, and how much the results of it were to be dreaded.

Nevertheless, the King, as if to mock at misfortune and to show his enemies the little uneasiness he felt, determined, at the commencement of the new year, 1706, that the Court should be gayer than ever. He announced that there would be balls at Marly every time he was there this winter, and he named those who were to dance there; and said he should be very glad to see balls given to Madame de Bourgogne at Versailles. Accordingly, many took place there, and also at Marly, and from time to time there were masquerades. One day, the King wished that everybody, even the most aged, who were at Marly, should go to the ball masked; and, to avoid all distinction, he went there himself with a gauze robe above his habit; but such a slight disguise was for himself alone; everybody else was completely disguised. M. and Madame de Beauvilliers were there perfectly disguised. When I say *they* were there, those who knew the Court will admit that I have said more than enough. I had the pleasure of seeing them, and of quietly laughing with them. At all these balls the King made people dance who had long since passed the age for doing so. As for the Comte de Brionne and the Chevalier de Sully, their dancing was so perfect that there was no age for them.

CHAPTER XXXIV

IN the midst of all this gaiety, that is to say on the 12th of February, 1706, one of our generals, of whom I have often spoken, I mean M. de Vendôme, arrived at Marly. He had not quitted Italy since succeeding to Maréchal de Villeroy, after the affair of Cremona. His battles, such as they were, the places he had taken, the authority he had assumed, the reputation he had usurped, his incomprehensible successes with the King, the certainty of the support he leaned on,—all this inspired him with the desire to come and enjoy at Court a situation so brilliant, and which so far surpassed what he had a right to expect. But before speaking of the reception which was given him, and of the incredible ascendancy he took, let me paint him from the life a little more completely than I have yet done.

Vendôme was of ordinary height, rather stout, but vigorous and active: with a very noble countenance and lofty mien. There was much natural grace in his carriage and words; he had a good deal of innate wit, which he had not cultivated, and spoke easily, supported by a natural boldness, which afterwards turned to the wildest audacity; he knew the world and the Court; was above all things an admirable courtier; was polite when necessary, but insolent when he dared —familiar with common people—in reality, full of the most ravenous pride. As his rank rose and his favour increased, his obstinacy, and pig-headedness increased too, so that at last he would listen to no advice whatever, and was inaccessible to all, except a small number of familiars and valets. No one better than he knew the subserviency of the French character, or took more advantage of it. Little by little he accustomed his subalterns, and then from one to the other all his army, to call him nothing but "Monseigneur," and "Your Highness." In time the gangrene spread, and even lieutenant-generals and the most distinguished people did not dare to address him in any other manner.

The most wonderful thing to whoever knew the King—so gallant to the ladies during a long part of his life, so devout the other, and often importunate to make others do as he did—was that the said King had always a singular horror of the inhabitants of the Cities of the Plain; and yet M. de Vendôme, though most odiously stained with that vice—so publicly that he treated it as an ordinary gallantry—never found his favour diminished on that account. The Court, Anet, the army, knew of these abominations. Valets and subaltern officers soon found the way to promotion. I have already mentioned how publicly he placed himself in the doctor's hands, and how basely the Court acted, imitating the King, who would never have pardoned a legitimate prince what he indulged so strangely in Vendôme.

The idleness of M. de Vendôme was equally matter of notoriety. More than once he ran the risk of being taken prisoner from mere indolence. He rarely himself saw anything at the army, trusting to his familiars when ready to trust anybody. The way he employed his day prevented any real attention to business. He was filthy in the extreme, and proud of it. Fools called it simplicity. His bed was always full of dogs and bitches, who littered at his side, the pups rolling in the clothes. He himself was under constraint in nothing. One of his theses was, that everybody resembled him, but was not honest enough to confess it as he was. He mentioned this once to the Princesse de Conti— the cleanest person in the world, and the most delicate in her cleanliness.

He rose rather late when at the army. * * * * In this situation he wrote his letters, and gave his morning orders. Whoever had business with him, general officers and distinguished persons, could speak to him then. He had accustomed the army to this infamy. At the same time he gobbled his breakfast; and whilst he ate, listened, or gave orders, many spectators always standing round . . . (I must be excused these disgraceful details, in order better to make him known). . . . On shaving days he used the same vessel to lather his chin in. This, according to him, was a simplicity of manner worthy of the ancient Romans, and which condemned the splendour and superfluity of the others. When all was over, he dressed; then played high at *piquet* or *hombre;* or rode out, if it was absolutely necessary. All was now over for the day. He supped copiously with his familiars: was a great eater, of wonderful gluttony; a connoisseur in no dish, liked fish much, but the stale and stinking better than the good. The meal prolonged itself in theses and disputes, and above all in praise and flattery.

He would never have forgiven the slightest blame from any one. He wanted to pass for the first captain of his age, and spoke with indecent contempt of Prince Eugène and all the others. The faintest contradiction would have been a crime. The soldier and the subaltern adored him for his familiarity with them, and the licence he allowed in order to gain their hearts; for all which he made up by excessive haughtiness towards whoever was elevated by rank or birth.

On one occasion the Duke of Parma sent the bishop

of that place to negotiate some affair with him; but M. de Vendôme took such disgusting liberties in his presence, that the ecclesiastic, though without saying a word, returned to Parma, and declared to his master that never would he undertake such an embassy again. In his place another envoy was sent, the famous Alberoni. He was the son of a gardener, who became an Abbé in order to get on. He was full of buffoonery; and pleased M. de Parma as might a valet who amused him, but he soon showed talent and capacity for affairs. The Duke thought that the night-chair of M. de Vendôme required no other ambassador than Alberoni, who was accordingly sent to conclude what the bishop had left undone. The Abbé determined to please, and was not proud. M. de Vendôme exhibited himself as before; and Alberoni, by an infamous act of personal adoration, gained his heart. He was thenceforth much with him, made cheese-soup and other odd messes for him; and finally worked his way. It is true he was cudgelled by some one he had offended, for a thousand paces, in sight of the whole army, but this did not prevent his advancement. Vendôme liked such an unscrupulous flatterer; and yet as we have seen, he was not in want of praise. The extraordinary favour shown him by the King—the credulity with which his accounts of victories were received—showed to every one in what direction their laudation was to be sent.

Such was the man whom the King and the whole Court hastened to caress and flatter from the first moment of his arrival amongst us. There was a terrible hubbub: boys, porters, and valets rallied round his postchaise when he reached Marly. Scarcely had he ascended into his chamber, than everybody, princes, bastards and all the rest, ran after him. The ministers followed: so that in a short time nobody was left in the *salon* but the ladies. M. de Beauvilliers was at Vau-

Marlborough bringing the cavalry into action at the end of the battle of Ramillies.
—p. 424.
From the painting by R. Caton Woodville.

cresson. As for me, I remained spectator, and did not go and adore this idol.

In a few minutes Vendôme was sent for by the King and Monseigneur. As soon as he could dress himself, surrounded as he was by such a crowd, he went to the *salon,* carried by it rather than environed. Monseigneur stopped the music that was playing, in order to embrace him. The King left the cabinet where he was at work, and came out to meet him, embracing him several times. Chamillart on the morrow gave a *fête* in his honour at L'Etang, which lasted two days. Following his example, Pontchartrain, Torcy, and the most distinguished lords of the Court, did the same. People begged and entreated to give him *fêtes;* people begged and entreated to be invited to them. Never was triumph equal to his; each step he took procured him a new one. It is not too much to say, that everybody disappeared before him; Princes of the blood, ministers, the grandest seigneurs, all appeared only to show how high he was above them; even the King seemed only to remain King to elevate him more.

The people joined in this enthusiasm, both in Versailles and at Paris, where he went under pretence of going to the opera. As he passed along the streets crowds collected to cheer him; they billed him at the doors, and every seat was taken in advance; people pushed and squeezed everywhere, and the price of admission was doubled, as on the nights of first performances. Vendôme, who received all these homages with extreme ease, was yet internally surprised by a folly so universal. He feared that all this heat would not last out even the short stay he intended to make. To keep himself more in reserve, he asked and obtained permission to go to Anet, in the intervals between the journeys to Marly. All the Court, however, followed him there, and the King was pleased rather than otherwise, at seeing Versailles half deserted for Anet, actually asking some if they had been, others, when they intended to go.

It was evident that every one had resolved to raise M. de Vendôme to the rank of a hero. He determined to profit by the resolution. If they made him Mars, why should he not act as such? He claimed to be appointed commander of the Maréchals of France, and although the King refused him this favour, he accorded him one which was but the stepping-stone to it. M. de Vendôme went away towards the middle of March to command the army in Italy, with a letter signed by the King himself, promising him that if a Maréchal of France were sent to Italy, that Maréchal was to take commands from him. M. de Vendôme was content, and determined to obtain all he asked on a future day. The disposition of the armies had been arranged just before. Tessé, for Catalonia and Spain; Berwick, for the frontier of Portugal; Maréchal Villars, for Alsace; Marsin, for the Moselle; Maréchal de Villeroy, for Flanders; and M. de Vendôme, as I have said, for Italy.

Now that I am speaking of the armies, let me give here an account of all our military operations this year, so as to complete that subject at once.

M. de Vendôme commenced his Italian campaign by a victory. He attacked the troops of Prince Eugène upon the heights of Calcinato, drove them before him, killed three thousand men, took twenty standards, ten pieces of cannon, and eight thousand prisoners. It was a rout rather than a combat. The enemy was much inferior in force to us, and was without its general, Prince Eugène, he not having returned to open the campaign. He came back, however, the day after this engagement, soon re-established order among his troops, and M. de Vendôme from that time, far from being able to recommence the attack, was obliged to keep strictly on the defensive while he remained in Italy. He did not fail to make the most of his victory, which, however, to say the truth, led to nothing.

Our armies just now were, it must be admitted, in by no means a good condition. The generals owed their promotion to favour and fantasy. The King thought he gave them capacity when he gave them their patents. Under M. de Turenne the army had afforded, as in a school, opportunities for young officers to learn the art of warfare, and to qualify themselves step by step to take command. They were promoted as they showed signs of their capacity, and gave proof of their talent. Now, however, it was very different. Promotion was granted according to length of service, thus rendering all application and diligence unnecessary, except when M. de Louvois suggested to the King such officers as he had private reasons for being favourable to, and whose actions he could control. He persuaded the King that it was he himself who ought to direct the armies from his cabinet. The King, flattered by this, swallowed the bait, and Louvois himself was thus enabled to govern in the name of the King, to keep the generals in leading-strings, and to fetter their every movement. In consequence of the way in which promotions were made, the greatest ignorance prevailed amongst all grades of officers. None knew scarcely anything more than mere routine duties, and sometimes not even so much as that. The luxury which had inundated the army, too, where everybody wished to live as delicately as at Paris, hindered the general officers from associating with the other officers, and in consequence from knowing and appreciating them. As a matter of course, there were no longer any deliberations upon the state of affairs, in which the young might profit by the counsels of the old, and the army profit by the discussions of all. The young officers talked only of pay and women; the old, of forage and equipages; the generals spent half their time in writing costly despatches, often useless, and sending them away by couriers. The luxury of the Court and city had spread into the army, so that delicacies were carried there unknown formerly. Nothing was spoken of but hot dishes in the marches and in the detachments; and the repasts that were carried to the trenches, during sieges, were not only well served, but ices and fruits were partaken of as at a *fête*, and a profusion of all sorts of liqueurs. Expense ruined the officers, who vied with one another in their endeavours to appear magnificent; and the things to be carried, the work to be done, quadrupled the number of domestics and grooms, who often starved. For a long time, people had complained of all this; even those who were put to the expenses, which ruined them; but none dared to spend less. At last, that is to say, in the spring of the following year, the King made severe rules, with the object of bringing about a reform in this particular. There is no country in Europe where there are so many fine laws, or where the observance of them is of shorter duration. It often happens, that in the first year all are infringed, and in the second, forgotten. Such was the army at this time, and we soon had abundant opportunities to note its incapacity to overcome the enemies with whom we had to contend.

The King wished to open this campaign with two battles; one in Italy, the other in Flanders. His desire was to some extent gratified in the former case; but in the other he met with a sad and cruel disappointment. Since the departure of Maréchal de Villeroy for Flanders, the King had more than once pressed him to engage the enemy. The Maréchal, piqued with these reiterated orders, which he considered as reflections upon his courage, determined to risk anything in order to satisfy the desire of the King. But the King did not wish this. At the same time that he wished for a battle in Flanders, he wished to place Villeroy in a state to fight it. He sent orders, therefore, to Marsin to take eighteen battalions and twenty squadrons of his army, to proceed to the Moselle, where he would find twenty others, and then to march with the whole into Flanders, and join Maréchal de Villeroy. At the same time he prohibited the latter from doing anything until this reinforcement reached him. Four couriers, one after the other, carried this prohibition to the Maréchal; but he had determined to give battle without assistance, and he did so, with what result will be seen.

On the 24th of May he posted himself between the villages of Taviers and Ramillies. He was superior in force to the Duke of Marlborough, who was opposed to him, and this fact gave him confidence. Yet the position which he had taken up was one which was well known to be bad. The late M. de Luxembourg had declared it so, and had avoided it. M. de Villeroy had been a witness of this, but it was his destiny and that of France that he should forget it. Before he took up this position he announced that it was his intention to do so to M. d'Orléans. M. d'Orléans said publicly to all who came to listen, that if M. de Villeroy did so he would be beaten. M. d'Orléans proved to be only too good a prophet.

Just as M. de Villeroy had taken up his position and made his arrangements, the Elector arrived in hot haste from Brussels. It was too late now to blame what had been done. There was nothing for it but to complete what had been already begun, and await the result.

It was about two hours after midday when the enemy arrived within range, and came under our fire from Ramillies. It forced them to halt until their cannon could be brought into play, which was soon done. The cannonade lasted a good hour. At the end of that time they marched to Taviers, where a part of our army was posted, found but little resistance, and made themselves masters of that place. From that moment they brought their cavalry to bear. They perceived that there was a marsh which covered our left, but which hindered our two wings from joining. They made good use of the advantage this gave them. We were taken in the rear at more than one point, and Taviers being no longer able to assist us, Ramillies itself fell, after a prodigious fire and an obstinate resistance. The Comte de Guiche at the head of the regiment of Guards defended it for four hours, and performed prodigies, but in the end he was obliged to give way. All this time our left had been utterly useless with its nose in the marsh, no enemy in front of it, and with strict orders not to budge from its position.

Our retreat commenced in good order, but soon the night came and threw us into confusion. The defile of Judoigne became so gorged with baggage and with the wrecks of the artillery we had been able to save, that everything was taken from us there. Nevertheless, we arrived at Louvain, and then not feeling in safety, passed the canal of Wilworde without being very closely followed by the enemy.

We lost in this battle four thousand men, and many prisoners of rank, all of whom were treated with much politeness by Marlborough. Brussels was one of the first-fruits he gathered of this victory, which had such grave and important results.

The King did not learn this disaster until Wednesday, the 26th of May, at his waking. I was at Versailles. Never was such trouble or such consternation. The worst was, that only the broad fact was known; for six days we were without a courier to give us details. Even the post was stopped. Days seemed like years in the ignorance of everybody as to details, and in the inquietude of everybody for relatives and friends. The King was forced to ask one and another for news; but nobody could tell him any. Worn out at last by the silence, he determined to despatch Chamillart to Flanders to ascertain the real state of affairs. Chamillart accordingly left Versailles on Sunday, the 30th of May, to the astonishment of all the Court, at seeing a man charged with the war and the finance department sent on such an errand. He astonished no less the army when he arrived at Courtrai, where it had stationed itself. Having gained all the information he sought, Chamillart returned to Versailles on Friday, the 4th of June, at about eight o'clock in the evening, and at once went to the King, who was in the apartments of Madame de Maintenon. It was known then that the army, after several hasty marches, finding itself at Ghent, the Elector of Bavaria had insisted that it ought at least to remain there. A council of war was held, the Maréchal de Villeroy, who was quite discouraged by the loss he had sustained, opposed the advice of the Elector. Ghent was abandoned, so was the open country. The army was separated and distributed here and there, under the command of the general officers. In this way, with the exception of Namur, Mons, and a very few other places, all the Spanish Low Countries were lost, and a part of ours, even. Never was rapidity equal to this. The enemies were as much astonished as we.

However tranquilly the King sustained in appearance this misfortune, he felt it to the quick. He was so affected by what was said of his body-guards, that he spoke of them himself with bitterness. Court warriors testified in their favour, but persuaded nobody. But the King seized these testimonies with joy, and sent word to the Guards that he was well contended with them. Others, however, were not so easily satisfied.

This sad reverse and the discontent of the Elector made the King feel at last that his favourites must give way to those better able to fill their places. Villeroy, who, since his defeat, had quite lost his head, and who, if he had been a general of the Empire, would have lost it in reality in another manner, received several strong hints from the King that he ought to give up his command. But he either could not or would not understand them, and so tired out the King's patience, at length. But he was informed in language which admitted of no misapprehension that he must return. Even then, the King was so kindly disposed towards him, that he said the Maréchal had begged to be recalled with such obstinacy that he could not refuse him. But M. de Villeroy was absurd enough to reject this salve for his honour; which led to his disgrace. M. de Vendôme had orders to leave Italy, and succeed to the command in Flanders, where the enemies had very promptly taken Ostend and Nieuport.

CHAPTER XXXV

MEANWHILE, as I have promised to relate, in a continuous narrative, all our military operations of this year, let me say what passed in other directions. The siege of Barcelona made no progress. Our engineers were so slow and so ignorant, that they did next to nothing. They were so venal, too, that they aided the enemy rather than us by their movements. According to a new rule made by the King, whenever they changed the position of their guns, they were entitled to a pecuniary recompense. Accordingly, they passed all their time in uselessly changing about from place to place, in order to receive the recompense which thus became due to them.

Our fleet, too, hearing that a much superior naval force was coming to the assistance of the enemy, and being, thanks to Pontchartrain, utterly unable to meet it, was obliged to weigh anchor, and sailed away to Toulon. The enemy's fleet arrived, and the besieged at once took new courage. Tessé, who had joined the siege, saw at once that it was useless to continue it. We had for some time depended upon the open sea for supplies. Now that the English fleet had arrived, we could depend upon the sea no longer. The King of Spain saw, at last, that there was no help for it but to raise the siege.

It was raised accordingly on the night between the 10th and 11th of May, after fourteen days' bombardment. We abandoned one hundred pieces of artillery; one hundred and fifty thousand pounds of powder;

thirty thousand sacks of flour; twenty thousand sacks of *sévade,* a kind of oats; and a great number of bombs, cannon-balls, and implements. As Catalonia was in revolt, it was felt that retreat could not take place in that direction; it was determined, therefore, to retire by the way of the French frontier. For eight days, however, our troops were harassed in flank and rear by Miquelets, who followed us from mountain to mountain. It was not until the Duc de Noailles, whose father had done some service to the chiefs of these Miquelets, had parleyed with them, and made terms with them, that our troops were relieved from these cruel wasps. We suffered much loss in our retreat, which, with the siege, cost us full four thousand men. The army stopped at Roussillon, and the King of Spain, escorted by two regiments of dragoons, made the best of his way to Madrid. That city was itself in danger from the Portuguese, and, indeed, fell into their hands soon after. The Queen, who, with her children, had left it in time to avoid capture, felt matters to be in such extremity, that she despatched all the jewels belonging to herself and her husband to France. They were placed in the custody of the King. Among them was that famous pear-shaped pearl called the *Pérégrine,* which, for its weight, its form, its size, and its water, is beyond all price and all comparison.

The King of Spain effected a junction with the army of Berwick, and both set to work to reconquer the places the Portuguese had taken from them. In this they were successful. The Portuguese, much harassed by the people of Castille, were forced to abandon all they had gained; and the King of Spain was enabled to enter Madrid towards the end of September, where he was received with much rejoicing.

In Italy we experienced the most disastrous misfortunes. M. de Vendôme, having been called from the command to go into Flanders, M. d'Orléans, after some deliberation, was appointed to take his place. M. d'Orléans set out from Paris on the 1st of July, with twenty-eight horses and five chaises, to arrive in three days at Lyons, and then to hasten on into Italy. La Feuillade was besieging Turin. M. d'Orléans went to the siege. He was magnificently received by La Feuillade, and shown all over the works. He found everything defective. La Feuillade was very young, and very inexperienced. I have already related an adventure of his, that of his seizing upon the coffers of his uncle, and so forestalling his inheritance. To recover from the disgrace this occurrence brought upon him, he had married a daughter of Chamillart. Favoured by this minister, but coldly looked upon by the King, he had succeeded in obtaining command in the army, and had been appointed to conduct this siege. Inflated by the importance of his position, and by the support of Chamillart, he would listen to no advice from any one. M. d'Orléans attempted to bring about some changes, and gave orders to that effect. But as soon as he was gone, La Feuillade countermanded those orders and had everything his own way. The siege accordingly went on with the same ill-success as before.

M. d'Orléans joined M. de Vendôme on the 17th of July, upon the Mincio. The pretended hero had just made some irreparable faults. He had allowed Prince Eugène to pass the Po, nearly in front of him, and nobody knew what had become of twelve of our battalions posted near the place where this passage had been made. Prince Eugène had taken all the boats that we had upon the river. We could not cross it, therefore, and follow the enemy without making a bridge. Vendôme feared lest his faults should be perceived. He wished that his successor should remain charged with them. M. d'Orléans, indeed, soon saw all the faults that M. de Vendôme had committed, and tried hard to induce the latter to aid him to repair them. But M. de Vendôme would not listen to his representations, and started away almost immediately to take the command of the army in Flanders, leaving M. d'Orléans to get out of the difficulty as he might.

M. d'Orléans, abandoned to himself (except when interfered with by Maréchal de Marsin, under whose tutelage he was), could do nothing. He found as much opposition to his plans from Marsin as he had found from M. de Vendôme. Marsin wished to keep in the good graces of La Feuillade, son-in-law of the all-powerful minister, and would not adopt the views of M. d'Orléans. This latter had proposed to dispute the passage of the Tanaro, a confluent of the Po, with the enemy, or compel them to accept battle. An intercepted letter, in cypher, from Prince Eugène to the Emperor, which fell into our hands, proved, subsequently, that this course would have been the right one to adopt; but the proof came too late; the decyphering table having been forgotten at Versailles! M. d'Orléans had in the mean time been forced to lead his army to Turin, to assist the besiegers, instead of waiting to stop the passage of the troops that were destined for the aid of the besieged. He arrived at Turin on the 28th of August, in the evening. La Feuillade, now under two masters, grew, it might be imagined, more docile. But no! He allied himself with Marsin (without whom M. d'Orléans could do nothing), and so gained him over that they acted completely in accord. When M. d'Orléans was convinced, soon after his arrival, that the enemy was approaching to succour Turin, he suggested that they should be opposed as they attempted the passage of the Dora.

But his advice was not listened to. He was displeased with everything. He found that all the orders he had given had been disregarded. He found the siege works bad, imperfect, very wet, and very ill-guarded. He tried to remedy all these defects, but he was opposed at every step. A council of war was held. M. d'Orléans stated his views, but all the officers present, with one honourable exception, servilely chimed in with the views of Marsin and La Feuillade, and things remained as they were. M. d'Orléans, thereupon, protested that he washed his hands of all the misfortunes that might happen in consequence of his advice being neglected. He declared that as he was no longer master over anything, it was not just that he should bear any part of the blame which would entail to those in command. He asked, therefore, for his post-chaise, and wished immediately to quit the army. La Feuillade and Marsin, however, begged him to remain, and upon second thoughts he thought it better to do so. The simple reason of all this opposition was, that La Feuillade, being very young and very vain, wished to have all the honours of the siege. He was afraid that if the counsel of M. d'Orléans prevailed, some of that honour would be taken from him. This was the real reason, and to this France owes the disastrous failure of the siege of Turin.

After the council of war, M. d'Orléans ceased to take any share in the command, walked about or stopped at home, like a man who had nothing to do with what was passing around him. On the night of the 6th to the 7th of September, he rose from his bed alarmed by information sent to him in a letter, that Prince Eugène was about to attack the castle of Pianezza, in order to cross the Dora, and so proceed to attack the besiegers. He hastened at once to Marsin, showed him the letter, and recommended that troops should at once be sent to dispute the passage of a brook that the enemies had yet to cross, even supposing them to be masters of Pianezza. Even as he was speaking, confirmation of the intelligence he had received was brought by one of our officers. But it was resolved, in the Eternal decrees, that France should be struck to the heart that day.

Marsin would listen to none of the arguments of M. d'Orléans. He maintained that it would be unsafe to leave the lines; that the news was false; that Prince Eugène could not possibly arrive so promptly; he would give no orders; and he counselled M. d'Orléans to go back to bed. The Prince, more piqued and more disgusted than ever, retired to his quarters fully resolved to abandon everything to the blind and deaf, who would neither see nor hear.

Soon after entering his chamber the news spread from all parts of the arrival of Prince Eugène. He did not stir. Some general officers came, and forced him to mount his horse. He went forth negligently at a walking pace. What had taken place during the previous days had made so much noise that even the common soldiers were ashamed of it. They liked him, and murmured because he would no longer command them. One of them called him by his name, and asked him if he refused them his sword. This question did more than all that the general officers had been able to do. M. d'Orléans replied to the soldier, that he would not refuse to serve them, and at once resolved to lend all his aid to Marsin and La Feuillade.

But it was no longer possible to leave the lines. The enemy was in sight, and advanced so diligently, that there was no time to make arrangements. Marsin, more dead than alive, was incapable of giving any order or any advice. But La Feuillade still persevered in his obstinacy. He disputed the orders of the Duc d'Orléans, and prevented their execution, possessed by I know not what demon.

The attack was commenced about ten o'clock in the morning, was pushed with incredible vigour, and sustained, at first, in the same manner. Prince Eugène poured his troops into those places which the smallness of our forces had compelled us to leave open. Marsin, towards the middle of the battle, received a wound which incapacitated him from further service, and was taken prisoner immediately after. Le Feuillade ran about like a madman, tearing his hair, and incapable of giving any order. The Duc d'Orléans preserved his coolness, and did wonders to save the day. Finding our men beginning to waver, he called the officers by their names, aroused the soldiers by his voice, and himself led the squadrons and battalions to the charge. Vanquished at last by pain, and weakened by the blood he had lost, he was constrained to retire a little, to have his wounds dressed. He scarcely gave himself time for this, however, but returned at once where the fire was hottest. Three times the enemy had been repulsed and their guns spiked by one of our officers, Le Guerchois, with his brigade of the old marine, when, enfeebled by the losses he had sustained, he called upon a neighbouring brigade to advance with him to oppose a number of fresh battalions the enemy had sent against him. This brigade and its brigadier refused bluntly to aid him. It was positively known afterwards, that had Le Guerchois sustained this fourth charge, Prince Eugène would have retreated.

This was the last moment of the little order that there had been at this battle. All that followed was only trouble, confusion, disorder, flight, discomfiture. The most terrible thing is, that the general officers, with but few exceptions, more intent upon their equipage and upon what they had saved by pillage, added to the confusion instead of diminishing it, and were worse than useless.

M. d'Orléans, convinced at last that it was impossible to re-establish the day, thought only how to retire as advantageously as possible. He withdrew his light artillery, his ammunition, everything that was at the siege, even at the most advanced of its works, and attended to everything with a presence of mind that allowed nothing to escape him. Then, gathering round him all the officers he could collect, he explained to them that nothing but retreat was open to them, and that the road to Italy was that which they ought to pursue. By this means they would leave the victorious army of the enemy in a country entirely ruined and desolate, and hinder it from returning into Italy, where the army of the King, on the contrary, would have abundance, and where it would cut off all succour from the others.

This proposition dismayed to the last degree our officers, who hoped at least to reap the fruit of this disaster by returning to France with the money with which they were gorged. La Feuillade opposed it with so much impatience, that the Prince, exasperated by an effrontery so sustained, told him to hold his peace and let others speak. Others did speak, but only one was for following the counsel of M. d'Orléans. Feeling himself now, however, the master, he stopped all further discussion, and gave orders that the retreat to Italy should commence. This was all he could do. His body and his brain were equally exhausted. After having waited some little time, he was compelled to throw himself into a post-chaise, and in that to continue the journey.

The officers obeyed his orders most unwillingly. They murmured amongst each other so loudly that the Duc d'Orléans, justly irritated by so much opposition to his will, made them hold their peace. The retreat continued. But it was decreed that the spirit of error and vertigo should ruin us and save the allies. As the army was about to cross the bridge over the Ticino, and march into Italy, information was brought to M. d'Orléans, that the enemy occupied the roads by which it was indispensable to pass. M. d'Orléans, not believing this intelligence, persisted in going forward. Our officers, thus foiled, for it was known afterwards that the story was their invention, and that the passes were entirely free, hit upon another expedient. They declared there were no more provisions or ammunition, and that it was accordingly impossible to go into Italy. M. d'Orléans, worn out by so much ; criminal disobedience, and weakened by his wound, could hold out no longer. He threw himself back in the chaise, and said they might go where they would. The army therefore turned about, and directed itself towards Pignerol, losing many equipages from our rear-guard during the night in the mountains, although that rear-guard was protected by Albergotti, and was not annoyed by the enemy.

The joy of the enemy at their success was unbounded. They could scarcely believe in it. Their army was just at its last gasp. They had not more than four days' supply of powder left in the place. After the victory, M. de Savoie and Prince Eugène lost no time in idle rejoicings. They thought only how to profit by a success so unheard of and so unexpected. They retook rapidly all the places in Piedmont and Lombardy that we occupied, and we had no power to prevent them.

Never battle cost fewer soldiers than that of Turin; never was retreat more undisturbed than ours; yet never were results more frightful or more rapid. Ramillies, with a light loss, cost the Spanish Low

Countries and part of ours: Turin cost all Italy by the ambition of La Feuillade, the incapacity of Marsin, the avarice, the trickery, the disobedience of the general officers opposed to M. d'Orléans. So complete was the rout of our army, that it was found impossible to restore it sufficiently to send it back to Italy, not at least before the following spring. M. d'Orléans returned therefore to Versailles, on Monday, the 8th of November, and was well received by the King. La Feuillade arrived on Monday, the 13th of December, having remained several days at Paris without daring to go to Versailles. He was taken to the King by Chamillart. As soon as the King saw them enter he rose, went to the door, and without giving them time to utter a word, said to La Feuillade, " Monsieur, we are both very unfortunate! " and instantly turned his back upon him. La Feuillade, on the threshold of the door that he had not had time to cross, left the place immediately, without having dared to say a single word. The King always afterwards turned his eyes from La Feuillade, and would never speak to him. Such was the fall of this Phaëton. He saw that he had no more hope, and retired from the army; although there was no baseness that he did not afterwards employ to return to command. I think there never was a more wrong-headed man or a man more radically dishonest, even to the marrow of his bones. As for Marsin, he died soon after his capture, from the effect of his wounds.

CHAPTER XXXVI

SUCH was our military history of the year 1706—a history of losses and dishonour. It may be imagined in what condition was the exchequer with so many demands upon its treasures. For the last two or three years the King had been obliged, on account of the expenses of the war, and the losses we had sustained, to cut down the presents that he made at the commencement of the year. Thirty-five thousand louis in gold was the sum he ordinarily spent in this manner. This year, 1707, he diminished it by ten thousand louis. It was upon Madame de Montespan that the blow fell. Since she had quitted the Court the King gave her twelve thousand louis of gold each year. This year he sent word to her that he could only give her eight. Madame de Montespan testified not the least surprise. She replied, that she was only sorry for the poor, to whom indeed she gave with profusion. A short time after the King had made this reduction,—that is, on the 8th of January, —Madame la Duchesse de Bourgogne gave birth to a son. The joy was great, but the King prohibited all those expenses which had been made at the birth of the first-born of Madame de Bourgogne, and which had amounted to a large sum. The want of money indeed made itself felt so much at this time, that the King was obliged to seek for resources as a private person might have done. A mining speculator, named Rodes, having pretended that he had discovered many veins of gold in the Pyrenees, assistance was given him in order that he might bring these treasures to light.

He declared that with eighteen hundred workmen he would furnish a million (francs' worth of gold) each week. Fifty-two millions a-year would have been a fine increase of revenue. However, after waiting some little time, no gold was forthcoming, and the money that had been spent to assist this enterprise was found to be pure loss.

The difficulty of finding money to carry on the affairs of the nation continued to grow so irksome that Chamillart, who had both the finance and the war departments under his control, was unable to stand against the increased trouble and vexation which this state of things brought him. More than once he had represented that this double work was too much for him. But the King had in former times expressed so much annoyance from the troubles that arose between the finance and war departments, that he would not separate them, after having once joined them together. At last, Chamillart could bear up against his heavy load no longer. The vapours seized him: he had attacks of giddiness in the head; his digestion was obstructed; he grew thin as a lath. He wrote again to the King, begging to be released from his duties, and frankly stated that, in the state he was, if some relief was not afforded him, everything would go wrong and perish. He always left a large margin to his letters, and upon this the King generally wrote his reply. Chamillart showed me this letter when it came back to him, and I saw upon it with great surprise, in the handwriting of the King, this short note: "Well! let us perish together."

The necessity for money had now become so great, that all sorts of means were adopted to obtain it. Amongst other things, a tax was established upon baptisms and marriages. This tax was extremely onerous and odious. The result of it was a strange confusion. Poor people, and many of humble means, baptised their children themselves, without carrying them to the church, and were married at home by reciprocal consent and before witnesses, when they could find no priest who would marry them without formality. In consequence of this there were no longer any baptismal extracts; no longer any certainty as to baptisms or births; and the children of the marriages solemnised in the way I have stated above were illegitimate in the eyes of the law. Researches and rigours in respect to abuses so prejudicial were redoubled therefore; that is to say, they were redoubled for the purpose of collecting the tax.

From public cries and murmurs the people in some places passed to sedition. Matters went so far at Cahors, that two battalions which were there had great difficulty in holding the town against the armed peasants; and troops intended for Spain were obliged to be sent there. It was found necessary to suspend the operation of the tax, but it was with great trouble that the movement of Quercy was put down, and the peasants, who had armed and collected together, induced to retire into their villages. In Perigord they rose, pillaged the *bureaux*, and rendered themselves masters of a little town and some castles, and forced some gentlemen to put themselves at their head. They declared publicly that they would pay the old taxes to King, curate, and lord, but that they would pay no more, or hear a word of any other taxes or vexation. In the end it was found necessary to drop this tax upon baptism and marriages, to the great regret of the tax-gatherers, who, by all manner of vexations and rogueries, had enriched themselves cruelly.

It was at this time, and in consequence, to some extent, of these events, that a man who had acquired the highest distinction in France was brought to the tomb in bitterness and grief, for that which in any other country would have covered him with honour. Vauban, for it is to him that I allude, patriot as he was, had all his life been touched with the misery of the people and the vexations they suffered. The knowledge that his offices gave him of the necessity for expense, the little hope he had that the King would retrench in matters of splendour and amusement, made him groan to see no remedy to an oppression which increased in weight from day to day. Feeling this, he made no journey that he did not collect information upon the value and produce of the land, upon the trade and industry of the towns and provinces, on the nature of the imposts, and the manner of collecting them. Not content with this, he secretly sent to such places as he could not visit himself, or even to those he had visited, to instruct him in everything, and compare the reports he received with those he had himself made. The last twenty years of his life were spent in these researches, and at considerable cost to himself. In the end, he convinced himself that the land was the only real wealth, and he set himself to work to form a new system.

He had already made much progress, when several little books appeared by Boisguilbert, lieutenant-general at Rouen, who long since had had the same views as Vauban, and had wanted to make them known. From this labour had resulted a learned and profound book, in which a system was explained by which the people could be relieved of all the expenses they supported, and from every tax, and by which the revenue collected would go at once into the treasury of the King, instead of enriching, first the traitants, the intendants, and the finance ministers. These latter, therefore, were opposed to the system, and their opposition, as will be seen, was of no slight consequence.

Vauban read this book with much attention. He differed on some points with the author, but agreed with him in the main. Boisguilbert wished to preserve some imposts upon foreign commerce and upon provisions. Vauban wished to abolish all imposts, and to substitute for them two taxes, one upon the land, the other upon trade and industry. His book, in which he put forth these ideas, was full of information and figures, all arranged with the utmost clearness, simplicity, and exactitude.

But it had a grand fault. It described a course which, if followed, would have ruined an army of financiers, of clerks, of functionaries of all kinds; it would have forced them to live at their own expense, instead of at the expense of the people; and it would have sapped the foundations of those immense fortunes that are seen to grow up in such a short time. This was enough to cause its failure.

All the people interested in opposing the work set up a cry. They saw place, power, everything, about to fly from their grasp, if the counsels of Vauban were acted upon. What wonder, then, that the King, who was surrounded by these people, listened to their reasons, and received with a very ill grace Maréchal Vauban when he presented his book to him. The ministers, it may well be believed, did not give him a better welcome. From that moment his services, his military capacity (unique of its kind), his virtues, the affection the King had had for him, all were forgotten. The King saw only in Maréchal Vauban a man led astray by love for the people, a criminal who attacked the authority of the ministers, and consequently that of the King. He explained himself to this effect without scruple.

The unhappy Maréchal could not survive the loss of his royal master's favour, or stand up against the enmity the King's explanations had created against him; he died a few months after consumed with grief, and with an affliction nothing could soften, and to which the King was insensible to such a point, that he made semblance of not perceiving that he had lost a servitor so useful and so illustrious. Vauban, justly celebrated over all Europe, was regretted in France by all who were not financiers or their supporters.

Boisguilbert, whom this event ought to have rendered wise, could not contain himself. One of the objections which had been urged against his theories, was the difficulty of carrying out changes in the midst of a great war. He now published a book refuting this point, and describing such a number of abuses then existing, to abolish which, he asked, was it necessary to wait for peace, that the ministers were outraged. Boisguilbert was exiled to Auvergne. I did all in my power to revoke this sentence, having known Boisguilbert at Rouen, but did not succeed until the end of two months. He was then allowed to return to Rouen, but was severely reprimanded, and stripped of his functions for some little time. He was amply indemnified, however, for this by the crowd of people, and the acclamations with which he was received.

It is due to Chamillart to say, that he was the only minister who had listened with any attention to these new systems of Vauban and Boisguilbert. He indeed made trial of the plans suggested by the former, but the circumstances were not favourable to his success, and they of course failed. Some time after, instead of following the system of Vauban, and reducing the imposts, fresh ones were added. Who would have said to the Maréchal that all his labours for the relief of the people of France would lead to new imposts, more harsh, more permanent, and more heavy than he protested against? It is a terrible lesson against all improvements in matters of taxation and finance.

But it is time, now, that I should retrace my steps to other matters, which, if related in due order of time, should have found a place ere this. And first, let me relate the particulars concerning a trial in which I was engaged, and which I have deferred allusion to until now, so as not to entangle the thread of my narrative.

My sister, as I have said in its proper place, had married the Duc de Brissac, and the marriage had not been a happy one. After a time, in fact, they separated. My sister at her death left me her universal legatee; and shortly after this, M. de Brissac brought an action against me on her account for five hundred thousand francs. After his death, his representatives continued the action, which I resisted, not only maintaining that I owed none of the five hundred thousand francs, but claiming to have two hundred thousand owing to me, out of six hundred thousand which had formed the dowry of my sister.

When M. de Brissac died, there seemed some probability that his peerage would become extinct; for the Comte de Cossé, who claimed to succeed him, was opposed by a number of peers, and but for me might have failed to establish his pretensions. I, however, as his claim was just, interested myself in him, supported him with all my influence, and gained for him the support of several influential peers: so that in the end he was recognised as Duc de Brissac, and received as such at the parliament on the 6th of May, 1700.

Having succeeded thus to the titles and estates of his predecessor, he succeeded also to his liabilities, debts, and engagements. Among these was the trial against me for five hundred thousand francs. Cossé felt so thoroughly that he owed his rank to me, that he offered to give me five hundred thousand francs, so as to indemnify me against an adverse decision in the cause. Now, as I have said, I not only resisted this demand made upon me for five hundred thousand francs, but I, in my turn, claimed two hundred thousand francs, and my claim, once admitted, all the personal creditors of the late Duc de Brissac (creditors who, of course, had to be paid by the new Duke) would have been forced to stand aside until my debt was settled.

I, therefore, refused this offer of Cossé, lest other creditors should hear of the arrangement, and force him to make a similar one with them. He was overwhelmed with a generosity so little expected, and we became more intimately connected from that day.

Cossé, once received as Duc de Brissac, I no longer feared to push forward the action I had commenced for the recovery of the two hundred thousand francs due to me, and which I had interrupted only on his account. I had gained it twice running against the late Duc de Brissac, at the parliament of Rouen; but the Duchesse d'Aumont, who in the last years of his life had lent him money, and whose debt was in danger, succeeded in getting this cause sent up for appeal to the parliament at Paris, where she threw obstacle upon obstacle in its path, and caused judgment to be delayed month after month. When I came to take active steps in the matter, my surprise—to use no stronger word—was great, to find Cossé, after all I had done for him, favouring the pretensions of the Duchesse d'Aumont, and lending her his aid to establish them. However, he and the Duchesse d'Aumont lost their cause, for when it was submitted to the judges of the council at Paris, it was sent back to Rouen, and they had to pay damages and expenses.

For years the affair had been ready to be judged at Rouen, but M. d'Aumont every year, by means of his letters of state, obtained a postponement. At last, however, M. d'Aumont died, and I was assured that the letters of state should not be again produced, and that in consequence no further adjournment should take place. I and Madame de Saint-Simon at once set out, therefore, for Rouen, where we were exceedingly well received, *fêtes* and entertainments being continually given in our honour.

After we had been there but eight or ten days, I received a letter from Pontchartrain, who sent me word that the King had learnt with surprise I was at Rouen, and had charged him to ask me why I was there: so attentive was the King as to what became of the people of mark, he was accustomed to see around him! My reply was not difficult.

Meanwhile our cause proceeded. The parliament, that is to say, the Grand Chamber, suspended all other business in order to finish ours. The affair was already far advanced, when it was interrupted by an obstacle, of all obstacles the least possible to foresee. The letters of state had again been put in, for the purpose of obtaining another adjournment.

My design is not to weary by recitals, which interest only myself; but I must explain this matter fully. It was Monday evening. The parliament of Rouen ended on the following Saturday. If we waited until the opening of the next parliament, we should have to begin our cause from the beginning, and with new presidents and judges, who would know nothing of the facts. What was to be done? To appeal to the King seemed impossible, for he was at Marly, and, while there, never listened to such matters. By the time he left Marly, it would be too late to apply to him.

Madame de Saint-Simon and others advised me, however, at all hazards, to go straight to the King, instead of sending a courier, as I thought of doing, and to keep my journey secret. I followed their advice, and setting out at once, arrived at Marly on Tuesday morning, the 8th of August, at eight of the clock. The Chancellor and Chamillart, to whom I told my errand, pitied me, but gave me no hope of success. Nevertheless, a council of state was to be held on the following morning, presided over by the King, and my petition was laid before it. The letters of state were thrown out by every voice. This information was brought to me at mid-day. I partook of a hasty dinner, and turned back to Rouen, where I arrived on Thursday, at eight o'clock in the morning, three hours after a courier, by whom I had sent this unhoped-for news.

I brought with me, besides the order respecting the letters of state, an order to the parliament to proceed to judgment at once. It was laid before the judges very early on Saturday, the 11th of August, the last day of the parliament. From four o'clock in the morning we had an infinite number of visitors, wanting to accompany us to the palace. The parliament had been much irritated against these letters of state, after having suspended all other business for us. The withdrawal of these letters was now announced. We gained our cause, with penalties and expenses, amid acclamations which resounded through the court, and which followed us into the streets. We could scarcely enter our street, so full was it with the crowd, or our house, which was equally crowded. Our kitchen chimney soon after took fire, and it was only a marvel that it was extinguished, without damage, after having strongly warned us, and turned our joy into bitterness. There was only the master of the house who was unmoved. We dined, however, with a grand company; and after stopping one or two days more to thank our friends, we went to see the sea at Dieppe, and then to Cani, to a beautiful house belonging to our host at Rouen.

As for Madame d'Aumont, she was furious at the ill-success of her affair. It was she who had obtained the letters of state from the steward of her son-in-law. Her son-in-law had promised me that they should not be used, and wrote at once to say he had had no hand in their production. M. de Brissac, who had been afraid to look me in the face ever since he had taken part in this matter, and with whom I had openly broken, was now so much ashamed that he avoided me everywhere.

CHAPTER XXXVII

IT was just at the commencement of the year 1706, that I received a piece of news which almost took away my breath by its suddenness, and by the surprise it caused me. I was on very intimate terms with Gualterio, the nuncio of the Pope. Just about this time we were without an ambassador at Rome. The nuncio spoke to me about this post; but at my age—I was but thirty—and knowing the unwillingness of the King to employ young men in public affairs, I paid no attention to his words. Eight days afterwards he entered my chamber—one Tuesday, about an hour after mid-day—his arms open, joy painted upon his face, and embracing me, told me to shut my door, and even that of my antechamber, so that he should not be seen. I was to go to Rome as ambassador. I made him repeat this twice over: it seemed so impossible. If one of the portraits in my chamber had spoken to me, I could not have been more surprised. Gualterio begged me to keep the matter secret, saying, that the appointment would be officially announced to me ere long.

I went immediately and sought out Chamillart, reproaching him for not having apprised me of this good news. He smiled at my anger, and said that the King had ordered the news to be kept secret. I admit that I was flattered at being chosen at my age for an embassy so important. I was advised on every side to accept it, and this I determined to do. I could not understand, however, how it was I had been selected. Torcy, years afterwards, when the King was dead, related to me how it came about. At this time I had no relations with Torcy; it was not until long afterwards that friendship grew up between us.

He said, then, that the embassy being vacant, the King wished to fill up that appointment, and wished also that a Duke should be ambassador. He took an almanack and began reading the names of the Dukes, commencing with M. de Uzès. He made no stop until he came to my name. Then he said (to Torcy), " What do you think of him? He is young, but he is good," &c. The King, after hearing a few opinions expressed by those around him, shut up the almanack, and said it was not worth while to go farther, determined that I should be ambassador, but ordered the appointment to be kept secret. I learnt this, more than ten years after its occurrence, from a true man, who had no longer any interest or reason to disguise anything from me.

Advised on all sides by my friends to accept the post offered to me, I did not long hesitate to do so. Madame de Saint-Simon gave me the same advice, although she herself was pained at the idea of quitting her family. I cannot refuse myself the pleasure of relating here what the three ministers each said of my wife, a woman then of only twenty-seven years of age. All three, unknown to each other, and without solicitation on my part, counselled me to keep none of the affairs of my embassy secret from her, but to give her a place at the end of the table when I read or wrote my despatches, and to consult her with deference upon everything. I have rarely so much relished advice as I did in this case. Although, as things fell out, I could not follow it at Rome, I had followed it long before, and continued to do so all my life. I kept nothing secret from her, and I had good reason to be pleased that I did not. Her counsel was always wise, judicious, and useful, and oftentimes she warded off from me many inconveniences.

But to continue the narrative of this embassy. It was soon so generally known that I was going to Rome, that as we danced at Marly, we heard people say, "Look! M. l'Ambassadeur and Madame l'Ambassadrice are dancing." After this I wished the announcement to be made public as soon as possible, but the King was not to be hurried. Day after day passed by, and still I was kept in suspense. At last, about the middle of April, I had an interview with Chamillart one day, just after he came out of the council at which I knew my fate had been decided. I learnt then that the King had determined to send no ambassador to Rome. The Abbé de La Trémoille was already there; he had been made Cardinal, and was to remain and attend to the affairs of the embassy. I found out afterwards that I had reason to attribute to Madame de Maintenon and M. du Maine the change in the King's intention towards me. Madame de Saint-Simon was delighted. It seemed as though she foresaw the strange discredit in which the affairs of the King were going to fall in Italy, the embarrassment and the disorder that public misfortunes would cause the finances, and the cruel situation to which all things would have reduced us at Rome. As for me, I had had so much leisure to console myself beforehand, that I had need of no more. I felt, however, that I had now lost all favour with the King, and, indeed, he estranged himself from me more and more each day. By what means I recovered myself it is not yet time to tell.

On the night between the 3rd and 4th of February, Cardinal Coislin, Bishop of Orléans, died. He was a little man, very fat, who looked like a village curate. His purity of manners and his virtues caused him to be much loved. Two good actions of his life deserve to be remembered.

When, after the revocation of the edict of Nantes, the King determined to convert the Huguenots by means of dragoons and torture, a regiment was sent to Orléans, to be spread abroad in the diocese. As soon as it arrived, M. d'Orléans sent word to the officers that they might make his house their home; that their horses should be lodged in his stables. He begged them not to allow a single one of their men to leave the town, to make the slightest disorder; to say no word to the Huguenots, and not to lodge in their houses. He resolved to be obeyed, and he was. The regiment stayed a month, and cost him a good deal. At the end of that time he so managed matters that the soldiers were sent away, and none came again. This conduct, so full of charity, so opposed to that of nearly all the other dioceses, gained as many Huguenots as were gained by the barbarities they suffered elsewhere. It needed some courage, to say nothing of generosity, to act thus, and to silently blame, as it were, the conduct of the King.

The other action of M. d'Orléans was less public and less dangerous, but was not less good. He secretly gave away many alms to the poor, in addition to those he gave publicly. Among those whom he succoured was a poor, broken-down gentleman, without wife or child, to whom he gave four hundred livres of pension, and a place at his table whenever he was at Orléans. One morning the servants of M. d'Orléans told their master that ten pieces of plate were missing, and that suspicion fell upon the gentleman. M. d'Orléans could not believe him guilty, but as he did not make his appearance at the house for several days, was forced at last to imagine he was so. Upon this he sent for the gentleman, who admitted himself to be the offender.

M. d'Orléans said he must have been strangely pressed to commit an action of this nature, and reproached him for not having mentioned his wants. Then, drawing twenty louis from his pocket, he gave them to the gentleman, told him to forget what had occurred, and to use his table as before. M. d'Orléans prohibited his servants to mention their suspicions, and this anecdote would never have been known, had it not been told by the gentleman himself, penetrated with confusion and gratitude.

M. d'Orléans, after he became cardinal, was often pressed by his friends to give up his bishopric. But this he would not listen to. The King had for him a respect that was almost devotion. When Madame de Bourgogne was about to be delivered of her first child, the King sent a courier to M. d'Orléans requesting him to come to Court immediately, and to remain there until after the delivery. When the child was born, the King would not allow it to be sprinkled by any other hand than that of M. d'Orléans. The poor man, very fat, as I have said, always sweated very much; on this occasion, wrapped up in his cloak and his lawn, his body ran with sweat in such abundance, that in the antechamber the floor was wet all round where he stood. All the Court was much afflicted at his death; the King more than anybody spoke his praises. It was known after his death, from his *valet de chambre*, that he mortified himself continually with instruments of penitence, and that he rose every night and passed an hour on his knees in prayer. He received the sacraments with great piety, and died the night following as he had lived.

Heudicourt the younger, a species of very mischievous satyr, and much mixed up in grand intrigues of gallantry, made, about this time, a song upon the grand *prévôt* and his family. It was so simple, so true to nature, withal so pleasant, that some one having whispered it in the ear of the Maréchal de Boufflers at chapel, he could not refrain from bursting into laughter, although he was in attendance at the mass of the King. The Maréchal was the gravest and most serious man in all France; the greatest slave to decorum. The King turned round therefore in surprise, which augmented considerably when he saw the Maréchal de Boufflers nigh to bursting with laughter, and the tears running down his cheeks. On turning into his cabinet, he called the Maréchal, and asked what had put him in that state at the mass. The Maréchal repeated the song to him. Thereupon the King burst out louder than the Maréchal had, and for a whole fortnight afterwards could not help smiling whenever he saw the grand *prévôt* or any of his family. The song soon spread about, and much diverted the Court and the town.

I should particularly avoid soiling this page with an account of the operation for fistula which Courcillon, only son of Dangeau, had performed upon him, but for the extreme ridicule with which it was accompanied. Courcillon was a dashing young fellow, much given to witty sayings, to mischief, to impiety, and to the filthiest debauchery, of which latter, indeed, this operation passed publicly as the fruit. His mother, Madame Dangeau, was in the strictest intimacy with Madame de Maintenon. They two alone, of all the Court, were ignorant of the life Courcillon led. Madame was much afflicted; and quitted his bed-side, even for a moment, with pain. Madame de Maintenon entered into her sorrow, and went every day to bear her company at the pillow of Courcillon. Madame d'Heudicourt, another intimate friend of Madame de Maintenon, was admitted there also, but scarcely anybody else. Courcillon listened to them, spoke devotionally to them, and uttered the reflections suggested by his state. They, all admiration, published everywhere that he was a saint. Madame d'Heudicourt and a few others who listened to these discourses, and who knew the pilgrim well, and saw him loll out his tongue at them on the sly, knew not what to do to prevent their laughter, and as soon as they could get away went and related all they had heard to their friends. Courcillon, who thought it a mighty honour to have Madame de Maintenon every day for nurse, but who, nevertheless, was dying of weariness, used to see his friends in the evening (when Madame de Maintenon and his mother were gone), and would relate to them, with burlesque exaggeration, all the miseries he had suffered during the day, and ridicule the devotional discourses he had listened to. All the time his illness lasted, Madame de Maintenon came every day to see him, so that her credulity, which no one dared to enlighten, was the laughing-stock of the Court. She conceived such a high opinion of the virtue of Courcillon, that she cited him always as an example, and the King also formed the same opinion. Courcillon took good care not to try and cultivate it when he became cured; yet neither the King nor Madame de Maintenon opened their eyes, or changed their conduct towards him. Madame de Maintenon, it must be said, except in the sublime intrigue of her government and with the King, was always the queen of dupes.

It would seem that there are, at certain times, fashions in crimes as in clothes. At the period of the Voysins and the Brinvilliers, there were nothing but poisoners abroad; and against these, a court was expressly instituted, called *ardente,* because it condemned them to the flames. At the time of which I am now speaking, 1703, for I forgot to relate what follows in its proper place, forgers of writings were in the ascendant, and became so common, that a chamber was established composed of councillors of state and others, solely to judge the accusations which this sort of criminals gave rise to.

The Bouillons wished to be recognised as descended, by male issue, of the Counts of Auvergne, and to claim all kinds of distinctions and honours in consequence. They had, however, no proofs of this, but, on the contrary, their genealogy proved it to be false. All on a sudden, an old document that had been interred in the obscurity of ages in the church of Brioude, was presented to Cardinal Bouillon. It had all the marks of antiquity, and contained a triumphant proof of the descent of the house of La Tour, to which the Bouillons belonged, from the ancient Counts of Auvergne. The Cardinal was delighted to have in his hands this precious document. But to avoid all suspicion, he affected modesty, and hesitated to give faith to evidence so decisive. He spoke in confidence to all the learned men he knew, and begged them to examine the document with care, so that he might not be the dupe of a too easy belief in it.

Whether the examiners were deceived by the document, or whether they allowed themselves to be seduced into believing it, as is more than probable, from fear of giving offence to the Cardinal, need not be discussed. It is enough to say that they pronounced in favour of the deed, and that Father Mabillon, that Benedictine so well known throughout all Europe by his sense and his candour, was led by the others to share their opinion.

After this, Cardinal de Bouillon no longer affected any doubt about the authenticity of the discovery. All his friends complimented him upon it, the majority to see how he would receive their congratulations. It was a chaos rather than a mixture, of vanity the most outrageous, modesty the most affected, and joy the most immoderate which he could not restrain.

Unfortunately, De Bar, who had found the precious document, and who had presented it to Cardinal de Bouillon, was arrested and put in prison a short time after this, charged with many forgeries. This event made some stir, and caused suspicion to fall upon the document, which was now attentively examined through many new spectacles. Learned men unacquainted with the Bouillons contested it, and De Bar was so pushed upon this point, that he made many delicate admissions. Alarm at once spread among the Bouillons. They did all in their power to ward off the blow that was about to fall. Seeing the tribunal firm, and fully resolved to follow the affair to the end, they openly solicited for De Bar, and employed all their credit to gain his liberation. At last, finding the tribunal inflexible, they were reduced to take an extreme resolution. M. de Bouillon admitted to the King, that his brother, Cardinal de Bouillon, might, unknown to all of them, have brought forward facts he could not prove. He added, that putting himself in the King's hands, he begged that the affair might be stopped at once, out of consideration for those whose only guilt was too great credulity, and too much confidence in a brother who had deceived them. The King, with more of friendship for M. de Bouillon than of reflection as to what he owed by way of reparation for a public offence, agreed to this course.

De Bar, convicted of having fabricated this document, by his own admission before the public tribunal, was not condemned to death, but to perpetual imprisonment. As may be believed, this adventure made a great stir; but what cannot be believed so easily is, the conduct of the Messieurs Bouillon about fifteen months afterwards.

At the time when the false document above referred to was discovered, Cardinal de Bouillon had commissioned Baluze, a man much given to genealogical studies, to write the history of the house of Auvergne. In this history, the descent, by male issue, of the Bouillons from the Counts of Auvergne, was established upon the evidence supplied by this document. At least, nobody doubted that such was the case, and the world was strangely scandalised to see the work appear after that document had been pronounced to be a forgery. Many learned men and friends of Baluze considered him so dishonoured by it, that they broke off all relations with him, and this put the finishing touch to the confusion of this affair.

On Thursday, the 7th of March, 1707, a strange event troubled the King, and filled the Court and the town with rumours. Beringhen, first master of the horse, left Versailles at seven o'clock in the evening of that day, to go to Paris, alone in one of the King's coaches, two of the royal footmen behind, and a groom carrying a torch before him on the seventh horse. The carriage had reached the plain of Bissancourt, and was passing between a farm on the road near Sèvres bridge and a *cabaret,* called the "Dawn of Day," when it was stopped by fifteen or sixteen men on horseback, who seized on Beringhen, hurried him into a post-chaise in waiting, and drove off with him. The King's carriage, with the coachman, footmen, and groom, was allowed to go back to Versailles. As soon as it reached Versailles the King was informed of what had taken place. He sent immediately to his four Secretaries of State, ordering them to send couriers everywhere to the frontiers, with instructions to the governors to guard all the passages, so that if these horsemen were foreign enemies, as was suspected, they would be caught in attempting to pass out of the kingdom. It was known that a party of the enemy had entered Artois, that they had committed no disorders, but that they were there still. Although people found it difficult, at first, to believe that Beringhen had been carried off by a party such as this, yet as it was known that he had no enemies, that he was not reputed sufficiently rich to afford hope of a large ransom, and that not one of our wealthiest financiers had been seized in this manner, this explanation was at last accepted as the right one.

So in fact it proved. A certain Guetem, a fiddler of the Elector of Bavaria, had entered the service of Holland, had taken part in her war against France, and had become a colonel. Chatting one evening with his comrades, he laid a wager that he would carry off some one of mark between Paris and Versailles. He obtained a passport, and thirty chosen men, nearly all of whom were officers. They passed the rivers disguised as traders, by which means they were enabled to post their relays [of horses]. Several of them had remained seven or eight days at Sèvres, Saint Cloud, and Boulogne, from which they had the hardihood to go to Versailles and see the King sup. One of these was caught on the day after the disappearance of Beringhen, and when interrogated by Chamillart, replied with a tolerable amount of impudence. Another was caught in the forest of Chantilly by one of the servants of M. le Prince. From him it became known that relays of horses and a post-chaise had been provided at Morlière for the prisoner when he should arrive there, and that he had already passed the Oise.

As I have said, couriers were despatched to the governors of the frontiers; in addition to this, information of what had taken place was sent to all the intendants of the frontier, to all the troops in quarters there. Several of the King's guards, too, and the grooms of the stable, went in pursuit of the captors of Beringhen. Notwithstanding the diligence used, the horsemen had traversed the Somme and had gone four leagues beyond Ham—Beringhen, guarded by the officers, and pledged to offer no resistance—when the party was stopped by a quartermaster and two detachments of the Livry regiment. Beringhen was at once set at liberty. Guetem and his companion were made prisoners.

The grand fault they had committed was to allow the King's carriage and the footmen to go back to Versailles so soon after the abduction. Had they led away the coach under cover of the night, and so kept the King in ignorance of their doings until the next day, they would have had more time for their retreat. Instead of doing this they fatigued themselves by too much haste. They had grown tired of waiting for a carriage that seemed likely to contain somebody of mark. The Chancellor had passed, but in broad daylight, and they were afraid in consequence to stop him. M. le Duc d'Orléans had passed, but in a post-chaise, which they mistrusted. At last Beringhen appeared in one of the King's coaches, attended by servants in the King's livery, and wearing his *cordon bleu,* as was his custom. They thought they had found a prize indeed. They soon learnt with whom they had to deal, and told him also who they were. Guetem bestowed upon Beringhen all kinds of attention, and testified a great desire to spare him as much as possible all fatigue. He pushed his attentions so far that they caused his failure. He allowed Beringhen to stop and rest on two occasions. The party missed one of their relays, and that delayed them very much.

Beringhen, delighted with his rescue, and very grateful for the good treatment he had received, changed places with Guetem and his companions, led them to

Ham, and in his turn treated them well. He wrote to his wife and to Chamillart announcing his release, and these letters were read with much satisfaction by the King.

On Tuesday, the 29th of March, Beringhen arrived at Versailles, about eight o'clock in the evening, and went at once to the King, who was in the apartments of Madame de Maintenon, and who received him well, and made him relate all his adventures. But the King was not pleased when he found the officers of the stable in a state of great delight, and preparing fireworks to welcome Beringhen back. He prohibited all these marks of rejoicing, and would not allow the fireworks to be let off. He had these little jealousies. He wished that all should be devoted to him alone, without reserve and without division. All the Court, however, showed interest in this return, and Beringhen was consoled by the public welcome he received for his fatigue.

Guetem and his officers, while waiting the pleasure of the King, were lodged in Beringhen's house in Paris, where they were treated above their deserts. Beringhen obtained permission for Guetem to see the King. He did more; he presented Guetem to the King, who praised him for having so well treated his prisoner, and said that war always ought to be conducted properly. Guetem, who was not without wit, replied, that he was so astonished to find himself before the greatest King in the world, and to find that King doing him the honour of speaking to him, that he had not power enough to answer. He remained ten or twelve days in Beringhen's house to see Paris, the Opera and the Comedy, and became the talk of the town. People ran after him everywhere, and the most distinguished were not ashamed to do likewise. On all sides he was applauded for an act of temerity, which might have passed for insolence. Beringhen regaled him, furnished him with carriages and servants to accompany him, and, at parting, with money and considerable presents. Guetem went on his parole to Rheims to rejoin his comrades until exchanged, and had the town for prison. Nearly all the others had escaped. The project was nothing less than to carry off Monseigneur, or one of the princes, his sons.

This ridiculous adventure gave rise to precautions, excessive in the first place, and which caused sad obstructions of bridges and gates. It caused, too, a number of people to be arrested. The hunting parties of the princes were for some time interfered with, until matters resumed their usual course. But it was not bad fun to see, during some time, the terror of ladies, and even of men, of the Court, who no longer dared go abroad except in broad daylight, even then with little assurance, and imagining themselves everywhere in marvellous danger of capture.

I have related in its proper place the adventure of Madame la Princesse de Conti with Mademoiselle Choin and the attachment of Monseigneur for the latter. This attachment was only augmented by the difficulty of seeing each other.

Mademoiselle Choin retired to the house of Lacroix, one of her relatives at Paris, where she lived quite hidden. She was informed of the rare days when Monseigneur dined alone at Meudon, without sleeping there. She went there the day before in a *fiacre*, passed through the courts on foot, ill clad, like a common sort of woman going to see some officer at Meudon, and, by a back staircase, was admitted to Monseigneur who passed some hours with her in a little apartment on the first floor. In time she came there with a lady's-maid, her parcel in her pocket, on the evenings of the days that Monseigneur slept there.

She remained in this apartment without seeing anybody, attended by her lady's-maid, and waited upon by a servant who alone was in the secret.

Little by little the friends of Monseigneur were allowed to see her; and amongst these were M. le Prince de Conti, Monseigneur le Duc de Bourgogne, Madame la Duchesse de Bourgogne, and M. le Duc de Berry. There was always, however, an air of mystery about the matter. The parties that took place were kept secret, although frequent, and were called *parvulos*.

Mademoiselle Choin remained in her little apartment only for the convenience of Monseigneur. She slept in the bed and in the grand apartment where Madame la Duchesse de Bourgogne lodged when the King was at Meudon. She always sat in an arm-chair before Monseigneur; Madame de Bourgogne sat on a stool. Mademoiselle Choin never rose for her; in speaking of her, even before Monseigneur and the company, she used to say " the Duchesse de Bourgogne," and lived with her as Madame de Maintenon did excepting that " darling " and " my aunt," were terms not exchanged between them, and that Madame de Bourgogne was not nearly so free, or so much at her ease, as with the King and Madame de Maintenon. Monsieur de Bourgogne was much in restraint. His manners did not agree with those of that world. Monseigneur le Duc de Berry, who was more free, was quite at home.

Mademoiselle Choin went on *fête*-days to hear mass in the chapel at six o'clock in the morning, well wrapped up, and took her meals alone, when Monseigneur did not eat with her. When he was alone with her, the doors were all guarded and barricaded to keep out intruders. People regarded her as being to Monseigneur, what Madame de Maintenon was to the

King. All the batteries for the future were directed and pointed towards her. People schemed to gain permission to visit her at Paris; people paid court to her friends and acquaintances, Monseigneur le Duc de Bourgogne sought to please her, was respectful to her, attentive to her friends, not always with success. She acted towards Monseigneur le Duc de Bourgogne like a mother-in-law, and sometimes spoke with such authority and bluntness to Madame de Bourgogne as to make her cry.

The King and Madame de Maintenon were in no way ignorant of all this, but they held their tongues, and all the Court who knew it, spoke only in whispers of it. This is enough for the present; it will serve to explain many things, of which I shall speak anon.

CHAPTER XXXVIII

ON Wednesday, the 27th of May, 1707, at three o'clock in the morning, Madame de Montespan, aged sixty, died very suddenly at the waters of Bourbon. Her death made much stir, although she had long retired from the Court and from the world, and preserved no trace of the commanding influence she had so long possessed. I need not go back beyond my own experience, and to the time of her reign as mistress of the King. I will simply say, because the anecdote is little known, that her conduct was more the fault of her husband than her own. She warned him as soon as she suspected the King to be in love with her; and told him when there was no longer any doubt upon her mind. She assured him that a great entertainment that the King gave was in her honour. She pressed him, she entreated him in the most eloquent manner, to take her away to his estates of Guyenne, and leave her there until the King had forgotten her or chosen another mistress. It was all to no purpose; and Montespan was not long before repentance seized him; for his torment was that he loved her all his life, and died still in love with her—although he would never consent to see her again after the first scandal.

Nor will I speak of the divers degrees which the fear of the devil at various times put to her separation from the Court; and I will elsewhere speak of Madame de Maintenon, who owed her everything, who fed her on serpents, and who at last ousted her from the Court. What no one dared to say, what the

King himself dared not, M. du Maine, her son, dared. M. de Meaux (Bossuet) did the rest. She went in tears and fury, and never forgave M. du Maine, who by his strange service gained over for ever to his interests the heart and the mighty influence of Madame de Maintenon.

The mistress, retired amongst the Community of Saint Joseph, which she had built, was long in accustoming herself to it. She carried about her idleness and unhappiness to Bourbon, to Fontevrault, to D'Antin; she was many years without succeeding in obtaining mastery over herself. At last God touched her. Her sin had never been accompanied by forgetfulness; she used often to leave the King to go and pray in her cabinet; nothing could ever make her evade any fast day or meagre day; her austerity in fasting continued amidst all her dissipation. She gave alms, was esteemed by good people, never gave way to doubt or impiety; but she was imperious, haughty and overbearing, full of mockery, and of all the qualities by which beauty with the power it bestows is naturally accompanied. Being resolved at last to take advantage of an opportunity which had been given her against her will, she put herself in the hands of Père de la Tour, that famous General of the Oratory. From that moment to the time of her death her conversion continued steadily, and her penitence augmented. She had first to get rid of the secret fondness she still entertained for the Court, even of the hopes which, however chimerical, had always flattered her. She was persuaded that nothing but the fear of the devil had forced the King to separate himself from her, that it was nothing but this fear that had raised Madame de Maintenon to the height she had attained; that age and ill-health, which she was pleased to imagine, would soon clear the way; that when the King was a widower, she being a widow, nothing would oppose their reunion, which might easily be brought about by their affection for their children. These children entertained similar hopes, and were therefore assiduous in their attention to her for some time.

Père de la Tour made her perform a terrible act of penitence. It was to ask pardon of her husband, and to submit herself to his commands. To all who knew Madame de Montespan this will seem the most heroic sacrifice. M. de Montespan, however, imposed no restraint upon his wife. He sent word that he wished in no way to interfere with her, or even to see her. She experienced no further trouble, therefore, on this score.

Little by little she gave almost all she had to the poor. She worked for them several hours a day, making stout shirts and such things for them. Her table, that she had loved to excess, became the most frugal; her fasts multiplied; she would interrupt her meals in order to go and pray. Her mortifications were continued; her chemises and her sheets were of rough linen, of the hardest and thickest kind, but hidden under others of ordinary kind. She unceasingly wore bracelets, garters, and a girdle, all armed with iron points, which oftentimes inflicted wounds upon her; and her tongue, formerly so dangerous, had also its peculiar penance imposed on it. She was, moreover, so tormented with the fear of death, that she employed several women, whose sole occupation was to watch her. She went to sleep with all the curtains of her bed open, many lights in her chamber, and her women around her. Whenever she awoke she wished to find them chatting, playing, or enjoying themselves, so as to re-assure herself against their drowsiness.

With all this she could never throw off the manners of a queen. She had an arm-chair in her chamber with its back turned to the foot of the bed. There was no other in the chamber, not even when her natural children came to see her, not even for Madame la Duchesse d'Orléans. She was oftentimes visited by the most distinguished people of the Court, and she spoke like a queen to all. She treated everybody with much respect, and was treated so in turn. I have mentioned in its proper place, that a short time before her death, the King gave her a hundred thousand francs to buy an estate; but this present was not gratis, for she had to send back a necklace worth a hundred and fifty thousand, to which the King made additions, and bestowed it on the Duchesse de Bourgogne.

The last time Madame de Montespan went to Bourbon she paid all her charitable pensions and gratuities two years in advance and doubled her alms. Although in good health she had a presentiment that she should return no more. This presentiment, in effect, proved correct. She felt herself so ill one night, although she had been very well just before, that she confessed herself, and received the sacrament. Previous to this she called all her servants into her room and made a public confession of her public sins, asking pardon for the scandal she had caused with a humility so decent, so profound, so penitent, that nothing could be more edifying. She received the last sacrament with an ardent piety. The fear of death which all her life had so continually troubled her, disappeared suddenly, and disturbed her no more. She died, without regret, occupied only with thoughts of eternity, and with a sweetness and tranquillity that accompanied all her actions.

Her only son by Monsieur de Montespan, whom she had treated like a mother-in-law, until her separation from the King, but who had since returned to her affection, D'Antin, arrived just before her death. She looked at him, and only said that he saw her in a very

different state to what he had seen her at Bellegarde.
As soon as she was dead he set out for Paris, leaving
orders for her obsequies, which were strange, or were
strangely executed. Her body, formerly so perfect,
became the prey of the unskilfulness and the ignorance
of a surgeon. The obsequies were at the discretion of
the commonest valets, all the rest of the house having
suddenly deserted. The body remained a long time
at the door of the house, whilst the canons of the
Sainte Chapelle and the priests of the parish disputed
about the order of precedence with more than indecency. It was put in keeping under care of the
parish, like the corpse of the meanest citizen of the
place, and not until a long time afterwards was it sent
to Poitiers to be placed in the family tomb, and then
with an unworthy parsimony. Madame de Montespan
was bitterly regretted by all the poor of the province,
amongst whom she spread an infinity of alms, as well
as amongst others of different degree.

As for the King, his perfect insensibility at the death
of a mistress he had so passionately loved, and for so
many years, was so extreme, that Madame de Bourgogne could not keep her surprise from him. He replied, tranquilly, that since he had dismissed her he
had reckoned upon never seeing her again, and that
thus she was from that time dead to him. It is easy
to believe that the grief of the children he had had by
her did not please him. Those children did not dare
to wear mourning for a mother not recognised. Their
appearance, therefore, contrasted with that of the children of Madame de la Vallière, who had just died, and
for whom they were wearing mourning. Nothing
could equal the grief which Madame la Duchesse d'Orléans, Madame la Duchesse, and the Comte de Toulouse exhibited. The grief of Madame la Duchesse
especially was astonishing, for she always prided her-

self on loving nobody; still more astonishing was the grief of M. le Duc, so inaccessible to friendship. We must remember, however, that this death put an end to many hopes. M. du Maine, for his part, could scarcely repress his joy at the death of his mother, and after having stopped away from Marly two days, returned and caused the Comte de Toulouse to be recalled likewise. Madame de Maintenon, delivered of a former rival, whose place she had taken, ought, it might have been thought, to have felt relieved. It was otherwise; remorse for the benefits she had received from Madame de Montespan, and for the manner in which those benefits had been repaid, overwhelmed her. Tears stole down her cheeks, and she went into a strange privacy to hide them. Madame de Bourgogne, who followed, was speechless with astonishment.

The life and conduct of so famous a mistress, subsequent to her forced retirement, have appeared to me sufficiently curious to describe at length; and what happened at her death was equally characteristic of the Court.

The death of the Duchesse de Nemours, which followed quickly upon that of Madame de Montespan, made still more stir in the world, but of another kind. Madame de Nemours was daughter, by a first marriage, of the last Duc de Longueville. She was extremely rich, and lived in great splendour. She had a strange look, and a droll way of dressing,—big eyes with which she could scarcely see, a shoulder that constantly twitched, grey hairs that she wore flowing, and a very imposing air. She had a very bad temper, and could not forgive. When somebody asked her if she said the *Pater*, she replied, yes, but that she passed by without saying it the clause respecting pardon for our enemies. She did not like her kinsfolk, the Matignons, and would never see nor speak to any of them. One day talking to the King at a window of his cabinet, she saw Matignon passing in the court below. Whereupon she set to spitting five or six times running, and then turned to the King and begged his pardon, saying, that she could never see a Matignon without spitting in that manner. It may be imagined that devotion did not incommode her. She herself used to tell a story, that having entered one day a confessional, without being followed into the church, neither her appearance nor her dress gave her confessor an idea of her rank. She spoke of her great wealth, and said much about the Princes de Condé and de Conti. The confessor told her to pass by all that. She, feeling that the case was a serious one, insisted upon explaining and made allusion to her large estates and her millions. The good priest believed her mad, and told her to calm herself; to get rid of such ideas; to think no more of them; and above all to eat good soups, if she had the means to procure them. Seized with anger she rose and left the place. The confessor out of curiosity followed her to the door. When he saw the good lady, whom he thought mad, received by grooms, waiting women, and so on, he had like to have fallen backwards; but he ran to the coach door and asked her pardon. It was now her turn to laugh at him, and she got off scot-free that day from the confessional.

Madame de Nemours had amongst other possessions the sovereignty of Neufchâtel. As soon as she was dead, various claimants arose to dispute the succession. Madame de Mailly laid claim to it, as to the succession to the principality of Orange, upon the strength of a very doubtful alliance with the house of Châlons, and hoped to be supported by Madame de Maintenon. But Madame de Maintenon laughed at her chimeras, as they were laughed at in Switzerland.

M. le Prince de Conti was another claimant. He based his right upon the will of the last Duc de Longueville, by which he had been called to all the Duke's wealth, after the Comte de Saint Paul, his brother, and his posterity. In addition to these, there were Matignon and the dowager Duchesse de Lesdiguières, who claimed Neufchâtel by right of their relationship to Madame de Nemours.

Matignon was an intimate friend of Chamillart, who did not like the Prince de Conti, and was the declared enemy of the Maréchal de Villeroy, the representative of Madame de Lesdiguières, in this affair. Chamillart, therefore, persuaded the King to remain neutral, and aided Matignon by money and influence to get the start of the other claimants.

The haughty citizens of Neufchâtel saw then all these suitors begging for their suffrages, when a minister of the Elector of Brandenbourg appeared amongst them, and disputed the pretensions of the Prince de Conti in favour of his master, the Elector of Brandenbourg (King of Prussia), who drew his claim from the family of Châlons. It was more distant, more entangled if possible, than that of Madame de Mailly. He only made use of it, therefore, as a pretext. His reasons were his religion, in conformity with that of the country; the support of the neighbouring Protestant cantons, allies, and protectors of Neufchâtel; the pressing reflection that the principality of Orange having fallen by the death of William III. to M. le Prince de Conti, the King (Louis XIV.) had appropriated it and recompensed him for it: and that he might act similarly if Neufchâtel fell to one of his subjects; lastly, a treaty produced in good form, by which, in the event of the death of Madame de Nemours, England and Holland agreed to declare for the Elector of Brandenbourg, and to assist him by force in procuring this little state. This minister of the Elector was in concert with the Protestant cantons, who upon his declaration at once sided with him; and who, by the money spent, the conformity of religion, the power of the Elector, the reflection of what had happened at Orange, found nearly all the suffrages favourable. So striking while the iron was hot, they obtained a provisional judgment from Neufchâtel, which adjudged their state to the Elector until the peace; and in consequence of this, his minister was put into actual possession, and M. le Prince de Conti saw himself constrained to return more shamefully than he had returned once before, and was followed by the other claimants.

Madame de Mailly made such an uproar at the news of this intrusion of the Elector, that at last the attention of our ministers was awakened. They found, with her, that it was the duty of the King not to allow this morsel to be carried off from his subjects; and that there was danger in leaving it in the hands of such a powerful Protestant prince, capable of making a fortified place of it so close to the county of Burgundy, and on a frontier so little protected. Thereupon, the King despatched a courier to our minister in Switzerland, with orders to go to Neufchâtel, and employ every means, even menaces, to exclude the Elector, and to promise that the neutrality of France should be maintained if one of her subjects was selected, no matter which one. It was too late. The affair was finished; the cantons were engaged, without means of withdrawing. They, moreover, were piqued into resistance, by an appeal to their honour by the electoral minister, who insisted on the menaces of Puysieux, our representative, to whose memoir the ministers of England and Holland printed a violent reply. The provisional judgment received no alteration. Shame was felt; and resentment was testified during six weeks; after which, for lack of being able to do better, this resentment was appeased of itself. It may be imagined what hope remained to the claimants of reversing at the peace this provisional judgment, and of struggling against a prince so powerful and so solidly supported. No mention of it was afterwards made, and Neufchâtel has remained ever since fully and peaceably to this prince, who was even expressly confirmed in his possession at the peace by France.

The armies assembled this year towards the end of May, and the campaign commenced. The Duc de Vendôme was in command in Flanders, under the Elector of Bavaria, and by his slothfulness and inattention, allowed Marlborough to steal a march upon him, which, but for the failure of some of the arrangements, might have caused serious loss to our troops. The enemy was content to keep simply on the defensive after this, having projects of attack in hand elsewhere to which I shall soon allude.

On the Rhine, the Maréchal de Villars was in command, and was opposed by the Marquis of Bayreuth, and afterwards by the Duke of Hanover, since King of England. Villars was so far successful, that finding himself feebly opposed by the Imperials, he penetrated into Germany, after having made himself master of Heidelberg, Mannheim, and all the Palatinate, and seized upon a number of cannons, provisions, and munitions of war. He did not forget to tax the enemy wherever he went. He gathered immense sums— treasures beyond all his hopes. Thus gorged, he could not hope that his brigandage would remain unknown. He put on a bold face and wrote to the King, that the army would cost him nothing this year. Villars begged at the same time to be allowed to appropriate some of the money he had acquired to the levelling of a hill on his estate which displeased him. Another than he would have been dishonoured by such a request. But it made no difference in his respect, except with the public, with whom, however, he occupied himself but little. His booty clutched, he thought of withdrawing from the enemy's country, and passing the Rhine.

He crossed it tranquilly, with his army and his immense booty, despite the attempts of the Duke of Hanover to prevent him, and as soon as he was on this side, had no care but how to terminate the campaign in repose. Thus finished a campaign tolerably brilliant, if the sordid and prodigious gain of the general had not soiled it. Yet that general, on his return, was not less well received by the King.

At sea we had successes. Frobin, with vessels more feeble than the four English ones of seventy guns, which convoyed a fleet of eighteen ships loaded with provisions and articles of war, took two of those vessels of war and the eighteen merchantmen, after four hours' fighting, and set fire to one of the two others. Three months after he took at the mouth of the Dwina seven richly-loaded Dutch merchant-ships, bound for Muscovy. He took or sunk more than fifty during this campaign. Afterwards he took three large English ships of war that he led to Brest, and sank another of a hundred guns. The English of New England and of New York were not more successful in Acadia; they attacked our colony twelve days running, without success, and were obliged to retire with much loss.

The maritime year finished by a terrible tempest upon the coast of Holland, which caused many vessels to perish in the Texel, and submerged a large number of districts and villages. France had also its share of these catastrophes. The Loire overflowed in a manner hitherto unheard of, broke down the embankments, inundated and covered with sand many parts of the country, carried away villages, drowned numbers of people and a quantity of cattle, and caused damage to the amount of above eight millions. This was another of our obligations to M. de la Feuillade—an obligation which we have not yet escaped from. Nature, wiser than man, had placed rocks in the Loire above Roanne, which prevented navigation to that place, the principal in the duchy of M. de la Feuillade. His father, tempted by the profit of this navigation, wished to get rid of the rocks. Orléans, Blois, Tours, in one word, all the places on the Loire, opposed this. They represented the danger of inundations; they were listened to, and although the M. de la Feuillade of that day was a favourite, and on good terms with M. Colbert, he was not allowed to carry out his wishes with respect to these rocks. His son, the M. de la Feuillade whom we have seen figuring with so little distinction at the siege of Turin, had more credit. Without listening to anybody, he blew up the rocks, and the navigation was rendered free in his favour; the inundations that they used to prevent have overflowed since at immense loss to the King and private individuals. The cause was clearly seen afterwards, but then it was too late.

The little effort made by the enemy in Flanders and Germany, had a cause, which began to be perceived towards the middle of July. We had been forced to abandon Italy. By a shameful treaty that was made, all our troops had retired from that country into Savoy. We had given up everything. Prince Eugène, who had had the glory of driving us out of Italy, remained there some time, and then entered the county of Nice.

Forty of the enemy's vessels arrived at Nice shortly afterwards, and landed artillery. M. de Savoie arrived there also, with six or seven thousand men. It was now no longer hidden that the siege of Toulon was determined on. Every preparation was at once made to defend the place. Tessé was in command. The delay of a day on the part of the enemy saved Toulon, and it may be said, France. M. de Savoie had been promised money by the English. They disputed a whole day about the payment, and so retarded the departure of the fleet from Nice. In the end, seeing M. de Savoie firm, they paid him a million, which he received himself. But in the mean time twenty-one of our battalions had had time to arrive at Toulon. They decided the fortune of the siege. After several unsuccessful attempts to take the place, the enemy gave up the siege and retired in the night, between the 22nd and 23rd of August, in good order, and without being disturbed. Our troops could obtain no sort of assistance from the people of Provence, so as to harass M. de Savoie in his passage of the Var. They refused money, militia, and provisions bluntly, saying that it was no matter to them who came, and that M. de Savoie could not torment them more than they were tormented already.

The important news of a deliverance so desired arrived at Marly on Friday, the 26th of August, and overwhelmed all the Court with joy. A scandalous fuss arose, however, out of this event. The first courier who brought the intelligence of it, had been despatched by the commander of the fleet, and had been conducted to the King by Pontchartrain, who had the affairs of the navy under his control. The courier sent by Tessé, who commanded the land forces, did not arrive until some hours after the other. Chamillart, who received this second courier, was piqued to excess that Pontchartrain had outstripped him with the news. He declared that the news did not belong to the navy, and consequently Pontchartrain had no right to carry it to the King. The public, strangely enough, sided with Chamillart, and on every side Pontchartrain was treated as a greedy usurper. Nobody had sufficient sense to reflect upon the anger which a master would feel against a servant who, having the information by which that master could be relieved from extreme anxiety, should yet withhold the information for six or eight hours, on the ground that to tell it was the duty of another servant!

The strangest thing is, that the King, who was the most interested, had not the force to declare himself on either side, but kept silent. The torrent was so impetuous that Pontchartrain had only to lower his head, keep silent, and let the waters pass. Such was the weakness of the King for his ministers. I recollect that, in 1702, the Duc de Villeroy brought to Marly the important news of the battle of Luzzara. But, because Chamillart was not there, he hid himself, left the King and the Court in the utmost anxiety, and did not announce his news until long after, when Chamillart, hearing of his arrival, hastened to join him and present him to the King. The King was so far from being displeased, that he made the Duc de Villeroy Lieutenant-General before dismissing him.

There is another odd thing that I must relate before quitting this affair. Tessé, as I have said, was charged with the defence of Toulon by land. It was a charge of no slight importance. He was in a country where nothing was prepared, and where everything was wanting; the fleet of the enemy and their army were near at hand, commanded by two of the most skilful captains of the day: if they succeeded, the kingdom itself was in danger, and the road open to the enemy even to Paris. A general thus situated would have been in no humour for jesting, it might have been thought. But this was not the case with Tessé. He found time to write to Pontchartrain all the details of the war and all that passed amongst our troops in the style of Don Quixote, of whom he called himself the wretched squire and the Sancho; and everything he wrote he adapted to the adventures of that romance. Pontchartrain showed me these letters; they made him die with laughing, he admired them so; and in truth they were very comical, and he imitated that romance with more wit than I believed him to possess. It appeared to me incredible, however, that a man should write thus, at such a critical time, to curry favour with a secretary of state. I could not have believed it had I not seen it.

www.ingramcontent.com/pod-product-compliance
Lightning Source LLC
Chambersburg PA
CBHW031305150426
43191CB00005B/82